THE FIRST ENGLISH BIBLE

The Bible was translated into English for the first time in the late 1300s by John Wyclif and his supporters. In the first study of the Wycliffite Bible for nearly a century, Mary Dove explains why people wanted an English translation, why many clergy opposed the idea, and why the church's attempt to censor the translation was unsuccessful. Based on intensive study of the surviving manuscripts, Dove takes the reader through every step of the conception, design and execution of the first English Bible. Illuminating examples are included at every point, and textual analyses and a complete list of surviving manuscripts are appended. Despite the meagre and inadequate resources with which the Wycliffites carried through their enormous enterprise, and the disagreements and changes of direction it involved, Dove demonstrates that the first English Bible initiated a tradition of scholarly, stylish and thoughtful biblical translation, and remains a major cultural landmark.

MARY DOVE is Reader in English at the University of Sussex.

CAMBRIDGE STUDIES IN MEDIEVAL LITERATURE

This series of critical books seeks to cover the whole area of literature written in the major medieval languages – the main European vernaculars, and medieval Latin and Greek – during the period c.1100–1500. Its chief aim is to publish and stimulate fresh scholarship and criticism on medieval literature, special emphasis being placed on understanding major works of poetry, prose, and drama in relation to the contemporary culture and learning which fostered them.

Recent titles in the series
Ralph Hanna, *London Literature, 1300–1380*
Maura Nolan, *John Lydgate and the Making of Public Culture*
Nicolette Zeeman *Piers Plowman and the Medieval Discourse of Desire*
Anthony Bale *The Jew in the Medieval Book: English Antisemitisms 1300–1500*
Robert J. Meyer-Lee *Poets and Power from Chaucer to Wyatt*
Isabel Davis *Writing Masculinity in the Later Middle Ages*
John M. Fyler *Language and the Declining World in Chaucer, Dante and Jean de Meun*
Matthew Giancarlo *Parliament and Literature in Late Medieval England*
D. H. Green *Women Readers in the Middle Ages*

A complete list of titles in the series can be found at the end of the volume.

THE FIRST ENGLISH BIBLE

The Text and Context of the Wycliffite Versions

MARY DOVE

CAMBRIDGE
UNIVERSITY PRESS

CAMBRIDGE UNIVERSITY PRESS
Cambridge, New York, Melbourne, Madrid, Cape Town, Singapore, São Paulo, Delhi

Cambridge University Press
The Edinburgh Building, Cambridge CB2 8RU, UK

Published in the United States of America by Cambridge University Press, New York

www.cambridge.org
Information on this title: www.cambridge.org/9780521880282

First published 2007
Reprinted 2009

Printed in the United Kingdom at the University Press, Cambridge

A catalogue record for this publication is available from the British Library

ISBN 978-0-521-88028-2 hardback

Contents

Illustrations

Acknowledgments

The following friends and colleagues generously shared ideas and information and offered suggestions while this work was in progress: Mishtooni Bose, Christopher de Hamel, Kantik Ghosh, Steve Halasey, Ralph Hanna, Anne Hudson, Michael Kuczynski, Ian Levy, Conrad Lindberg, Michelle O'Malley, Shannon McSheffrey, Paul Needham, Barbara Pertzel, Derrick Pitard, Anne Karin Ro, Wendy Scase, James Simpson, Clive Sneddon, Fiona Somerset, Toshiyuki Takamiya, Norman Vance, Brian Young, and two anonymous readers on behalf of the Cambridge University Press. I am particularly grateful to Simon Hunt for allowing me to make reference to his unpublished dissertation, to Vybarr Cregan-Reid for his help with technical issues, and to Dora, George, Ruth and Stephen.

I am grateful to librarians at the following libraries and institutions for making manuscripts available and taking time to discuss them with me: the Bodleian Library, University of Oxford; the Bridwell Library at Southern Methodist University; the British Library; Cambridge University Library; Christ Church, Oxford; Columbia University Library; Corpus Christi College, Cambridge; Corpus Christi College, Oxford; Emmanuel College, Cambridge; Gloucester Record Office; Hereford Cathedral Library; the John Rylands University Library, the University of Manchester; Lambeth Palace Library; the London Library; Magdalene College, Cambridge; the Marquis of Bath's Library at Longleat; Norwich Corporation Library; the Queen's College, Oxford; the William H. Scheide Library; St John's College, Cambridge; St John's College, Oxford; Trinity College, Cambridge; Trinity College, Dublin; the Van Kampen Collection; Wadham College, Oxford; Worcester College, Oxford, and York Minster Library. Many thanks to Consuelo Dutschke, Director of the Digital Scriptorium, Lynda McLeod of Christie's, and the private owners of manuscripts of the Wycliffite Bible who have permitted me to include details of their copies in the Index of Manuscripts.

This project could not have been completed without the research leave and financial assistance provided by the School of English and American Studies and the School of Humanities at the University of Sussex, and by the Arts and Humanities Research Council and the British Academy. I should also like to thank the Rockefeller Foundation for generously accommodating me in their Study Centre at Bellagio, and the President and Fellows of Clare Hall, Cambridge, where most of this book was written.

Abbreviations

BRUO	A. B. Emden, *A Biographical Register of the University of Oxford to AD 1500*, 3 vols. (Oxford: Clarendon Press, 1957–9)
BS	*Biblia Sacra Iuxta Latinam Vulgatam Versionem*, 18 vols. (Rome: Vatican, 1926–1995)
CCCM	Corpus Christianorum Continuatio Mediaeualis
CCSL	Corpus Christianorum Series Latina
CHB, I	P. R. Ackroyd and C. F. Evans, eds., *The Cambridge History of the Bible*, Volume 1: *From the Beginnings to Jerome* (Cambridge University Press, 1970)
CHB, II	G. W. H. Lampe, ed., *The Cambridge History of the Bible*, Volume 2: *The West From The Fathers To The Reformation* (Cambridge University Press, 1969)
DDC	Augustine, *De Doctrina Christiana*, ed. J. Martin, CCSL XXXII (Turnhout: Brepols, 1962)
Deanesly, *LB*	Margaret Deanesly, *The Lollard Bible and Other Medieval Biblical Versions* (Cambridge University Press, 1920)
De Hamel, *Book*	Christopher De Hamel, *The Book: A History of the Bible* (London: Phaidon, 2001)
EETS	Early English Text Society (o.s. = old series; n.s. = new series)
EV	Earlier Version of the Wycliffite Bible
Fristedt, *WB, I*	Sven L. Fristedt, *The Wycliffe Bible, Part I. The Principal Problems Connected with Forshall and Madden's Edition*, SSE 4 (Stockholm: Almqvist and Wiksell, 1953)
Fristedt, *WB, II*	Sven L. Fristedt, *The Wycliffe Bible, Part II*: *The Origin of the First Revision as Presented in* De

	Salutaribus Documentis, SSE 21 (Stockholm: Almqvist and Wiksell, 1969)
Fristedt, *WB, III*	Sven L. Fristedt, *The Wycliffe Bible, Part III*: *Relationships of Trevisa and the Spanish Medieval Bibles*, SSE 28 (Stockholm: Almqvist and Wiksell, 1973)
FZ	W. W. Shirley, ed., *Fasciculi Zizaniorum Magistri Johannis Wyclif cum Tritico*, Rolls Series 5 (London, 1885)
Ghosh, *WH*	Kantik Ghosh, *The Wycliffite Heresy: Authority and the Interpretation of Texts* (Cambridge University Press, 2001)
Hudson, *PR*	Anne Hudson, *The Premature Reformation: Wycliffite Texts and Lollard History* (Oxford: Clarendon Press, 1988)
Hudson, *SEWW*	Anne Hudson, ed., *Selections from English Wycliffite Writings* (Cambridge University Press, 1978)
Hunt, *TFST*	Simon Hunt, 'An Edition of Tracts in Favour of Scriptural Translation and of Some Texts connected with Lollard Vernacular Biblical Scholarship', DPhil thesis, 2 vols., University of Oxford (1994)
Ker, *MLGB*	Neil R. Ker and Andrew G. Watson, *Medieval Libraries of Great Britain: A List of Surviving Manuscripts*, 2nd edn (London: Royal Historical Society, 1964)
Ker, *MMBL*	Neil R. Ker, *Medieval Manuscripts in British Libraries*, vol. I (Oxford: Clarendon Press, 1969), vol. II (1977), vol. III (1983), vol. IV (1992), vol. V (2000)
LALME	Angus McIntosh, M. L. Samuels and Michael Benskin, *A Linguistic Atlas of Late Mediaeval English*, 4 vols. (Aberdeen University Press, 1986)
Lewis, *NT*	John Lewis, *The New Testament of Our Lord and Saviour Jesus Christ Translated out of the Latin Vulgat by John Wiclif* (London: Page, 1731)
Lindberg, *Baruch*	Conrad Lindberg, ed., *The Middle English Bible 2*: *The Book of Baruch* (Oslo: Norwegian University Press, 1985)

Lindberg, *EV* — Conrad Lindberg, ed., *The Earlier Version of the Wycliffite Bible*, vol. I, SSE 6 (Stockholm: Almqvist and Wiksell, 1959), vol. II, SSE 8 (1961), vol. III, SSE 10 (1963), vol. IV, SSE 13 (1965), vol. V, SSE 20 (1969), vol. VI, SSE 29 (1973), vol. VII, SSE 81 (1994), vol. VIII, SSE 87 (1997)

Lindberg, *Judges* — Conrad Lindberg, ed., *The Middle English Bible* 3: *The Book of Judges* (Oslo: Norwegian University Press, 1989)

Lindberg, *KHB* — Conrad Lindberg, ed., *King Henry's Bible, MS Bodl 277: the Revised Version of the Wyclif Bible*, vol. I SSE 89 (Stockholm: Almqvist and Wiksell, 1999), vol. II SSE 94 (2001), vol. III SSE 98 (2002), vol. IV SSE 100 (2004)

Lindberg, *MSS* — Conrad Lindberg, 'The Manuscripts and Versions of the Wycliffite Bible: A Preliminary Survey', *Studia Neophilologica* 42 (1970), 333–47

Lindberg, *PE* — Conrad Lindberg, ed., *The Middle English Bible* 1: *Prefatory Epistles of St. Jerome* (Oslo: Norwegian University Press, 1978)

LV — Later Version of the Wycliffite Bible

MED — H. Kurath, S. M. Kuhn *et al.*, eds., *Middle English Dictionary* (Ann Arbor: University of Michigan Press, 1952–2001)

ODNB — H. G. C. Matthew and Brian Harrison, eds., *The Oxford Dictionary of National Biography*, 61 vols. (Oxford University Press, 2004)

PL — Patrologia Cursus Completus Series Latina, ed. J.-P. Migne

RBMA — F. Stegmüller and N. Reinhardt, *Repertorium Biblicum Medii Aevi*, 11 vols. (Madrid: Consejo Superior de Investigaciones Científicas, 1950–80)

Sharpe, *HLW* — Richard Sharpe, *A Handlist of the Latin Writers of Great Britain and Ireland before 1540* (Turnhout: Brepols, 2001)

SSE — Stockholm Studies in English

WB — Wycliffite Bible

WB — Josiah Forshall and Frederic Madden, eds., *The Holy Bible, Containing the Old and New Testaments, with the Apocryphal Books, in the Earliest English*

Versions Made from the Latin Vulgate by John Wycliffe and His Followers, 4 vols. (Oxford: Clarendon Press, 1850)

WW, *NT* John Wordsworth and Henry Julian White, *Nouum Testamentum Domini Nostri Iesu Christi Latine Secundum Editionem Sancti Hieronymi*, 3 parts (Oxford: Clarendon Press, 1889–1954)

Manuscript sigla

I retain the sigla used by Josiah Forshall and Frederic Madden as far as possible, but where they use the same siglum for more than one manuscript, or more than one siglum for the same manuscript, a choice has had to be made. Conrad Lindberg's two-letter sigla are potentially ambiguous: the sigla including a _ are my own.

For further details of all manuscripts, see the Index of manuscripts of the Wycliffite Bible (pp. 281–306).

A	Corpus Christi College Oxford 4
A	British Library Royal 1. C. VIII
a	Bodley 183
α	British Library Harley 1666
B	Bodleian Douce 370
B	British Library Royal 1. C. IX
b	Bodleian Rawlinson C. 259
b	British Library Harley 2249
B_554	Bodley 554
β	University College Oxford 96
C	Bodleian Douce 369 part 1
C	British Library Cotton Claudius E.II
c	Gonville and Caius College Cambridge 343/539
ç	John Rylands Library Eng. 82
Ca (Lindberg)	see C_U_6680
C_J_E.14	St John's College Cambridge E. 14
C_J_G.26	St John's College Cambridge G. 26
C_U_6680	Cambridge University Library Additional 6680
C_U_6682	Cambridge University Library Additional 6682
C_U_6683	Cambridge University Library Additional 6683
D	see U
D	British Library Lansdowne 454

d	Magdalene College Cambridge Pepys Library 1603
D_72	Trinity College Dublin 72
D_74	Trinity College Dublin 74
D_76	Trinity College Dublin 76
E	Bodley 959
E	British Library Arundel 104
e	British Library Harley 5017
F	Trinity College Dublin 66
F	Sion College ARC L 40.2 / E1
f	British Library Harley 3903
G	British Library Egerton 617/618
G	Lincoln College Oxford Latin 119
g	British Library Additional 10596
ȝ	Cambridge University Library Ll. 1. 13
H	Cambridge University Library Additional 6681
H	Corpus Christi College Oxford 20
Ha (Lindberg)	see b
I	Bodley 277
i	British Library Additional 10046
ı	Cambridge University Library Kk. 1. 8
J	Jesus College Cambridge 30
K	Bodleian Douce 369 part 2
K	Bodleian Fairfax 2
k	British Library Additional 10047
L	Bodley 296
l	Bodleian Rawlinson C. 237/238
L_o	Marquess of Bath Longleat 3
M	British Library Royal 1. B. VI
M	Queen's College Oxford 388
m	Bodleian Rawlinson C. 257
N	Sidney Sussex College Cambridge 99
N	St John's College Oxford 7
n	Bodleian Dugdale 46
O	Magdalene College Cambridge F. 4. 6
O	New College Oxford 66
o	British Library Harley 6333
P	Bodleian Rawlinson C. 258
P	Emmanuel College Cambridge 21
p	Emmanuel College Cambridge 108
P_P	Penn University Library Philadelphia 120

P_S	W. H. Scheide Library Princeton 12
Q	National Library of Scotland Edinburgh Advocates 18. 6. 7
Q	Cambridge University Library Mm. 2. 15
q	Van Kampen MS 637
R	Cambridge University Library Dd. 1. 27
r	John Rylands Library Eng. 80
Ry (Lindberg)	see R_91
R_77	John Rylands Library Eng. 77
R_81	John Rylands Library Eng. 81
R_83	John Rylands Library Eng. 83
R_88	John Rylands Library Eng. 88
R_89	John Rylands Library Eng. 89
R_91	John Rylands Library Eng. 91
S	New York Public Library 67
S	Corpus Christi College Cambridge Parker Library 147
s	Jesus College Cambridge 47
T	Trinity College Dublin 75
T	Trinity College Cambridge B. 2. 8
t	Cambridge University Library Gg. 6. 8
U	British Library Additional 11858
U	Lambeth Palace London 25
u	British Library Harley 1212
V	New College Oxford 67
V	Lambeth Palace London 1033
W	Yale University Beinecke Library 125
W	Norfolk Heritage Centre I h 20
w	Magdalene College Cambridge Pepys 2073
W_o	Herzog-August-Bibliothek Wolfenbüttel Guelf. Aug. A. 2
X	Christ Church Oxford 145
X	Hereford Cathedral Library O. VII. 1
x	Lambeth Palace London 369
Y	British Library Additional 15580
Y	Trinity College Dublin 67
y	British Library Additional 15521
Z	Cambridge University Library Ee. 1. 10

Introduction

'The heart of Lollardy,' David Daniell says, 'was its English Bible', and the first complete translation of the Bible from Latin into English, by the Oxford philosopher and theologian John Wyclif and men associated with him, is generally recognized as the most substantial achievement of the Wycliffite movement. Studies of the writings of the Wycliffites have shifted, in the past thirty years, from the periphery to the centre of research into the literature, history and culture of England at the end of the Middle Ages, but this is the first book on the Wycliffite translation of the Bible since Margaret Deanesly's *The Lollard Bible and Other Medieval Biblical Versions*, published just after the First World War.

This new study examines both the text and the context of the first English Bible. It begins by positioning the decision to translate the Bible in the context of the rise of lay literacy and the emergence of vernacular culture, and by assessing the nature and impact of the opposition to biblical translation. The arguments for a Bible in English were extremely strong, but clerical antagonism towards the Bible associated with Wyclif culminated, in 1409, in the promulgation of ecclesiastical legislation prohibiting the use of any recent, unlicensed translation. This prohibition remained in place until 1529. While a number of magnates and members of religious orders are known to have owned Wycliffite Bible manuscripts, most pre-Reformation owners were reluctant to name themselves in their copies, because possession of scripture in English was *prima facie* grounds for suspicion of heresy, and a heresy trial could result in imprisonment, excommunication and even death by burning. Nevertheless, some two hundred and fifty manuscripts of the Wycliffite Bible, or parts of it, survive, considerably more than of any other text in Middle English (details of all surviving mansucripts known to me are listed in the Index of manuscripts of the Wycliffite Bible). More than a third of the manuscripts contain a lectionary indicating which epistles and gospels are to be read at mass throughout the year, suggesting that the stationers who produced them anticipated a predominantly devout and orthodox readership.

Early evidence names Wyclif, Nicholas Hereford and John Trevisa as translators of the first English Bible, but in pre-Reformation copies attributions of authorship are extremely scarce. I trace the fascinating history of speculation about the identity of the translators, ranging from scrupulous bibliographical and historical scholarship to the frank guess on the part of the early eighteenth-century Cambridge theologian Daniel Waterland that John Purvey had an important role. My view is that Wyclif instigated the project, that work began in the early 1370s in the Queen's College, Oxford, and that Wyclif, Hereford and Trevisa all played a part in the translation. My investigation of the editorial decisions made during the translation process, my analysis of the development of the translation itself, my exploration of the relationship between translation and interpretation, and my estimate of the level of accuracy of the text – or rather, texts – are all based on internal evidence from Wycliffite Bible manuscripts. There is no external evidence, and I have found myself using the word 'probably' again and again.

The textual tradition is highly complex, and the endemic complications of medieval textual production must have been exacerbated by the increasing suspicion with which Wyclif and his associates were regarded, especially after Wyclif's withdrawal from Oxford to Lutterworth in the autumn of 1381. A project of enormous dimensions was matched with changing personnel and limited and aleatory resources; plans made at one stage may have seemed hopelessly unrealistic at another. The project was certainly not defined down to the last detail from the start and professionally executed in impeccable order, like the project of an ideal applicant to a twenty-first-century research-funding body. Editorial decisions were probably made very informally, and there were some changes of direction which seem to have led to disagreement among the translators. The logistical difficulties of the enterprise serve to heighten our estimate of the translators' overall achievement.

Only twenty complete Wycliffite Bibles survive, with evidence for perhaps seventeen more (these Bibles and other select manuscripts are fully described in Appendix 4). Several of these Bibles make frequent appearances in these pages. The scribes who wrote them were clearly professionals, and the English Bible closely resembles the late-medieval Latin Bible in format and decoration as well as content. More than two-thirds of surviving manuscripts contain only books of the New Testament. Josiah Forshall and Frederic Madden, in their admirable 1850 edition of the Wycliffite Bible (which was twenty years in the making), presented two versions of the translation side by side, 'Earlier' and 'Later', the Earlier Version a closely literal rendering of the Latin Bible and the Later Version a more idiomatic revision. Manuscripts of the Later Version outnumber manuscripts of the Earlier Version by more than five to one. The distinctiveness of the versions is confirmed and elaborated on here, although Conrad Lindberg's extensive editorial work on the Wycliffite Bible has demonstrated that revision was an ongoing process throughout the translation project, and, indeed, after the Later Version had been completed. For all books of the Bible except Judges and Baruch, which are edited in both versions by Lindberg, we still depend on Forshall and Madden's edition of the Later Version, the base text of which, British Library Royal 1. C. VIII, is in part a revised version of the Later Version (from Genesis to Numbers 20 and from Psalms to the end of the Old Testament). All readings from the Later Version included in this study have, however, been checked against the manuscripts, and additions and select emendations to Forshall and Madden's text of the Later Version are recorded in Appendix 2. A new edition of the Later Version of the Wycliffite Bible, much to be desired, seems unlikely to appear any time soon, but one of the aims of this study is to prepare the ground for a new edition.

Why were two separate versions of the translation in circulation? Wycliffite Bibles in the Earlier Version differ from Bibles in the Later Version in content (the contents of the versions are detailed in Appendix 1), in the underlying Latin text and in translational idiom. The implications of the differences between the two versions for the translation process as a whole are examined here for the first time. I argue that the Earlier Version was never intended to be copied as a translation in its own right, but that the translators producing the Later Version lost control of what happened to the Earlier Version in the early 1380s. The Wycliffites who arranged to have the Bible copied in the Earlier Version almost certainly knew that stylistic and textual work on the translation were still in progress, but they chose to go ahead without waiting for the Later Version to be completed. The independence of the versions is underlined by the fact that in the New Testament a few manuscripts of the Earlier Version contain textual revisions not found in the Later Version.

The translator who represents himself as being in charge of the production of the Later Version composed two English prologues, a prologue to the Prophets (prefixed to the book of Isaiah), and a prologue to the Bible as a whole (which I shall refer to as the Prologue with a capital 'P'). Although the Prologue is consensually attributed to Purvey, there is no evidence for this, and in these pages it is treated as an anonymous work. Both English prologues help us to understand the translators' purposes (although the writer may not in fact speak for them all), their expectations of their readers, and the ways in which they interpreted the biblical text and invited their readers to interpret the biblical text. They did not leave the reader alone with the biblical text and the Holy Spirit for guidance. The prologue to the Prophets asserts that Isaiah is 'ful opyn' (readily comprehensible), but proceeds to give advice about how to interpret 'þe derk (obscure) places of þe profetis'. The Prologue initiates English readers into the tradition of biblical interpretation, from Augustine of Hippo to the fourteenth-century Franciscan Nicholas of Lyra.

The final chapter of the Prologue claims that the text of the first English Bible is both clear and accurate. The translators are careful to avoid adding words unnecessarily, but where an exact translation of the Latin is obscure they often include explanatory glosses within the text, and sometimes also in the margin. The glosses derive principally from a translation of Lyra, made, I argue, by the translators themselves to assist with the revision process. Throughout the Old Testament, the translators seem to have intended to draw the reader's attention to differences between the Latin text and the Hebrew original, but the programme of marginal glosses survives only in an incomplete state (for additions to Forshall and Madden's record of the glosses, see Appendix 2). During the revision process, the translators made considerable efforts to establish an authoritative text of the Latin Bible, and the text of the Later Version is, as the Prologue claims, more accurate than the text of 'comune Latyn Biblis', and much more accurate than the Earlier Version, although it seems to have been completed in haste. Select readings from the Earlier and Later Versions are compared with each other, and with readings from a selection of late-medieval Latin Bibles and French Bibles, in Appendix 3.

As a result of the Wycliffite enterprise, the biblical canon in its entirety was made accessible for the first time to the reader literate in English but not in Latin. Forshall and Madden were confident that this was one of the principal causes of the Reformation, but our evaluation of the effects of the translation must be far more cautious and provisional, and far less partisan (I have done my utmost to avoid slanted preconceptions throughout this book). One effect of the Wycliffite enterprise which has scarcely been recognized is that the English reader literate in Latin could for the first time read the whole Bible in his or her native tongue, in a translation commanding confidence and respect as a literal and meaningful rendering of a carefully edited original. For such a reader, reading in translation would defamiliarize the well-known Latin, and sharpen awareness that the Latin was a translation, too. Chaucer may have been one such reader. The preface to the *Treatise on the Astrolabe* seems to be his contribution to the debate about the desirability or otherwise of biblical translation, the subject of the first chapter of this book.

It should be noted that all biblical references (unless otherwise stated) are to the Vulgate Bible, and in Psalms to the Gallican Psalter, unless otherwise stated.

CHAPTER I

The Bible debate

The earliest unambiguous reference to John Wyclif as a translator of holy scripture takes us to the heart of the medieval English debate about the desirability of translating the Bible from Latin into English. The chronicler Henry Knighton, a canon at the Augustinian Abbey of St Mary in Leicester, combines a statement that Wyclif has translated the gospel with an argument about why it should never have been translated. In his composite chronicle entry on the Wycliffite heretics and their errors, dated 1382 but written c. 1390, he laments that

Magister Iohannes Wyclif evangelium quod Cristus contulit clericis et ecclesie doctoribus, ut ipsi laycis et infirmioribus personis secundum temporis exigenciam et personarum indigenciam cum mentis eorum esurie dulciter ministrarent, transtulit de latino in anglicam linguam non angelicam. Unde per ipsum fit vulgare et magis apertum laicis et mulieribus legere scientibus quam solet esse clericis admodum litteratis et bene intelligentibus, et sic evangelica margarita spargitur et a porcis conculcatur.[1]

(Master John Wyclif translated from Latin into the English language – very far from being the language of angels![2] – the gospel that Christ gave to the clergy and doctors of the church, for them to administer sweetly as mental nourishment to laypeople and to the infirm, according to the necessity of the time and the people's need. As a consequence, the gospel has become more common and more open to laymen and even to women who know how to read than it customarily is to moderately well-educated clergy of good intelligence. Thus the pearl of the gospel is scattered abroad and trodden underfoot by swine.)

[1] Geoffrey H. Martin, ed., *Knighton's Chronicle, 1337–1396* (Oxford: Clarendon Press, 1995), pp. 242–4 (my translation). On the date of Knighton's entry on Wyclif and the Wycliffites, referring to events of 1381–7, see pp. xvi–xvii, 283 (Knighton mentions Nicholas Hereford's imprisonment in 1387, but not his rehabilitation in 1392); on Knighton and Lollardy, see pp. xlii–xlvi.

[2] An ironic reference to Bede's story about Gregory the Great and the English slaves ('non angli sed angeli'): *Ecclesiastical History of the English People*, ed. B. Colgrave and R. A. B. Mynors, vol. I (Oxford: Clarendon Press, 1969), pp. 134–5.

Knighton has in mind the verse from Matthew's Gospel 'Do not give anything holy to dogs, or throw your pearls in front of pigs, in case they should tread them beneath their feet' (7:6).[3] He has no doubt that Matthew's words can be interpreted in relation to the laity trampling on sacred scripture; the 'evangelica margarita' was one of the privileges Christ reserved for the clergy, and above all the most highly educated, the doctors. The fact that Wyclif was one of these (he became a doctor of divinity in 1371/2) must have exacerbated Knighton's distress.[4]

It seems to Knighton that because Wyclif has translated the *evangelium* (by which he probably means the Gospels, but may mean the New Testament, or even 'scripture' more generally), the average cleric in England at the end of the fourteenth century has less access to the gospel in Latin than a literate layperson has to the gospel translated into English. Since biblical translation makes the gospel *vulgare* and *apertum*, smudging the traditional boundaries between clergy and laity – laymen even think their mother-tongue is 'better and worthier than the Latin language' ('melior et dignior quam lingua latina') – it is (in Knighton's view) one of the signs of the proximity of the end of the world that Wyclif should have undertaken it.[5] Wyclif's is not so much a translation as an apocalyptic deformation of the gospel.

Knighton's testimony about Wyclif's involvement in biblical translation is important, since he was (as the editor of his Chronicle, Geoffrey Martin, demonstrates) 'a close observer of the phenomenon [of Lollardy] with access to some particular sources of information about it'.[6] The process of formation of the Wycliffite Bible, and the roles played by Wyclif and others in the project, will be investigated later in this study. Here, we are concerned with the expectations about the consequences of translation of those who did, and those who did not, want the Bible to be translated, and what these expectations reveal about the cultural, political and religious

3 Unless otherwise stated, translations from the Latin Bible are my own, and as literal as possible.

4 On Wyclif's career, see *BRUO*, III.2103–6; Anne Hudson and Anthony Kenny, *ODNB* LX (2004), pp. 616–30; Andrew E. Larsen, 'John Wyclif, c. 1331–1384', in Ian C. Levy, ed., *A Companion to John Wyclif: Late Medieval Theologian* (Leiden: Brill, 2006), pp. 1–65; Michael Wilks, 'John Wyclif: Reformer', in Hudson, ed., *Wyclif: Political Ideas and Practice: Papers by Michael Wilks* (Oxford: Oxbow, 2000), pp. 1–15, and Herbert B. Workman, *John Wyclif: A Study of the English Medieval Church*, 2 vols. (Oxford: Clarendon Press, 1926). Larsen argues that Wyclif was born between 1330 and 1335, probably closer to 1335 (pp. 9–12).

5 Knighton quotes the eight signs of the end of the world from Guillaume de Saint-Amour's antifraternal *De Periculis Nouissimorum Temporum*, written in 1255; Martin, pp. 244–50 (quot. at 248).

6 'Knighton's Lollards', in Margaret Aston and Colin Richmond, eds., *Lollardy and the Gentry in the Later Middle Ages* (Stroud: Sutton, 1997), pp. 28–40, quot. at 28; also Hudson, *PR*, pp. 43–4, 240–2.

contexts within which the Latin Bible was translated into English for the first time. It makes sense to Knighton that the translator of the gospel is a declared heretic. His understanding of the hierarchical relation between Christ, doctors, clergy, laymen and the *infirmiores* (women, children and lunatics) precludes orthodox clerics translating the Bible. He had evidently been privy to debates about biblical translation, since he rehearses here two of the arguments recorded elsewhere: that translation derogates from the privilege of the clergy, and that it renders scripture liable to fall into disrepute. The name of Wyclif, however, is not mentioned in any of the large number of texts arguing for or against an English Bible. Only one, the Dominican Thomas Palmer's determination against translation, c. 1401–7, associates the Bible with the Lollards.[7]

Like Knighton, Palmer cites Matthew on not throwing pearls in front of pigs as a proof-text against translation. 'Holy scripture', he argues, 'ought not to be communicated to sinful men in its totality, orally or in writing.'[8] The objection Palmer advances is that Christ gave the traitor Judas, who was 'both a dog and a pig', the eucharist, the holiest of sacraments. If a priest must give the sacrament to a communicant whom he knows to be 'either a dog through infidelity or a pig through filthiness of sins', then by the same token he must not keep holy scripture from a sinful man.[9] Palmer predictably replies that a priest may indeed withhold the sacrament from a notorious sinner, although not from the sinner whose offences are hidden.[10]

Palmer would certainly have been aware of the context in which Pope Innocent III quotes the same verse from Matthew's Gospel, in a letter of 1199 to the laity of Metz, in north-eastern France. The Archbishop of Metz has informed him, says the Pope, that laypeople have translated the Gospels, the Pauline Epistles, the Psalms, Gregory the Great's moral commentary on the book of Job and many other books into French, and some readers of these translations have been reported as preaching, assembling in 'occultis conventiculis' ('secret conventicles'), and failing to honour the sacerdotal office, by omission and by commission.[11] Innocent exhorts the people of Metz not to be like the 'dogs and pigs' of Matthew's Gospel, heretics who reverence neither scripture nor sacraments nor priests. At the same time,

[7] On Palmer, see *BRUO*, III.1421–2, and Sharpe, *HLW*, p. 674; his *determinacio* is preserved in Trinity Coll. Camb. 347, fols. 2v–47v, ed. Deanesly, *LB*, pp. 418–37. On the date, see Hudson, 'The Debate on Bible Translation, Oxford 1401', in *Lollards and their Books* (London: Hambledon Press, 1985), pp. 81–2. Lollards are mentioned in Deanesly, *LB*, p. 421/13–15, p. 425/24; see Ghosh, *WH*, p. 100.

[8] 'Sacra scriptura non est malis totaliter communicanda voce vel scriptura', Deanesly, *LB*, p. 429/23–4. Palmer cites the work of another Oxford Dominican, Nicholas Gorham's *In Apocalypsim*, in support.

[9] 'Vel canem per infidelitatem vel porcum per spurcitiam peccatorum'; *LB*, p. 432/29–30, 36–7.

[10] *LB*, p. 433.

[11] PL CCXIV.695–9; see Deanesly, *LB*, p. 31. *Moralia in Iob* was one of the most widely circulated commentaries throughout the Middle Ages.

Innocent's letter and the chapter of Pope Gregory IX's *Decretals* quoting Innocent's letter *Cum ex iniuncto* assert that 'desire to understand the holy scriptures and eagerness to exhort in accordance with them is not to be reproved but rather commended',[12] and Malcolm Lambert is almost certainly right that Innocent was 'anxious not to extinguish [the] enthusiasm' generated by followers of Peter Valdes.[13]

There is no evidence that the church was hostile to the French Bible completed in around 1260, possibly under the auspices of the Dominicans.[14] Even so, the canon *Cum ex iniuncto* associates lay study of the Bible, particularly in translation, with the likelihood of heretical activity, and from the early thirteenth century onwards there was tension between clerical approval of lay access to the Bible in principle and fear of the consequences in practice.[15]

In England in the late fourteenth century, fear of the consequences of biblical translation is voiced particularly emphatically by friars, and in Wyclif's *Opus Evangelicum*, written in his retirement in Lutterworth (1383–4), it is friars who are identified as the dogs and pigs of Matthew 7:6. Friars claim, according to Wyclif, that the dogs are the laity from whom sacred scripture should be withheld, but they themselves are barking dogs who 'argue aimlessly and uselessly about the text of scripture'.[16] Two of the three surviving Oxford determinations on biblical translation were written by friars, the Dominican Palmer and the Franciscan William Butler, both coming down against translation.[17] The third determination, a debate between two doctors coming down in favour of translation, was written

12 'Desiderium intelligendi divinas scripturas et secundum eas studium adhortandi reprehendum non sit, sed potius commendandum', *Decretal. Gregor.* IX, lib.v, tit.vii, c. 12; ed. E. Richter and E. L. Friedberg, *Corpus Iuris Canonici*, vol. II (Leipzig: Tauchnitz, 1881), 784–7, quot. at 785.

13 *Medieval Heresy*, 3rd edn (Oxford: Blackwell, 2002), p. 82; see further Leonard E. Boyle, 'Innocent III and Vernacular Versions of Scripture', in Katherine Walsh and D. Wood, eds., *The Bible in the Medieval World: Essays in Memory of Beryl Smalley*, Studies in Church History, Subsidia 4 (Oxford: Blackwell, 1985), pp. 97–107. On Valdes and the early Waldenses, see Lambert, *Medieval Heresy*, pp. 70–80.

14 Clive T. Sneddon, 'The "Bible du XIIIe siècle": its Medieval Public in the Light of its Manuscript Tradition', in W. Lourdaux and D. Verhelst, eds., *The Bible and Medieval Culture* (Louvain University Press, 1979), pp. 140, 135, 137. See further pp. 83–4, below.

15 Deanesly's account of the clerical response to translations in European vernaculars is pervasively slanted towards prohibition and discouragement, *LB*, pp. 18–88. For a more balanced account, see *CHB*, II.338–491.

16 'Circa textum scripture diffuse et inutiliter altercantur': *Opus Evangelicum*, ed. Johann Loserth, vol. II (London: Wyclif Society, 1895), p. 387/34–5. Matt. 7:6 is the core text of Book III, chs. 38–9, pp. 383–90. On the date, see Williell R. Thomson, *The Latin Writings of John Wyclif* (Toronto: University of Toronto Press, 1983), p. 220. On Matt. 7:6, see further Christina von Nolcken, 'Lay Literacy, the Democratization of God's Law and the Lollards', in John L. Sharpe III and Kimberly Van Kampen, *The Bible As Book: The Manuscript Tradition* (London: British Library, 1998), pp. 182–4.

17 On Butler, see *BRUO*, I.329, and Sharpe, *HLW*, p. 757; his *determinacio* is preserved in Merton Coll. Oxf. 68, fols. 102r–204v, ed. Deanesly, *LB*, pp. 401–18.

by the secular cleric Richard Ullerston of the Queen's College.[18] Butler's and Ullerston's determinations are both dated 1401: in Oxford at the turn of the fifteenth century, as Anne Hudson says, 'the question of biblical translation could [still] be debated openly, without accusations of heresy being levelled against defenders of the [positive] view'.[19] Yet all three texts speak of profound clerical anxieties about lay access to the Bible.

Like Knighton, Palmer is anxious to keep the boundaries between clergy and laity clearly marked. Knighton's 'moderately well-educated clergy' are not educated well enough for Palmer's purposes: every nation, Palmer argues, needs *clerici* who are sufficiently learned in the language in which scripture is preserved to be able 'to interpret scripture to the people by way of circumlocution'.[20] Knighton supposes that as a consequence of Wyclif's translation laymen and women understand the gospel in English more readily than the average cleric understands it in Latin, as though the only barrier to understanding were the language itself. Palmer would have regarded this as simplistic. *Circumlocutio* – taking a roundabout approach to the words of scripture, glossing and interpreting them for the laity – is necessary, Palmer believes, because access to the naked text, uninterpreted scripture, gave rise to the Arian, Sabellian and Nestorian heresies in the early church, and *a fortiori* could lead 'simple people' into error.[21] With little or no knowledge of the church's tradition of interpretation, an area of knowledge in which doctors of divinity are expert, the laity cannot hope to read and immediately understand what they are reading. For fear of heresy, laypeople should not be allowed to read scripture *ad libitum* even in Latin, according to Butler.[22] Palmer and Butler write as though the threat of heresy were potential rather than actual, but, in the same year in which Butler and Ullerston were writing their determinations on biblical translation, the statute *De Heretico Comburendo* was enacted, signalling a determination to eradicate heresy, specifically the Wycliffite heresy.[23]

18 On Ullerston, see *BRUO*, III. 1928–9, and Sharpe, *HLW*, pp. 516–17. His incomplete, unedited *determinacio* is in Vienna, Österreichische Nationalbibl. 4133, fols. 195r–207v; see Hudson, 'The Debate on Bible Translation', pp. 69–81.

19 Ibid., p. 83, on the dating of Butler's and Ullerston's treatises, see pp. 67, 75.

20 'Populo per circumlocutionem scripturas interpretari'; Deanesly, *LB*, p. 435/13–17.

21 *LB*, p. 422/9–12.

22 *LB*, p. 401/14–15; the arguments in favour of translation to which Butler is replying have been excised from the MS (fols. 118–20).

23 *De Heretico Comburendo* became law on 10 March 1401. Alison McHardy argues that the mandate sent to England by Boniface IX in 1395 was sufficient for the execution of heretics without the need for a statute, but that there was a wish on the part of the Commons for a strong deterrent, '*De Heretico Comburendo*, 1401', in Aston and Richmond, eds., *Lollardy and the Gentry*, pp. 112–26. See

Palmer assumes that laypeople reading the Bible in English will have access to only one of the senses of scripture, the literal sense. He cites against translation the text at the heart of Gregory the Great's advocacy of spiritual senses, 'littera occidit, spiritus autem vivificat' ('the literal sense kills, whereas the spirit gives life', 2 Cor. 3:6).[24] Gregory famously interpreted an obscure verse of Deuteronomy as an Old Testament anticipation of Paul's contrast between the spirit and the letter: 'If you find a bird's nest in a tree or on the ground, and the mother-bird is sitting on her young, you shall not take her along with her young, but you shall let her go' (Deut. 22:6). Paraphrasing Gregory, Palmer interprets this verse as meaning that the 'sensus litteralis, qui est quasi magister aliorum sensuum, dimitti debet, et pulli eius retineri, allegoriae et anagogicae' ('the literal sense, which is as it were the master and teacher of the other senses, ought to be left behind, and its young, that is the allegorical and anagogical senses, retained').[25] How, Palmer implies, could the laity hope to understand this obscure verse of Deuteronomy, which is not about birds at all?

Palmer is, however, tweaking Gregory, in a gesture towards late-medieval understanding of the senses of scripture. Gregory does not say the literal sense is *magister*; on the contrary, the thrust of his argument is that the spiritual senses are *altiora* ('higher') than the literal. In the fourteenth-century schools, on the other hand, it was a commonplace that the literal sense was the central and dominant sense. The Franciscan biblical scholar Nicholas of Lyra had definitively stated this, on the authority of Augustine, in the prologue to his hugely influential commentary on the Bible, 1322–31:

> Sicut edificium declinans a fundamento disponitur ad ruinam, sic expositio mystico discrepans a sensu litterali reputanda est indecens et inepta, vel saltem minus decens ceteris paribus et minus apta, et ideo volentibus proficere in studio sacre scripture necessarium est incipere ab intellectu sensus litteralis.[26]

(Just as a building which begins to part company with its foundations is inclined to collapse, so a mystical exposition which deviates from the literal sense must

also Paul Strohm, *England's Empty Throne: Usurpation and the Language of Legitimation, 1399–1422* (New Haven: Yale University Press, 1998), pp. 32–62.

24 Deanesly, *LB*, p. 424/28.

25 *LB*, p. 424/26–28; cf. Gregory, *Homiliae in Hiezechielem*, ed. M. Adriaen, CCSL CXLII (Turnhout: Brepols, 1971), pp. 420–2. Palmer's 'allegorical' sense includes the moral sense. See also Ghosh, *WH*, p. 102.

26 From the second prologue to the *Postilla Litteralis, Biblia Latina cum Postillis Nicolai de Lyra*, 4 vols., vol. I (Venice, 1481) [there is no modern edition of the *Postilla*]; trans. Alastair J. Minnis and A. B. Scott with David Wallace, eds., in *Medieval Literary Theory and Criticism c. 1100–c. 1375: The Commentary-Tradition* (Oxford: Clarendon Press, 1988), p. 268. On Lyra's prologue, and its dependence on Augustine, see further pp. 133–5, below.

be considered unseemly and inappropriate, or at any rate less seemly and less appropriate than other interpretations. So those who wish to make headway in the study of holy scripture must begin by understanding the literal sense.)

Yet if the literal sense is dominant, as Lyra claims and Palmer admits, it scarcely makes sense for the Oxford friar to argue, as Gregory had done, that the literal sense must be dismissed in favour of spiritual senses. Only in relation to a peculiarly abstruse verse with no meaningful literal sense does Palmer's argument stand up, and even then it depends on the assumption that the understanding of 'simple people', knowing basic grammar (if they know anything at all), is confined to the literal sense. His model of pedagogy, as Rita Copeland argues, is a highly traditional one, according to which there is a symbolic boundary between those who understand scripture on the literal, grammatical level, and 'those assumed to be endowed with reason and hermeneutical perspicacity (men, clergy, *litterati*)', for whom the 'higher', spiritual senses of scripture are reserved.[27] Given this model, a translation of the Bible into English, without *circumlocutio*, cannot fail to lead those Palmer calls 'idiote circa scripturam' ('illiterates where scripture is concerned'), astray.[28]

The same text cited by Palmer against translation of the Bible, 'the literal sense kills, whereas the spirit gives life' (2 Cor. 3:6), is the first of three objections against translation refuted in the tract 'The holi prophete Dauid seiþ', probably written before 1390.[29] At first sight it may seem odd that the writer of 'The holi prophete Dauid seiþ', arguing for translation, agrees with Palmer that Paul's words, 'by auctorite of þe Hooly Goost', mean that the Mosaic law of the Old Testament must be read spiritually and not literally, because the 'cerymonyes eiþer [or] sacrifices of þe elde law [Old Testament], wiþoutyn goostli vndirstondyng of þe new lawe [New Testament], sleeþ men bi errour of mysbileue'.[30] The writer does not, however, share Palmer's assumption that those he calls 'symple men of witt'[31] are incapable of spiritual interpretation. It is the enemies of translation

[27] 'Childhood, Pedagogy and the Literal Sense', in Wendy Scase, Rita Copeland and David Lawton, eds., *New Medieval Literatures* I (Oxford University Press, 1997), p. 138; see also Copeland, *Pedagogy, Intellectuals and Dissent in the Later Middle Ages: Lollardy and Ideas of Learning* (Cambridge University Press, 2001), pp. 55–98, and, on Butler and Palmer, pp. 103–4.

[28] Deanesly, *LB*, p. 425/22–25. Palmer argues that the Jews killed Christ because he taught them to understand scripture spiritually.

[29] Camb. UL Ff. 6. 31 (pt. 2), fols. 1r–16r, ed. Deanesly, *LB*, pp. 445–56; selections ed. Stephen Shepherd, in Jocelyn Wogan-Browne, Nicholas Watson, Andrew Taylor and Ruth Evans, eds., *The Idea of the Vernacular: An Anthology of Middle English Literary Theory, 1280–1520* (Exeter University Press, 1999), pp. 149–56. Deanesly rightly says (pp. 269–70) that this treatise closely reflects Wyclif's thought, and it shares some material with the Prologue to WB see p. 18, below.

[30] Deanesly, *LB*, p. 452/31–4. [31] *LB*, p. 453/15.

who read too literally, understanding 'þe lettre sleeþ' to mean 'hooli writ is harmful to men, and fals and repreuable (open to reproof) siþþen þat it sleeþ men by deeþ of synne (through sin which kills the soul)'.[32]

This is sophistry, in the writer's view, for scripture is never false and never open to reproof.[33] Those who say so are 'proude clerkis' who are heading for hell:

þe more þei cunne [know] Cristis lawe þe more þey make hem self dampnable for here [their] hiȝ cunnyng and here wickid lyuynge, and þe symple men for here lytyl cunnyng groundyn him silf þe more in meknesse, and bisie hem to lerne þe wei of saluacioun. Þus þouȝ þei haue not tyme and leiser to turne and turne aȝen þe bokis of goddis lawe [the Bible] to cunne þe lettere þerof, þei han and kepyn þe fruit and þe veri sentence [true meaning] of al þe lawe of God þourȝ kepyng of duble charite [love of God and of one's neighbour].[34]

The true literal sense and true spiritual sense of scripture, its overall 'sentence', is the law of love. The writer describes six ways of arriving at understanding of this 'sentence': by prayer; by penitence; by faith; by being prepared to listen to what wiser people say; by reading the text of the New Testament; and by studying 'þe trewe and opyn (plain, literal) exposicion of hooli doctours and oþere wise men as þei may eseli and goodli come þerto'.[35] The right attitude alone is not enough, nor is it sufficient to trust to one's own interpretation.

A late fourteenth-century sermon on the text 'attendite popule meus legem meam', 'my people, vndirstonde ȝe my lawe' (Ps. 77:1), suggests that the arguments against translation of the Bible could sometimes be used by the laity as an excuse for leaving the study of scripture to the clergy. The preacher imagines one of his hearers objecting to being told he should understand the Bible: 'þou seist, parauntur [perhaps], it is forbede [forbidden] by ȝou prestes and prelates of holychurche anny lewde [uneducated] man to entermette of [meddle with] holy writte'. The preacher does not allow the layman to get away with this: 'Sir, I sey naye: but itt is forbede anny lewde man to mysvse holywritt, for þei þat entermetten þerof withowte techynge and cunnynge vndirstondeþ it amysse'.[36] Yet the fact that the body of this sermon is an exposition of the twelve articles of the Apostles' Creed suggests no very high expectations of the

[32] *LB*, p. 452/14–16.

[33] Here his thought is very close to Wyclif's: see pp. 69 and 194, below.

[34] *LB*, p. 453/17–25.

[35] *LB*, p. 451/23–43 and 452/1–12, quot. 10–12.

[36] Ed. Woodburn O. Ross, sermon 3 for Trinity xix, *Middle English Sermons, Edited from BM MS Royal 18 B XXIII* (London, 1940; EETS o.s. 209), p. 13; see Janet Coleman, *English Literature in History 1350–1400: Medieval Readers and Writers* (London: Hutchinson, 1981), pp. 204–5.

laity's understanding, and 'The holi prophete Dauid seiþ' recommends the New Testament for study, not holy writ as a whole.

One of the points at issue in the debate on biblical translation was whether the whole Bible should be made available to the laity, or only portions of it. Palmer cites as one of the arguments of those favouring translation that 'it is said that the Venerable Bede translated the whole Bible into the English language . . . and he would not have done so had it not been lawful'.[37] Palmer replies that even if he had done so the church has not approved any translation made by Bede – evidently, and tellingly, he is of the opinion that any translation, new or old, requires ecclesiastical approval – and in fact 'Bede only translated such parts of scripture as are necessary for salvation'.[38] To the argument that 'omnis lex', the whole of God's law, which confers life and death, needs to be available in the common tongue, he replies 'not every truth is to be written in English, since many are lacking in usefulness'.[39] Besides, 'according to the Lollards, all truth is contained in sacred scripture, because it contains the first truth, which contains all other truths', and therefore the truth is as fully present in any one part as in any other part.[40]

Whatever Palmer might argue, there was already a complete English Bible by the time he wrote his determination. Before 1397, Thomas of Gloucester, youngest son of Edward III, owned a copy, now British Library Egerton 617/618; in that year, it was listed among his forfeited possessions.[41] John Hus, writing in Prague, a city in which a number of English Wycliffites had taken refuge from persecution, reported in 1411 that 'people from England say that [Wyclif] himself translated the whole Bible from Latin into English'.[42] No doubt the Wycliffites in Bohemia wanted to maximize

37 'Dicitur quod Beda venerabilis totam scripturam transtulit in linguam Anglicam . . . quod non fecisset nisi licuisset', Deanesly, *LB*, p. 419/17–18, and see pp. 133–5. Cuthbert's Letter on the Death of Bede says Bede translated John 1:1–6:9: Colgrave and Mynors, eds., *Bede's Ecclesiastical History*, p. 583. Ranulf Higden says Bede translated the Gospel of John: *Polychronicon*, V, xxiv, ed. Joseph Rawson Lumby, *Polychronicon Ranulphi Higden*, vol. VI (London, 1976; Rolls Series), p. 224.

38 'Beda non transtulit eam [scripturam] nisi quoad necessaria ad salutem': Deanesly, *LB*, p. 435/31–5; cf. p. 437/22–23. Butler concedes that translations might have been allowable in the past, when few people would have had access to them, but are not in his own day, when they would be widely disseminated: *LB*, p. 405/36 to p. 406/9, and pp. 133–4

39 'Non omnis veritas est scribenda in Anglico, quia multe sunt inutiles', Deanesly, *LB*, p. 421/12–13; for the pro-translation argument, p. 418/28–30.

40 'Omnis veritas continetur in sacra scriptura secundum Lollardos, quia continet primam veritatem que continet omnes alias veritates', ibid., p. 421/13–15. Palmer is evidently thinking of Wyclif's own writings here; see pp. 27–9, below.

41 The first vol. (Genesis–Psalms) is now missing; see the description in Appendix 4, pp. 246–7, below.

42 'Per Anglicos dicitur quod ipse totam bibliam transtulit de latino in anglicum': 'Contra Iohannem Stokes', ed. Jaroslav Eršil, *Magistri Iohannis Hus Opera Omnia*, vol. 22: *Polemica* (Prague, 1966), pp. 61–2.

Wyclif's role in the translation, but, as we shall see, from the beginning, in the early 1370s, Wyclif and the translators planned to translate holy scripture in its entirety.[43] To us, who take for granted the Bible as book, it seems natural that a decision to translate the Bible into English meant a decision to translate all the books of the Bible. In Wyclif's Oxford, however, it seemed natural that some books of the Bible should be translated into English and not others, for there had been a long history of highly selective translation.[44]

However accurate Knighton's claim that Wyclif himself translated the *evangelium* may be, it is certainly true that the Gospels are what Knighton would have expected Wyclif to choose to translate. As a prologue to Matthew in two late manuscripts of the Wycliffite Bible (c. 1425–50) puts it, 'Þouȝ al holi writt is ful trewe, nedeful [necessary] and comfortable to mankynde, neþeles þe holy gospel, as þe herte and spirit þerof, is moost profitable to synful men.'[45] The anti-translation argument that 'many truths are lacking in usefulness' is rebutted – the whole of holy writ is *nedeful* – but the Gospels are the most necessary part. A note at the beginning of Matthew's Gospel in a complete Wycliffite Bible dated 1408, Bodleian Fairfax 2, says 'mark wel þis booc and alle þe bookis swynge [following]', as though the preceding Old Testament had not needed to be read quite so attentively.[46]

The centrality of the Gospels is asserted several times in the collection of tracts in favour of biblical translation preserved in Cambridge University Library Ii. 6. 26, a collection probably made by a Wycliffite c. 1410, containing a mixture of orthodox and specifically Lollard material (very little of it, however, manifestly heretical).[47] The second of these tracts, beginning 'Oure Lord Jesu Crist verry God and man', which in four of the seven extant copies is one of the prologues to the Wycliffite translation of Clement of Llanthony's Gospel harmony, *Unum ex Quattuor* (*Oon of Foure*), argues

43 See ch. 4, below.

44 On translation of the Bible into English before Wyclif, see David Daniell, *The Bible in England: Its History and Influence* (New Haven: Yale University Press, 2003), pp. 19–65; Deanesly, *LB*, pp. 131–55; David C. Fowler, *The Bible in Early English Literature* (London: Sheldon Press, 1977) and *The Bible in Middle English Literature* (Seattle: University of Washington Press, 1984); J. Burke Severs, ed., *A Manual of the Writings in Middle English, 1050–1400* (New Haven: Connecticut Academy of Arts and Sciences 1970), pp. 381–409, 534–52, and Geoffrey Shepherd, 'English Versions of the Scriptures Before Wyclif', *CHB*, II.362–87.

45 *WB*, IV.681^{b}/1–2; 3p (see list of manuscript sigla, pp. xiv–xvi, above, and Index of MSS of the Wycliffite Bible, pp. 281–306, below) are dated c. 1450 in *WB*, I.liv, lvi, but this date is probably too late.

46 Fol. 312r. On the date, see p. 39, below, and the description in Appendix 4.

47 On the twelve treatises in this MS, see Hudson, *PR*, p. 424, and Hunt, *TFST*, I.72–129 (on the date of the collection, 76–8; on Lollard material in the collection, 123–27). Deanesly attributes them to John Purvey, *LB*, pp. 270–4, but this cannot be sustained: see pp. 76–9, below.

that 'Cristyn men owen [ought] myche to trauel [labour] nyȝt and day about þe tixt of holy writ, and nameli [especially] þe gospel in here modir tunge, siþen Jesu Christ . . . tauȝte þis gospel wiþ his blessed mouþ'.[48] 'Alle þing þat man nediþ, boþe bodily and gostly, is conteyned in [God's] blissid lawe, and specialy in þe gospel', says the seventh tract in this collection, which shares much of its material with the Wycliffite *Pater Noster II*.[49] Both the third and the fourth tracts in the collection specifically commend 'þe gospel in our moder tunge', and the third contrasts the absolute truth of the gospel with the mingled truth and falsehood of chronicles, saints' lives and the writings of philosophers.[50]

In his determination in favour of biblical translation, Ullerston quotes Robert Grosseteste, Bishop of Lincoln 1235–53, to the effect that a poorly educated priest would do well to 'repetere in septimana nudum [unglossed] textum evangelii diei dominice'[51] ('recorde. . in þe woke þe nakid tixt of þe Soundaie gospel', as the words are translated in the tract 'First seiþ Bois', a tract in favour of translation closely related to Ullerston's determination).[52] If the priest prepares for mass in this way, says Grosseteste, and supposing he understands Latin well enough to start with, his parishioners will at least hear the 'historiam grossam' ('groos story'), the whole literal narrative of the gospel for the day, in English. In his own voice, Ullerston comments that it would be better for children to construe the (Latin) Gospel in prose

48 Fols. 22r–25r, ed. Hunt, *TFST*, II.282–8 (also *WB*, I.xiv–xv), quot. at fol. 23r, II.283/21–4. On this treatise, see Hunt, I.92–7. It is prefixed to WB John in D_76, fols. 99r–100r, and to WB Matt. in R_77, fols. 15r–16r (see p. 52, below), and in Dresden Sächsische Landesbibl. Od. 83, fols. 17v–19r; see Appendix 1. *Oon of Foure* is unedited: see Sharpe, *HLW*, pp. 87–8.

49 Inc. 'Siþen þat þe trouþe of God stondiþ not in oo langage', fols. 41v–46r, ed. Hunt, *TFST*, II.313–20, quot. at fol. 43r, II.314/40–2; also ed. Hudson, *SEWW*, pp. 107–9, 189–91. On this treatise, see Hunt, I.103–9. *Pater Noster II* is ed. Thomas Arnold, *Select English Works of John Wyclif*, vol. III (Oxford: Clarendon Press, 1871), pp. 98–100; Hunt argues that 'Siþen þat þe trouþe' is 'an adept reworking' of *Pater Noster II*; I.104–8 (quot. at 105).

50 Treatise three inc. 'Many croniculis ben fals but al þe gospel is trwe. Oure Lorde Jesu Crist lord of trouþe', fols. 25r–26v, ed. Hunt, *TFST*, II.289–91, and see I.97. Treatise four inc. 'And anoþer sentens come[n]dynge þe gospel in our moder tunge. cristen men, vnderstonden', fols. 26v–28v, ed. Hunt, II.292–5, and see I.97–8.

51 Fol.198v; from the sermon 'Scriptum est de Leuitis'. See S. Harrison Thomson, *The Writings of Robert Grosseteste, Bishop of Lincoln* (Cambridge University Press, 1940), no. 31 (p. 176). Ghosh comments on the controversial implications, by 1401, of the phrase 'nudum textum' (of which Ullerston seems unaware): *WH*, p. 108.

52 Bois = Boethius; ed. Curt F. Bühler, 'A Lollard Tract: On Translating the Bible into English', *Medium Ævum* 7 (1938), 167–83, quot. at 175/169–70. Hunt compares the treatise with Ullerston's *determinacio*, *TFST*, I.220–6, concluding that the order of its arguments is confused, but that it shows some interesting knowledge of English history and custom not evidenced by Ullerston. The treatise was twice printed in the Reformation, as 'A compendious olde treatyse shewynge howe that we ought to haue the scripture in Englysshe': see Hudson, 'The Debate on Bible Translation', p. 68.

than to study pagan poets and Bibles in verse.[53] Boys destined for the priesthood, the first, longest and most academic of the twelve tracts in favour of translation tells us,[54] learn to read the Psalms, the Gospels and the Epistles in grammar schools, schools which were established (the writer reminds us) by the church's own canon law.[55] The way in which the boys learn is to 'writen in Englische wiþ þe Latyn', that is, write an English translation alongside or between the lines of the Latin, so as to be able to 'rede it aȝen if it nede [should it be necessary] to haue it freschly in mynde'.[56] These facts are cited as evidence that the church endorses translation, but they also provide evidence for the existence of an inner canon within the biblical canon as a whole.[57] The fact that Rolle's *Psalter*, a translation of the Psalms with an English commentary, was revised by Wycliffites,[58] and that Wycliffites compiled *Glossed Gospels* in English,[59] is a clear indication that, in common with their orthodox contemporaries, they conceived of an inner canon of biblical books that were especially profitable and necessary.

The pattern of extant manuscripts of the Wycliffite Bible tends to confirm this. Only a small proportion of the 250 or so surviving Wycliffite Bible manuscripts are complete Bibles. There are only five complete Bibles in the Earlier Version (one of them made up of two manuscripts now separated, Trinity College Dublin 66 and British Library Additional 15580), and fifteen complete Bibles in the Later Version.[60] Counting manuscripts which are

53 Vienna, Österreichische Nationalbibl. 4133, fol. 205r.

54 Inc. 'Alle cristine peple stant in þre maner of folke', CUL Ii. 6. 26, fols. 1r–22r, ed. Hunt, *TFST*, II.265–81. On this treatise, see Hunt, *TFST*, I.87–92, and on the relationship between lines 24–59 of this treatise and *Dives and Pauper* see *TFST*, I.88.

55 Fols. 6v–7r; Hunt, *TFST*, II.262/174–83. The canon to which the treatise refers is *Decretal. Gregor.* IX, lib.v, tit.v, c. iv, *Quia nonnullis* (Innocent III); ed. Richter and Friedberg, *Corpus Iuris Canonici*, II.770. 'Pestil' (181) may mean the Pauline Epistles or the Pauline and Catholic Epistles.

56 Fol. 7r; Hunt, *TFST*, II.262/183–4.

57 See David Lawton, 'Englishing the Bible', in David Wallace, ed., *The Cambridge History of Medieval Literature* (Cambridge University Press, 1999), p. 455.

58 On Rolle's *Psalter*, c. 1340, see the treatise 'First seiþ Bois', ed. Bühler, 'A Lollard Tract', p. 175/182–6; ed. H. R. Bramley, *The Psalter or Psalms of David . . . by Richard Rolle* (Oxford: Clarendon Press, 1884). A new edition is being prepared by Jill C. Havens and Karl Gustaffson. On the Wycliffite revisions of Rolle, see Dorothy Everett, 'The Middle English Prose Psalter of Richard Rolle of Hampole', *Modern Language Review* 17 (1922), 217–27, 337–50, and 18 (1923), 381–93; Hudson, *PR*, pp. 259–64, and Hudson, 'The Variable Text', in A. J. Minnis and Charlotte Brewer, eds., *Crux and Controversy in Middle English Textual Criticism* (Cambridge University Press, 1992), pp. 55–8. Hudson is preparing an edition of Everett's R[evised]V[ersion]1 and RV2 for the EETS.

59 On the *Glossed Gospels* see Henry Hargreaves, 'Popularising Biblical Scholarship: the Role of the Wycliffite *Glossed Gospels*', in Lourdaux and Verhelst, eds., *The Bible and Medieval Culture*, pp. 171–89; Copeland, *Pedagogy, Intellectuals and Dissent*, pp. 130–9; Hudson, 'The Variable Text'; pp. 51–5; Hudson, *PR*, pp. 248–59, and p. 142, below. There is no modern edition.

60 EV: *AL*_o*W*_o*X* | *F* + *Y* (lacks Psalms, see Index of MSS of WB); LV: ACC_U_6680EGIKM PP_SQRSX; in U, the Pentateuch is in EV. (See the list of manuscript sigla, above, and Appendix 4 and the Index of MSS of WB, below.)

now separate but were probably once part of the same Bible as evidence for one Bible, and counting complete or incomplete Old Testaments (although they may well never have been part of complete Bibles), there is evidence for at the most five more Bibles in the Earlier Version and twelve in the Later Version.[61] By far the most frequently copied Old Testament book is Psalms; it survives in forty-two manuscripts.[62] Some 176 manuscripts contain solely books from 'þe testament of crist', 109 of these being complete or partial New Testaments, thirty-three of these containing Gospels only and thirty-four of these containing books from Romans to the Apocalypse only.[63] The concordance to the Wycliffite Bible compiled in the early fifteenth century is a concordance to the New Testament only.[64] In the records of heresy trials in the diocese of Coventry and Lichfield between 1486 and 1522, books of the Old Testament are mentioned nine times and books of the New Testament twenty-one times.[65]

These figures are in accordance with the recommendation made in the first chapter of the Prologue to the Wycliffite Bible, that 'cristen men and wymmen, olde and ȝonge, shulden studie fast [intently] in þe newe testament, for it is of ful autorite and opyn to vndirstonding of simple men'.[66] Yet in the same chapter of the Prologue the reader literate in English but not in Latin is assured that, according to Augustine, anyone who maintains meekness and charity truly understands 'al holi writ', and that therefore the 'simple man of wit' should not be too frightened to study it.[67] Contrariwise, Augustine threatens the *clerk*, the Latin-literate reader, that if he reads the Bible blinded by pride in his 'verrey vndirstondyng of hooly writ, wiþouten charite', he will 'go quyk [alive] in to helle'.[68] The translators of the Wycliffite Bible aimed to make the whole of scripture available in the vernacular, so that the growing body of people literate in English but not in Latin would have full access to it, without the need for a Latin-literate intermediary, who was all too likely in their view to be a 'worldli clerk' with

61 EV: *BCGHK*; LV: DFHLNOR_91VWY | B + e (see Index of MSS) b + *U* (see Index of MSS).

62 Nineteen copies in complete Bibles; 10 in complete or partial OTs; 13 copies of Ps. alone, or with other selected books (see the Index of MSS of WB).

63 See the Index of MSS of WB. Some of the MSS containing Gospels and some containing Rom.–Apoc. doubtless once formed complete NTs. The figure 176 includes MSS containing OT lectionaries, on which see pp. 61–2, below.

64 See Sherman M. Kuhn, 'The Preface to a Fifteenth-Century Concordance', *Speculum* 43 (1968), 258–73, and Hudson, *PR*, pp. 234–5.

65 Shannon McSheffrey and Norman Tanner, eds., *Lollards of Coventry 1486–1522* Camden Society (Cambridge, 2003), p. 343. See also Hudson, *PR*, pp. 232–3, 470–2.

66 *WB*, I.2/31–2.

67 *WB*, I.2/36–8.

68 *WB*, I.2/42 to 3/1; *Enarrationes in Psalmos*, [Ps. 54:16], ed. E. Dekkers and J. Fraipont, CCSL XXXIX (Turnhout: Brepols, 1956), pp. 668–9. The same passage of Augustine is cited in a very similar context in 'The holi prophete Dauid seiþ', ed. Deanesly, *LB*, p. 449/26–27.

his own agenda. Nevertheless, holiness of life was not a sufficient condition for true understanding of the Bible. Intensive study was necessary as well.

Copeland attributes to the Lollards a new pedagogical model, one that refuses to acknowledge a boundary between lay and clerical potential for learning.[69] The first of the tracts in Cambridge University Library Ii. 6. 26, 'Alle cristine peple stant in þre maner of folke', argues that 'lewed curatis', men who have care of souls but little or no education in Latin, need scripture in English to enable them to teach the people, for 'now it is fulfillid þat þe prophete seid: *parvuli petierunt panem et non erat qui frangeret eis*' ('the children looked for bread and there was nobody to break it for them', Lam. 4:4)'.[70] There are those who argue, says the tract (including Butler and Palmer, though nobody is named), that laypeople should not read the Bible because it 'haþ so manye vnderstondynges literal and spiritual þat þe lewid pepel may not vnderstonde it'.[71] The writer replies that 'þe most part' of priests 'vnderstonden not holy write ne þe gospel neiþer literalliche ne spiritualiche', neither in English nor in Latin, and even the wisest clerks living do not understand 'al þe gospel ne al þe sauter ne al holy write litterallich and spiritualiche'.[72] Learned laypeople may understand both Latin and English better than unlearned priests do.[73]

If the laity do not know God's law, and are therefore 'redi to rebelle aȝens here souereyns' and commit all manner of unlawfulness, the church is to blame.[74] This point is evidently made in response to an implied argument given voice in 'Oure Lord Jesu Crist verry God and man', the second of the collection of tracts in favour of translation: 'wordely [worldly] clirkis crien and seyn holy writt in Englische wolde make men at debate, and sougitis [subjects] to be rebel aȝeyns here soueryns'.[75] The uprising of 1381 certainly raised the level of clerical anxiety about the potentially radical consequences of the teachings of Wyclif. Michael Wilks argues that the rebels were demanding the *reformatio regni* Wyclif's writings ask the king to undertake,[76] and (according to the St Albans chronicler) John Ball, whom

69 *Pedagogy, Intellectuals and Dissent*, pp. 99–140, and 'Childhood, Pedagogy and the Literal Sense', pp. 147–56.

70 Fols. 3r–v; Hunt, *TFST*, II.258/72, 259/80–2. The argument is made on the authority of 'sicut populus sic sacerdos' (Is. 24:2; Hos. 4:9), II.258/67–8.

71 Fol. 7r; Hunt, *TFST*, II.262/188 to 263/191.

72 Cf. 'Tanta est enim divinae scripturae profunditas, ut non solum simplices et illiterati sed etiam prudentes et docti non plene sufficiant ad ipsius intelligentiam indagandam', *Cum ex iniuncto*, ed. Richter and Friedberg, *Corpus Iuris Canonici*, II.785.

73 Fol. 7r–v; Hunt, *TFST*, II. 263/194–6, 199–202. See also Ghosh, *WH*, pp. 97, 108, and Hudson, 'Lollardy: the English Heresy?', in *Lollards and their Books*, p. 156.

74 Fol. 19v; Hunt, *TFST*, II.276/571–2.

75 Fol. 24r–v; Hunt, *TFST*, II. 284/68–70.

76 '*Reformatio Regni*: Wyclif and Hus as Leaders of Religious Protest Movements', in Hudson, ed., *Wyclif: Political Ideas and Practice*, pp. 63–84, esp. 81.

the rebels liberated from the Archbishop of Canterbury's prison, was a long-time teacher of Wyclif's perverse doctrines.[77] William Courtenay, the successor to Thomas Sudbury, the Archbishop of Canterbury murdered by the rebels in June 1381, argued that heresy must be ruthlessly suppressed to avoid further unrest.[78]

The availability of the Bible in English was drawn into the orbit of clerical anxiety not because scripture advocates dissension – to say so would 'sclaundre God, auctor of pees'[79] – but because the English Bible was associated with Wyclif, and because the *clerici* were fearful that laypeople who became familiar with the book invoked as the source of all authority might feel confident to discuss questions going to the heart of the church as an institution and the relationship between church and state. The maintenance of heretical opinions by Oxford scholars was condemned by William Barton, Chancellor of the University, in May 1381, and, in the late autumn, Wyclif withdrew from Oxford to the parish of Lutterworth, of which he had been rector since 1374.[80]

'Alle cristine peple stant in þre maner of folke' cautiously limits lay reading and discussion of scripture to the private domain. Many have been converted by the teachings of 'lewed men and wymen', the writer says, and Augustine 'was conuertid bi his moder þere alle þe clirkis of cristendom myȝten not conclude [convince] hym ne conuerte him', but laypeople should not 'dispute þe feiþ or make argumentis aȝenes þe feiþ in audience of þe pepel', lest the listeners should fall into 'hard temptacion' or 'gret doute'.[81] A distinction is made in this tract between the 'lewed pepel þat ben iclepid ydiotis', illiterates who can be taught only the bare basics of Christian faith, and intelligent, 'well-letterid' laypeople who may 'hauen lykynge (take pleasure) in Goddis lawe' in spite of not being literate in Latin.[82] Christ's words about not casting pearls before swine apply to 'ydiotis', who 'han no lykynge in gostly þingis', but not to English-literate laypeople, who can

77 *Chronicon Angliae*, ed. E. M. Thompson, Rolls Series (London, 1869), pp. 320–1; on Ball's role in the uprising, see Steven Justice, *Writing and Rebellion: England in 1381* (Berkeley: University of California Press, 1994), pp. 103–11, and on Wyclif and the uprising, Hudson and Kenny, *ODNB* LX (2004), p. 619.

78 Joseph Dahmus, *William Courtenay, Archbishop of Canterbury, 1381–1396* (Philadelphia: Pennsylvania State University Press, 1966), p. 297, and Margaret Aston, 'Lollardy and Sedition, 1381–1431', *Past and Present* 17 (1960), 1–44.

79 'Oure Lord Jesu Crist verry God and man', fol. 24v; Hunt, *TFST*, II.284/72–3. See Ghosh, *WH*, p. 239.

80 Hudson and Kenny, *ODNB* LX, p. 619, and *FZ*, pp. 110–13.

81 Fols. 20v–21r; Hunt, *TFST*, II.595–99/601–6. See also 'Oure Lord Jesu Crist verry God and man', fol. 23v; Hunt, *TFST*, II.283/51–3, and Ghosh, *WH*, pp. 89–91.

82 Fol. 8v; Hunt, *TFST*, II.265/249; 264/241; 265/261–2. Hunt rightly says that 'this division of the laity is uncommon, at least in Lollard writers'. II.468.

and should be taught.[83] When 'a man of lawe' quoted the law of God in the Gospel of Luke, Christ replied, 'You have answered rightly' (Luke 10:27–8); 'He seide not as men don þese dayes "who made þe borel [ignorant] clerk so hardi to rede Goddis lawe?" but he preised him for his redynge.'[84] This echoes the scornful question put into the mouth of 'worldli clerkis' in the final chapter of the Prologue to the Wycliffite Bible: 'what spiryt makiþ idiotis hardi to translate now þe Bible into English?'[85] Certainly not, the worldly clerks imply, the Holy Spirit. Because they refuse to acknowledge that scripture needs to be interpreted to the laity by way of *circumlocutio* rather than translated literally, the translators are accused of being illiterates, their education notwithstanding. They might have retorted with a point from the pro-translation tract 'First seiþ Bois', that the apostles themselves 'ben clepid ydiotes' in the Latin Bible; John and Peter are described as 'sine litteris et idiotae' ('uneducated and illiterate men', Acts 4:13).[86]

THE TRUTH OF SCRIPTURE

The model of the relation between clergy and laity in the friars' determinations against biblical translation, as Kantik Ghosh argues, is uncompromisingly hierarchical and supervisory.[87] One of Butler's fears is that the dissemination of translations of scripture may result in inaccurate texts ('libri mendosi') which will lead their readers into error.[88] To the argument that not all Latin Bibles are free from misreadings either, he replies that the church has ensured that scripture is now taught and written in universities, so that 'if books contain errors, they can easily be corrected'.[89] As long as the Latin Bible remains within a controlled clerical environment, Butler's anxiety is allayed. Ullerston understands the issues better. He is aware that the Franciscan polymath Roger Bacon believed that the text of the Latin Bible copied in the universities and disseminated throughout the length and breadth of Europe was an inaccurate one. In the late 1260s, Bacon had argued that what he called the Parisian copy-text ('exemplar Parisiense') of the Bible, which he dates to the late 1220s, was more corrupt than earlier

[83] Fols. 9v–10r; Hunt, *TFST*, II.265/263 to 266/276. [84] Fol.12r; Hunt, *TFST*, II. 268/335–44.
[85] *WB*, I.59/4–5.
[86] Bühler, 'A Lollard Tract', p. 172/66; cf. WB in EV, 'ydiote, *or vnlerid man*' (1 Cor. 14:16), Lindberg, *EV*, VIII.111 (gloss *om. OX*). See also David Lawton, 'Englishing the Bible', in Wallace, ed., *The Cambridge History of Medieval Literature*, pp. 475, 480.
[87] Butler's even more than Palmer's; see Ghosh, *WH*, pp. 93–100.
[88] In his first argument against translation, incomplete at the beginning; Deanesly, *LB*, p. 401/6–7.
[89] 'Ecclesia ordinavit universitates in quibus docentur scripturae et scribuntur libri qui si falsi sunt possunt corrigi', *LB*, p. 401/11–12; see Ghosh, *WH*, pp. 92–3.

texts of the Latin Bible, and that the *Correctorium Bibliae* ('corrected' text) produced by the Dominicans at the University of Paris, and promulgated by the Dominican General Chapter in 1236, only multiplied error.[90] In Ullerston's determination, the doctor who argues against translation cites Bacon's opinion as a reason against translating the Latin Bible into English: 'si ab olim translacio erat fidelis et modo corrupta, periculosum est secundum illam transferre' ('if formerly the translation was faithful and is now corrupt, it is dangerous to translate according to it').[91] Bacon, says Ullerston, attributes the corrupt nature of the translation to ignorance of the original languages, 'sicut, inquit, patet per totam Bibliam' ('as, he says, is apparent throughout the Bible'). Bacon spoke with authority, as he himself knew some Hebrew, as well as Greek.[92]

The Latin Bible in the late Middle Ages descended from translations of the Jewish and Christian Scriptures made by Jerome (c. 346–420) and earlier translators.[93] Around 380, Jerome was commissioned by Pope Damasus to revise the existing Latin translations of the Greek New Testament.[94] He completed his revision of the Latin Gospels by 383/4, and continued to work on translation of the biblical text until 405.[95] At that point, the Latin Bible incorporating Jerome's translations consisted of the following elements: Jerome's revision of Old Latin translations of books of the Jewish Scriptures made from the Greek of the Septuagint (Jerome revised at least the Old Latin Job and Psalms);[96] Jerome's translation of all the books of the Jewish Scriptures directly from the Hebrew (a Latin translation without any precursors); unrevised Old Latin translations of books and parts of

90 *Opus Tertium* (c. 1266–8), ed. J. S. Brewer, *Rogeri Bacon Opera Quedam Hactenus Inedita*, Rolls Series (London, 1859), pp. 92–7; cf. Bacon's *Opus Minus*, 1267, ed. Brewer, pp. 330–49, and his *Compendium Studii*, pp. 438–9, 464–6. See also Hudson, *SEWW*, p. 174; Raphael Loewe, 'The Medieval History of the Latin Vulgate', *CHB*, II.147–51, and Beryl Smalley, *The Study of the Bible in the Middle Ages*, 3rd edn (Oxford: Blackwell, 1983), pp. 329–33. On textual criticism of the Bible, and the *correctoria*, see n. 108, below.

91 Vienna, Österreichische Nationalbibl. 4133, fol. 195v (discussion of the biblical text is not included in 'First seiþ Bois').

92 See Deanna Copeland Klepper, 'Nicholas of Lyra and Franciscan Interest in Hebrew Scholarship', in Philip D. W. Krey and Lesley Smith, eds., *Nicholas of Lyra: the Senses of Scripture* (Leiden: Brill, 2000), pp. 295–6, and Smalley, *The Study of the Bible in the Middle Ages*, pp. 332–3.

93 See H. F. D. Sparks, 'Jerome as Biblical Scholar', *CHB*, II.510–41; E. F. Sutcliffe, 'Jerome', *CHB*, II.80–101, and H. J. White, 'Vulgate', in James Hastings, ed., *A Dictionary of the Bible*, vol. IV (Edinburgh: Clark, 1902), pp. 873–90.

94 See Sparks, 'Jerome as Biblical Scholar', *CHB*, I.513–4, and White, 'Vulgate', pp. 873–4. The first certain evidence for a Latin translation of the NT is c. 180, see Pierre Nautin, 'Bibelübersetzungen I', *Theologische Realencyclopëdie*, vol. VI (Berlin: De Gruyter, 1980), p. 172.

95 White, 'Vulgate', p. 876.

96 Jerome revised the OL Psalms twice: his first translation is the 'Roman Psalter', his second is the 'Gallican Psalter', popularized by Alcuin, and he also translated Psalms from the Hebrew: see Sparks, 'Jerome as Biblical Scholar', *CHB*, I.514.

books included in the Septuagint but not in the Jewish Scriptures; Jerome's revision of the Old Latin translations of the Gospels from the original Greek,[97] and the rest of the New Testament in an Old Latin translation from the original Greek – revised, but perhaps not by Jerome.[98]

In the Old Testament, Old Latin translations from the Septuagint and, in the New Testament, alternative Old Latin translations of the Gospels continued to exist alongside Jerome's translations, so that the Latin Bible entered the Middle Ages in a state of considerable textual complexity. Awareness of the wide variety of texts and readings preserved in biblical manuscripts and biblical commentaries resulted in many attempts at establishing a correct and consistent text of the Latin Bible. The first attempt was made by Cassiodorus in the middle of the sixth century.[99] Alcuin, commissioned by Charlemagne in 797 to establish a correct text, sent from Tours to York (he was a Northumbrian by birth) for manuscripts representing the Italo-Northumbrian branch of the biblical textual tradition, then and now regarded very highly. He did not, however, have the time for intensive textual-critical work. His contemporary Theodulf of Orleans, members of the School of Auxerre (particularly Haimo) during the ninth century, Lanfranc of Bec in the late eleventh century and the Cistercian Stephen Harding in the middle of the twelfth century, all made significant contributions to the study of the text of the Bible.[100]

Wyclif, in his major work on the Bible, *De Veritate Sacrae Scripturae* ('On the Truth of Holy Scripture', 1377–8), reminds his readers of the well-known fact that 'Saint Jerome . . . in his own time was harshly criticized [as a translator] by Augustine and his other rivals.'[101] Familiar with Old Latin translations, and believing the Greek textual tradition of the Jewish Scriptures to be superior to the Hebrew tradition, Augustine regarded as unsound

97 Ibid., 527–9.

98 Sparks argues that Jerome did not revise the other books of the NT: ibid., 519–22. For a contrary view see White, 'Vulgate', p. 874.

99 Ibid., p. 878.

100 On the history of the text of the Latin Bible, see Samuel Berger, *Histoire de la Vulgate pendant les premiers siècles du moyen âge* (Paris, 1893) (to the end of the Merovingian period); Richard Gameson, ed., *The Early Medieval Bible: its Production, Decoration and Use* (Cambridge University Press, 1994); Laura Light, 'Versions et revisions du texte biblique', in Pierre Riché and Guy Lobrichon, eds., *Le Moyen Age et la Bible* (Paris: Beauchesne, 1984), pp. 55–93 (ninth/thirteenth cents.); Loewe, 'The Medieval History of the Latin Vulgate', *CHB*, II.102–54, and White, 'Vulgate', pp. 877–9, 886–9.

101 'Beatus Ieronymus . . . tempore suo passus est ab Augustino et aliis emulis suis calumpniam', *De Veritate Sacrae Scripturae*, I, 11; ed. Rudolf Buddensieg, vol. I (London: Wyclif Society, 1905), p. 232/17–20. On the date, see Thomson, *The Latin Writings of John Wyclif*, pp. 55–7. On the reception of Jerome's translation, see Sparks, 'Jerome as Biblical Scholar', *CHB*, I.544–6; Loewe, 'The Medieval History of the Vulgate', *CHB*, II.102, and White, 'Vulgate', p. 876.

Jerome's decision to translate the Jewish Scriptures from Hebrew.[102] Ullerston's tract argues, against Bacon's low view of the text of the 'Paris Bible', that an established text will always be preferred to a new text, until the new text becomes established in its turn. Augustine, Ullerston says, thought Jerome's translation of the Jewish scriptures from the Hebrew inferior to translations from the Greek of the Septuagint, but 'because the church prefers Jerome's translation, Augustine, if he were alive now, would have chosen it above all others'.[103] Sympathetic to Wyclif, although not himself a Wycliffite, Ullerston determines in favour of translation, while at the same time upholding the authority of tradition.[104]

Bacon's harsh words about the text of the 'Paris Bible' properly relate more generally to the text of Latin Bibles written from about 1200 onwards; the notion of a specifically Parisian text cannot be sustained, as Guy Lobrichon demonstrates.[105] Post-1200 Latin Bibles characteristically include a considerable degree of interpolation, derived from glosses and from the writings of the Fathers, as well as textual errors and inferior readings.[106] Ignorance of the original languages of scripture was, however, beginning to be remedied. Stephen Harding consulted Jewish rabbis when preparing his recension of the Old Testament,[107] and the thirteenth-century *correctoria* frequently note differences between Latin and Hebrew readings.[108] Bacon greatly admired Grosseteste, who learnt Greek late in life, and promoted, among other linguistic projects, a new translation of the Psalms from the Hebrew.[109] The most significant work of biblical textual scholarship in the later Middle Ages, the Franciscan Nicholas of Lyra's *Postilla Litteralis*, is

102 Gerald Bonner, 'Augustine as Biblical Scholar', *CHB*, I.544–6.

103 'Quia ecclesia prefert translacionem Ieronimi, ipsam pre ceteris preellegit Augustinus, si modo viveret': Vienna, Österreichische Nationalbibl. 4133, fol. 200r; see Ghosh, *WH*, pp. 104–5.

104 On Ullerston's Wycliffite sympathies, see Hudson, 'The Debate on Bible Translation', pp. 79–80. Ghosh notes that Ullerston concedes Bacon's point that 'translaciones longius derivate sunt imperfecciores', but falls back on arguing that knowledge of things signified is more important than changing verbal signs: *WH*, p. 105.

105 'Les éditions de la Bible Latine dans les universités du XIIIe siècle', in Giuseppe Cremascoli and Francesco Santi, eds., *La bibbia del XIII secolo: storia del testo, storia dell'esegesi* (Florence: SISMEL, 2004), pp. 15–34. Pecia copying, says Lobrichon, could have led to systematization, but only three Parisian pecia bibles have been identified, pp. 24–25.

106 Laura Light, 'French Bibles c. 1200–30: a new look at the origin of the Paris Bible', in Gameson, ed., *The Early Medieval Bible*, p. 157; also ch. 6, below.

107 Smalley, *The Study of the Bible in the Middle Ages*, pp. 79, 81. Harding's Bible is now Dijon, Bibl. de la Ville 9bis.

108 See Gilbert Dahan, *L'exégèse chrétienne de la Bible en Occident médiéval: XIIe–XIVe siècle* (Paris: Cerf, 1999), pp. 161–238, and ch. 6 and Appendix 3, below.

109 Klepper, 'Nicholas of Lyra and Franciscan Interest in Hebrew Scholarship', in Krey and Smith, eds., *Nicholas of Lyra*, pp. 292–3; Smalley, *The Study of the Bible in the Middle Ages*, p. 343, and Margaret T. Gibson, *The Bible in the Latin West* (Indiana: University of Notre Dame Press, 1993), pp. 12, 66–7.

informed throughout the Old Testament by his familiarity with the writings of 'Rashi' (Solomon ben Isaac of Troyes, 1045–1105) and other medieval Jewish scholars of scripture.[110]

Following Bacon, Lyra cautions his readers against trusting the Hebrew tradition uncritically; he believes that the Jews have deliberately corrupted their own ancient texts where they referred openly to the divinity of Christ – 'a charge almost as old as Christian scholarship itself', as Deanna Klepper says.[111] Special cases excepted, however, Lyra's commentary strongly reinforced Bacon's argument that biblical scholars needed to return, in the Old Testament, to Jerome's translation of the *hebraica veritas*, the authentic Hebrew text.[112] When Wyclif, at the height of his academic career in Oxford, decided to take the ambitious step of lecturing on the entire Bible, he was heavily dependent on Lyra,[113] whom he regarded as a 'novellus tamen copiosus et ingeniosus postillator scripture' ('a recent and yet copious and clever interpreter of the Bible').[114]

Wyclif's unprinted *Postilla* on the whole Bible does not, however, follow Lyra in commenting on the Bible from Genesis to the Apocalypse; no doubt he wanted the shape of his commentary to appear quite different from Lyra's. Begun in the early 1370s, but probably revised and completed during his years in Lutterworth, the *Postilla* divides the Bible into eight parts, a division borrowed from the Franciscan Petrus Aureoli and resting on Aristotelian determinations about the *causa formalis*, that is, the generic and stylistic characteristics of biblical books.[115] The five surviving parts of

110 On Lyra's life (1270–1349) and works, see Krey and Smith, eds., *Nicholas of Lyra*, pp. 1–12; on Rashi, p. 1 and *passim*. Scholars of the school of Rashi also write under this name.

111 'Nicholas of Lyra and Franciscan Interest in Hebrew Scholarship', p. 296; see also p. 31, below.

112 *Opus Minus*, ed. Brewer, p. 332; Smalley, *The Study of the Bible in the Middle Ages*, p. 331. 'Hebraica veritas' is Jerome's phrase: see *Epistola LVII ad Pammachium*, VII, 4, ed. G. J. M. Bartelink, *Liber de Optimo Genere Interpretandi*, *Mnemosyne*, supplement 61 (Leiden, 1980), pp. 15, 80.

113 Gustav A. Benrath says: '[d]ie Benutzung der Postille Lyras ist in Wyclifs Bibelkommentar vom Anfang bis zum Ende auf Schritt und Tritt nachweisbar': *Wyclifs Bibelkommentar* (Berlin: De Gruyter, 1966), p. 10. Smalley points out that the incipit and explicit of Wyclif's postill on Job are the same as Lyra's: 'John Wyclif's *Postilla super Totam Bibliam*', *Bodleian Library Record* 4 (1953), 190.

114 *De Veritate Sacrae Scripturae*, I, 12; ed. Buddensieg, I.275.

115 On Wyclif's *Postilla*, see Benrath, *Wyclifs Bibelkommentar*, and Smalley, 'John Wyclif's *Postilla super Totam Bibliam*', 186–205. Thomson dates it 1371–6 (*The Latin Writings of John Wyclif*, pp. 192–215), but Pamela Gradon argues that the work could not have been delivered orally as it stands, and that it was probably revised in Lutterworth: 'Wyclif's *Postilla* and his Sermons', in Helen Barr and Ann M. Hutchison, eds., *Text and Controversy from Wyclif to Bale: Essays in Honour of Anne Hudson* (Turnhout: Brepols, 2005), p. 75; Gradon demonstrates the close relation between Wyclif's *Postilla* and his sermons, pp. 67–77. The eight-part division of the Bible occurs in Aureoli's *Compendium Litteralis Sensus Totius Divinae Scripturae*, ed. P. Seeboeck (Quaracchi, 1896). On the influence of Aristotle on biblical *accessus*, see Alastair J. Minnis, *Medieval Theory of Authorship: Scholastic Literary Attitudes in the Later Middle Ages*, 2nd edn (Aldershot: Scolar Press, 1988).

Wyclif's *Postilla* are Job–Ecclesiastes, books which teach, according to Aureoli, 'dialectically and disputatively'; Psalms–Song of Songs–Lamentations, which teach 'hymnically and as if poetically and singingly (*decantative*)'; the Prophets, who teach 'prophetically and declaringly (*declarative*)'; and, more conventionally, the Gospels, and the other books of the New Testament.[116] There are two postills on the Song of Songs, the prologue to the second postill being, as Smalley demonstrates, the inaugural lecture Wyclif delivered when he incepted as a doctor of divinity.[117]

If Wyclif does not make a great deal of the generic and stylistic determinants of the parts derived from Aureoli, it is doubtless because his chief concern is with interpretive issues relating to the Bible as a whole. For each biblical book, he depends on Lyra for an overall framework of interpretation, and comes into his own only in discussions of the issues raised by individual chapters or verses. The postill on the Prophets contains some of the most interesting material in the surviving commentary. In the prologue to the postill, Wyclif argues, following Augustine, that biblical rhetoric is different from pagan rhetoric in that the sense does not depend on rhetorical flourishes, and laments that rhetoricians in his own day, too, labour over tropes at the expense of meaning.[118] Again following Augustine, Wyclif gives the first verse of Genesis as an example of the multiple meanings of unembellished scripture. Wyclif has learned from Lyra and from Richard FitzRalph, Archbishop of Armagh, to enlarge the domain of the literal sense to include all manner of figurative senses intended by the author.[119] Citing the *Hexameron* of Grosseteste, an author whom he holds in high regard and frequently quotes in the *Postilla*, Wyclif explains that in the first verse of Genesis there is a threefold allegorical sense, a sixfold tropological (moral) sense and a twofold anagogical sense.[120] Nevertheless, argues Wyclif,

116 *Compendium Litteralis Sensus*, pp. 28–29. The three parts that do not survive are the Pentateuch, the historical books, and Prov.–Wisd.–Ecclus.

117 St John's Coll. Oxf. 171, fols. 323v–326v; Smalley, 'Wyclif's *Postilla* on the Old Testament and his *Principium*', in *Oxford Studies Presented to Daniel Callus, O.P.* (Oxford: Clarendon Press, 1964), pp. 271–9. The second postill is incomplete.

118 Magdalen Coll. Oxf. lat. 55, fol. 1r; Benrath, *Wyclifs Bibelkommentar*, pp. 64–5; Rita Copeland, 'Rhetoric and the Politics of the Literal Sense in Medieval Literary Theory: Aquinas, Wyclif, and the Lollards', in Piero Boitani and Anna Torti, eds., *Interpretation: Medieval and Modern* (Cambridge University Press, 1993), p. 16.

119 See Alastair J. Minnis, '"Authorial Intention" and "Literal Sense" in the Exegetical Theories of Richard FitzRalph and John Wyclif: An Essay in the Medieval History of Biblical Hermeneutics', *Proceedings of the Royal Irish Academy*, vol. 75, Section C, no. 1 (Dublin, 1975).

120 Magdalen Coll. Oxf. lat. 55, fols. 1r–v; see Benrath, *Wyclifs Bibelkommentar*, p. 65. On Wyclif's indebtedness to Grosseteste, see R. W. Southern, *Robert Grosseteste: the Growth of an English Mind in Medieval Europe*, 2nd edn (Oxford: Clarendon Press, 1992), pp. 298–315.

because the author undoubtedly intended all these senses they should all be called literal senses.

Later in the postill on the Prophets, Wyclif, following Lyra, makes a more elementary point about authorial intention: both the Old and the New Testaments 'often speak figuratively (*parabolice*) when there is no literal sense', as in Judges 9:8 where the trees of the wood are said to speak.[121] This 'parabolic' sense, intended by the human author of scripture, should also be called literal. In his commentary on Daniel, Wyclif refers to cases where there is more than one literal sense – what Lyra calls the double (or triple, or quadruple) literal sense – but Wyclif argues that some literal senses take precedence over others, though all are authentic. His example, taken from the second prologue to Lyra's *Postilla Litteralis*, is that God says concerning Solomon, 'I shall be to him a father and he shall be to me a son' (1 Chron. 17:13), whereas the same verse is cited in Hebrews 1:5 as said literally of Christ, and this literal sense is therefore *principalior*, 'more principal' – a deliberate catachresis, although the literal sense according to which the son is Solomon is still a principal sense.[122] In his commentary on Galatians, Wyclif cites the same example, but his point there is that the literal sense is identical with the fullness of God's authorial intention, so that one cannot speak of 'gradus autorisacionis sensuum scripture' ('grades of authenticity of senses of scripture').[123]

The absolute truth of scripture is the topic of Wyclif's disputation with the Oxford Carmelite John Kynyngham, at about the time he incepted as a doctor.[124] Among the texts discussed by Kynyngham and Wyclif are the words of the prophet Amos to Amaziah the priest, 'I am not a prophet, neither am I the son of a prophet, but a herdsman, pulling up sycamore trees' (Amos 7:14).[125] Wyclif discusses the same text in his postill on the

[121] Commenting on Jer. 31:12, Magdalen Coll. Oxf. lat. 117, fol. 107v; see Benrath, *Wyclifs Bibelkommentar*, p. 76; Mary Dove, 'Literal Senses in the Song of Songs', in Krey and Smith, eds., *Nicholas of Lyra*, p. 132, and Christopher Ocker, *Biblical Poetics before Humanism and Reformation* (Cambridge University Press, 2002), pp. 142–9.

[122] Commenting on Dan. 8, Magdalen Coll. Oxf. lat. 117, fol. 201v; see Benrath, *Wyclifs Bibelkommentar*, p. 76. On the same example in the Prologue to WB, see pp. 134–5, below.

[123] Gal. 4:24, Vienna, Österreichische Nationalbibl. 1342, fols. 227v–228r; see Benrath, *Wyclifs Bibelkommentar*, pp. 371–3, quot. at 372/1, and Ghosh, *WH*, pp. 41–2.

[124] See J. A. Robson, *Wyclif and the Oxford Schools* (Cambridge University Press, 1961), pp. 162–70, and Ian C. Levy, 'Defining the Responsibility of the Late Medieval Theologian: the Debate between John Kynyngham and John Wyclif', *Carmelus* 49 (2002), 5–29. On Kynyngham (also Kenningham / Cunningham), see *BRUO*, II.1077, and on the date of this debate, see Thomson, *The Latin Writings of John Wyclif*, pp. 227–9.

[125] *FZ*, pp. 7–8, 21–9, 48–55, 458–9; see Smalley, 'Wyclif's *Postilla* on the Old Testament', pp. 284–6, and Levy, 'Defining the Responsibility of the Late Medieval Theologian', 16–20.

Prophets, depending on the same theory of *ampliacio temporis* ('extension of time') which he elaborates in the disputation.[126] Amos, argues Wyclif, is extending the present tense of the verb 'to be'; he cannot mean what Gregory the Great and the *Glossa Ordinaria* take him to mean – that he is not a prophet at the moment of speaking because he is not experiencing a prophetic vision.[127] Wyclif likes Lyra's explanation, that Amos means that he is not (has not been and will not be) a false prophet; but he also suggests to Kynyngham that Amos may mean that he is not a prophet by 'kind', that is, by being the son of a prophet.[128] At any rate, what Amos says must be true, and true of past and future as well as present, because all times are simultaneously present to God.[129] It is unthinkable that scripture should ever be false *de vi sermonis*, 'by virtue of what it says', even if it seems to be false from a grammatical point of view and from the point of view of common sense.[130] Scripture has its own specialized mode of speaking, and always speaks the truth.

In the first book of *De Veritate Sacrae Scripturae*, Wyclif makes a powerful and subtle case that both the Old and the New Testaments are the word of God and totally authentic, 'for the law contained in the Church's manuscripts, commonly called "writ" (*scriptura*), is the law God gave to his church' (church, that is, including the Jews of the Old Testament), and God would never permit his church to be deprived of his law.[131] Wyclif goes on to rehearse the points his opponents make about the long history of textual corruption. First, even if the text of the Jewish Scriptures had originally been given *indefectibiliter*, 'incorruptibly', 'it does not seem necessary to believe that Ezra correctly restored it' after the return from the Babylonian exile (4 Ezra 14).[132] Secondly, 'it is not necessary to believe that St Jerome translated incorruptibly': Augustine and others certainly did not think so.[133] Thirdly, the corrupt nature of modern scribes makes it

126 Magdalen Coll. Oxf. lat. 117, fols.237v–238r; see Benrath, *Wyclifs Bibelkommentar*, pp. 77–9.

127 Magdalen Coll. Oxf. lat. 117, fol.273v, cf. *FZ*, pp. 7–8; see Levy, 'Defining', 17.

128 *FZ*, p. 459; see Levy, 18–19.

129 See Levy, 'Defining', 10–11, and Beryl Smalley, 'The Bible and Eternity: John Wyclif's Dilemma', *Journal of the Warburg and Courtauld Institutes* 27 (1964), 73–89.

130 *FZ*, p. 459; see Levy, 'Defining', 19.

131 'Lex codicum ecclesie, vocata vulgariter scriptura, sit lex, quam deus dedit sue ecclesie', I, 10; Buddensieg, I.206/15–17. On the meaning of *ecclesia*, see I.228/12–13.

132 'Non videtur oportere credere quod Hesdras recte restituit scripturam hebraicam', I, 11; Buddensieg, I.232/13–16. According to the apocryphal 4 Ezra 14, Ezra dictated a perfect text by divine inspiration to five scribes for forty days.

133 'Nec oportet . . . credere, quod beatus Ieronymus indefectibiliter transtulit', I, 11; Buddensieg, I.232/16–19. Wyclif refers to Augustine's *Epist.* LXXXII [to Jerome], ed. Alois Goldbacher, CSEL XXXIV (Vienna: Tempsky, 1898), pp. 351–87.

impossible to be sure that the text of the Latin Bible has been corrected where it was in error.[134]

Contra, Wyclif maintains that there are three things it is necessary for himself and his readers to believe. First, the Jewish Scriptures (the twenty-two books accepted by both Jews and Christians, as detailed by Jerome in his prologue to the First Book of Kings) are absolutely authentic,[135] and 'there is no difference in sense found in our Latin books and the books of the Jews'.[136] Secondly, Jerome's translation is commended by the 'the holiness of his life' to which Augustine testifies, as much as by his linguistic expertise and faithful rendering of the original languages of scripture.[137] Thirdly, the deficiencies of contemporary texts of the Bible are the consequence of the sin of the church. 'Manuscripts', that is, particular texts of the Bible, 'are nothing but substitutes, necessary for a limited time only; the meaning, however, is always required, and thus it is necessary that the Catholic faith should reside within the entire Mother Church' ('codices non sunt nisi supposiciones pro tempore necessarii, semper autem sensus requiritur, et sic necesse est in tota matre ecclesia esse fidem catholicam').[138]

Ghosh argues that Wyclif 'takes the easy way out' here; that he 'is indeed aware of the central relevance of textual matters to his ideology of authority, but refuses to acknowledge this relevance'.[139] This seems unjust to Wyclif, who is concerned to defend the overall veracity of the Bible against assertions that textual errors undermine its holiness. He did not reach the position he espouses in *De Veritate Sacrae Scripturae* easily; it was partly because of the textual problems associated with the late-medieval Bible, highlighted by Lyra, that the young Wyclif was exercised about the lack of congruence between the Bible as physical book and the nature of the writing contained in it. Wyclif recalls that in his immaturity, perhaps while a boy at grammar school,[140] he was 'painfully entangled in understanding and defending scripture *de virtute sermonis*', which evidently means, in this context, 'according to the literal, grammatical sense'.[141] He had not realized at that stage that scripture should be interpreted 'pure ad sensum autoris'

[134] I, 11; Buddensieg, I.232/21–23.

[135] I, 11; Buddensieg, I.233/22–24. On Jerome's prologue to 1 Kings, the *Prologus Galeatus*, see *RBMA*, no. 323, and pp. 92–4, below.

[136] 'Inter nostros libros latinos et suos hebreos non est in sensu diversitas', I, 11; Buddensieg, I.234/2–3.

[137] I, 11; Buddensieg, I.234/24. Augustine's letter 'De Sanctitate Ieronymi', 233/25, is not otherwise known.

[138] I, 11; Buddensieg, I.235/12–15.

[139] *WH*, p. 59.

[140] *De Veritate*, I, 4; Buddensieg, I.87.

[141] 'Fui anxie intricatus ad intelligendum ac defendendum istas scripturas de virtute sermonis', I.6; Buddensieg, I.114/1–3. On Wyclif's use of the phrase *de virtute sermonis* to mean 'strictly literal sense' and 'intended literal sense', see Ian C. Levy, trans., *John Wyclif: On the Truth of Holy Scripture* (Kalamazoo, Michigan 2001; published for TEAMS by Medieval Institute Publications), p. 33.

('entirely according to the sense intended by its author'): not its human author, that is, but God.[142] Wyclif is here tracing, through his own intellectual history, the entire trajectory of meaning of *sensus litteralis* in the Middle Ages. God, Wyclif says, later made it clear to him that what is written in a Bible is not in itself holy; it is 'no more than the trace of a tortoise-shell on a stone, unless it can be called holy on account of the way in which it leads the faithful by hand into knowledge of heavenly scripture'.[143]

Ghosh observes in this passage 'the characteristic vertical movement of Wyclif's thought: '"Scripture" is identical with Christ and the will of God . . . the book itself is quite irrelevant'.[144] It is true that only according to the fifth and lowest of Wyclif's modes of scripture is 'holy scripture taken to be the manuscripts . . . which are designed to recall the first truth',[145] while the highest of Wyclif's five modes of scripture refers to scripture as an 'open book' (Dan. 7:10), identified as the 'Book of Life' (Apoc. 20:12), in which is inscribed all truth.[146] In a highly elusive discussion of the biblical apocrypha, Wyclif says we should not think of the 'book of life' as being limited to the biblical canon.[147] He has in mind the New Testament apocrypha as well as the Old Testament apocrypha, for he specifies the Gospel of Nicodemus as well as Wisdom, Ecclesiasticus, Judith, Tobit and the Maccabees, claiming (not without justification) that what Jerome says about the books of the Old Testament apocrypha applies in the same way to 'the Gospel of Nicodemus and those others which the church has decided neither to condemn explicitly, nor explicitly to canonize' ('evangelio Nichodemi et aliis, quos decrevit ecclesia nec dampnare nec explicite canonizare').[148]

Yet although the Bible as book is, for Wyclif, scripture in the fifth and lowest mode, it cannot be called 'irrelevant'. Wyclif's Neoplatonist concept of scripture is grounded in the material presence of the Latin Bible, the most

142 I, 9; Buddensieg, I.183/15. See Copeland, 'Rhetoric and the Politics of the Literal Sense', p. 16 and Ghosh, *WH*, pp. 42–5.

143 'Non plus quam vestigium testudinis super saxum . . . sacra autem nullo modo dicitur, nisi propter manuduccionem qua inducit fideles in noticiam scripture celestis', I, 6; Buddensieg, I.114/25 to 115/3.

144 *WH*, p. 56.

145 'Quinto modo sumitur scriptura sacra pro codicibus . . . que sunt signa memorandi veritatem priorem', I, 6; Buddensieg, I.108/15 to 109/2.

146 I, 6; Buddensieg, I.114/9–12. On Wyclif's five modes of holy scripture, see Ghosh, *WH*, pp. 54–6; Levy, *John Wyclif: On the Truth of Holy Scripture*, pp. 14–16; Minnis, '"Authorial Intention" and "Literal Sense"', 25–27, and Smalley, 'The Bible and Eternity'. Levy maintains against Ghosh, Minnis and Smalley that 'Wyclif . . . fits quite comfortably within a continuum of biblical exegesis stretching from Augustine to Aquinas': *John Wyclif: On the Truth of Holy Scripture*, p. 8.

147 I, 11; Buddensieg, I.241–2.

148 I, 11; Buddensieg, I.242/9–11. On Wyclif and the apocrypha, see Hudson, *PR*, p. 230; on the apocrypha in WB, see pp. 92–102, below.

highly valued of books in the medieval West. His search for the truth of holy writ seems to have originated in an awareness of the incommensurability of material and spiritual value: he realized, he says, that truth was not to be found 'de pellis bestiarum', that is, in the vellum of manuscript pages.[149] Twice during his discussion of textual matters he asserts that individual biblical manuscripts are of no more worth than the beasts from which they were made.[150] Even so, it seems to this reader that he protests too much. If the potentially defective biblical text is where enquiry into the truth of scripture begins, it surely follows that each and every Bible is a pearl without price.

PRECEDENTS

Wyclif's assertion that the truth of the Latin Bible was guaranteed by the holiness of Jerome potentially put a weapon into the hands of opponents of translation. In the final chapter of the Prologue to the Wycliffite Bible, they are represented as arguing that 'if men now weren as holi as Jerom was, þei miȝten translate out of Latyn into English, as he dide out of Ebru and out of Greek into Latyn, and ellis þei shulden not translate now . . . for defaute (lack) of holynesse and of kunnyng'.[151] The reply of the writer of the Prologue, on behalf of the translators, is that Jerome was less holy than the apostles and evangelists, that the translators who translated the Jewish scriptures into the Greek of the Septuagint were not nearly as holy as Moses and the prophets who wrote them, and that the church has approved even translations by 'open eretikis', by which he means Jews cunningly mistranslating their own scriptures to prevent the Messiah being identified with Christ.[152]

The history of the transmission of scripture, as texts advocating translation point out, was a history of translation. The precedents they cite are not properly part of the Bible debate, since they are matters of fact; only the accuracy of the facts can be called into question, and some of the objections postulated by writers arguing for translation are palpably absurd. According to the tract 'Alle cristine peple stant in þre maner of folke', some opponents of translation 'seyn þat crist tauȝtte þe peple þe gospel and þe *pater noster* ["Our Father"] frist in Latyn, and þerfor it schulde not be translated into Englische, but it is not so'. Because the King of Heaven wanted his law and gospel to be taught 'opinly to þe pepel', Christ taught in Hebrew,

149 I, 6; Buddensieg, I.114/4.
150 I, 11; Buddensieg, I, 238/3–4, 244/8–10.
151 *WB*, I.58/22–25.
152 *WB*, I.58/26–35. The authorities cited for deliberate mistranslation are Jerome's first prologue to Job and his prologue to Daniel: *RBMA*, nos. 344 and 494.

the language of the people to whom he preached. Therefore, 'as nedeful as it was to translate þe gospel from Ebrewe in to Grwe (Greek) and in to Latyn for helpe of þe peple þat couden noon (knew no) Ebrwe, now it is nedful and leful to translate in to Englysche for helpe of Englisch peple'.[153] The spokesman for the translators of the Wycliffite Bible claims that their opponents ask how 'idiotis' dare to translate the Bible into English when 'þe foure greete doctouris [Ambrose, Augustine, Jerome and Gregory the Great] dursten neuere do þis?'[154] He invents this 'lewid' (idiotic) question to enable him to remind his English readers that the doctors 'ceessiden neuere til þei hadden holy writ in here modir tunge of here owne puple', that is, Latin, for 'Latyn was a comoun langage to here puple . . . as Englishe is comoune langage to oure puple.'[155]

Chaucer also takes the opportunity provided by writing a prologue to a work translated from Latin to point out that the Latin language was once a mother-tongue. In the prologue to the widely copied translation of the *Treatise on the Astrolabe* he made for his son, Lowys (probably completed in 1391), he writes: 'Latyn folk had [the contents of this treatise] first out of othere dyverse langages, and writen hem in her owne tunge, that is to seyn, in Latyn.' The goal of understanding can be reached by way of any language, as 'diverse pathes leden diverse folk the righte way to Rome', and the language of the Romans was once itself a vernacular.[156] As Andrew Cole points out, Chaucer designates Richard II 'lord of this [English] langage', for Chaucer and his contemporaries regarded writing in the vernacular as 'a national matter and therefore an international affair'.[157] Cole argues that Chaucer's apologia for using a 'superfluite of wordes' in his translation is a response to the discussion about specific strategies for translating Latin into English in the Prologue to the Wycliffite Bible (strategies we shall consider in due course).[158] Although this is certainly an interesting possibility, Chaucer's prologue is so allusive that it is hard to be sure of anything except that he is showing awareness of the Bible debate, from the point of view of a practising translator.[159]

Chaucer may have known the 'Dialogus inter Dominum et Clericum' prefixed by another practising translator, John Trevisa, to his translation of

[153] Fol. 6r–v; Hunt, *TFST*, II.261/160 to 262/168. See Ghosh, *WH*, p. 91.
[154] *WB*, I.59/4–6. [155] Ibid., I.9–10, 13–14.
[156] Larry D. Benson, ed., *The Riverside Chaucer* (Oxford University Press, 1988), p. 662/39–40.
[157] 'Chaucer's English Lesson', *Speculum* 77 (2002), 1135; *The Riverside Chaucer*, p. 662/57.
[158] 'Chaucer's English Lesson', 1161–4; see pp. 145–8, below.
[159] See Glending Olsen, 'Geoffrey Chaucer', in Wallace, ed., *The Cambridge History of Medieval English Literature*, pp. 582–3; Alcuin Blamires, 'The Wife of Bath and Lollardy', *Medium Aevum* 58 (1989), 240, and Ralph Hanna, 'The Difficulty of Ricardian Prose Translation: The Case of the Lollards', *Modern Language Quarterly* 51 (1991), 322.

Ranulf Higden's *Polychronicon* (1387).[160] Like the prologue to the *Astrolabe*, Trevisa's 'Dialogus' is at an oblique angle to the Bible debate. The Lord, who favours translation (of Higden, and of the Bible), is in a position to command the Clerk to translate; the Clerk is not opposed to translation, but invites the Lord to persuade him.[161] Responding to the argument of the Clerk that translation is unnecessary where the original text is 'boþe good and fayr', the Lord learnedly points out (for among other things this prologue is an exercise in flattery) that by this reasoning those who translated the Jewish scriptures into Greek – Aquila, Symmachus, Theodotion and Origen – were all 'lewedlych [fruitlessly] ocupyed', since the inspiration of the Holy Spirit had ensured that the original Hebrew was accurate and elegant; yet in fact these translators are 'hyȝlych ypreysed of al holy cherche'.[162] Moreover, the Lord argues, there would be no point in preaching in Latin, however good, to men who only knew English, and if a translation is to be made for purposes of preaching, then it may as well be preserved in written form. If preaching in English is 'good and neodful', then translation is also necessary and good.[163]

The Clerk expresses anxiety that an inaccurate translation (of the *Polychronicon*) might result in 'blame'; Trevisa may be thinking of a point made in 'First seiþ Bois', that Jerome made many enemies through translating the Bible (as well as incurring Augustine's criticism), as he complains in the first and second epistles prefixed to the Latin Bible and to the Earlier Version of the Wycliffite Bible.[164] In spite of this, says 'First seiþ Bois', and in spite of Jerome's admission that he has made errors in translation,[165] in his prologue to Kings Jerome claims. 'I am not knowyng to myself in any maner me to haue changyd any þinge from þe Ebrew trewiþ' (a literal rendering of 'mihi

160 Along with a translation of Richard FitzRalph's anti-fraternal *Defensio Curatorum*. Ed. Ronald Waldron, 'Trevisa's Original Prefaces on Translation: A Critical Edition', in E. D. Kennedy, R. Waldron and J. S. Wittig, eds., *Medieval English Studies Presented to George Kane* (Cambridge: Brewer, 1988), pp. 285–99, and by J. A. Burrow and Thorlac Turville-Petre, eds., *A Book of Middle English* (Oxford: Blackwell, 1992), pp. 213–20. See Fiona Somerset, *Clerical Discourse and Lay Audience in Late Medieval England* (Cambridge University Press, 1998), pp. 64–8, 78–93.

161 The *Polychronicon* was translated at the request of Trevisa's patron, Thomas, Lord Berkeley. On the limited audience for Trevisa's text, see Somerset, *Clerical Discourse and Lay Audience*, p. 100, and on Trevisa as a translator of the Bible see pp. 71–3, below.

162 Waldron, 'Trevisa's Original Prefaces on Translation', p. 291/91–2, 100 to 292/109. Trevisa also mentions a 'fifth translation' from Hebrew to Greek, the anonymous 'Quinta', p. 291/103. Theodotion is named in the rubrics in Daniel in WB as the translator of the non-canonical parts of this book: *WB*, III.634, 662.

163 Waldron, p. 292/118–21 and p. 293/152–3.

164 Bühler, 'A Lollard Tract', p. 177/262 to 178/277; *Epistola LIII ad Paulinum*; *RBMA*, no. 284, and *Praefatio in Pentateucum ad Desiderium*; *RBMA*, no. 285; see Appendix 1, and p. 86, below.

165 Jerome confesses he has erred, using the proverbial expression 'errasse humanum est et confiteri errorem prudentis', in *Epistola LVII ad Pammachium*, XII, 3; ed. Bartelink, *Liber de Optimo Genere Interpretandi*, pp. 20, 113.

omnino conscius non sim mutasse me quippiam de hebraica veritate').[166] As if following this train of thought, the Lord reminds the Clerk that even the holiest men made more than one attempt at biblical translation: 'Orygenes [Origen] made twey translacions and Jerom translatede þryes þe Sauter'.[167] What he wants is not 'þe beste [translation] þat myȝte be, for þat were an ydel desyre vor eny man þat is now here alyue', but 'a skylfol (competent) translacion þat myȝte be knowe and vnderstonde'.[168] Although he is here referring to his request for a translation of the *Polychronicon*, his reassurance might apply with even more force to the translation of the Bible he is advocating. In view of the long history of translation of the Bible, he cannot understand why English speakers should be deprived of a translation.

The history of the Bible in the vernacular, in England and in Europe, is sketched in several texts arguing for biblical translation, including 'First seiþ Bois' and the final chapter of the Prologue to the Wycliffite Bible. The Prologue introduces the history of translation with the exclamation: 'Lord God, siþen at þe bigynnyng of feiþ so manie men translatiden into Latyn, and to greet profyt of Latyn men, lat oo [one] symple creature of God translate into English, for profyt of English men.'[169] The 'simple creature' who proves to be interested in the history of language and the history of institutions will, after all, be following the precedent set by Bede, who translated the Bible ('or a grete parte of þe Bibile', says the tract 'First seiþ Bois') into 'Saxon', the English vernacular of his time,[170] and by King Alfred, founder of Oxford, who translated 'þe bigynning of þe Sauter' (Psalms 1–50).[171] He will also be giving English people the access to scripture in the vernacular already enjoyed by the Czechs, the 'Britons' (Welsh?) and the

166 Bühler, 'A Lollard Tract', p. 177/250–2; *RBMA*, no. 323.

167 Waldron, p. 293/154–5, 160–1. Trevisa is referring to Origen's revision of the Septuagint and his *Hexapla*, on which see M. Wiles, 'Origen as Biblical Scholar', *CHB*, II, p. 458. On Jerome's translations of the Psalms, see n. 96, above.

168 Waldron, p. 293/160–4.

169 *WB*, I.59/26–28. The preceding quotation from Augustine's *De Doctrina Christiana* speaks of the innumerable translations of scripture into Latin (II, xi, 16); ed. J. Martin, CCSL XXXII (Turnhout: Brepols, 1962), p. 42/21–26. Su Fang Ng thinks the writer is advocating multiple translations of the Bible into English, but this seems unlikely in view of his promotion of WB: 'Translation, Interpretation and Heresy: The Wycliffite Bible, Tyndale's Bible and the Contested Origin', *Studies in Philology* 98 (2001), 328.

170 *WB*, I.59/29–30. Trevisa and 'First seiþ Bois' both say Bede translated the Gospel of John: Waldron, 'Trevisa's Original Prefaces on Translation', p. 292/142–4 and Bühler, 'A Lollard Tract', p. 174/133–5; on the authority of Cuthbert and Higden, see n. 37, above.

171 *WB*, I.59/30–2. Cf. Bühler, 'A Lollard Tract', p. 174/149–50 and Waldron, 'Trevisa's Original Prefaces on Translation', p. 292/137–8; on the authority of Higden, *Polychronicon*, VI, i; ed. Lumby, VI.356. See also Deanesly, *LB*, pp. 134–6, and Geoffrey Shepherd, *CHB*, II.370–1.

French – and, we might add, French speakers in England.[172] 'First seiþ Bois' lists Spanish, French, German, Italian and Flemish as languages into which scripture has been translated; 'Alle cristine peple stant in þre maner of folke' says people can hear scripture in their own language in Rome, the rest of Italy, France and Germany; and Ullerston lists Wendels (Slavs), Armenians, French, Germans and Spaniards.[173] Unsurprisingly, there is no mention in these texts of the Waldenses as instigators of translation of the Bible into medieval European vernaculars.[174]

The passage of the Prologue to the Wycliffite Bible adducing precedents for translation concludes: 'lat þe Chirche of Engelond appreue þe trewe and hool translacioun of symple men þat wolden for no good in erþe, bi here witing [knowledge] and power, putte awei þe leste truþe, ȝea þe leste lettre eiþer title [jot or tittle] of holy writ'.[175] In spite of this moving plea, the Wycliffite Bible was not approved by the English church, and the advocates of biblical translation lost the legal battle to be allowed open access to the law of God in their mother-tongue in 1409. Archbishop Thomas Arundel's articles against heresy, usually called the *Constitutions*, were promulgated at the London Council at St Paul's on 14 January of that year, after having been issued at the Provincial Council at Oxford in 1407.[176] In the context of the Bible debate, it is ironic that the preamble to the seventh article of the *Constitutions*, concerning the Bible in English, makes Jerome's comments on the difficulty of translating scripture the justification for forbidding further translation:

Periculosa quoque res est, testante beato Hyeronymo, textum sacre scripture de uno in aliud ydioma transferre, eo quod in ipsis translationibus non de facili idem sensus in omnibus sensus retinetur, prout idem beatus Hyeronymus, etsi inspiratus fuisset, se in hoc saepius fatetur errasse.[177]

(It is a difficult and dangerous thing, as St Jerome testifies, to translate the text of holy scripture from one language into another, inasmuch as in such translations

[172] *WB*, I.59/29–33. Andrew Breeze argues that 'Britons' means Welsh (although in fact there are no scriptures in medieval Welsh): 'The Wycliffite Bible Prologue on the Scriptures in Welsh', *Notes and Queries* n.s. 46 (1999), 16–17. On the medieval French Bible, see pp. 83–4, below.

[173] Bühler, 'A Lollard Tract', p. 173/113–17, 125–27; 'Alle cristine peple', fol. 13v, Hunt, *TFST*, II. 270/390–5; Vienna, Österreichische Nationalbibl. 4133, fol. 198r. On vernacular translations of the Bible in medieval Europe, see *CHB*, II.338–491.

[174] But no surviving MSS of biblical translations clearly linked with Waldenses pre-date the sixteenth century: see Euan Cameron, *Waldenses: Rejections of Holy Church in Medieval Europe* (Oxford: Blackwell, 2000), pp. 216–20, 300.

[175] *WB*, I.58/35–8; cf. Matt. 5:18.

[176] C. R. Cheney, *Medieval Texts and Studies* (Oxford: Clarendon Press, 1973), pp. 123, 172.

[177] David Wilkins, ed., *Concilia Magnae Britanniae et Hiberniae*, vol. III (London, 1737), p. 317.

the same meaning is only with difficulty fully conveyed. St Jerome, although he was inspired, confesses that he often erred in this respect.)

In reality, as Rita Copeland points out, 'Jerome's theoretical interests in translation bear little resemblance to those positions for which his authority is invoked', and here his 'open-ended theoretical and practical questions contract into the rigid dictum that linguistic idiom resists and precludes translation'.[178]

Translations of the Bible are therefore prohibited, whether 'per viam libri vel libelli aut tractatus . . . iam noviter tempore dicti Johannis Wycliff, sive citra, compositus, aut in posterum componendus, in parte vel in toto, publice vel occulte' ('by way of a book, pamphlet or treatise . . . newly composed in the time of the said John Wyclif, or since then, or that may in future be composed, in part or in whole, publicly or privately'). The inhibition is to remain in place until such time as a translation is approved by the diocesan bishop or by a provincial council: in the event, it remained in place in all dioceses until 1529. As he said in a letter to Pope John XXIII in 1412, accompanying a copy of the *Constitutions*, Arundel believed that

ille pestilens et damnandae memoriae miserrimus Johannes Wycliff, serpentis antiqui filius . . . ipsam ecclesiae sacrosanctae fidem et doctrinam sanctissimam totis conatibus impugnare studuit, novae ad suae malitiae complementum scripturarum in linguam maternam translationis practica adinventa.[179]

(the pestilent and wretched John Wyclif, of cursed memory, son of the old serpent . . . endeavoured by every means to attack the very faith and sacred doctrine of holy church, devising, to fill up the measure of his malice, the expedient of a new translation of the scriptures into the mother-tongue.)

In spite of the very strong arguments advanced in favour of translation, and in spite of the fact that the opponents of translation never at any time offered any specific criticisms of the text of the Wycliffite Bible,[180] the association of the first English Bible with a man whom the church regarded as a notorious heretic made it impossible for those in favour of translation to persuade the ecclesiastical authorities to approve it. The consequences of the legislation of 1409 will be explored in the next chapter.

[178] *Pedagogy, Intellectuals and Dissent*, pp. 202–3, and see Copeland, 'The Fortunes of "Non Verbum pro Verbo": Or, Why Jerome Is Not a Ciceronian', in Roger Ellis, ed., *The Medieval Translator: The Theory and Practice of Translation in the Middle Ages*, vol. I (Cambridge University Press, 1989), pp. 27–8.

[179] Wilkins, *Concilia*, III.350.

[180] See Deanesly, *LB*, p. 15, and pp. 174–5, below.

CHAPTER 2

Censorship

Archbishop Arundel's articles against heresy to a large extent reaffirm earlier ecclesiastical legislation concerning the responsibility of the higher clergy to be watchful and to nip error in the bud.[1] What was new in 1409 was that for the first time the English Church withheld approval from a specified translation of the Bible. In his *determinacio* on biblical translation, probably written not long before the Oxford Council at which the *Constitutions* were issued, Palmer infers from the fact that no translation of the Bible into English has been formally approved by the Church that all existing translations are suspect.[2] Undoubtedly he anticipated, or knew, that the Archbishop would censor the Bible associated with Wyclif. The Wycliffite treatise *De Oblacione Iugis Sacrificii*, written in 1413, calls Arundel 'þe grettist enmy þat Crist haþ in Ynglond'.[3] Nicholas Watson argues that Arundel's *Constitutions* were 'the capstone of [an] increasingly systematic campaign of opposition to the Lollards', and 'one of the most draconian pieces of censorship in English history'.[4] Everything Ullerston had advocated in the debate about biblical translation, says Watson, received a resounding 'no' from the English Church in 1409: no vernacular scripture translated recently enough to be clearly understood (neatly side-stepping the question of whether earlier translations had needed formal approval); no vernacular theology; no lay access to clerical learning. The *Constitutions*, in Watson's

[1] See Ian Forrest, 'Ecclesiastical Justice and the Detection of Heresy in England, 1380–1430', DPhil thesis, University of Oxford (2003); on restraining the preaching of heresy, H. Leith Spencer, *English Preaching in the Late Middle Ages* (Oxford University Press, 1993), pp. 174–6.

[2] See p. 14, above.

[3] Ed. Hudson, *The Works of A Lollard Preacher*, EETS 317 (Oxford University Press, 2001), p. 167; on the date, pp. xlix–l. On the context of the *Constitutions* in Arundel's career, see Peter McNiven, *Heresy and Politics in the Reign of Henry IV: The Burning of John Badby* (Woodbridge: Boydell Press, 1987), pp. 114–16; see also Hudson, *PR*, pp. 82–7.

[4] 'Censorship and Cultural Change in Late-Medieval England: Vernacular Theory, the Oxford Translations Debate and Arundel's *Constitutions* of 1409', *Speculum* 70 (1995), 822–64, quots. at 825, 826. James Simpson also calls the *Constitutions* 'draconian': *The Oxford English Literary History, Volume 2. 1350–1547: Reform and Cultural Revolution* (Oxford University Press, 2002), p. 464.

view, inaugurated a major cultural change and profoundly affected the nature of religious writing in the vernacular.

In his comments about the censorship of biblical translation in Arundel's *Constitutions*, Watson echoes the words Thomas More puts into the mouth of the young man who is his debating-partner in *A Dialogue Concerning Heresies*, published in the year More became Henry VIII's Chancellor, 1529. 'Euery man knoweth,' says the youth, that 'the clergy of this realme hath forboden all the peple to haue any scripture translated into our tonge', and he says he concurs with the common view that this is 'an euyll made lawe'.[5] So it would be if it were the law, replies the Chancellor. He positions Arundel's article on biblical translation in what he understands to be its anti-Wycliffite context ('after that it was perceyued what harme the people toke by the translacyon, prologes and gloses of Wyclyffe and also of some other that after hym holpe to set forth his secte'), and also in the context the preamble to the article offers ('for as moche as it is daungerouse to translate the texte of scripture out of one tonge into another, as holy saynt Hyerom [Jerome] testyfyeth, for as moche as in translacyon it is harde alwaye to kepe the same sentence hole'), before going on to translate the article word for word as it appears in print in William Lyndwood's *Provinciale seu Constitutiones Anglie*, making sure the Latin-literate reader knows where to find the passage in this glossed edition of the Constitutions of the Province of Canterbury.[6]

The English Church cannot be said to censor translation when translations 'well done of olde before Wyclyffys dayes' may be read, and new translations may be read as soon as they have been examined and if necessary emended. Only the specific translations made by the heretics Wyclif and William Tyndale fall under the prohibition.[7] Crucially, recalling the wording of Arundel's letter to Pope John XXIII,[8] More reads the Archbishop's charge that Wyclif 'toke vpon him of a malycious purpose to translate [the Bible] of new' (p. 314/26–27) as confirmation of the existence of a previous and orthodox English translation. After all, Lyndwood's gloss on *noviter*, in

5 *A Dialogue Concerning Heresies*, III, xiiii, ed. Thomas C. M. Lawler, Germain Marc'hadour and Richard C. Marius, *The Complete Works of St. Thomas More*, vol. VI (New Haven: Yale University Press, 1981), p. 314/19, 12–14.

6 *Dialogue*, III, xiiii; p. 315/20–35; in the 1525 Antwerp edition of the *Provinciale*, Book V, ch. 2, *De magistris et potestate docendi*, fols. ccvi^{r-v}. More gives the running-head, *de magistris*, p. 316/16–18. For the text of the article, see p. 36, above.

7 *Dialogue*, III, xiiii; p. 316/2–9. On the ironic strategies of the *Dialogue* as a whole, see Brian Cummings, 'Reformed Literature and Literature Reformed', in Wallace, ed., *The Cambridge History of Medieval Literature*, pp. 834–9.

8 See p. 36, above.

the phrase 'iam noviter tempore dicti Johannis Wycliff, sive citra, compositus', specifies that translations made before the time of Wyclif are exempt from the prohibition.[9] In line with Lyndwood's interpretation, the date of Bodleian Fairfax 2, a complete Wycliffite Bible originally dated 1408, has been altered to look like 1308.[10] More says that he himself has seen 'bybles fayre & old wryten in Englyshe whych haue ben knowen & sene by the byshop of the dyocyse & left in ley mennys handys & womens to suche as he knew for good & catholyke folke'.[11] These Bibles cannot, in More's mind, have anything to do with Wyclif, chief of all heretics, who 'purposely corrupted that holy texte, malycyously plantyng therein suche wordys as myght in the reders erys serue to the profe of suche heresyes as he went about to sow, which he not onely set forth with his own translacyon of the Byble, but also with certayne prologes & glosys which he made thervpon'.[12]

As Margaret Deanesly reminds us, More knew and cared a great deal more about Tyndale's New Testament, published on the Continent three years before the *Dialogue Concerning Heresies* was published, than about Wyclif's Bible.[13] More supposes Wyclif's malice would have manifested itself in the same way as Tyndale's, through deliberate corruption of the text: as Brian Cummings argues, 'errors of language and of theology are for More virtually synonymous'.[14] More takes Arundel on trust that Wyclif's translation was heretical, particularly since he knows that the prologue to an English Bible exhibited at St Paul's Cross at the time Richard Hunne was posthumously denounced as a Lollard heretic, in 1514, had been seen to contain manifest heresies (though he does not recall specific details), and that this 'gaue the readers vndouted occasyon to thynke that the boke was wryten after Wyclyffs copy and by hym translated into our tonge'.[15] Conversely, the impeccably Catholic contexts in which he has seen handsome old English

9 Lyndwood's gloss reads 'apparet quod libros, libellos vel tractatus in anglicis . . . prius translatos de textu scripture legere non est prohibitum', fol. ccvi^{v}. Cf. John Lewis, *The History of the Life and Sufferings of the Reverend and Learned John Wicliffe* (London: Knaplock, 1720), pp. 329–30.

10 The fourth 'c' has been erased in the date 'm.cccc & viiij', fol. 385r; see *WB*, I.xlviii; De Hamel, *Book*, p. 177, and Appendix 4, below.

11 *Dialogue*, III, xv; p. 317/11–14. More perhaps assumes they have been licensed because of the terms of the *Constitutions*.

12 *Dialogue*, III, xiiii; p. 314/23, 28–32, p. 315/1.

13 *LB*, pp. 1–17. The printing of Tyndale's New Testament was begun in Cologne and completed in Worms in 1526; see De Hamel, *Book*, pp. 241–3.

14 *The Literary Culture of the Reformation: Grammar and Grace* (Oxford: Oxford University Press, 2002), p. 192.

15 *Dialogue*, III, xv; p. 330/20–22. More says he does not know whether this Bible was burned or not; in his view it would have been a good idea to preserve it, because of all the rumours that have surrounded the case, p. 330/22–26. On Hunne and on the exhibited Prologue, see further pp. 126 and 136, below.

Bibles – probably including Bodley 277, an outstandingly lavishly decorated Bible given by Henry VI to the London Charterhouse[16] – declare to More their non-Wycliffite origins. Ownership of scripture in English is suspicious only if there are grounds for suspecting the owner of heresy.

The young man of the *Dialogue Concerning Heresies* has one more telling point to make: it cannot be accidental that so few people own Bibles in English when so many would like to do so; it must be in the Church's interest to keep it that way.[17] More's reply is pragmatic. Heretics may be prepared to 'lay theyr money togyder and make a purse amonge them for the pryntyng of an euyll made or euyll translated boke',[18] knowing that it risks being proscribed and burned, since the financial loss will not fall on any one person; but a printer is not going to risk the outlay involved in publishing the whole Bible in English if he is not sure whether the translation falls under Arundel's prohibition, and will therefore need to be approved.[19] More professes himself surprised that God has not put it into the mind of a 'good vertuous man' to translate the Bible 'in faythfull wyse', and to have it approved by the whole clergy, or at least one bishop. He guesses, however, that no bishop would be prepared to go it alone in this delicate matter.[20]

At this point, More rehearses the reasons why the clergy are not eager for the Bible to be available in English.[21] We have already encountered these reasons in the late-medieval debate about biblical translation, but here there is the additional class-conscious twist that 'the worse sort' desire it more 'than them we fynde far better'.[22] Claiming not to accept the arguments against translation, More reminds the young man of the crucial legal point that the *Constitutions* of 1409 accept translation in principle.[23] He then reverts to consideration of the process by which an English Bible might be approved, speculating that the licensing Arundel mentions presumably includes the emending of errors, unless the translator is a heretic and the

[16] Fol. 375r; see Hudson, *PR*, p. 23, and Appendix 4, below.

[17] 'Surely so is it not for nought that the englysshe byble is in so fewe mennes handes whan so many wolde so fayne haue it', *Dialogue*, III, xvi; p. 331/13–15.

[18] As members of the Colins family did, paying 20s for an English Bible, with several people probably contributing to the cost: *The Acts and Monuments of John Foxe*, ed. S. R. Cattley and J. Pratt, vol. IV (London: Religious Tract Society, 1877), p. 237; see Hudson, 'Lollard Book Production', p. 132. For other instances, see Hudson, *PR*, p. 233.

[19] *Dialogue*, III, xvi; p. 331/16–27. More supposes that even printers and booksellers were unsure about the date and origins of WB.

[20] Ibid., p. 331/27–35.

[21] Ibid., pp. 332–4.

[22] Ibid., p. 332/4–5. If More's intended mode is anti-clerical satire, the arguments against translation are straightforwardly presented.

[23] Ibid., pp. 337–41; on the *Constitutions*, p. 340/29–32.

translation therefore faulty through and through.[24] A translation might be made by one man, 'or by dyuers dyuydynge the laboure amonge theym, and after conferrynge [collating] theyr seuerall partys togyther eche with other'.[25] Then the translation would need to be approved, and the printing authorized, and the bishop would according to 'hys dyscrecyon and wysedome delyuer [the Bible] to suche as he perceyueth honeste, sad [serious] and vertuous, wyth a good monycyon & fatherly counsayll to vse it reuerently with humble hart and lowly mynde'. The Bible should be returned to the bishop on the death of the borrower, 'so that as nere as may be deuysed no man haue it but of the ordinaryes [bishop's] hande'.[26]

Evidently More is thinking of schemes like the fifteenth-century 'common-profit' books: books composed or purchased from that part of a deceased person's estate designated for charitable works, and made available to the poor on permanent loan in return for the prayers of the readers for the soul of the testator.[27] A bishop, More thinks, would happily lay out the £10 or £15 such a scheme would cost (evidently he does not expect more than a handful of people to have English Bibles on loan in any one diocese). Not everyone would benefit from being loaned a whole Bible; the bishop might decide to provide Matthew, Mark and Luke but not John, Acts but not the Apocalypse, the letter to the Ephesians but not the letter to the Romans. Sometimes it might be necessary for the bishop to take back a Bible he has loaned, lest his children in God should damage themselves by misinterpreting it.[28] As the young man retorts, laymen and women would probably prefer to buy their own Bibles rather than submit to such a scheme.

More's hypothetical episcopally controlled translation presupposes a model of the relation between clergy and laity that is, like William Butler's a century before, uncompromisingly hierarchical and supervisory (doubtless he is aware that the scheme he suggests is implausible). English Bibles can safely be left in the hands of laymen and women just so long as the bishop knows these people to be 'good & catholyke folke'. The Reformers were certainly wise to assume that under a Catholic dispensation English Bibles were dangerous for them to have and to hold. On a flyleaf of the Wycliffite Bible which is now William H. Scheide 12 at Princeton, Richard Bowyer, son of Thomas Bowyer, a London grocer, records that his father received

[24] Ibid., p. 340/35–6, p. 341/1–3.
[25] Ibid., p. 341/10–13. More does not mention from what originals a translation might be made.
[26] Ibid., p. 341/13–19, 22–23.
[27] Wendy Scase, 'Reginald Pecock, John Carpenter and John Colop's "Common-Profit" Books: Aspects of Book Ownership and Circulation in Fifteenth-Century London', *Medium Ævum* 61 (1992), 261–74.
[28] *Dialogue*, III, xvi; p. 341/33–4, p. 343/27–35, p. 344/6–9.

this 'singuler jewell of antiquite & carefully preserved in the daungerous tyme of Quene Mary' on his marriage to his second wife, Joane Mery, in 1531.[29] Joane had been 'brought up by her Uncle Willyam Mery grocer of London, in whose house the true relygion of the Ghospell of our Saviour Jesus Christ [that is, Lollardy] was zealously professed, and the sayd Joane therein instructed and trayned in her youthe'. Her Bible passed to Richard's elder brother, Thomas, a lawyer of the Middle Temple. Writing in what he calls 'this most happy raigne of Good Queene Elizabeth', Thomas says that he 'doth veryly by Gods grace purpose to kepe this boke which in those superstitious tymes was kept in huggremuggre', and to leave it to his heirs 'as a perpetuall monument' (fol. 404r).

Before Mary's accession in 1553, Thomas Bowyer the elder, who after his marriage to Joane 'was grown to that estimation creaditt and welth in London that he was in election to be Alderman', made his ownership of this 'singuler jewell', which cost John H. Scheide £2375 in 1931,[30] sufficiently widely known for it to come to the attention of John Bale, during the period (c. 1548–52) when the Protestant polemicist and bibliographer was engaged upon preparing the manuscript index of British writers from which his printed *Scriptorum Illustrium Maioris Brytanniae . . . Catalogus* (1557–9) derives.[31] The index contains the following entry under the name Ioannes Wiclevus:

Bibliorum libros omnes in anglicum idioma transtulit adhibitis praefationibus, prologus uniuersalis de tota Bibliorum summa, qui continet xv. capita incipit *Viginti quinque libri veteris testamenti sunt libri fidei.*[32]

(He translated all the books of the Bible into common English with their individual prologues [and with] an overall prologue, a synopsis of the whole Bible, containing fifteen chapters, beginning: *Twenty-five books of the Old Testament are books of faith.*)

Bale records that these details derive from a copy 'ex domo magistri Bower', from Master Bowyer's household. Written above the prologue to the

[29] P_S (see list of manuscript sigla, pp. xiv–xvi above), fol. 403v; Percy A. Bowyer, 'Notes Concerning the Bowyer Family', *Sussex Archaeological Collections* 64 (1923), 105–8; for the ownership notes in this MS, see Appendix 4.

[30] It was sold by Alexander Peregrine Fuller-Acland-Hood to Quaritch in that year, and purchased by Scheide.

[31] John N. King, *ODNB* III.483. The index is preserved in Bodl. Selden supra 64, ed. Reginald Lane Poole and Mary Bateson, *Index Britanniae Scriptorum: John Bale's Index of British and Other Writers* (Woodbridge: Brewer, 1990).

[32] I.e., 'Fyue and twenty bookis of þe olde testament ben bookis of feiþ', the opening of the Prologue to WB, *WB*, I.1/1; fol. 94r, Poole and Bateson, *Index*, p. 266. In the *Catalogus* (*Scriptorum Illustrium Maioris Brytanniae . . . Catalogus*, 2 vols., Basle, 1557–9), Bale lists the Prologue, titled *Elucidarium Bibliorum*, and the Bible itself, separately: vol. I (Basel, 1557), pp. 451, 456.

Apocalypse in Bowyer's Bible is a note by Bale: 'Hunc prologum Gilberti Porretani in Apocalipsim transtulit Joannes Wiclevus in Anglicum sermonem' ('John Wyclif translated this prologue of Gilbert de la Porrée on the Apocalypse into English').[33] In his *Catalogus*, Bale records that Wyclif 'Transtulit in Anglicum sermonem Biblia tota adhibitis praefationibus atque argumentis cuique libro suis' ('translated the whole Bible into English, with prologues and synopses attached to each book').[34]

Both the city merchant Bowyer and the ex-Carmelite Bale were adherents of what they call the 'true religion', Protestantism, prematurely revealed to the English nation by Wyclif, the 'stella matutina' ('morning star') of the Reformation, as he was first called by Bale in the earlier version of his catalogue of writers.[35] At the time Bale saw Bowyer's Bible, in the reign of the godly but ailing Edward VI, renewed persecution by the Antichrist in the form of the Catholic Mary must have seemed all too likely. Creating a record of what Wyclif's Bible contained, and preserving it like a rare gem, were twin gestures towards ensuring the ultimate triumph of 'the true relygion of the Ghospell of our Saviour Jesus Christ'. The Bible had never been printed, although the Prologue had appeared as an anonymous work in 1536,[36] and Robert Crowley, printing it as *The Pathwaye to Perfect Knowledge* in 1550, asserts that it is 'The true copye of a Prolog wrytten about two C. yeres paste by John Wyckliffe (as maye justly be gatherid bi that, that John Bale hath written of him in his boke entitled the Summarie of famouse writers of the Ile of great Britain)'. In fact, in the *Summarium* there is no reference to the Prologue, although Bale asserts that Wycif translated the whole Bible.[37] Crowley is extrapolating from the fact that the Prologue he prints 'is founde written in an olde English Bible bitwixt the olde Testament and the Newe, whych Bible remaynith now in the kyng hys maiesties [Edward VI's] Chamber'.[38] The name of Wyclif verifies the text's religious content for Crowley as it falsifies it for More, while (unless kept in

[33] P_S, fol. 397r; see *RBMA*, no. 839; although the prologue was attributed to Gilbert de la Porrée in the late Middle Ages, the author is uncertain. This is the prologue to Apoc. normally found in WB in LV, ed. *WB*, IV.639–40; see Appendix 1, and p. 106, below.

[34] *Catalogus*, I.456.

[35] *Illustrium Maioris Britanniae Scriptorum . . . Summarium* (Wesel, 1548), fol. 154v; see Margaret Aston, *Lollards and Reformers: Images and Literacy in Late Medieval Religion* (London: Hambledon Press, 1984), pp. 244–5.

[36] Printed by John Gough, *The Dore of Holy Scripture*; on the author, fol. Bii^{v}.

[37] *Summarium*, fol. 157v, but perhaps *Introductorium scripturae* (fol. 157r) should be understood as referring to the Prologue (there is no incipit).

[38] Presumably Q, in which the Prologue is found in this position, fols. 275r–90v; see Appendix 4. In 1519, the Bible is recorded as belonging to 'Stephanus Tomson, sacri palacii notarii' (fol. 307r), i.e., the Palace of Westminster; see Hudson, *PR*, p. 234.

hugger mugger) rendering its owner liable to persecution in superstitious times.

A Protestant king might reasonably have a Wycliffite Bible at hand, but Catholic royal owners of English Bibles presumably cannot have regarded the translation as being in any way tainted with heresy. As we have seen, Henry VI donated Bodley 277 (edited by Conrad Lindberg as *King Henry's Bible*) to the London Charterhouse.[39] Henry VII owned British Library Royal 1. C. VIII,[40] and the Wycliffite Bible now in Wolfenbüttel[41] belonged to Thomas of Lancaster, son of Henry IV, before he was created Duke of Clarence in 1412.[42] Thomas of Gloucester, youngest son of Edward III, owned British Library Egerton 617/618; it was listed among his forfeited possessions, and valued at 40 shillings, in 1397.[43] Henry IV owned an English Bible that cannot now be identified: when Thomas Marlborough, a London bookseller, was indicted for having it in his possession, in 1419, it was valued at £5, not much less than the King's Latin Bible, £6 13s 4d.[44] This must have been a quite outstandingly sumptuous copy, but the three surviving Bibles known to have been in royal hands before the Reformation are all large and handsome volumes, certainly professionally produced, probably in London.[45]

It was Thomas of Gloucester's English Bible, prominently displayed in the British Museum, which caught the attention of the Catholic historian Francis Gasquet in the 1890s, leading him, in his essay on 'The Pre-Reformation English Bible', to consider the implications of the high quality of production of manuscripts of the medieval English Bible, of the number of copies recorded in orthodox Catholic contexts, of the number of copies apparently intended for liturgical use, and of the number of copies

[39] De Hamel, *Book*, pp. 183–5, figs.130–1; see Appendix 4.

[40] His arms are incorporated in the lower border of fol. 1r, originally the wrapper of the MS; see A. I. Doyle, 'English Books In and Out of Court from Edward III to Henry VII', in V. J. Scattergood and J. W. Sherborne, eds., *English Court Culture in the Later Middle Ages* (London: Duckworth, 1983), p. 169, and Anne Hudson, 'Lollard Book Production', in Jeremy Griffiths and Derek Pearsall, eds., *Book Production and Publishing in Britain 1375–1475* (Cambridge University Press, 1989), p. 129. For a description of A, the base text of LV in *WB*, see Appendix 4.

[41] Herzog-August-Bibliothek, Cod. Guelf. Aug. A. 2; see Index of MSS.

[42] De Hamel, *Book*, pp. 173–4; fig.122; Doyle, 'English Books In and Out of Court', pp. 168–9; W. Milde, ed., *Mittelalterliche Handschriften der Herzog August Bibliothek: 120 Abbildungen* (Frankfurt: Klostermann, 1972), pp. 182–3.

[43] Gloucester also owned the Gospels in English, valued at 6s 8d; see Doyle, 'English Books In and Out of Court', p. 168; Jeanne E. Krochalis, 'The Books and Reading of Henry V and His Circle', *The Chaucer Review* 23 (1988), p. 51; De Hamel, *Book*, pp. 173–4, fig. 116, and Appendix 4.

[44] Henry Summerson, 'An English Bible and Other Books Belonging to Henry IV', *Bulletin of the John Rylands Library* 79 (1997), 109–15. Could this be Bodl. 277?

[45] See De Hamel, *Book*, p. 174, and Doyle, 'English Books In and Out of Court', p. 169.

bequeathed in wills to heirs, churches or religious institutions (ownership of which was therefore openly acknowledged when the will was proved in the ecclesiastical court).[46] Gasquet revisits More's arguments that the pre-Reformation Church did not censor scripture in the vernacular, and argues that the Bible known as Wycliffite is the authorized, or at least 'semi-official and certainly perfectly orthodox', medieval translation.[47]

Gasquet's *The Old English Bible and Other Essays* appeared in the wake of Pope Leo XIII's *Apostolicae Curae* (1896), a bull which exacerbated Catholic–Protestant relations in England by declaring that 'ordinations carried out according to the Anglican (Church of England) rite have been, and are, absolutely null and utterly void'. Gasquet, Abbot-General of the English Benedictines, was a member of Pope Leo's commission on Anglican orders, and his attempts to exonerate the pre-Reformation English Church from the charge of censorship, and to wrest the medieval Bible from association with Wyclif, were predictably unwelcome to Protestant scholars, 'so damaging' were they, as Herbert Workman said, 'to the reputation of Wyclif, so subversive of Protestant tradition'.[48] To add insult to injury, Gasquet's tone was far from conciliatory: he ignored the evidence provided by records of heresy trials, and his claim that the Wycliffites had no particular interest in the scriptures in English was patently unsustainable.[49]

'Nothing,' said Arthur Ogle, reviewing *The Old English Bible* in 1901, 'has worked more powerfully to divorce [Englishmen's] hearts from the mediaeval type of discipline and authority than the fact that the first translators of the English Bible achieved their task under the censure of authority.'[50] Clerical censorship, in other words, was perceived as a necessary precondition for lay empowerment. The bitterness of the debate Gasquet inaugurated reminds us how much was at stake: if the first English Bible was not produced by Wyclif and the Wycliffites, and was not censored by Arundel, the history of the late medieval English Church and of the liberation of the

[46] F. A. Gasquet, 'The Pre-Reformation English Bible', in *The Old English Bible and Other Essays* (London: Nimmo, 1897), pp. 102–55 (on MSS of WB, pp. 139–46); the essay was first published in the *Dublin Review* 115 (1894), 122–52. Part II of the essay, replying to critics, contains no new evidence: *The Old English Bible*, pp. 156–78.

[47] Ibid., pp. 137–8.

[48] Herbert B. Workman, 'The First English Bible', *London Quarterly Review* 135 (1921), 191. Workman also writes of his 'reverence' for Purvey, ibid.

[49] *The Old English Bible*, pp. 126–30; evidently he had not read the Prologue to WB, see p. 129. David Knowles castigates his inaccuracies in 'Cardinal Gasquet as an Historian', in C. L. N. Brooke and G. Constable, eds., *The Historian and Character, and Other Essays* (Cambridge University Press, 1963), pp. 240–63.

[50] *Church Quarterly Review* 51 (1901), 139. F. G. Kenyon, *Our Bible and the Ancient Manuscripts*, 2nd edn (London: Eyre and Spottiswode, 1896), pp. 204–8, and F. D. Matthew, 'The Authorship of the Wycliffite Bible', *English Historical Review* 10 (1895), 91–9, also dismiss Gasquet's arguments.

English people at the Reformation would need to be completely rewritten. In the event, Deanesly's *The Lollard Bible* (1920) re-established the medieval English Bible as the Wycliffite Bible, prohibited by Arundel.[51] Workman, reviewing *The Lollard Bible*, says that Deanesly has utterly refuted Gasquet's contention that the church did not discourage biblical translation, and has shown that 'the old Protestant tradition was correct'.[52] In his view, Arundel's *Constitutions* were a crafty compromise, since the system of licences enabled the church to keep the English Bible out of the hands of the poor while evading a charge of outright suppression.[53]

LICENCES

If there was a system of licences, very little evidence of its operation has survived. The Carthusian Nicholas Love makes much to-do about obtaining a licence from Arundel for his *Mirror of the Blessed Life of Jesus Christ*, a translation and adaptation of the *Meditationes Vitae Christi*.[54] A memorandum detailing the process, included in about a third of the surviving manuscripts, claims that the work was presented to the Archbishop in London 'in about 1410', and that after examining the work 'per dies aliquot' ('for some days') he personally approved and commended it in every particular, and decreed that it should be made publicly available 'ad fidelium edificacionem et hereticorum sive lollardorum confutacionem' ('for the edification of the faithful and the confutation of heretics or lollards').[55] Love desired his *Mirror* both to be and to be seen to be authorized scripture for the laity, approved not just by a diocesan bishop, as the 1409 *Constitutions* required, but by the primate of all England – an 'official alternative', Kantik Ghosh suggests, 'to the Lollard Bible'.[56]

51 Deanesly argues specifically against Gasquet, *LB*, pp. 382–4.

52 'The First English Bible', 198, but see p. 9, above.

53 Ibid., 199; also Workman, *A Study of the English Medieval Church*, I.195. Workman points out that Gasquet's arguments incited scholars to discover other medieval English translations of scripture, e.g., Anna C. Paues, *A Fourteenth Century English Biblical Version Consisting of a Prologue and Parts of the New Testament* (Cambridge University Press, 1902).

54 Pseudonymously attributed to Bonaventura; ed. M. Stallings-Tany, *Ioannis de Cavlibus Meditaciones Vite Christi*, CCCM CLIII (Turnhout: Brepols, 1997); see Ghosh, *WH*, p. 247.

55 Michael M. Sargent, ed., *Mirror of the Blessed Life of Jesus Christ* (New York: Garland, 1992), p. 7; on the MSS including the memorandum, pp. xlv, cxxv; see Ghosh, *WH*, pp. 147–73, and Hudson, *PR*, pp. 437–40. A. I. Doyle suggests that the correct date is 1409, since Arundel was granted a confraternity in Mount Grace Priory in that year: 'Reflections on Some Manuscripts of Nicholas Love's *Myrour of the Blessed Lyf of Jesu Christ*', *Leeds Studies in English* n.s. 14 (1983), 83.

56 Ghosh, *WH*, p. 147; Ghosh argues that Bonaventura's notion of meditative discourse is 'premised . . . on a near-complete elision of the literal words of the Bible', p. 155, and that Love's adoption of this discourse is 'self-conscious and polemical' (p. 154).

Whether Arundel read Love's work as scrupulously as the memorandum suggests may well be doubted. A more realistic scenario is that he or a deputy checked that the English text was indeed a translation of the highly respectable *Meditationes*,[57] and that the passages of polemic against the Lollards, and the appended treatise on the sacrament, were fully orthodox.[58] *The Mirror of our Lady*, written for the Bridgettine nuns of Syon, Middlesex, after 1415 (the year of Syon's foundation) and before about 1450, gives a quite different description of the process of obtaining a licence: 'Forasmuche as it is forbode vndyr payne of cursynge that no man schulde haue ne drawe [translate] eny text of holy scripture Englisshe withoutte lycence of the bysshope diocesane . . . I asked and haue licence of oure bysshope [the Bishop of London] to drawe suche thinges in to Englysshe to yowre gostly comforte and proffite'.[59] Both his own and the nuns' consciences, the writer says, may thereby be 'the more sewre [secure] and clere'. Apparently the writer has been licensed as a trustworthy translator by the diocesan bishop; there is no suggestion that the bishop asked to see the result. Elsewhere, the writer of the *Mirror* speaks of the readers rather than the translation needing to be licensed: 'Of the psalmes I have drawen but fewe, for ye may have them of Rychard Hampoules [Rolle's] drawynge' – too early to fall under Arundel's prohibition – 'and out of Englisshe Bibles, if ye have lysence thereto'.[60]

The only Wycliffite Bible manuscript including a reference to something like a licence is John Rylands Library Eng. 77, a handsome New Testament in the Later Version with fine gold initials at the opening of each book, written around 1400 [see fig. 1].[61] A mid-fifteenth-century note in this manuscript says that it cost £4 6s 8d, and that it was 'over seyne [scrutinized] and redd be Doctor Thomas Ebbrall and Doctor Yve or þ^t^ [before] my moder bought it' [see fig. 2].[62] Thomas Eborall (d. 1471) and William Ive were Oxford graduates and successive masters (between 1444 and 1471) of Whittington College, a college of secular clergy founded by the executors

57 On the audience of the *Meditationes* and the *Mirror*, see Ghosh, *WH*, p. 248.

58 See Ghosh, *WH*, p. 148, and Sargent, *Mirror of the Blessed Life of Jesus Christ*, pp. xliv–lviii. The *Mirror* as approved in 1409/10 may be a revised version of an earlier text: see Doyle, 'Reflections', 82–93.

59 Aberdeen UL 134, fol. 56r; Henry Hargreaves, '*The Mirror of Our Lady*', *Aberdeen University Review* 42 (1968), 277; in John H. Blunt, ed., *The Myroure of Oure Ladye*, EETS e.s. 19 (London, 1873), p. 71. On the licensing of *The Mirror*, see Hargreaves, '*The Mirror*', 277–80.

60 Blunt, *The Myroure of Oure Ladye*, p. 3. On Rolle's *Psalter*, c. 1340, see p. 17, above.

61 Ker, *MMBL*, III.404–5; see also Hudson, *PR*, pp. 23–4, and Index of MSS, below. Ker dates the MS s. xiv/xv (p. 404). The initials are gold on a mauve or blue background, with the other colour as outline, and there are demi-vinet extenders in gold, blue and mauve.

62 R_77, fol. 267v.

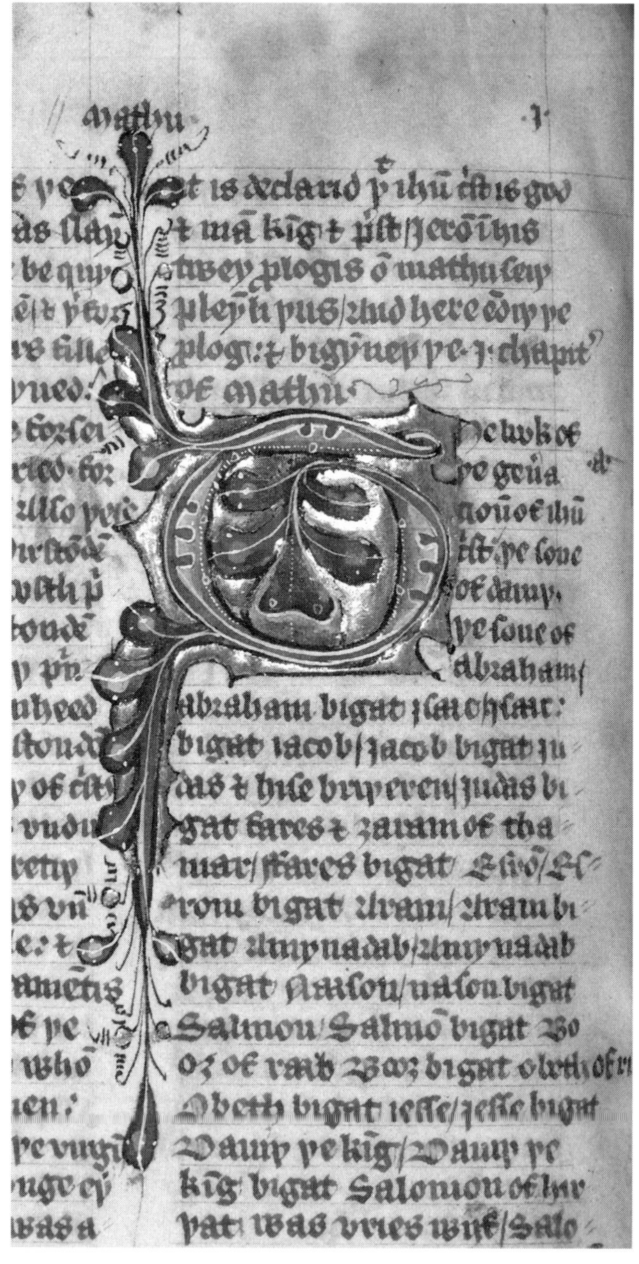

Figure 1. Initial at the opening of Matthew, John Rylands Library Eng. 77, fol. 16v. London (?), c. 1400.

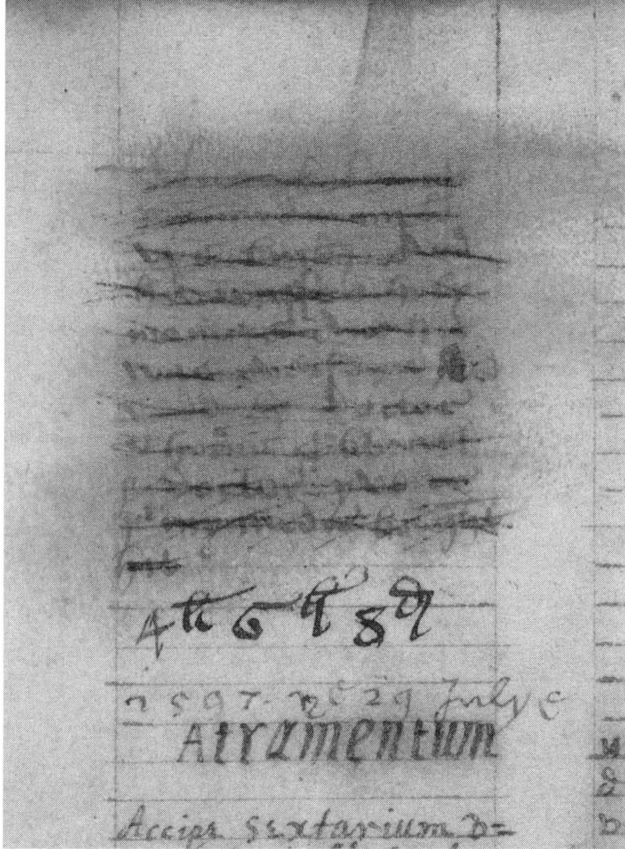

Figure 2. The 'licence' in John Rylands Library Eng. 77, fol. 267v.

of Richard Whittington, in part to supply priests to pray for the souls of Richard and his wife Alice, buried in the neighbouring Church of St Michael Paternoster Royal in the City of London, near St Paul's Church.[63] The master of the College was also rector of the church.

As Ralph Hanna points out, Eborall and Ive were both active in the suppression of heresy. Ive rebuked the London Carmelites for asserting the absolute poverty of Christ, and Eborall was among the theologians who determined that the writings of Reginald Pecock were heretical.[64] Pecock,

[63] Eborall was master and rector from 1444–64 and Ive from 1464–70; *BRUO*, pp. 622–3, 1008–9.

[64] 'English Biblical Texts before Lollardy', in Fiona Somerset, Jill C. Havens and Derrick G. Pittard, eds., *Lollards and their Influence in Late Medieval England* (Woodbridge: Boydell Press, 2003), p. 150.

who had been Eborall's predecessor as master of Whittington College, was convicted and deprived of the see of Chichester in 1457.[65] Yet the two examiners of John Rylands Library Eng. 77 also owned texts that imply a less hard-line orthodoxy. Ive owned Wyclif's *De Mandatis Divinis* ('On the Ten Commandments');[66] Eborall owned part of the New Testament in English, and *The Pore Caitif*, a text drawn into the Lollard ambit by the interpolation of Wycliffite material.[67] Wendy Scase has shown that Pecock, while master of Whittington College, was interested in schemes to provide the poor with books containing sound spiritual education in English, as a way of combatting the teachings London Lollards were circulating among themselves.[68] Perhaps he felt that the contents of 'common-profit' books were not scrutinized sufficiently closely before being made available on permanent loan.

A common-profit miscellany funded from the estate of John Colop, who was involved in the administration of the Whittington charity while Pecock and then Eborall were masters of the College, includes *Proper Will* and epistles associated with the author of *The Cloud of Unknowing*, the Carmelite Richard Lavenham's *Litil Tretys on the Seven Deadly Sins*, and the Wycliffite tract 'The holi prophete Dauid seiþ', which argues that priests should not prevent simple people from knowledge of God's law.[69] Colop's miscellany, for which he may have collected material in advance of his death,[70] also contains a portion of the *Glossed Gospels* (the section on the sacrament of the altar from the long Matthew),[71] remedies against 'foure

65 See Wendy Scase, 'Reginald Pecock', in *Authors of the Middle Ages*, ed. M. C. Seymour, vol. III, no. 8 (Aldershot: Variorum, 1996).

66 In Magdalen Coll. Oxf. lat. 98; see Ralph Hanna, 'English Biblical Texts Before Lollardy', in Somerset *et al.*, *Lollards and Their Influence in Late Medieval England*, p. 150.

67 Ibid. The wording of the will of 1465 by which Eborall acquired biblical material in English is ambiguous: 'two volumes of Gospels (or gospel lections?) and Epistles (or epistle lections?) in Latin and English', *BRUO*, p. 623; possibly the biblical text was in both languages, as in Eton 24 (dated 1455), where each chapter of Apoc. in Latin is followed by an English translation; see Ker, *MMBL*, II.650–1. On *The Pore Caitif*, see M. Teresa Brady, '*The Pore Caitif*: an Introductory Study', *Traditio* 10 (1954), 529–48, and Hudson, *PR*, p. 425.

68 'Reginald Pecock', p. 90, and Scase, 'Reginald Pecock, John Carpenter and John Colop's "Common-Profit" Books', 265–6. On St Paul's as the centre of the London book trade, see C. Paul Christianson, *Memorials of the Book Trade in Medieval London: The Archives of Old London Bridge* (Cambridge University Press, 1987), pp. 48–9. On Lollard book production in London, see also pp. 53, 77, below.

69 CUL Ff. 6. 31; Scase, 'Reginald Pecock, John Carpenter and John Colop's "Common-Profit" Books', 267–9, and A. I. Doyle, 'The European Circulation of Three Latin Spiritual Texts', in Minnis, ed., *Latin and Vernacular*, p. 133. On 'The holi prophete Dauid seiþ', see pp. 12–13, above.

70 The MS is in two distinct parts, originally with separate foliations; Scase, 'Reginald Pecock, John Carpenter and John Colop's "Common-Profit" Books', 264. John's younger relative Richard (d. 1476) was a stationer, 262.

71 Part 2, fols. 27v–36r; see Hargreaves, 'Popularising Biblical Scholarship: the Role of the Wycliffite *Glossed Gospels*', in Lourdaux and Verhelst, eds., *The Bible and Medieval Culture*, p. 185.

errours which letten (prevent) þe verrey knowyng of holy writt' ('wordly maner', 'fleschly lust', 'fals couetise' and 'veyn glorie'),[72] and a selection of biblical texts on three topics: 'How thu schuldest not adde ne abrigge ouȝt [anything], change not ne countre not þe biddingis of god'; 'Sewe [follow] not wittis ne lawis of mon', and 'Wo for lust of gloteny'.[73] As Scase and Mishtooni Bose point out, Pecock evidently regards the first part at least as a Lollard text, for he counters its assertion that the curse on anyone who adds to or takes away from the prophecies in the book of Revelation (Apoc. 22:18–19) 'spekiþ nat of alle þe wordis of þis book [of the Apocalypse only] but of alle þe wordis of holi writ in the Bible'.[74] Pecock supposes that the writer is arguing against all glossing and commentary whatever rather than (as is surely the case) arguing for an accurate rendition of the naked text and for the primacy of its literal meaning.

In Bose's words, 'the particular network of literary practices [including interpretive practices] that fostered the compiling of this enigmatic codex remains largely inscrutable'.[75] Colop's miscellany is neither patently orthodox nor patently heterodox.[76] If his executors had asked Eborall to look through the volume before loaning it out, would he have had (as Pecock clearly would) any anxieties about the appropriateness of its contents for simple laypeople? Would he have felt differently about authorizing a volume for the use of unknown poor readers than he felt about authorizing the New Testament of a woman who, Hanna observes, must have been wealthy as well as literate in English, and shrewd enough to know the terms of Arundel's *Constitutions*? 'Mother, Eborall and Ive', says Hanna, 'testify to a situation thoroughly removed from the crusades of extirpation by which Lollardy is often known to us. Here we witness a transaction involving all the trappings at least of orthodoxy, with Lollard scripture at its centre'.[77] Nevertheless, this transaction seems to be *sui generis*. The note is an informal record, and no bishop was involved in approving the translation or the reader. *The Mirror of Our Lady* suggests that reader and translator, but not the translation itself, need to be licensed; More apparently thinks

[72] Part 2, fols. 98v–99v. [73] Part 1, fols. 61r–v; 61v–62v; 62v–63r.

[74] Part 1, fol. 61v. Scase, 'Reginald Pecock, John Carpenter and John Colop's "Common-Profit" Books', 267; Mishtooni Bose, 'Reginald Pecock's Vernacular Voice', in Somerset *et al.*, eds., *Lollards and their Influence*, pp. 230–1. Pecock's argument is in his *Repressor of Over Much Blaming of the Clergy*, ed. Churchill Babington, vol. I, Rolls Series (London, 1860), p. 55. 'How thu schuldest not adde ne abrigge' also cites Deut. 4:2 and seven other texts, all of which, the writer argues, should be interpreted as referring to the Bible as a whole.

[75] 'Reginald Pecock's Vernacular Voice', p. 231.

[76] James Simpson warns against 'distinguishing too readily between the orthodox and heterodox in the early fifteenth century': 'Saving Satire after Arundel's Constitutions: John Audelay's "Marcol and Solomon"', in Barr and Hutchison, eds., *Text and Controversy*, p. 386.

[77] 'English Biblical Texts before Lollardy', p. 151.

both translation and reader need to be licensed. If there had been frequent applications for licences, the outline at least of the legal process would surely have been less ambiguous.

Certainly the 1409 *Constitutions* refer to the translation, not the translator or reader, needing to be approved. The editors and scribes of those Wycliffite Bible manuscripts that contain selected books, chapters and verses of the Bible, rather than a continuous biblical text, may well have been hoping to evade the legislation by concealing the fact that the extracts derived from a complete (and therefore Wycliffite) Bible.[78] Sven Fristedt makes this case in relation to Cambridge University Library Ee. 1. 10, which once contained an abridged version of the whole of the Old Testament.[79] One would have thought that Eborall and Ive, given a complete New Testament to examine, would have looked carefully for any heretical prologues or glosses. In that case, the prologues to Matthew in John Rylands Library Eng. 77 would, one might think, have given them pause. The first prologue, beginning 'Seynt Austyn seiþ in þe secunde book Of Crysten Doctryne', based almost entirely on Augustine's *De Doctrina Christiana*, is one of the prologues to Matthew in the *Glossed Gospels*;[80] the third is the usual and unexceptionable Later Version prologue.[81] The second prologue to Matthew in this manuscript, however, 'Oure Lord Jesu Crist verry god and man', is the second of the tracts in favour of translation in Cambridge University Ii. 6. 26.[82] This text claims that 'Euery cristen man or woman haþ taken þe staat, autorite and bonde of God in his cristendom to be a disciple of holy write and a real techer þerof, vp[on] peyne of dampnacion in al his lijf', and bitingly asks 'What Antecrist dare for schame of cristen men lette lewide men to lerne her lesson so hard [insistently] comaundid of God?'[83]

78 They include ç (extracts from Kings–Chron. and Sapiential books in LV), f (Job, Tobit in LV), R_83 (extracts from Sapiential books in LV), R_89 (extracts from Prophets in ELV), g (Tobit, Dan. 13 in LV), Bodl. 771 (extracts from OT and NT in EV), Bodl. Douce 36 (Tobit in LV), Bodl. Laud misc. 182 (extracts from NT in LV), Huntington 501 (extracts from Prol. to WB and OT in ELV), and Keio UL 170 X 9. 6 (extracts from Prol. to WB and OT in LV); see also Index of MSS. The summary of Gen.–James 1 in Trin. Coll. Oxf. 93 makes use of LV, but is only partially dependent on WB.

79 Fristedt, *WB*, *II*.liii. Z now contains only 2 Chron.–2 Macc. 15:10; see Henry Hargreaves, 'An Intermediate Version of the Wycliffite Old Testament', *Studia Neophilologica* 28 (1956), 129–47, and Appendix 4, below.

80 R_77, fols. 13r–15r; prologue to the 'intermediate' gloss on Matthew, and also one of the prologues to *Oon of Foure*, ed. Hunt, *TFST*, II.370–82 (R_77 ends at II.375/153); the part contained in R_77 is also ed. *WB*, I.44–9; on the MSS, see Hunt, *TFST*, I.190–2 (and on R_77, I.163). On the relationship between 'Seynt Austyn seiþ' and the Prol. to WB, see p. 130, below.

81 'Matheu þat was of Judee, as he is set first in ordre', *WB*, IV.2; *RBMA*, no. 590 + 589; see Appendix 1 for the contents of WB, and p. 106, below.

82 R_77, fols. 15r–16r; see p. 15, above.

83 Hunt, *TFST*, II.284/61–7; R_77 shares the reading of 63–4 with o and Dresden Sächsische Landesbibl. Od. 83, Hunt, *TFST*, II.287.

This prologue to Matthew is not heretical, but its language is undoubtedly inflammatory, and it implies a context of Lollard discourse about the deficiencies of the ecclesiastical hierarchy. If Eborall and Ive read it, they must have seen that the corollary of its argument for unhindered access to scripture in English is that the terms of Arundel's *Constitutions* are contrary to the will of God. Possibly they appreciated the irony of their own position in relation to what they were reading; possibly they had some sympathy with the prologue-writer (though, if so, they doubtless thought he underestimated the need for the laity to be guided in the interpretation of scripture); possibly they looked only at the non-controversial opening (as Wycliffites hoped orthodox clergy would do). They may not have read the prologues at all, but simply checked that the English biblical text, or at least the beginning of Matthew, was a faithful rendition of the Latin. Eborall may have checked the text against his own English Gospels and Epistles. Possibly they thought they were being asked to license the reader as much as the text, in which case her very request, whatever else they may have known of her, demonstrated her anxious orthodoxy.

In the absence of any other evidence of licensing of Wycliffite Bible manuscripts, we can only speculate about the implications of the Eborall and Ive instance. Certainly a considerable number of apparently unlicensed copies of the Wycliffite Bible, or parts of it, were in unquestionably orthodox ownership before the Elizabethan Settlement.[84] Apart from the copies in royal ownership already mentioned, William Weston, last Lord Prior of St John's of Jerusalem at Clerkenwell, owned the New Testament in the Later Version now Magdalene College Cambridge Pepys 2073;[85] Anne Danvers gave John Rylands Library Eng. 81 (a New Testament in the Earlier Version) to her 'mastre confessor and his bretherne encloosed in Syon', sending it by her son on Mid-Lent Sunday, 1517, and asking the monks to pray for her family, alive and dead (their names are listed), and for John and Thomas, servants of William Danvers;[86] British Library Additional 10596 (Tobit and Susanna in the Later Version) belonged to the nuns of Barking

[84] See Hudson, *PR*, 23, and *WB*, I.xxi.

[85] Fol. 351v; Rosamond McKitterick and Richard Beadle, *Catalogue of the Pepys Library at Magdalen College Cambridge*, vol. V, i (Cambridge: Brewer, 1992), p. 50; see Gasquet, *The Old English Bible*, p. 143. On the presence of religious dissidents in Clerkenwell, see Maureen Jurkowski, 'Lollard Book Producers in London in 1414', in Barr and Hutchison, eds., *Text and Controversy*, pp. 219–22.

[86] R_81, fol.153v; Ker, *MMBL*, III.406–7; see Gasquet, *The Old English Bible*, pp. 144–5. On the donation, and the fact that Syon owned a copy of the Wycliffite *Glossed Gospels*, see Vincent Gillespie, 'The Mole in the Vineyard', in Barr and Hutchison, eds., *Text and Controversy*, p. 159, and on the lost libraries of Syon, pp. 131–61, and 'The Book and the Brotherhood: Reflections on the Lost Library of Syon Abbey', in A. S. G. Edwards, Vincent Gillespie and Ralph Hanna, eds., *The English Medieval Book: Studies in Memory of Jeremy Griffiths* (London: British Library, 2000), pp. 185–208.

Abbey;[87] Edmund Bonner, Bishop of London under Henry VIII, Edward VI, Mary and Elizabeth, owned Lambeth Palace 25 (a complete Bible);[88] Norwich Cathedral Priory owned Columbia University Plimpton 269 (a New Testament, lacking the Gospels, in the Later Version);[89] the Franciscan house at Shrewsbury owned Bodley 771 (extracts from the Old and New Testaments in the Earlier Version);[90] Bodleian Rawlinson c. 258 (a New Testament in the Later Version) belonged to the Dominican recluse John Lacy, who copied and illuminated St John's College Oxford 94 (containing the Hours of the Virgin and Middle English devotional texts) between 1420 and 1434.[91] Lacy was associated with Newcastle from at least 1408, and an erased inscription (fol. 1r) links this New Testament with the house of the Dominican recluses in Newcastle.[92] St John's College Cambridge E. 14, containing the Psalms, the Canticles and the Athanasian Creed in the Later Version, and the five Sapiential books (Proverbs–Ecclesiasticus), was owned by Clemens Ridley, servant to Robert Shurton, priest, who bequeaths his soul to God 'and to the Blessed Virgin Mary and all the saints', and his body to be buried at St Katherine-iuxta-Turrem, London.[93]

A wide range of religious orders, military, monastic, fraternal and eremitical, is represented in this list, and Danvers's donation to Syon shows that scripture in English, like common-profit books, was seen to be exchangeable for prayer for souls in purgatory. Giving her New Testament to a religious foundation would mean, Danvers must have hoped, that prayers would be said for her family in perpetuity, certainly for longer than the twenty-two years the house at Syon had remaining to it before it was dissolved. This transaction seems a world away from any hint of heresy, so that the idea of asking whether Danvers's New Testament had been licensed by a diocesan bishop or by a provincial council in accordance with the *Constitutions* of 1409 is apparently otiose. Nevertheless, giving the book away during her lifetime meant that Danvers secured the prayers of priests for the souls of her family without leaving a volume of scripture in English to be declared as part of her estate. A cleric, John Hopton, chaplain of the chantry of St Nicholas in Holy Trinity Church, Goodramgate, York, and a layman, Philip Baunt, a Bristol merchant, willed their English Gospels, in 1394 and

[87] Ker, *MLGB*, p. 6; see Gasquet, *The Old English Bible*, p. 142.

[88] Ibid., p. 143, and Appendix 4, below. [89] Ker, *MLGB*, p. 138. [90] Ibid., p. 179.

[91] Ralph Hanna, *A Descriptive Catalogue of the Western Medieval Manuscripts of St John's College Oxford* (Oxford University Press, 2002), pp. 125–30.

[92] *P*, fol.1r; Ker, *MLGB*, pp. 134, 284. On Lacy's association with Newcastle, see Hanna, *A Descriptive Catalogue*, p. 209.

[93] C_J_E.14, flyleaf, in a s.xv hand; M. R. James, *A Descriptive Catalogue of the Manuscripts in the Library of St John's College Cambridge* (Cambridge University Press, 1913), p. 150.

1404 respectively, to St Nicholas's chantry and to a chaplain of St Mary Redcliffe, but William Danvers, who took his mother's New Testament to Syon for her, may perhaps have suggested the scheme as a way of avoiding potential embarrassment to him.[94]

In any case, several members of religious orders, a few clerics and at least one layman apparently regarded unlicensed ownership of unlicensed scripture in English as unproblematic. Gasquet accounts for the situation by arguing that the medieval English Bible was a non-Wycliffite translation approved by the church, and Michael Wilks, though arguing from very different kinds of evidence, also thinks its origins were non-Wycliffite.[95] In the next chapter, I argue that the medieval English Bible is indeed the Wycliffite Bible, but, as Hudson says, there is no evidence that the controversy inaugurated by Arundel produced 'the easy tests of identity through the rendering of certain biblical words that characterize the arguments between Thomas More and William Tyndale'.[96] Rather than leading to the enforcement of legislation for the approval of individual volumes containing scripture, or scriptural passages, in English, Arundel's *Constitutions* seem to have resulted in a situation whereby the perceived orthodoxy of the owner was made to vouch for the orthodoxy of the translation owned.[97] Laypeople were less likely than clergy – *a fortiori* less likely than members of religious orders – to be confident about their perceived orthodoxy. In the one case in which an English New Testament was approved by clerics for a laywoman, there is no suggestion that any emendation or excision was asked for, even though we should have expected that what we recognize as Wycliffite prologues would signal that this was the translation specifically prohibited by Arundel.

We do not know this woman's name, and the fact that manuscripts of the Wycliffite Bible so rarely contain records of pre-Reformation lay

94 For Hopton's will, see James Raine, ed., *Testamenta Eboracensia, or Wills Registered at York*, pt. I (London: Surtees Society, 1834), p. 196, and for Baunt's will, *William Barrett, The History and Antiquities of the City of Bristol* (Bristol: William Pine, 1789), p. 583; see *WB*, I.xxxii, and Gasquet, *The Old English Bible*, pp. 143–4. Hopton also owned a 'psalterium glosatum' and 'unum librum qui vocatur Speculum Ecclesiae'.

95 Wilks questions whether Wyclif would have approved of a literal translation of the Bible for laypeople, and argues that Sven L. Fristedt and Conrad Lindberg's work on the MSS of WB shows there is no evidence linking MSS of WB in EV with Wyclif: 'Misleading Manuscripts: Wyclif and the Non-Wycliffite Bible', *Studies in Church History* 11 (1975), 147–61. Hudson finds Wilks's case 'unconvincing', *PR*, pp. 154–7, 240, as does the present writer.

96 Hudson, *PR*, p. 24. David Crystal, however, thinks that words used in the English Bible would have been perceived to have a 'Wycliffian identity': *The Stories of English* (London: Penguin Books, 2005), p. 240.

97 As Shannon McSheffrey also argues: 'Heresy, Orthodoxy and English Vernacular Religion', *Past and Present* 186 (2005), 68–70; see also McSheffrey and Tanner, eds., *Lollards of Coventry*, pp. 31–2.

ownership and only infrequently contain records of pre-Reformation clerical ownership suggests a widely felt fear that possession of scripture in English might be regarded as incriminating by the authorities of church and state. This fear was well founded. In 1416, Archbishop Henry Chichele directed the Bishop of London to publish a 'statute against heretics', requiring bishops and archdeacons to 'enquire diligently at least twice a year about people suspected of heresy' because they attended conventicles, stood out from the usual run of the faithful in their way of life, professed errors or heretical opinions, or owned 'libros suspectos in lingua vulgari anglicana conscriptos' ('suspect books written in the common tongue, English').[98] The previous year, John Claydon, an illiterate skinner who lived in Aldersgate, was indicted as a relapsed heretic (he had been convicted and imprisoned by Robert Braybrooke, Bishop of London 1381–1404), tried before Chichele, delivered to the secular arm and burned principally because he had had made for him and read to him a copy of the Wycliffite book *The Lanterne of Liȝt* and professed to agree with its opinions, which are detailed in Chichele's *Register*.[99] Palmer was one of the doctors who examined the book. Biblical books in English were evidently 'suspect' too: William Harry of Tenterden, who fled to London after Chichele ordered a large-scale arrest of suspected heretics in Kent in May 1428, confessed in Convocation in July that he had 'read various books of holy scripture in the common tongue' and had often attended conventicles with men suspected of Lollardy.[100] He abjured, but for lack of sufficient surety for good behaviour was imprisoned at the Archbishop's pleasure. We do not know when or whether he was released.

Geoffrey Blyth, Bishop of Coventry and Lichfield 1503–30, explains to the Bishop of Lincoln in a letter dated 3 November 1511 that gaoling suspected heretics is not only a good way of persuading them to abjure but also a good way of getting episcopal hands on 'right many dampnable books, which shall noye [harm] no more by Goddes grace'.[101] We might assume that the books confiscated by Blyth were overtly Wycliffite, were it not that the records of heresy hearings before Blyth and his predecessor, John Hales,

98 E. F. Jacob, ed., *The Register of Henry Chichele, Archbishop of Canterbury, 1414–1443*, vol. III (Oxford: Clarendon Press, 1945), p. 18. On the legal proceedings against Lollards in the Convocation of the Province of Canterbury, see vol. I (1943), pp. cxxix–cxliv. For Henry V's statute against Lollards in 1414, see Wilkins, *Concilia*, III.358–60, and *The Register of Henry Chichele*, vol. IV (1947), p. 145.

99 Ibid., pp. 132–8; see Hudson, *PR*, pp. 167, 211–14.

100 *The Register of Henry Chichele*, III.189–90; see Aston, *Lollards and Reformers*, pp. 78–9. On fears of a heretical insurgency in 1428, see pp. 76–81.

101 McSheffrey and Tanner, eds., *Lollards of Coventry*, pp. 139–40. Blyth's annotations on the Prologue to WB survive; see p. 174, below, and the description of MS S in Appendix 4.

preserved in the Lichfield Court Book, frequently refer to books owned by alleged Lollards as 'books containing heresy' or 'books of heretical depravity', when the books which are identified in the records are predominantly biblical: Tobit, for example, is mentioned in depositions four times, the Gospels are mentioned six times and the Pauline Epistles eight times.[102]

There is evidence that the Coventry deponents themselves thought that possession of scripture in English was incriminating. On 5 November 1511 Alice Rowley, widow of William, a draper and sometime mayor of Coventry, deposed that before being taken into custody she gave Joan Smyth, also widow of a sometime mayor but since remarried, 'duos libros, unum de mandatis, alium de epistolis Jacobi' ('two books, one on the commandments and the other the Catholic Epistles' – or perhaps just the Epistle of James).[103] On the same day, Matthew Markelond (aka Maclyn), a fuller, deposed that when he had abjured twenty-five years previously, during the episcopate of John Hales, 'he burned a book he owned, the Gospels in English' ('cremavit librum quem in Anglic' de evangeliis habuit'), presumably because of the risk involved in keeping it; and Thomas Clerc, a hosier, deposed that his wife Cristiana knew about an 'extremely bad book' he owned and 'wanted him to burn it'.[104] Markelond continued to be familiar with the Gospels in English; on 31 October 1511 Robert Hachet, a lawyer, deposed that Markelond knew by heart the gospel beginning 'In principio', that is, John's Gospel (perhaps just the first chapter).[105] Hudson is doubtless right that memorization was 'a skill deliberately chosen for its evangelizing potential', rather than 'a poor alternative to reading'.[106]

On the basis of the admittedly patchy records that survive – and even the evidence that does survive, as Hudson points out, is 'selected, formulaic, and by definition hostile'[107] – McSheffrey states that 'the simple possession of scripture in English was never the sole basis for an accusation of heresy in the later fifteenth or early sixteenth centuries'.[108] On the face of it this is reassuring, but even if it could be proved to be true of all dioceses from

102 McSheffrey, 'Heresy, Orthodoxy and English Vernacular Religion', 61; *Lollards of Coventry*, p. 343. Separate deponents may, of course, be referring to a single copy. For other examples, see Hudson, *PR*, pp. 22, 166–7, 186–8, 231.

103 On Rowley and Smyth, *Lollards of Coventry*, pp. 27, 315; on Rowley's books, pp. 46, 155; on the concealing of books, see also pp. 208, 217–8, 245, and Hudson, *PR*, pp. 168, 460–1.

104 *Lollards of Coventry*, pp. 152, 188; on the destruction of books, see also pp. 106, 126, 185, and Hudson, *PR*, p. 168.

105 *Lollards of Coventry*, pp. 45, 124.

106 *PR*, p. 191; on memorization, pp. 190–2.

107 *PR*, pp. 32–41 (quot. at 39). The surviving records are detailed by David M. Smith, *A Guide to Bishops' Registers of England and Wales: A Survey from the Middle Ages to the Abolition of Episcopacy in 1641* (London: Royal Historical Society, 1981).

108 'Heresy, Orthodoxy and English Vernacular Religion', 63; also *Lollards of Coventry*, pp. 22–3.

1380 to 1535, the likeliest way for suspected Lollards to 'reveal themselves', as Hudson points out, 'was by their ownership of [English] books',[109] so that even if possession of scripture in English never stood alone in an indictment it may sometimes or often have been the crucial factor in the prosecution and trial of an alleged Lollard. Demonstratively orthodox behaviour, such as having one's English New Testament scrutunized by two doctors of divinity, makes sense in this context.

Social status and influence doubtless played a part in persuading the ecclesiastical authorities not to enquire over-zealously about ownership of English scripture, but according to her own testimony Alice Rowley, who may have been of similar status to the owner of John Rylands Library Eng. 77, put herself in the position of being overheard by John Cropwell, a wire-drawer and servant of Joan Smyth, talking about heretical opinions with Thomas Bown, a shoemaker, in the nave of the Benedictine Priory Church in Coventry.[110] The penance Blyth imposed on Rowley, following her abjuration in January 1512, was that, carrying her own faggot on her shoulder, she should watch the burning of her friend Joan Warde (aka Wasshingburn, who had relapsed after abjuring some twenty years previously, and was executed on 15 March 1512), and that she should then leave the wood with an offering of twelve pence at the shrine of Mary of the Tower in the Carmelite friary, a popular place of pilgrimage.[111] The records say nothing more about Rowley, but on 4 April 1520 Joan Smyth, Robert Hachet, Thomas Bown and four others went to the stake as relapsed heretics.[112]

LITURGICAL USE

One of the features of John Rylands Library Eng. 77 that Eborall and Ive probably did recognize, and which may have contributed to their approval of the book as orthodox, is that it opens with a liturgical calendar incorporating a lectionary according to the established Use of Sarum (Salisbury), indicating which epistles and gospels are read at mass throughout the year.[113] Thomas of Gloucester's Bible, written before 1397, contains one, and at least

109 *PR*, p. 166; also Deanesly, *LB*, pp. 352–3.

110 *Lollards of Coventry*, pp. 37, 158.

111 Ibid., pp. 9, 238–40, 241.

112 Ibid., pp. 9–10; John Foxe, *Actes and Monuments* (London: John Day, 1563), pp. 420–1. Rowly perhaps died before 1520. Foxe suggests a degree of reluctance on Blyth's part to deliver these heretics to the secular arm, perhaps because he was unwilling to create martyrs.

113 R_77, fols. 4r–12r. Some MSS include a separate Calendar and Lectionary, e.g., Trinity Coll. Camb. B. 10. 20 and Bodl. Fairfax 11.

two others were probably written before 1400.[114] A complete calendar-plus-lectionary contains three elements: the temporal, which comprises dominicals and ferials (Sundays and weekdays) and festivals throughout the Christian year, beginning with the first Sunday of Advent; the sanctoral, which comprises the proper of saints (individual saints' days throughout the Christian year, usually beginning with St Andrew's Eve, 29 November) and the common of saints (days celebrating a species of saint, such as virgin, confessor or martyr); and, thirdly, the commemorations (days of special observance or special need, for instance 'for reyn').[115] The lectionary in John Rylands Library Eng. 77 contains all these, but (as is very often the case) combines the common of saints with the proper of saints rather than listing them separately.[116]

The rubric usually found at the beginning of the lectionary in the Later Version of the Wycliffite Bible explains that it is a 'rule [canon-table] þat telliþ in whiche chapitris of þe bible ȝe mai fynde þe lessouns, pistlis and gospels, þat ben rad in þe chirche al þe ȝeer'.[117] The system for finding the lections in the biblical text is explained: the tables give the name of the biblical book, the number of the chapter, the opening and closing words of each lection and a letter between 'a' and 'g', and this letter is written in the margin beside the opening of the lection.[118] The end of the lection

[114] *G*, 618, fols. 160r–177r, with the opening words of the lections in Latin and EV, Bodl. Hatton 111, fols. 13v–34r, and *S*, fols. 1r–3v, in EV. In c and Emmanuel Coll. Camb. 34, a lectionary in LV includes a note relating to the liturgical effect of leap years which is dated 1397, but since the note was probably originally copied from a calendar, the date provides only a *terminus post quem*. P. R. Robinson, however, dates the Emmanuel MS to 1397: *Catalogue of Dated and Datable Manuscripts c. 737–1600 in Cambridge Libraries*, vol. I (Cambridge: Brewer, 1988), no. 186, p. 64.

[115] Ed. from *AY*, with additional material from the LV Lectionaries in Ek*MM*RX, *WB*, IV.683–98. See Hudson, *PR*, p. 198.

[116] There are two common orders for lectionaries in WB MSS: (1) temporal, commemorations, proper of saints combined with common of saints ('alle vnder oon as þei fallin in þe ȝeer bi ordre', P, fol. 4r), and (2) temporal, proper of saints, common of saints, commemorations. Neil R. Ker records several lectionaries with order (1) as lacking the common of saints, including Chetham 6723, R_76R_77R_78R_80 and R_91 (*MMBL*, III.355, 404–6, 414), as does *WB* (Ek*MM*R) (IV.696). Other Lectionaries with order (1): aC_U_6683PpS, Bancroft 128, BL Harl. 4890, Bodl. 531 and 665, Bodl. Douce 265, Fairfax 11, Lyell 26 and Selden supra 49. MS 3 lacks both the proper of saints and the common of saints; Bodl. Fairfax 21 lacks the commemorations. In Bodl. Selden supra 51, one calendar incorporates lections for the proper of saints, fols. 13v–25r, and a second calendar incorporates lections for the temporal and the commemorations, fols. 25v–32v. In K, the temporal and proper of saints are combined within each month (beginning Jan.), with dominicals and ferials listed at the end of each month and commemorations listed in the lower part of fols. 192v–193r; book and chapter numbers and indexing letters of each lection are provided, but not the opening and closing words, fols. 188r–193v.

[117] MSS *M*R; for (slight) variations, see *WB*, IV.683.

[118] See De Hamel, *Book*, p. 181 and fig. 127 (from an MS in a private collection).

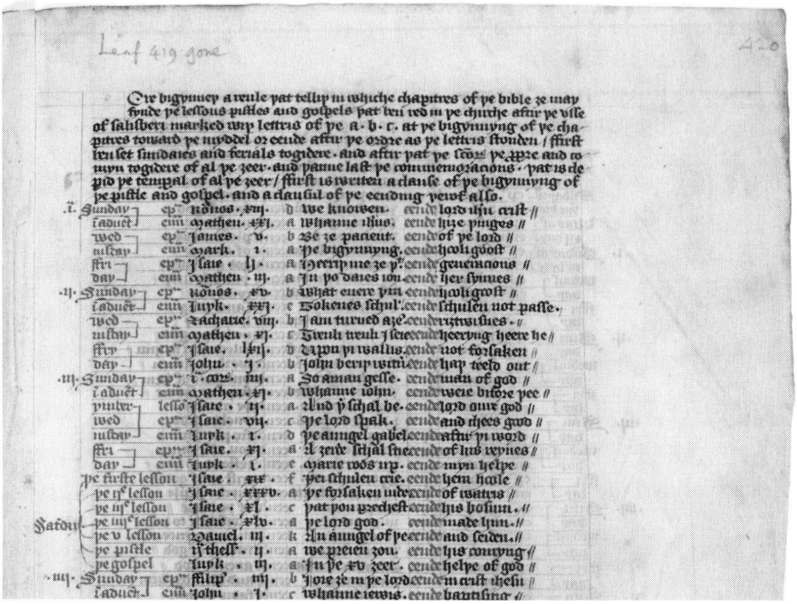

Figure 3. Opening of the Lectionary in Cambridge University Library Dd. 1. 27, fol. 420r. London (?), c. 1430.

is marked with a marginal //. The tables are normally ruled with great care, so that all the items of information can be readily located (see fig. 3). The close association between lectionary and biblical text is suggested by Corpus Christi College Cambridge 440 and Cambridge University Library Additional 6684, in which a lectionary indicating only the gospel lections is prefixed to a text of the Gospels, and by St John's College Cambridge E. 13, in which a lectionary indicating only the epistle lections is prefixed to a New Testament opening with the Epistle to the Romans. In some cases, in the absence of a lectionary, lections are indicated by rubrics within the biblical text. At the beginning of Matthew in Cambridge University Additional 6682 a rubric tells readers they are about to read 'þe gospel of þe natyuyte of oure lady & of concepcioun',[119] and in John Rylands Library Eng. 84 rubrics indicating lections occur throughout the part of Acts that is in the Earlier Version (7:31–10:6, which includes the lection for the feast

[119] C_U_6682, fol. 1v; 8 Sept., see *WB*, IV.694.

of the Conversion of St Paul).[120] Thomas of Gloucester's Bible has rubrics indicating the beginning and ending of every lection as well as a lectionary.

More than a third of the c. 250 surviving Wycliffite Bible manuscripts – at least eighty-nine – include a lectionary, complete or partial, and in two-thirds of the manuscripts including a lectionary, as in John Rylands Library Eng. 77, the lectionary comes first, and is followed by the New Testament, or part of it.[121] Eborall and Ive are therefore likely to have seen other manuscripts similar to the one they were asked to approve. The proportions and format of this volume are characteristic of a Wycliffite Lectionary and New Testament – 268 folios; folio size 190 by 130 millimetres; written space 122 by 80 millimetres; two columns of 36 lines with the bounding-lines carefully ruled; the hand a good, even *textualis*. It is also characteristic that the decoration is of high quality and the production professional in every respect.[122]

The stationers who oversaw the production of manuscripts of the Wycliffite Bible evidently anticipated that buyers would want to know which lections were going to be read at mass on any particular day, and to want to be able to find them. Further confirmation of this is provided by the fact that, because one or more of the lections at mass could be a reading from the Old Testament, the text of the Old Testament mass-lections is added to the New Testament (or part of the New Testament) in twenty-five manuscripts of the Wycliffite Bible, and the Old Testament lections are written in full within a lectionary in at least four others.[123] Even if the user of a lectionary were to have access to a copy of the Old Testament to look up the lections,[124] a note in a complete Bible in the Later Version, Hereford Cathedral O. VII. 1, explains why it would be difficult to follow an Old Testament lection from the information given in the Lectionary alone:

120 At fols. 34r, 35r, 36v, 38v; Ker, *MMBL*, III.408. The MS from which this part derives presumably had such rubrics throughout. The Latin incipits of lections are included within the text in BL Royal 1. A. X, from Matt. to 1 Cor. On the rubrics in *Y*, see De Hamel, *Book*, p. 181.

121 See the Index of MSS. R_79 does not now contain a lectionary, but there are subdividing letters in the margin linking this NT to a lectionary, as there are in Thomas Downe's NT (now in Bel Air, California, see Index of MSS); for other examples, see Hudson, *PR*, p. 198. Where only a summary description of contents is now available, the presence of a lectionary is likely not to have been noted: eighty-nine is therefore a conservative estimate.

122 Ker, *MMBL*, III.404, n. 61, above, and pp. 88–92, below.

123 The OT lections are written in full within the lectionary in Bodley 531, Dunedin Public Lib. Reed fragment 20, Longleat 5, Tokyo Takamiya (Sotheby's, 3.7.84, lot 6), and Van Kampen 641. The Dunedin and Takamiya leaves are probably from the same MS, see Index of MSS. The two quires of OT lections in Van Kampen 641 were presumably at some stage removed from a WB in NT; see Von Nolcken, 'Lay Literacy, the Democratization of God's Law and the Lollards', p. 186.

124 Some lectionaries, however, indicate NT lections only, e.g. Bodl. Douce 265, Gough Eccl. Top.5, and Fairfax 21.

it is to undirstonde [be understood] þat not ech lessone of þe oolde lawe is writen in þe Bible word bi word as it is red in chirche, but sum is taken a resoun [section] of o [one] chapitre and þe remenaunt of anoþer, and summe ben taken of mo chapitris, and þat in diverse placis, and ȝit not accordinge fulli to þe text of þe Bible . . . and also in many lessouns þe chirche haþ set to [added] boþe bigynnyngis and endingis þat ben not in þe Bible.[125]

This sounds wordy, but liturgical practice is notoriously hard to describe.

The Old Testament lections follows the order temporal, proper of saints, common of saints and commemorations.[126] Several of the lections for the common of saints are taken from Wisdom, an apocryphal book (although always included in Wycliffite Bibles), and Queen's College Oxford 388, a complete Wycliffite Bible in the Later Version, provides a reason for this: '[Wisdom] is red in holi cherche in lessouns of þe masse, for þe mater þerof is goostli and profecie of þingis to comynge'.[127] In Cambridge University Additional 6683, the Old Testament lections contain running-heads for ease of reference. A manuscript like this one, with a lectionary, a New Testament and a full text of the Old Testament lections (some fifteen such manuscripts survive, complete or in part), would have provided its owners with a text of all the lections at mass throughout the year, plus a foolproof way of locating the lections for each day. As usual, however, we do not know who the medieval owners were: the first recorded owner of Cambridge University Additional 6683 is post-Reformation and post-Mary.[128]

The volume Eborall and Ive approved (or are said to have approved) does not contain Old Testament lections; but the devout female owner, and her son, could have prepared themselves for mass by reading in English the New Testament lections they would hear read in Latin, very likely in St Michael Paternoster Royal. Whether they would have had their English New Testament with them at mass is a moot point; it might not be prohibited for a layperson privately to read an approved translation in church,

[125] The note is at the end of the lectionary, fol. 5v. The example given is the epistle inc. 'In þat tyme ȝifte shal be born', which 'bigynneþ in Isaiah xix c. toward þe ende [Is. 19:21], and þe remenaunt is in diverse placis of þe chapitre suyinge'.

[126] Order (2) in note 118, above. The temporal begins with the first epistle of the first Friday in Advent, inc. 'heeriþ me ȝe þat suen' (Is. 51:1, C_U_6683, fol. 269r); the proper of saints begins with the first epistle of the Vigil of St Andrew, inc. 'Þe blessyng of þe lord is on þe head' (Ecclus 44:25, fol. 302r); the common of saints begins with the first epistle of the vigil of an apostle (again, beginning at Ecclus 44:25, fol. 307r); the commemorations begin with the first epistle of the commemoration of Our Lady from Easter until Trinity Sunday (fol. 311r) and end with the mass of requiem, inc. 'In þo daies collacioun or spekinge togidere maad Iudas' (2 Macc. 12:38, fol. 312r). The text in C_U_6683 is in LV, though idiosyncratic in many details. Where the same OT lection is prescribed for more than one day, only the first few words are given at the repeat; Ker notices this in relation to York Minster XVI. N. 7 (*MMBL*, IV.752).

[127] *WB*, III.84. On the apocrypha, see pp. 92–102, below.

[128] A. Babington, 1560, fol.1r.

to aid understanding of the Latin, but, considerations of security and conservation aside, a man who chose not to name himself or his mother in his book of English scripture is unlikely to have wanted his ownership of it publicly demonstrated. Henry Hargreaves has shown that a passage in *The Mirror of our Lady* discouraging the Bridgettine sisters at Syon from looking at translated scripture during the offices (as opposed to reading it in advance), on the grounds that they should focus their attention on the Latin, was in all likelihood added to the text.[129] Possibly the practice had become widespread and was perceived to be disruptive.

Like the epistles and gospels, individual psalms can readily be located in Wycliffite Bibles, since, as De Hamel shows, the format of the Wycliffite Psalms resembles the format of a liturgical Psalter (there is, however, no 'rule' for locating the proper psalms).[130] The Wycliffite Psalms – usually with the biblical and non-biblical Canticles, and sometimes with the Athanasian creed and the *Dirige* (the office for the dead) as well[131] – also occur as separate and conveniently small volumes of English scripture, and the Psalms have been removed from St John's College Oxford 7, an otherwise complete Old Testament, presumably for convenience of use.[132] One manuscript of the Wycliffite Psalms has each verse in Latin and in English, as in Rolle's Psalter.[133] Psalms were customarily identified by their Latin openings (so *Beatus vir*, Ps. 1), and these are nearly always included in Wycliffite Psalms. A wealthy medieval owner of British Library Arundel 104, a complete Bible in the Later Version, excised illuminated initials from Latin manuscripts to paste into his English Psalms (the English initials were, of course, in most cases different from the Latin).[134] In this and in most manuscripts of the Wycliffite Psalms, alternating blue and red one-line capitals mark the opening of each verse of each psalm, so that the psalm could be read antiphonally where appropriate, or a listener could keep track of the text of a psalm read or sung antiphonally.[135]

129 '*The Mirror of Our Lady*', p. 279. 130 *Book*, pp. 182–3 and figs. 128–9.

131 Including *Te Deum*, an early Christian hymn. The opening words of the Athanasian Creed are 'Quicunque vult'; K includes a summary of the Canticles with book and chapter numbers, and the Quicunque vult, fols. 187r–v. D_72 includes the *Dirige*, fols. 93r–96r; Yale University Beinecke Lib. 360 includes the Office of the Dead, the Litany, the Hours of the Virgin, and other liturgical material.

132 See Index of MSS; on the absence of Psalms in N, see Hanna, *A Descriptive Catalogue of the Western Medieval Manuscripts of St John's College*, p. 9, and the Index of MSS, below.

133 BL Harley 1896, which also contains the Canticles and the Athanasian Creed. The Wycliffite Psalms 1–83 are also in Latin and English in Worcs. Cath. F. 172, fols. 186v–213v.

134 See Stella Panayotova, 'Cuttings from an Unknown Copy of the Magna Glossatura in a Wycliffite Bible', *The British Library Journal* 25 (1999), 85–100, and De Hamel, *Book*, pp. 182–3 and fig. 129, which shows the 'S' for *Salvum me fac*, in LV 'God make þou me saaf' (Ps. 69, fol. 354r). Many of the pasted-in initials have since been removed again.

135 This practice is borrowed from Latin Bibles: see De Hamel, *Book*, p. 128 and fig. 91.

The Wycliffite Old Testament lections include some details of liturgical practice suggesting that the focus is indeed on the hearer. 'On Cristemasse morn þe firste lessoun at þe firste masse . . is sungen in þe pulpit' by two voices, explains the compiler of the lectionary, one singing the words of Isaiah 9:2, 6–7 and the other answering. The response is 'as it were a glose of text' ('a gloss on the text'), and the biblical text is underlined in red to distinguish it from the gloss. This responsorial lection begins:

[voice 1:]	Þe peple of folk þat walkiden in derknessis
[voice 2:]	whom þe enemye wiþ trecherous gile put out of paradijs & ledde hem bi þraldom in to helle
[voice 1:]	say [saw] a greet li ȝt
[voice 2:]	þere schoon greet liȝtis boþe at mydnyȝt & vnto þe herdemen [shepherds]
[voice 1:]	to hem wonyinge in þe kingdom of schadewe of deeþ
[voice 2:]	liȝt euerlastinge & þe verri aȝenbiynge [redemption] . . .

The second lection for the first mass of Christmas is the same verses of Isaiah without the responses.[136] The compiler of the Old Testament lectionary clearly has two aims: to provide his reader with an English translation of the responsory, and to alert him or her to what to expect, visually and aurally. The text can only be sung in Latin.

Private lay reading of lections in English, before or during mass, is one thing, but were the lections read publicly in English, or in Latin and English, at mass?[137] Gasquet believes they were, 'frequently if not ordinarily'.[138] Hudson says that although it is 'hard to prove' that Wycliffite Bibles were read in churches, they may originally have been intended for that purpose.[139] English Psalters and English New Testaments with lectionaries are typically of a size to be carried and handled by individuals, but the large format of complete Wycliffite Bibles suggests more public use. Thomas of Gloucester's Bible, A. I. Doyle says, 'must be meant for display and use on a

[136] [illegible], fols. [illegible]. The text of the second lection is in LV, whereas in the responsorial lection the biblical text is translated directly from the Latin, presumably because the responses had to be translated from scratch. The text of this reponsorial lection is identical in OT lectionaries in EV and LV, and in BL Harley 1029 and 1710.

[137] Deanesly doubts whether translations were used even privately in church, and says that the canon-tables enabling readers to find the epistle and gospel lections in Clement of Llanthony's *Unum ex Quattuor* were 'in all probability for private study': *LB*, p. 176.

[138] *The Old English Bible*, p. 152.

[139] 'Lollard Book Production', pp. 131–2; see also Hudson, *PR*, p. 199.

lectern'.[140] There is no reason why Gloucester should not have ordered his chaplains to read aloud from his English Bible in his chapel: the epistle and gospel lections could easily be located, since his Bible includes the kind of lectionary we are familiar with, and rubrics indicating the beginning and ending of each lection as well. Eleven other complete Wycliffite Bibles contain lectionaries.[141] The London Carthusians to whom Henry VI gave the large and lavish Bible now Bodley 277 evidently made intensive use of it alongside Latin Bibles, for notes in the margins indicate the comparative length of passages in English and in Latin.[142] Both, or English alone, may have been read in the refectory, but a rubric on the opening page of the Psalter points out that it 'cantatur in choro' ('is sung [in Latin] in the choir').

All questions of legality aside, we have to wonder whether lections read aloud in English in the Earlier Version of the Wycliffite Bible would have been comprehensible to people listening. One of the reasons the translators opted for an English text that followed the Latin closely, without any substantial additional material, was presumably that they wanted readers to be able to study the English alongside the Latin. The Earlier Version would certainly not have made transparent sense to a listener hearing it for the first time, but might have made good sense to a listener who had studied it beforehand. A cleric reading the lections aloud in the Earlier Version, and to a lesser extent in the Later Version, would also have needed to look them over in advance in order to read them with understanding. We also have to wonder whether the explanatory glosses included in the text of the Wycliffite Bible were intended to be read aloud.[143] It would be awkward (in some cases very awkward) to do so, but it would be difficult to avoid, since the glosses are by no means regularly underlined in red, as the translators planned.

There are two Wycliffite Bible manuscripts, both in the Harleian collection, that look particularly like service-books: they are in fact *comites*, missal lectionaries containing full texts of the epistle and gospel lections at mass throughout the year (Old Testament and New Testament lections, in the Earlier Version, in the order temporal, proper of saints, common of saints and commemorations).[144] Both are clearly written but not beautiful

140 'English Books In and Out of Court', p. 168.

141 MSS *Æ*EKMPP_SSW_o*XX* and C_U_6680.

142 De Hamel, *Book*, pp. 184–5 and figs. 130–1.

143 On glosses, see pp. 152–72, below.

144 BL Harley 1029 and 1710. In β, a copy of the Prologue to the Wycliffite Bible is followed by the gospel lections for Holy Week and Easter, fols. 97r–109v. Bodl. Hatton 111 contains the office of Compline in English, fols. 2r–9v. Eborall's MS of gospels and epistles may also have been a *comes*: see p. 50, above.

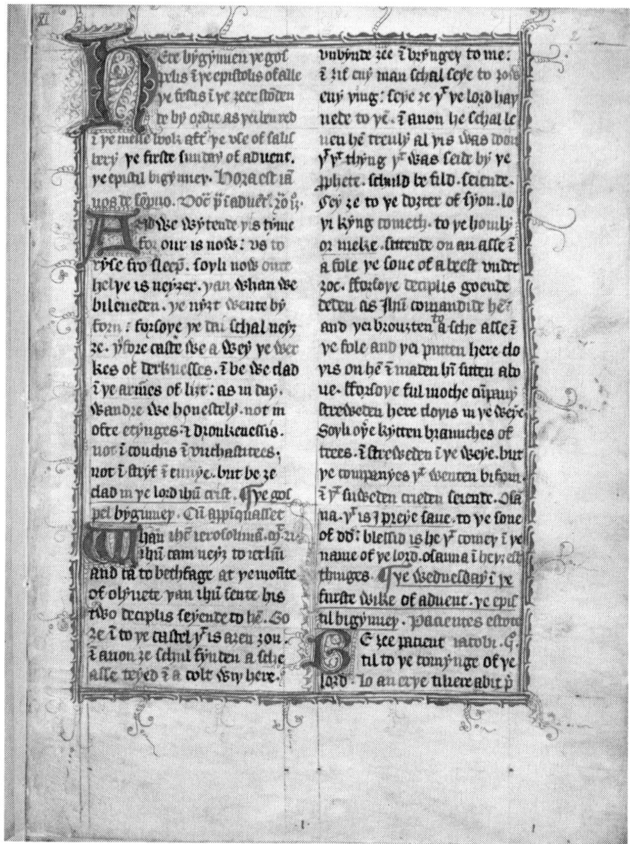

Figure 4. Opening of a *comes* (missal lectionary), British Library Harley 1710, fol. 2r. East Midlands (?), c. 1390–1400.

volumes, for use rather than pleasure (see fig. 4). As Gasquet points out, one of them, Harley 1710 (c. 1390–1400), belonged to a chantry priest, Sir Roger Lyne of St Swithun's, London Stone, in the City of London.[145] Cataloguing this manuscript in around 1720, Humfrey Wanley commented that its existence 'is a sort of proof that in times of Popery, the reading Gods word in our mother-tongue, was not denied by authority; and this is also asserted by Sir Thomas More'.[146] Elsewhere, Wanley notes that 'More

[145] 'Roger Lyne chantre prest of saynt swythyns at london stone', in a s. xv/xvi hand, fol. 1r; Gasquet, *The Old English Bible*, p. 152. The dialect of the MS is markedly East Midland.

[146] Humfrey Wanley, D. Casley and W. Hocker, eds., *A Catalogue of the Harleian Manuscripts in the British Museum*, vol. II (London, 1808), p. 182. Wanley had reached BL Harley 2408 when he died in 1726; see p. 74, below.

wrote, that there were [in the time of Wyclif] divers translations of scripture into English, allowed by authority.'[147] A 'sort of proof' falls short of a certainty: it is possible that Lyne read epistle and gospel lections in English in St Swithun's, but he may have used his missal lectionary merely for private study, or he may have read it to, or with, parishioners who preferred not to risk owning scripture in the vernacular themselves – although this was against the letter of Arundel's *Constitutions*. Public reading of scripture in English sounds more of an affront to the *Constitutions* than private reading, but reading and thinking beforehand, alone or in a group, was potentially far more subversive.

Both Wanley and Gasquet echo More's claim that the medieval English Bible was 'allowed by authority'. Gasquet's essay infuriated his Protestant readers, but the complexity of the evidence demands a less partisan appraisal of Arundel's attempt to censor the first English Bible than either Gasquet or his critics were able to offer. There is, as we have seen, some truth in what Gasquet claims. Manuscripts of the Wycliffite Bible continued to be written in large numbers, particularly New Testaments, and some were in unquestionably orthodox ownership. Many were apparently intended for devout readers who attended mass regularly, and some may have been used during mass. Lections from the Wycliffite Bible may in certain circumstances have been read aloud. The proposed system of licences does not seem to have been generally enforced, and probably could not have been enforced in a manuscript as opposed to a print culture.

Few people, on the other hand, could feel confident about owning scripture in English, because this laid them permanently open to suspicion of heresy, with potentially life-threatening consequences. Not only indicted Lollards but also devout and pious owners like Anne Danvers gave copies away. Although the common opinion that 'the clergy of this realme hath forboden all the peple to haue any scripture translated into our tonge' (as reported by the young man in the *Dialogue Concerning Heresies*) was not strictly accurate, and although the first English Bible was far more widely available than Arundel, in his desire to protect the English Church from error and heresy, would have wished, after the *Constitutions* of 1409 the Christian community for which Arundel was responsible was more anxiety-ridden and less united than it had been before the work of translation began. Arundel ensured that the history of the first English Bible and its translators, the subject of the next chapter, cannot be separated from the history of the English Reformation.

147 In his description of BL Harley 1666, *A Catalogue of the Harleian Manuscripts*, II.169.

CHAPTER 3

The translators

The title of Josiah Forshall and Frederic Madden's edition of the first complete Bible in English, one of the outstanding works of medieval scholarship in the Victorian period, claims that it was 'made from the Latin Vulgate by John Wycliffe and his followers'. Forshall and Madden claim that:

> It may be impossible to determine with certainty the exact share which Wycliffe's own pen had in the translation, but there can be no doubt that he took a part in the labour of producing it, and that the accomplishment of the work must be attributed mainly to his zeal, encouragement and direction. It was not probably until his later years that Wycliffe matured so extensive a design. He was led to the undertaking slowly and gradually; and it was not completed until after several preliminary efforts.[1]

Their 'no doubt' notwithstanding, Forshall and Madden admit that the evidence for Wyclif's involvement in the translation is presumptive, not conclusive. Their joint introduction to the edition was, however, written under very difficult circumstances, and Madden's diary suggests they may not have been in complete agreement. On 7 May 1850, Madden wrote that Forshall was 'virtually in confinement'. Thomas Gaisford, Dean of Christ Church, urged him on behalf of the Clarendon Press to write the introduction himself, but he says 'it would not be fair to complete [it] without the cooperation and concurrence of Mr Forshall . . . after a co-operation of more than twenty years'. On 21 June, Madden reports that 'we do not quite agree as to the form or matter of the first few paragraphs. It is of no great moment, but I should have preferred writing it by myself.'[2]

Madden first called the work which had occupied Forshall and himself for so long the 'Wycliffite Bible' in his diary-entry for 24 April 1832, where he says that they 'intend to devote every day to the collation of [the] Wycliffite Bible', while the British Museum, where they were both employed, was

[1] *WB*, I.6. [2] Bodl. Eng. hist. c. 163, pp. 132, 173.

closed for the annual holiday.[3] This title of convenience, associating the earliest English Bible with Wyclif but not specifying him as translator, has become customary. Is it, however, justified?

We have seen that Knighton, Arundel and Hus, writing c. 1390, in 1407 and in 1411 respectively, associate the English Bible with Wyclif; Knighton and Arundel confidently, Hus by hearsay. The first time Wyclif unambiguously argues that readers literate in English but not in Latin should have access to scripture in the vernacular is in his *Trialogus* (1382–3), written in Lutterworth.[4] Claiming divine authorization for the work of translation, Wyclif says the Holy Spirit 'vult vulgares codices de lege nova vel veteri studeri et legi' ('wishes manuscripts of both the New Testament and the Old Testament to be read and studied in the common tongue'), because scripture contains all truth.[5] A new kind of reader, situated outside the University, will then be in a position to share Wyclif's detestation of those 'doctores novelli' who sophistically claim that infinitely truthful scripture contains logical falsehoods.[6] In his *De Triplico Vinculo Amoris* (1383), Wyclif refers to scripture in English as an actuality: he castigates the folly of those 'who wish to condemn scriptures as heretical when they are written in English and have harsh things to say about sin'.[7] An argument supporting translation is that Richard II's queen, Anne of Bohemia, owns Gospels in her mother-tongue, Czech, and also in German and Latin.[8]

In *De Veritate Sacrae Scripturae*, there is no mention of translation, but Wyclif prophesies woe to the church whose clerics are more concerned with temporal dominion and with human traditions of their own making than with preaching the law of God, which is the totality of scripture.[9] 'Spiritual profit is infinitely better than temporal', he concludes, 'and spiritual profit cannot be acquired apart from the teaching of holy scripture'.[10] An argument sometimes advanced against the necessity of preaching in the

[3] Bodl. Engl. hist. 148, p. 111.

[4] On the date of the *Trialogus*, see Thomson, *The Latin Writings of John Wyclif*, p. 79.

[5] Ed. Gotthard Lechler (Oxford: Clarendon Press, 1869), p. 240/12–13.

[6] *Trialogus*, p. 241/3–4. On Wyclif's hatred of sophists, see Ian C. Levy, *John Wyclif: Scriptural Logic, Real Presence, and the Parameters of Orthodoxy* (Milwaukee: Marquette University Press, 2003), pp. 102–5.

[7] 'Qui volunt dampnare scripta tamquam heretica propter hoc quod scribuntur in anglico et acute tangunt peccata'; ed. Rudolf Buddensieg, *John Wiclif's Polemical Works in Latin*, vol. II (London: Wyclif Society, 1883), p. 168/6–8. On the date, see Thomson, *The Latin Writings of John Wyclif*, p. 294.

[8] *John Wiclif's Polemical Works in Latin*, vol. II, p. 168/9–11. Cf. the claim in 'First seiþ Bois' that Thomas Arundel said at Queen Anne's funeral that 'sche hadde on Engliche al þe foure Gospeleris wiþ þe doctoris vpon hem': ed. Bühler, 'A Lollard Tract', p. 178/291–8.

[9] *De Veritate*, IV, 20; ed. Buddensieg, II.129–42.

[10] 'Infinitum melius lucrum spirituale quam temporale, spirituale autem non potest acquiri sine doctrina scripture sacre', IV, 20; II.142/18–20.

vernacular, says Wyclif, is the 'lie [*ficticia*] that it is no longer necessary', and the reasons given are twofold: that 'quelibet vetula scit satis simbolum et oracionem dominicam, et hoc sufficit ad salutem' ('every old woman knows the Creed and the Lord's Prayer well enough, and that is sufficient for salvation'), and that theologians have the reputation of being heretics, and are all too likely to spread error.[11] The arguments advanced against preaching the law of God come from the same armoury as the arguments against biblical translation: that only what is necessary for salvation needs to be known and that exposure to scripture leads to heresy.[12] John Kynyngham, the Oxford Carmelite who debated the senses of scripture with Wyclif in the early 1370s, makes the related point that notorious heresies have arisen from biblical verses being interpreted according to the strictly grammatical sense, whereas they in fact invite interpretation according to the full sense intended by the author. Kynyngham is taking a leaf out of Wyclif's book here.[13]

Countering those who oppose preaching scripture in its entirety, Wyclif argues that 'it is necessary to preach to the very end of the world'.[14] There can be no doubt of his commitment to the truth of scripture. Was he, however, involved in the work of translation? The Wycliffite refugees in Prague who said that 'Wyclif himself translated the whole Bible' were certainly exaggerating, but it is unlikely that Wyclif played no role at all in the translation that was, according to Arundel, his (devilish) 'invention'. Given what we know about Arundel's *Constitutions*, we should not expect to find Wyclif's name recorded in Wycliffite Bible manuscripts before the Reformation; nor do we. On Arundel's authority, More believed Wyclif had translated the Bible, but he thought the English Bibles he had seen (except for the one exhibited at the Hunne hearing) were translated before the time of Wyclif. John Leland, whose searches supplied John Bale with invaluable information on Wyclif's writings, does not mention Wyclif as a translator of the Bible.[15] The first significant post-Reformation evidence

11 Ibid., IV, 21; II.179/7–11.

12 Richard Ullerston quotes Jerome to the effect that when scripture is available in the common tongue a 'garrula anus' or 'delirus senex', among other incompetent or sophistical readers, may make scripture mean what they want it to mean. *Epistola LIII ad Paulinum*, ed. Lindberg, *PE*, pp. 99–101/22–41; Vienna, Osterreichische Nationalbibl. 4133, fol. 195v; see also Ghosh, *WH*, p. 88.

13 *FZ*, pp. 41–2; the point is well discussed by Levy, 'Defining the Responsibility of the Late Medieval Theologian', 23–26.

14 'Necesse est predicare usque ad finem mundi', *De Veritate*, IV, 21; II.179/14–15.

15 Leland, *Commentarii de Scriptoribus*, ed. Anthony Hall, vol. II (Oxford, 1709), pp. 378–81. On Leland material about Wyclif not included in Hall's edition, see James P. Carley, 'Cum excuterem puluerem et blattas: John Bale, John Leland, and the *Chronicon Tinemutensis coenobii*', in Barr and Hutchison, eds., *Text and Controversy*, pp. 184–7.

naming the English Bible as Wyclif's comes from Bale, and from the printer Robert Crowley, who says in his editions of *Piers Plowman* in 1550 that Wyclif 'translated the Holye Bible into the Englishe tonge'.[16] Crowley's edition of the Prologue to the Wycliffite Bible, published as *The Pathwaye to Perfect Knowledge* in the same year, attributes the Prologue to Wyclif. The content of the Prologue has always strongly encouraged the association of the English Bible with Wyclif and his followers.[17]

Early evidence names one other candidate for translator of the whole English Bible: John Trevisa, who is said by William Caxton to have translated the Bible 'atte request of Thomas Lord Barcley (Berkeley)', his patron.[18] In the Translators' Preface to the King James ('Authorized') Version of the Bible (1611), itself one of the richest and most acrimonious documents in the debate about biblical translation, Miles Smith claims that 'in our King Richard the Seconds dayes, John Trevisa translated [the Bible] into English, and many English Bibles in written hand are yet to be seene with divers [various others] translated as it is very probable in that age'.[19] We might have expected the translators of the King James Bible to be eager to name Wyclif's translation as a precedent, but Wyclif had been appropriated by the Puritan wing of the Church of England as a proto-Genevan Reformer, and Smith, who distances himself from the Puritans almost as far as he distances himself from Roman Catholics, probably preferred to credit Trevisa and unnamed others with the translation rather than cede the first English Bible to fellow-Anglicans he regarded as zealots.

Trevisa argues indirectly for biblical translation in his 'Dialogus inter Dominum et Clericum', and he translated the apocryphal Gospel of Nicodemus.[20] He was admitted as a fellow of the Queen's College, Oxford, in 1369, in the same year as Nicholas Hereford (c. 1345–after 1417), who is named in the first part of Bodleian Douce 369 as the translator of the

16 Sig. *ii [STC 19906/7/7a]; see Hudson, 'No Newe Thyng', in *Lollards and their Books*, pp. 247–8. On Bale, see pp. 42–3, above.

17 See ch. 5, below.

18 In the prologue to Caxton's edition of Trevisa's translation of Ranulf Higden's *Polychronicon* (London, 1482); Caxton perhaps misunderstood the 'Dialogus inter Dominum et Clericum'. Somerset points to the relation between Berkeley and Thomas of Gloucester, who owned two (perhaps three) of the books Trevisa translated for Berkeley (*Clerical Discourse and Lay Audience*, p. 76). Bale repeats Caxton's assertion in *Scriptorum Illustrium Maioris Brytanniae . . . Catalogus*, vol. I, p. 518. On Trevisa as translator of the Bible, see David C. Fowler, 'John Trevisa and the English Bible', *Modern Philology* 58 (1960), 81–98, and *The Life and Times of John Trevisa, Medieval Scholar* (Seattle: University of Washington Press, 1995), pp. 225–32.

19 Ed. David Daniell, *The Bible in English*, p. 783. Daniell restates with approval Fowler's case for Trevisa as translator, pp. 91–5.

20 See Fowler, *The Life and Times of John Trevisa*, pp. 120–45, and on the Gospel of Nicodemus, p. 30, above.

Earlier Version as far as Baruch 3:20.[21] Hereford was an important disseminator of Wyclif's ideas at least from 1382 until 1391.[22] Wyclif lived in the Queen's College from 1374, probably until his withdrawal to Lutterworth in 1381.[23] Trevisa was expelled in 1378–9, with other 'southerners', who took with them several books which would have been relevant to the translation project, including Nicholas of Lyra's *Postilla* on Psalms and on Proverbs.[24] Taken together, these facts make it not unlikely that Trevisa was one of the translators involved in the production of the Wycliffite Bible.[25] Sven Fristedt moved from thinking it likely that Trevisa was involved to having 'no doubt' about it.[26] In 'Who Wrote Wiclif's Bible?', Conrad Lindberg agrees that Trevisa was probably one of the translators of the Earlier Version, and he argues that the vocabulary of the Prefatory Epistles and the Pentateuch shows 'good agreement' with the vocabulary of Trevisa's translations.[27] Lindberg, however, has always insisted on Wyclif's pre-eminent role in the translation project, whoever else may have been involved at different stages, and he argues for Wyclif as author of the Prologue as well.[28]

In manuscripts of the Wycliffite Bible, the translation is commonly attributed to Wyclif from the seventeenth century onwards – by Andrew Cook, for instance, who was given Bodleian Laud misc. 33 (part of the New Testament in the Later Version) in 1615.[29] Humphrey Haggat, who gave an Old Testament in the Later Version to St John's College Oxford in 1620, attributes the translation to 'Master John Wickliffe in the time of King Edward the Third' (who died in 1377).[30] Thomas Fairfax (Third Baron Fairfax, d. 1671), who bequeathed his manuscript collection to the Bodleian Library, wrote in Bodleian Fairfax 11, a sumptuous lectionary and

21 Fowler, 'John Trevisa and the English Bible', pp. 88–9. *C* ends at Bar. 3:20, fol. 250r: Henry Hargreaves, 'The Vernacular Scriptures: the Wycliffite Versions', *CHB*, II.400; De Hamel, *Book*, p. 171, and see further pp. 103–4, below. On Hereford, see *BRUO*, II.913–15; Simon Forde, *ODNB* XXVI (2004), pp. 763–5; Hudson, *PR*, pp. 176–8, 241–2, and pp. 78–9, 81 below.

22 See Martin, ed., *Knighton's Chronicle*, pp. 277–83; *BRUO*, II.913–15; Simon Forde, *ODNB*; and Hudson, *PR*, pp. 176–8.

23 Fowler, 'John Trevisa and the English Bible', p. 89.

24 Ibid., pp. 93–4.

25 See Hudson, *PR*, pp. 394–7; she concludes her discussion with a verdict of 'not proven', p. 397.

26 *WB*, *II*.xlviii; his study of Trevisa's methods as a translator of Higden convinced him (*WB*, *III*, esp. pp. 39–40), and he says he has 'no doubt' in 'A Note on Some Obscurities in the History of the Lollard Bible', *Stockholm Studies in Modern Philology* n.s. 4 (1972), 43.

27 *Stockholm Studies in Modern Philology* n.s. 7 (1984), 135; 'A Note on the Vocabulary of the Middle English Bible', *Studia Neophilologica* 57 (1985), 129–30.

28 Although he says in 1985 that Wyclif's role was 'probably restricted to initiating and supervising the work', *Baruch*, p. 50. He suggests that Wyclif wrote the Prologue in 'Who Wrote Wyclif's Bible?', p. 134, and argues that ch.10, parts of ch.13 and the second half of ch.15 are 'clearly later additions': 'Literary Aspects of the Wyclif Bible', *Bulletin of the John Rylands Library* 77:3 (1995), 85.

29 Fol. 2v; date, fol. 145r (*WB*, I.xlvi is incorrect here).

30 N, fol. 1r; see the Index of MSS.

New Testament in the Later Version, 'Wickliff's Translation of the New Testament'.[31]

The New Testament in the Later Version was the most recognizable portion of what we know as the Wycliffite Bible, but ecclesiastical historians and antiquarians recognized that it was not the only surviving medieval English New Testament, and that both translations existed as part of entire Bibles in medieval English. Thomas James, in his *Treatise of the Corruption of Scripture, Councels and Fathers by the Prelats, Pastors and Pillars of the Church of Rome, for Maintenance of Popery and Irreligion*, dated what we call the Earlier Version to 1290.[32] Archbishop James Ussher agreed with James that the first translation was made 'long before Wyclifs translation', although he seems to have seen at least two copies of the Earlier Version.[33] The time-gap between the translations was narrower according to Thomas Fuller, although he still exaggerates the linguistic differences; he associates them with the two translators tradition had named, the earlier with Wyclif and the later with Trevisa.[34] Henry Wharton comes to the same conclusion in the commentary appended to his edition of Ussher's *Historia Dogmatica* (1689). Wharton argues that the passage about abuses at the University of Oxford in the Prologue to the Wycliffite Bible could not have been written by Wyclif, an eminent doctor of that university.[35] He observes that the Prologue properly belongs to the version to which it is (sometimes) prefixed, because this version lacks 3 Ezra (also known as 2 Esdras), rejected in the Prologue on the authority of Jerome, but included in the other version.[36] Because the biblical verses translated in the final chapter of the Prologue accord exactly with what is now known as the Later Version, and the Prologue cannot have been written by Wyclif, the 'Prologue-version', Wharton concludes, is not Wyclifs, and must therefore be Trevisa's.[37]

[31] Fol. ii^r; it was recorded as having been 'bought in Scotland', fol. iii^r.

[32] London: Lownes, 1612, pp. 30, 74. On James's veneration of Wyclif, see James Crompton, 'John Wyclif: A Study in Mythology', *Transactions of the Leicestershire Archaeological and Historical Society* 42 (1966–7), 13.

[33] *Jacobi Usserii, Armachani Archiepiscopi, Historia Dogmatica . . . de Scripturis et Sacris Vernaculis* (London, 1690), p. 155 (Ussher died in 1656); see *WB*, I.xxi. Ussher says there are three copies of this earlier translation in Oxford: in the Bodleian, in Christ Church (145) and in the Queen's College (but M is in LV).

[34] *The History of the Worthies of Britain*, vol. I (London, 1662), p. 204.

[35] *Auctarium Historiae Dogmaticae Jacobi Usserii* [appended to Ussher's *Historia Dogmatica*] (London, 1689), pp. 424–5. For this passage, in ch.13 of the Prologue, see *WB*, I.51/7 to 52/25, and pp. 107–113, below. Although Wharton has seen Q, he quotes from Crowley's 1550 edition.

[36] *WB*, I.2/18–19; Jerome's prologue to 1 Ezra, *RBMA*, no. 330; see Appendix 1 and pp. 100–1, below. For WB MSS containing the Prologue, see ch. 5, nn. 80–3, below.

[37] *Auctarium Historiae Dogmaticae Jacobi Usserii*, pp. 426–7; see also C. Oudin, *Commentarius de Scriptoribus Ecclesiae Antiquis*, vol. III (Leipzig, 1722), pp. 1044–48, and *WB*, I.xxi.

When the Anglo-Saxonist Humfrey Wanley began cataloguing Robert Harley's library, in 1708, he knew from his contributions to the 'Great' Catalogue of English and Irish manuscripts inspired by Edward Bernard (1697) that the medieval English Bible was sometimes but by no means always ascribed to Wyclif. In that catalogue, Bishop John Moore's Bible, now Cambridge University Library Dd. 1. 27, is described as 'Wicliffi Biblia integra' ('a complete Wyclif Bible'),[38] but another complete Bible in the Later Version, Hereford Cathedral O. VII. 1, is described as being 'in an ancient English translation'.[39] Trevisa is not mentioned in Bernard's catalogue in connection with translation of the Bible. Cataloguing the Harleian collection, Wanley was reluctant to commit himself to naming Wyclif. No translator is mentioned in connection with British Library Harley 272 (a New Testament) or 327 (Romans to the end of the New Testament), and Wanley says that 1212 (another New Testament) is said to be one of Wyclif's versions 'by many', but not necessarily by himself.[40] In his description of Harley 1666, the Prologue to the Wycliffite Bible, Wanley comments that the contents of the Prologue 'agree well enough with the person and opinions of Wycliffe; who is also commonly said to have translated the Bible into English; though I could never yet see such a book with his name written therein by the first hand [the scribe's]'.[41] This is laudably cautious. Wanley is inclined to trust More's authority on the existence of pre-Wycliffite translations and on the openness of the pre-Reformation church to scripture in English, but his position is unusual.

Following Wharton's conclusions about Trevisa, which Wanley regarded as mistaken,[42] Protestant scholars were anxious to reinstate Wyclif's claim to the version they call the 'common' version, that is, the Later Version. Proposing the first edition of the Wycliffite Bible in 1719 (a proposal that came to nothing), John Russell says that Trevisa's 'pretensions' to authorship will be 'considered and confuted'.[43] Ignoring Wharton's observations, Russell clings to the fact that Bale's description of Wyclif's Bible 'agrees exactly'

[38] 'Codices Manuscripti Johannis Mori Episcopi Norvic.', in Edward Bernard *et al.*, eds., *Catalogi Librorum Manuscriptorum Angliae et Hiberniae* (Oxford: Sheldonian Theatre, 1697), no.9341, p. 365/458r. See the description in Appendix 4, below.

[39] 'Codices Manuscripti Ecclesiae Herefordensis', *Catalogi Librorum Manuscriptorum*, no. 1798, p. 45/346r. See the description in Appendix 4, below.

[40] Humfrey Wanley, D. Casley and W. Hocker, eds., *A Catalogue of the Harleian Manuscripts in the British Museum*, vol. I (London, 1808), pp. 101–2, 200, 599. He mentions Wyclif in connection with nos. 940 and 984, pp. 479, 499. For all these MSS, see the Index of MSS. Wanley had reached no. 2408 at his death in 1726.

[41] *A Catalogue of the Harleian Manuscripts*, II.169.

[42] As reported by Daniel Waterland, *The Works of Daniel Waterland*, vol. X (Oxford, 1823), pp. 356–7.

[43] *Proposals for Printing by Subscription, the Holy Bible . . . Translated into English by John Wickleffe*, 1 August 1719, pasted into G, fols. i–ii. Russell says that the text will be transcribed from Lincoln Coll. Oxf. MS (Latin 119) in the OT and from Robert Keck's MS (now BL Harl. 5017) in the NT.

with the 'common' version – 'unless it be in this, that it does not deserve the many slanders which [Papists] have been pleased to throw upon it'. The 'other' version, with Jerome's prologues (that is, the Earlier Version), should, Russell thinks (following James and Ussher), be dated 'many years before Wickleffe'.

In his *History of the Life and Sufferings of the Reverend and Learned John Wicliffe* (1721), a riposte to attempts to diminish Wyclif's reputation and cast doubt on every aspect of the historical accounts,[44] John Lewis supplies an annotated version of Bale's catalogue of Wyclif's writings, noting under the entry on Wyclif's translation of the Bible three manuscripts: Cambridge University Library Kk. 1. 8 (Prologue and New Testament), Trinity College Cambridge B. 2. 8 (Pentateuch) and Emmanuel College Cambridge 34, a New Testament and lectionary including, as Lewis says, a note relating to 1397 and the date 1383.[45] All these are in the Later Version. The first edition of any part of the Wycliffite Bible except the Prologue is Lewis's 1731 edition of the New Testament in what we know as the Later Version, with a substantial history of the Bible in English.

The Cambridge theologian Daniel Waterland had told Lewis in 1728 that in spite of Russell's arguments about the antiquity of the earlier version he believed that both versions were Wyclif's, because of attributions in manuscripts and earlier authorities, and because of the fact that the 'common' translator clearly had the older version in front of him.[46] He was sure that the 'common' version could not be Trevisa's.[47] Lewis agrees with Russell and Waterland about Wyclif's authorship of the version he prints, the 'common' version, but supposes that it is the 'revised' version that is 'more rare and scarce'.[48] This confusion is reproduced in the introduction to Henry Hervey Baber's reprint of Lewis's text of the New Testament, in 1810.[49] When Baber visited Madden in May 1829 'respecting the publication of Wickliffe's Old Test[ament]', Madden confided in his diary that he

44 Especially that of A. Varillas, trans. Matthias Earbery, *The Pretended Reformers* (London: Smith, 1717).

45 *History of the Life* (London: Knaplock), pp. 143–74, details of WB MSS p. 149; see Index of MSS, below, and, on the Emmanuel MS, ch. 2, n. 114, above. 1383 is in a s. xvi/xvii hand, but Lewis apparently accepts it. On Lewis's account of Wyclif's writings, see Matti Peikola, *Congregation of the Elect: Patterns of Self-Fashioning in English Lollard Writings*, Anglicana Turkuensia 21 (Turku: University of Turku Press, 2000), pp. 43–5.

46 Letter dated 20 Jan. 1828, *The Works of Daniel Waterland*, vol. X, pp. 274–6.

47 Ibid., X.276.

48 Lewis, *NT*, pp. 5–9. The base text of the Gospels is Bodl. Gough Eccl. Top. 5 (then owned by Lewis), and of the rest of the NT an MS then belonging to Edward Dering, Bart. (now British and Foreign Bible Society Eng. 1, 2). Both are in LV. Some variants from Waterland's collation of ten Cambridge MSS are recorded.

49 *The New Testament Translated from the Latin in the Year 1380 By John Wiclif* (London: Hamilton, 1810), pp. lii–lxxii; see *WB*, I.xxi.

had difficulty in convincing Baber that he had the versions the wrong way round, but Madden's knowledge of the manuscripts in the British Museum (where he was an assistant keeper) enabled him to prove that the 'common' version of the Old Testament was the revised version ('not that of Wiclif but of the writer of the Prologue').[50] At first, Forshall and Madden set out, with Baber, to edit the Old Testament; it was not until 1842 that they decided to edit the New Testament as well, pointing out to the Curators of the Press that the New Testament had never been printed in the Earlier Version.[51]

Waterland was responsible for bringing a new name into the history of the translators of the Wycliffite Bible. He realized that the Prologue to the Wycliffite Bible could not have been written by Wyclif, who died in 1384, since a passage castigating the University of Oxford refers to events of the late 1380s.[52] Looking for a candidate for the authorship of the Prologue and the Prologue-version of the Bible, someone closely associated with Wyclif, Waterland guessed (his own word) that John Purvey was the author of the Prologue-version: '[Purvey] is the man I pitch upon, for the Translator of the Bible, and composer of that Prologue.'[53] Waterland based his guess primarily on what Bale says about Purvey, particularly that he was 'Lollardorum librarium et Wiclevi glossatorem' ('book-keeper of the Lollards and annotator of Wyclif's works').[54] Bale derived this information from the Carmelite Thomas Netter's *Doctrinale Antiquitatum Fidei Cathholicae Ecclesiae* (1423–30).[55]

Waterland also notes that Bale attributes to Purvey the commentary on the Apocalypse now known as *Opus Arduum* (on what grounds is not known, and Bale is probably mistaken),[56] and a number of other works. Two, which do not survive, are described by Netter: *De Compendiis Scripturarum, Paternarum Doctrinarum et Canonum*, arguing from biblical, patristic and canon-law sources that bishops and clergy have a duty to preach and that royalty, knights, military men, laymen and women are entitled to

[50] 31 May 1829, Bodl. Engl. hist. c. 147, fols. 118r–119r; see also *WB*, I.xxi–xxiii.

[51] Baber resigned in Nov. 1829: Bodl. Engl. hist. c. 147, fol. 135v; Bodl. MS Engl. hist. c. 155, pp. 10–11.

[52] 17 August 1729, *The Works of Daniel Waterland*, X.360–1; *WB*, I.51/7 to 52/11; see further pp. 119–13, below.

[53] *The Works of Daniel Waterland*, X.361.

[54] Bale, *Scriptorum Illustrium Maioris Brytanniae . . . Catalogus*, I.541–3 (quot. at 542).

[55] Netter mentions Purvey and works attributed to Purvey at 1, i; 2, lxx, lxxiii, and 6, xiii, xvii and cxvii; ed. B. Blanciotti, 3 vols. (Venice, 1757–9), I.33; II.619, 637; III.110, 127 and 732. In a note at I.33, Netter calls Purvey 'doctor eximius' and Wyclif's 'interpres'. Bale also derives information from Knighton, ed. Martin, *Knighton's Chronicle*, pp. 291–3, and from *FZ*, pp. 383–407; see Hudson, 'John Purvey: A Reconsideration of the Evidence for his Life and Writings', in *Lollards and their Books*, pp. 86–95, and Hudson, *ODNB* XLV (2004), pp. 587–8.

[56] See Hudson, 'A Neglected Wycliffite Text', *in Lollards and their Books*, pp. 43–66, esp. 56–7.

preach, and *Libellus de Oratione*, including criticism of liturgical practice.[57] Bale also attributes to Purvey a work called 'Ad Parliamentum Angliae', probably the *Lollard Disendowment Bill* of 1410 (again, Bale's source for the attribution is unknown).[58] Eleven other works attributed to Purvey by Bale can be identified with the errors the Carmelite Richard Lavenham extracts out of the 'libelli Purvey Lollardi'.[59]

Accounts of Purvey's writings before Waterland pitched upon him, then, demonstrate that he was an active Wycliffite but provide next to no evidence linking him with translation of the Bible. One piece of evidence which Waterland used to link Purvey with biblical translation comes from Trinity College Dublin 75, a manuscript containing the Prologue to the Wycliffite Bible, and the New Testament and prologues to individual books of the New Testament in a mix of Earlier and Later Versions.[60] This manuscript contains the motto 'Christus homo factus J.P. prosperet actus', and a monogram spelling 'Peruie', which may or may not refer to the follower of Wyclif.[61] Another item the manuscript contains is a copy of a letter to Cardinal Henry Beaufort, Bishop of Winchester, from John Witton, curate of Chedynfolde, Surrey, rejecting accusations of heresy (written after 1427, when Beaufort became cardinal), and John Scattergood and Guido Latré suggest that Witton owned the manuscript.[62] New evidence uncovered by Maureen Jurkowski suggests that in fact Beaufort may have been the owner. She argues that the manuscript could have come into his hands at the same time as his servant, John Pirie, obtained the goods of Thomas Lyttleton, a parchmener, and Nicholas atte Cok, a brewer, who had been indicted for sheltering Purvey and two other rebels after the Oldcastle uprising in 1414, and who had subsequently fled from justice.[63] If Jurkowski is right, and Trinity College Dublin 75 belonged to Purvey and subsequently to

[57] On *De Compendiis*, see *Doctrinale*, 2, lxx, lxxiii; I.619, 637, and, on *Libellus*, 6, xiii, xvii and cxvii; III.110, 127 and 732. From 2, lxxiii it seems that *De Compendiis* was solely concerned with preaching, but see Hudson, 'John Purvey', p. 94. On the *Libellus*, see Hudson, *Two Wycliffite Texts: The Sermon of William Taylor 1406, The Testimony of William Thorpe 1407*, EETS o.s. 301 (Oxford University Press, 1993), pp. xxiii–xxiv, and *ODNB* XLV.587.

[58] Hudson, 'John Purvey', pp. 92, 98–9; the *Lollard Disendowment Bill* is ed. Hudson, *SEWW*, no. 27.

[59] *FZ*, pp. 383–99; see Hudson, 'John Purvey', pp. 91, 99.

[60] On this MS, see Appendix 4, and p. 105, below.

[61] *The Works of Daniel Waterland*, X.362, 395; motto, fol.1r; monogram, fol. 217v; the monogram is reproduced in *WB*, I.lxi. Hudson rejects the association: 'John Purvey', pp. 102–3.

[62] Fols. 255r–257r. John Scattergood and G. Latré, 'Trinity College Dublin MS 75: A Lollard Bible and some Protestant owners', in J. Scattergood and J. Boffey, eds., *Texts and their Contexts: Papers for the Early Book Society* (Dublin: Four Courts Press, 1997), pp. 223–40.

[63] 'Lollard Book Producers in London in 1414', in Barr and Hutchison, eds., *Text and Controversy*, pp. 209–10. Lyttleton and atte Cok's possessions were seized by the Middlesex escheator, for the Crown, before Pirie obtained them (their recorded goods were of little value). Jurkowski thinks this manuscript may be the 'Biblia' listed among his forfeited possessions (see following n.), but the contents hardly amount to a 'Bible', and the listed Bible was probably in Latin.

Beaufort, the member of Beaufort's staff who copied Witton's letter also had access to another Wycliffite Bible manuscript from which he copied the Old Testament lections which follow the letter, in the same hand (fols. 257r–281r). While Beaufort might have taken steps to procure scripture in English, and enabled and encouraged the copying of more, it is much likelier that Witton owned the manuscript, and probable that no part of it was written before c. 1425.

A stronger piece of evidence linking Purvey with biblical translation is the inventory of his books made while he was in prison after the Oldcastle uprising (he died in prison in May 1414). This includes items that could have been used by the translators of the Wycliffite Bible, including Bede's commentary on the Pauline Epistles and Lyra's postill on the same books.[64] The note at Baruch 3:20 in one Wycliffite Bible manuscript, 'Here endiþ the translacioun of N and now bigynneþ þe translacioun of J and of oþere men',[65] reinforces the evidence for Nicholas Hereford as a translator but scarcely improves the case for Purvey: the 'J' could refer to John Purvey, John Wyclif, John As[h]ton,[66] or many another.

When Forshall and Madden began work on their edition in 1829, they accepted Waterland's identification of Purvey as one of the translators, but they surmised that Purvey's role was limited to his being one of the translators responsible for the Earlier Version.[67] In the introduction to their edition, however, they follow Waterland in attributing the Prologue and the Later Version to Purvey,[68] on the grounds that the Prologue must have been written by the same person who wrote *The Thirty-Seven Conclusions* (*Ecclesiae Regimen*), a text edited by Forshall.[69] The content of this Wycliffite text, say Forshall and Madden, 'very nearly coincides' with the articles Purvey abjured in 1401, and with Lavenham's list of Purvey's errors and heresies.[70] The differences between the Prologue to the Wycliffite Bible and *The Thirty-Seven Conclusions*, and between that tract and the documentation of Purvey's errors, now seem as significant as the similarities.[71] Nonetheless, Forshall and Madden's edition turned Waterland's guess into

64 Maureen Jurkowski, 'New Light on John Purvey', *English Historical Review* 110 (1995), 1184.

65 Z, fol. 61v. The note was discovered by Hargreaves in 1956: see further pp. 103–4, below.

66 See Martin, ed., *Knighton's Chronicle*, pp. 279–91; *BRUO*, I.67, Hudson, *PR*, pp. 77–78 and *passim*, and T. F. Henderson (rev. Zoë Lawton), *ODNB* II (2004), pp. 788–9.

67 20 June 1829, Bodl. Engl. hist. c. 147, fol. 120r.

68 In spite of finding Waterland's evidence unsatisfactory, *WB*, I.xxiv–xxv; see Hudson, 'John Purvey', p. 103.

69 *WB*, I.xxv; ed. Josiah Forshall, *Remonstrances against Romish Corruptions of the Church: Addressed to the People and Parliament of England in 1395, 18 Ric. II* (London: Longman, 1851).

70 *WB*, I.xxvi–xxviii; *FZ*, pp. 383–99.

71 See Hudson, 'John Purvey', pp. 103–4.

accepted fact, and the Prologue to the Wycliffite Bible and the Later Version of the Wycliffite Bible have been attributed to Purvey ever since.[72] The fact remains, however, that only Nicholas Hereford can with confidence be named as one of the translators of the Wycliffite Bible.

Whoever the individual translators were, the production of the first English Bible was conceived as a group endeavour. The translators did far more than turn the Latin Bible into English. Their hugely ambitious project involved editorial, hermeneutic and linguistic biblical scholarship. Aware that one of the most telling arguments against biblical translation was the danger of translating from a corrupt text of the Latin Bible, the translators wanted to give their English readers a Bible they could rely upon as an apt and accurate rendering of a carefully edited original. The project is outlined in the final chapter of the Prologue, written after Wyclif's death but recalling a process Wyclif, I believe, played an important part in determining and developing. First, 'þis symple creature hadde myche trauaile wiþ diuerse felawis and helperis to gedere [collect] manie elde Biblis' in order to establish a corrected and authoritative Latin text. Secondly, they studied this authoritative text with the aid of commentaries and glosses, 'and especially Lire [Lyra] on the old testament'; thirdly, they consulted linguistic authorities in order to elucidate 'harde wordis and harde sentencis', and, fourthly, they produced a clear and accurate English translation.[73] What is being sketched here in the final chapter of the Prologue is the whole trajectory of the Wycliffite Bible enterprise.[74]

With a task of such magnitude, several scholars must have been involved at any one time.[75] Lindberg's most recent hypothesis is that Wyclif began to establish a critical text of the Latin Bible 'as soon as or soon after he came to Oxford' (probably c. 1350). He then prepared an interlinear gloss, which was turned into a continuous text and then into a more idiomatic text, the Earlier Version being finished around 1380 and the Later Version around 1390.[76] Previously, Lindberg had suggested that work on the project began

[72] Ibid., pp. 103–8. Hargreaves calls his study of Psalms in LV 'The Latin Text of Purvey's Psalter': *Medium Aevum* 24 (1955), 73–90. Lindberg also attributes the revision of LV tentatively to Purvey, *KHB*, I.47; see further pp. 101, 150–2 below.

[73] *WB*, 1, 57/7–15. See Hudson's notes on these four stages, *SEWW*, pp. 162–3.

[74] Hudson, *PR*, p. 243. As she points out, *WB*, I.xxii, Fristedt, *WB*, I.137, and Hargreaves, 'The Latin Text of Purvey's Psalter', 73, all assume that this passage relates to the production of LV only.

[75] See Hudson, 'Wyclif and the English Language', in Anthony Kenny, ed., *Wyclif in his Times* (Oxford: Clarendon Press, 1986), p. 92, and *PR*, p. 242.

[76] Lindberg, *EV*, VIII.71 (1997). Wyclif was a Bachelor of Arts by the late spring of 1356; on the date of Wyclif's matriculation, see Andrew E. Larsen, 'John Wyclif, c. 1331–1384', in Levy, ed., *A Companion to John Wyclif*, pp. 9–11. On the supposed interlinear translation, see also Lindberg, *Judges*, p. 74, and pp. 137–8, below.

in about 1370 and lasted for two decades, with four translators working on the Earlier Version (with assistants) and two translators (with assistants) working on the Later Version.[77] Six or seven main translators sounds about right, with most of them probably working both on the initial translation and on the revision, at least in the 1370s. Everything points to the fact that from the outset the translation of the Bible was envisaged as a process, culminating in a text that could be understood by readers whose only language was English. Starting with a 'construe' and revising in the direction of readability in the target language was, after all, a recognized method of translation, as Beryl Smalley pointed out in response to Margaret Deanesly's argument that the extreme literalness of the Earlier Version meant that the Wycliffite Bible was never intended to be used 'for devotional purposes'.[78] In the *Mirror of the Blessed Life of Jesus Christ*, Nicholas Love translates 'benedicta es tu in mulieribus (Luke 1:28)' as 'blessed be þou in women, or aboue al women', providing an example in miniature of the process.[79]

Lindberg may be right that Wyclif began contemplating an English Bible early in his Oxford career, but we shall see that there is no evidence that the earliest translation was interlinear, and a starting-date of 1370 for collaborative work is perhaps a little early. David Fowler believes that by 1372 John Trevisa was working with Wyclif and other Queensmen on the project.[80] I think it likely that the project was in the planning stages at the beginning of the 1370s, at the same time as Wyclif was planning his *Postilla* on the whole Bible, and that work on the translation started before the middle of the decade. Forshall and Madden voice the assumptions of their age and indeed of the whole of Christian tradition when they say that 'the New Testament was naturally the first object'.[81]

[77] Conrad Lindberg, 'The Language of the Wyclif Bible', in W.D. Bald and H. Weinstock, eds., *Medieval Studies Conference Aachen 1983: Language and Literature* (Frankfurt: Lang, 1984), pp. 103, 106.

[78] Margaret Deanesly, *The Significance of the Lollard Bible* (London: Athlone, 1951), p. 6; Smalley, review of Deanesly, *Medium Ævum* 22 (1953), 51; see also Von Nolcken, 'Lay Literacy, the Democratization of God's Law and the Lollards', in Sharpe and Van Kampen, eds., *The Bible As Book*, p. 179; Fristedt, *WB*, *III*.39, and Clive R. Sneddon, 'Rewriting the Old French Bible: The New Testament and Evolving Reader Expectations in the Thirteenth and Early Fourteenth Centuries', in Rodney Sampson and Wendy Ayres-Bennett, eds., *Interpreting the History of French: A Festschrift for Peter Rickard* (Amsterdam: Rodopi, 2002), pp. 45–51.

[79] Ed. Sargent, p. 23.

[80] *The Life and Times of John Trevisa*, p. 229; cf. Fristedt, *WB*, *II*.xlviii–xlix, lxiii–lxiv. In his review of Hudson, *PR*, Fowler contests her argument that translation began c. 1380, *Studies in the Age of Chaucer* 12 (1990), 296–305.

[81] *WB*, I.xv.

The claim made by William Smith of Leicester, in 1389, that for eight years he had been working hard at copying 'sacred texts from the gospel and the epistles of Paul and other epistles and doctors of the church in the vernacular' ('libros solempnes . . . in materna lingua de euangelio, de epistolis Pauli et aliis epistolis et doctoribus'),[82] has been read as confirming that the New Testament alone had been translated by the early 1380s.[83] Hudson favours Deanesly's suggestion that Smith is referring to the *Glossed Gospels*, which may well be right.[84] All the internal textual evidence, however, points to the fact that the Old Testament, not the New Testament, was the translators' first object. The Gospels, as Hudson says, 'were only reached [in the Earlier Version] at a stage when the original literary method had already been substantially modified in the direction of fluency'.[85]

Having been associated with three Oxford colleges as well as the Queen's College – Merton, Balliol and Canterbury College – Wyclif was well placed to organize the gathering of the necessary resources, including Bibles, commentaries, lexicons, the paraphernalia of work-in-progress, a place to keep all these things plus space for the translators to work. While Wyclif was in Oxford there is every reason to suppose that the translation was made there. The naming of Hereford in the first part of Bodleian Douce 369 is in line with this: he is far more likely to have been working on the translation while living in the Queen's College before 1382 than while in prison in Italy and in England, as he was for most of the period 1382–87. The very strong contemporary evidence linking Wyclif with the translation implies that at the least he initiated the project and actively supervised it.

Hudson comments that Wyclif's attitude towards translation was 'amazingly nonchalant', citing his comment in *De Contrarietate Duorum Dominorum* that burning manuscripts of God's law is fruitless, 'for language, whether Hebrew, Greek, Latin or English, is nothing but the clothing of the law of the Lord' ('Lingua enim, sive hebrea, sive greca, sive latina, sive anglica est quasi habitus legis domini').[86] Wyclif was certainly less exercised

[82] Martin, ed., *Knighton's Chronicle*, pp. 534–5. Two Leicester Lollards summoned to trial in Dorchester in 1389 were William Parmenter and Michael Scrivener; see Hudson, *PR*, p. 76.

[83] By Fristedt, *WB*, *II*.73–4, and Hargreaves, 'The Vernacular Scriptures: the Wycliffite Versions', *CHB*, II.393. Lindberg suggests Wyclif translated NT and left OT to his helpers, *EV*, V.92.

[84] Hudson, *PR*, pp. 76, 249; Deanesly thinks Smith is referring to the whole of WB in EV as well as the *Glossed Gospels*, *LB*, p. 278.

[85] *PR*, p. 240. Lindberg assumes that the work began with the Prefatory Epistles: 'From Jerome to Wyclif, an Experiment in Translation: the First Prologue', *Studia Neophilologica* 63 (1991), 143–5. See further pp. 137–45, below.

[86] Hudson, 'Wyclif and the English Language', p. 90; Wyclif, *Polemical Works*, II.700/29–31.

than Trevisa or Ullerston – or Jerome – show themselves to be by the difficulties of translating the Bible, but if one wishes to get an enormous project off the ground over-confidence is no bad thing. The next chapter considers just what the 'Bible' was that Wyclif and his colleagues set out to clothe in English.

CHAPTER 4

The canonical scriptures

At the point when they were making decisions about how to proceed with the work, what did Wyclif and the translators expect a Bible to contain and to look like? We might have expected that they would take the Bible in French as a model, since French Bibles were available in England from the late thirteenth century onwards, and the French Bible, in the form of the *Bible historiale complétée*, was the vernacular Bible with which Chaucer and his educated contemporaries were brought up.[1] The *Bible historiale complétée* was not, however, a translation of the Latin Bible *tout court* but a blend of Peter Comestor's *Historia Scholastica* and the biblical text, and it incorporated many interpretive glosses (the book of Genesis, for example, was heavily glossed from the *Glossa Ordinaria*).[2] The inter-relations between the various versions of the French Bible of the late Middle Ages, customarily called the *Bible du XIIIe siècle*, the *Bible historiale* and the *Bible historiale complétée*, are dauntingly complex, but Clive Sneddon argues that the success of the *Bible historiale complétée* 'seems to imply that readers wanted to have all the books of the Bible in their possession', but 'were not too particular about the actual source translated'.[3] Although composite, the *Bible historiale complétée* was still regarded as 'a Bible'; the copy the Lollard sympathizer John Cheyne bequeathed to his son in 1413 is called 'a Bible in French'.[4]

[1] Gibson, *The Bible in the Latin West*, p. 13; see also pp. 70–1. Dudley R. Johnson argues that the *Bible historiale* was a source of Chaucer's Monk's Tale: 'The Biblical Characters of Chaucer's Monk', *PMLA* 66 (1951), 827–43.

[2] Clive R. Sneddon, 'The "Bible du XIIIe siècle": Its Medieval Public in the Light of its Manuscript Tradition', in Lourdaux and Verhelst, eds., *The Bible and Medieval Culture*, pp. 127–40, esp. pp. 129, 132; see also C. A. Robson, 'Vernacular Scriptures in France', *CHB*, II.436–52, and Samuel Berger, *La Bible française au Moyen Age* (Paris, 1884).

[3] 'The "Bible du XIIIe siècle"', p. 131. Sneddon has recently argued that the *Bible du XIIIe siècle* was made in Orléans for the family of Louis IX in the late 1240s, and was available in Paris by 1260: 'On the Creation of the Old French Bible', *Nottingham Medieval Studies* 46 (2002), 25–44.

[4] BN fr. 156, fol. 3v; see Sneddon, 'The "Bible du XIIIe siècle"', p. 140. On Cheyne, see Nigel Saul, *ODNB* XI.376.

If Sneddon is right that readers of French Bibles did not concern themselves over-much with sources, the translators of the Wycliffite Bible were much more particular on their readers' behalf. As Oxford scholars, their Bible was of course the Latin Bible, and there is no evidence that they considered translating anything other than the text of the Latin Bible, and no sign that they made use of any of the versions of the French Bible,[5] although, contrariwise, the Anglo-Norman translation of Genesis to Tobit in British Library Royal 1. C. III, made at the end of the fourteenth century, contains translational glosses in English which often coincide with the Earlier Version of the Wycliffite Bible.[6] The success of the composite *Bible historiale complétée* among educated English laypeople perhaps encouraged the Wycliffite translators to choose a different direction, and make their English Bible as much like the Latin Bible as possible, and as literal a rendering of the Latin as possible. From a theological point of view, this is what we should expect: Wyclif argued that the totality of God's law should be available in English, but also that God's law contains everything necessary for salvation, when understood in the light of Christ. This by no means implies a rejection of the tradition of scriptural interpretation, as we shall see, but it does make the text of scripture of equal authority with the human person of Christ, the Word.[7]

Complete Latin Bibles had only been produced on anything like a commercial scale since the early thirteenth century. In the early Middle Ages, pandects (manuscript-volumes containing all the books of the Old and New Testaments) were enormous and very rare. The oldest surviving one-volume Bible, the *Codex Amiatinus*, written in Northumbria around 700, has 1030 folios measuring 505 by 340 millimetres, and weighs 34 kilograms.[8] Nearly half the surviving biblical manuscripts before 800 were manuscripts of the Gospels alone.[9] The first production of Bibles on a large scale was in the early ninth century in Tours, instigated by Alcuin, Abbot of St Martin's but originally from the Cathedral School at York. Each 'Tours Bible' had about 450 large folios and took some six months to make.[10] In a poem written

[5] See Lindberg, *EV*, II.25, correcting *EV*, I.25.

[6] On this MS, which belonged to Reading Abbey, see Berger, *La Bible française au Moyen Age*, pp. 231–7, 386; 'les eawes del diluuie en vnderent flowed' (Gen. 7:6, EV and LV, *WB*, I.91); 'espres sprinkled' (Gen. 31:12, EV, *WB*, I.143); 'a soun signe bekkening' (Gen. 42:6, EV, *WB*, I.) [etc.].

[7] See Levy, *John Wyclif*, pp. 112–22, and pp. 193–7, below.

[8] Now Florence, Biblioteca Medicea-Laurenziana Amiatino 1; see De Hamel, *Book*, pp. 33–4 and figs. 16–17; the leaves measure 505 by 340mm, p. 34.

[9] 'Over 43 per cent', according to Patrick McGurk, 'The Oldest Manuscripts of the Latin Bible', in Gameson, ed., *The Early Medieval Bible*, p. 4.

[10] David Ganz, 'Mass Production of Early Medieval Manuscripts: The Carolingian Bibles from Tours', in Gameson, ed., *The Early Medieval Bible*, p. 55. Ganz points out that the order of books in Tours

to accompany a presentation copy, Alcuin marvels at the fact that a single book can encompass such manifold riches: 'Continet iste uno sancto sub corpore codex / Hic simul hos totos munera magna Dei' ('this manuscript contains here within one holy corpus all these books, God's great gifts, at one and the same time').[11] The owners of 'Tours Bibles' were cathedral churches, religious houses and great princes; purchasing a Bible was beyond the means of the individual scholar. It was not until the late twelfth century that developments in the technology of manuscript production in France enabled Latin Bibles of a manageable size and affordable price to be produced.[12] From the 1230s onwards, multiple copies of Bibles written on ultra-thin 'uterine' vellum were sold by the Paris stationers to friars, monks and secular scholars, and were disseminated throughout Europe.[13]

The order of the biblical books, which had previously been variable in a number of respects,[14] became largely standardized in Latin Bibles written in France from 1200 onwards.[15] In broad terms, the order of the Old Testament books derived from the Hebrew scriptures was superseded by the order derived from the Greek Septuagint.[16] In the former, there was a tripartite division: the historical books, the prophetical books and the writings. The books of Kings (the last of the historical books) are followed by the books of Isaiah and the other Prophets, and after the Prophets come Job, Psalms, the Books of Solomon (Proverbs, Ecclesiastes and the Song of Songs) and Wisdom and Ecclesiasticus, and the later writings, including the books of Chronicles and Maccabees. The order in which Old Testament books customarily appear in Latin Bibles written in France after 1200, derived from the Septuagint, is: the Pentateuch[17] (Genesis, Exodus, Leviticus, Numbers,

Bibles is variable, and that under Alcuin's successor, Fridugisus (804–34), the epistle to the Laodiceans is included (p. 57). See also De Hamel, *Book*, fig.20, p. 37.

11 Ganz, 'Mass Production of Early Medieval Manuscripts', p. 56.

12 See Light, 'French Bibles c. 1200–30', and De Hamel, *Book*, pp. 114–39. Fig. 83, p. 118, shows a life-size example.

13 De Hamel argues that it was in particular the Dominican and Franciscan friars who created the demand for such Bibles (*Book*, pp. 129–33); see also Smalley, *The Study of the Bible in the Middle Ages*, pp. 196–263, and Smalley in Lampe, ed., *CHB*, II.204–9.

14 See Berger, *Histoire de la Vulgate*, pp. 331–41.

15 See Light, 'French Bibles c. 1200–30', pp. 155, 161–3, and De Hamel, *Book*, pp. 120–2. The characteristic components of the Vulgate before the thirteenth century, including the prologues, are conveniently detailed by De Hamel, pp. 22–4. The Latin–English glossary in BL Add. 34305 follows the older biblical order (see Index of MSS).

16 The Septuagint order is the order in which Augustine lists the OT books in *DDC*, II, viii, 13/39–40; see Light, 'French Bibles c. 1200–30', p. 161. Theodulfian Bibles and Stephen Harding's Bible order the OT books according to Jerome's discussion in his *Prologus Galeatus* (on which, see pp. 92–4, 200, below), Light, ibid.

17 The word is not used in Middle English; in the second Prefatory Epistle, it is translated 'þe fyue bokis of Moyses': Lindberg, *PE*, p. 152/5–6.

Deuteronomy); the historical books (Joshua, Judges, Ruth, 1–4 Kings, 1–2 Chronicles-Prayer of Manasseh,[18] 1–3 Ezra,[19] Tobit, Judith, Esther); the wisdom books (Job, the Gallican Psalter,[20] Proverbs, Ecclesiastes, the Song of Songs, Wisdom, Ecclesiasticus);[21] the Major Prophets (Isaiah, Jeremiah–Lamentations–Baruch–Epistle of Jeremiah,[22] Ezekiel, Daniel–Susanna–Bel and the Dragon); the Minor [shorter] Prophets (Hosea, Joel, Amos, Obadiah, Jonah, Micah, Nahum, Habakkuk, Zephaniah, Haggai, Zechariah, Malachi), and 1–2 Maccabees. In the New Testament, the customary order in French Bibles after 1200 is: the Gospels (Matthew, Mark, Luke, John); the Pauline Epistles (Romans, 1–2 Corinthians, Galatians, Ephesians, Philippians, Colossians, [Laodiceans],[23] 1–2 Thessalonians, 1–2 Timothy, Titus, Philemon, Hebrews); the Acts of the Apostles; the Catholic Epistles (James, 1–2 Peter, 1–3 John, Jude), and the Apocalypse.[24]

As well as the biblical books themselves, Latin Bibles typically included prologues to the Bible as a whole and to individual books of the Bible, many of them derived from the writings of Jerome. These Latin Bible prologues include two Prefatory Epistles, beginning 'Frater Ambrosius' (Jerome's *Epistola LIII ad Paulinum*) and 'Desiderii mei' (Jerome's *Praefatio in Pentateucum ad Desiderium*), and prologues to the following books:

[18] The Prayer of Manasseh (2 Chron. 37) is not part of the Hebrew scriptures or the Septuagint, but is sometimes included among the Canticles, and is included in many late-medieval Latin Bibles and in the thirteenth-century French Bible: see Appendix 3. On its origins, see George W. E. Nickelsburg, in John Barton and John Muddiman, eds., *The Oxford Bible Commentary* (Oxford University Press, 2001), pp. 770–1.

[19] 3 Ezra is commonly but not invariably included; see further Appendix 3 and pp. 100–1, below.

[20] Translated from Greek into Latin, revised by Jerome, and established as the 'common' Latin Psalter by Alcuin: see White, 'Vulgate', in Hastings, ed., *A Dictionary of the Bible*, IV.874–5. There are, however, parallel Gallican and Hebrew Psalters in Bodl. Lyell 7 (the Hebrew is incomplete), Bodl. Kennicott 15 and Bodl. Laud Lat. 13; cf. De Hamel, *Book*, fig.7, p. 19 (MS in a private collection). BL Royal I. B. XII, written by William de Hales in 1254, has the Hebrew Psalter only. Some Bibles, esp. Bibles written in England, lack Psalms (e.g. BL Royal 1. A. XI): see De Hamel, *Book*, pp. 128–9. The Latin–English glossary in BL Add. 34305 also lacks Psalms; see Index of MSS.

[21] The Prayer of Solomon is included in some post-1200 Bibles as ch. 52 of Ecclus (= 2 Chron. 6:13–20), e.g. BL Royal I. E. IX, Bodl. Canon. Bib. Lat. 47 and 52 and Bodl. Lyell 7, but it is more often omitted. WB does not include it.

[22] The book of Baruch was often lacking in Latin Bibles before 1200, and the order Jeremiah, Lamentations, Baruch, Epistle of Jeremiah (= Bar. 6) is new in 'Paris Bibles'; P.-M. Bogaert, 'Le nom de Baruch dans la littérature pseudépigraphique: l'Apocalypse syriaque et la livre deutérocanonique', in W. C. van Unnik, ed., *La Littérature juive entre Tenach et Mischna* (Leiden: Brill, 1974), pp. 66, 61. Baruch was originally lacking in the Old French Bible (BXIII), see Sneddon, 'Rewriting the Old French Bible', p. 36.

[23] Laodiceans is more often omitted than included; it is present in e.g. Bodl. Lat. bibl. f. 3 and Bodl. Laud Lat. 13, and inserted in the margin at the end of the Pauline Epistles in Bodl. Lyell 7. See further Appendix 3 and p. 95, below.

[24] Acts may also follow the Catholic Epistles (which are also called Canonical Epistles, or Epistles of the Christian Faith, or the Seven Epistles).

Joshua, Kings, Chronicles, Ezra, Tobit, Judith, Esther, Job (two prologues), Psalms, Proverbs, Isaiah, Jeremiah, Baruch, Ezekiel, Daniel, Hosea, each of the Minor Prophets, the Gospels, the Pauline Epistles, Acts and the Apocalypse.[25] Latin Bibles written in France from 1200 onwards typically include new prologues to Ecclesiastes, Amos, Matthew and the Apocalypse, and two to Maccabees.[26] From 1230 onwards, 'Paris Bibles' also typically include new prologues to 2 Chronicles and Wisdom, and the short prologues to each of the Pauline Epistles common in the earlier Middle Ages, but often lacking in Bibles written in France between 1200 and 1230.[27] 'Paris Bibles' also typically include an alphabetical list of the meaning of Hebrew names, beginning '*Aaz* apprehendens' ('*Aaz* means "seizing"').[28]

In the Wycliffite translation, the books of the Bible, throughout the Old and New Testaments, appear in the same order in which they appear in Latin Bibles written in France after 1200.[29] The prologues included in the Earlier Version of the Wycliffite Bible are the same as the prologues found in the 'Paris Bible', except that the new prologue to Matthew is lacking and the pre-1200 prologue to the Apocalypse is retained.[30] In the Old Testament, however, all the prologues from Ezekiel onwards are omitted (for reasons we shall consider in the next chapter), and there are several Earlier Version manuscripts, including the complete Bibles Longleat 3, Christ Church Oxford 145 and Corpus Christi College Oxford 4, that lack some or all of the New Testament prologues.[31] The text '*Aaz* apprehendens' is never found in Wycliffite Bible manuscripts, but is so common in Latin Bibles from about 1230 onwards that a decision must have been made by Wyclif and the translators to exclude it as extraneous to the Bible proper.

From about 1230 onwards, the *capitula*-lists (summaries of the contents of biblical books chapter by chapter) found in earlier Latin Bibles are typically replaced by the new chapter divisions and numbers devised in the university of Paris at the beginning of the thirteenth century, probably

25 *RBMA*. nos. 284, 285 [both included in Lindberg, *PE*], 311, 323, 328, 327, 330, 332, 335, 341 + 343, 344, 357 (uncommon), 457, 482, 487, 491 (uncommon), 492, 494, 500, 507, 510, 515, 519 + 517, 524, 521, 526, 528, 531, 534, 538, 539, 543, 551, 572, 590, 607, 620, 633, 640, 684, 700, 707, 715, 728, 736, 747, 752, 765, 772, 780, 783, 793, 809 and 834.

26 Light, 'French Bibles c. 1200–30', pp. 163–6; *RBMA*, nos. 462, 513, 547, 553, 589 and 839.

27 Light, 'French Bibles c. 1200–30', pp. 166–7, 173–6; *RBMA*, nos. 327 and 468. Ker lists the 'complete' set of prologues normally found in 'Paris Bibles', *MMBL*, I.96–7.

28 *RBMA*, no. 7709 (Stephen Langton, but probably the work of Remigius of Auxerre, no.7192.1); see Light, 'French Bibles c. 1200–30', p. 156.

29 Except for the omission of 3 Ezra in LV; see n. 19, above.

30 See Appendix 1, below, which contains full details of the order and contents of WB in EV and in LV.

31 For details, see the Index of MSS, and pp. 105–6, below.

by Stephen Langton.[32] In Wycliffite Bible manuscripts, in the Earlier and Later Versions, the chapter-numbers are always clearly indicated (usually in red, or deep-blue and red, roman numerals), and each chapter also has a decorated initial (typically a 2 or 3-line deep-blue letter flourished in red). Scribes of Wycliffite Bible manuscripts sometimes write the final words of a chapter in the right-hand side of the column, leaving a gap on the left – a practice which had helped to draw the eye to the break between chapters, when chapters were identified by their opening words rather than by their number (see fig. 5).[33] These scribes were evidently well accustomed to writing Latin Bibles.

As in late-medieval Latin Bibles, there are rubrics in Wycliffite Bible manuscripts indicating the beginnings and endings of prologues and of biblical books (at the end of Jeremiah a rubric contextualizing Lamentations has become part of the biblical text),[34] and also rubrics introducing 'þe scripture of Ezechie [Hezekiah] kyng of Juda whanne he hadde be sijk and hadde rekyuered of his sikenesse' (Is. 38:9), the Prayer of Jeremiah and the Epistle of Jeremiah, and specifying which parts of Daniel and Esther are in the Septuagint but not the Hebrew.[35] There are running-heads for ease of reference, although in Latin Bibles and in a few Wycliffite Bible manuscripts running-heads are omitted in Psalms.[36] Usually the name of the book is a running-head on both verso and recto, but some scribes writing Wycliffite Bible manuscripts follow the Latin Bible practice of extending the name in Lombardic capitals across the whole opening (see (JO)SUE, fig. 5).[37]

At the openings of biblical books, in the Earlier Version and in the Later Version, there is often a gold initial on a coloured background and an elaborately decorated bar border in gold and several colours (particularly deep blue, light blue, mauve, orange and pink, in the period c. 1390–1420). Otherwise, the opening initial and bar border are typically in deep blue and red, flourished in both colours. The historiated initials common in Latin

32 Light, 'French Bibles c. 1200–30', pp. 168–70. It is quite common for such Bibles to have both the older chapter divisions and indications of the new chapter numbers (ibid., p. 171); see e.g. Bodl. Kennicott 15 (Paris, c. 1200–1210). There is an NT *capitula*-list in English in K, fols. 385v–388v (the same list survives partially in Lambeth Palace 547); see Appendix 4.

33 There are chapter-breaks of this kind in BC_U_6680eIKQRSU*X*; see the descriptions of these MSS in Appendix 4.

34 A gloss at Jer. 52:34 points this out: 'al þis til in to þe ende of þe chapetre semiþ addid of sum expositur [summe expositouris E] to continue þe sentence to þe chapetris sewinge, for it is not in Ebreu neþer in bokis amendid, Lire here [i.e., see Lyra's gloss on this verse]' (marg. EGKPQU text Y), cf. *WB*, III.471.

35 *WB*, III.292, III.483, III.495; see further pp. 99–100, below.

36 De Hamel, *Book*, p. 182; running-heads are lacking in Ps. in *A*AL_oZ.

37 As in IR*X* and the first part of P_S; see De Hamel, *Book*, figs. 96–7, pp. 137, 139. In *C* and in the early part of *E*, the name is on the verso only, see Appendix 4.

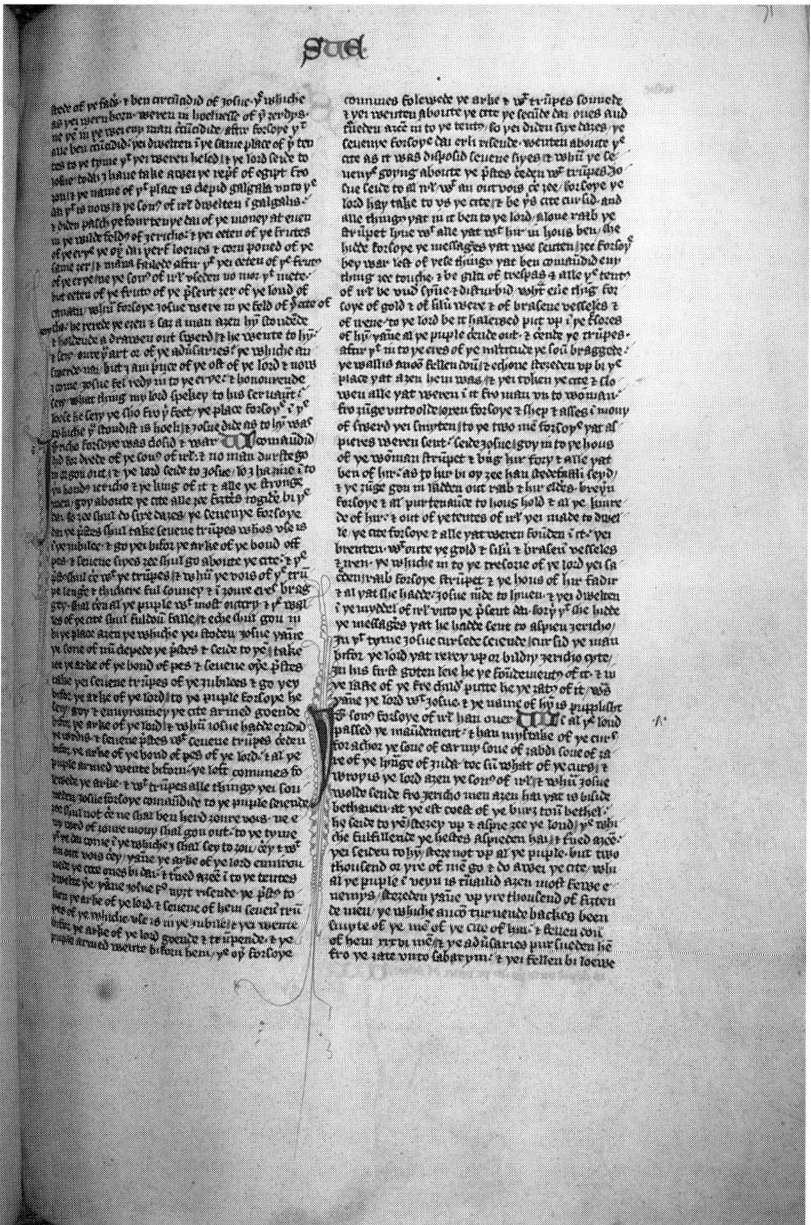

Figure 5. Chapter-divisions and running-head written in traditional style, Christ Church Oxford 145, fol. 71r, c. 1390–1400.

Figure 6. John the Evangelist, British Library Royal 1. C. VIII, fol. 325v. London (?), c. 1400–10.

Bibles, particularly at the opening of Genesis and the Gospels, and in the Psalter, are almost never found in Wycliffite Bible manuscripts, however luxurious. No doubt Kathleen Scott is right that the Wycliffites deliberately eschewed pictorial imagery in sacred texts.[38] There are, however, miniatures of the evangelists and apostles in the Bible now in Wolfenbüttel made for Thomas of Lancaster, brother of Henry V, c. 1400.[39] There is a miniature of John the Evangelist with his eagle at the opening of John in British Library Royal 1. C. VIII, c. 1400–10 (see fig. 6) and in British Library Arundel 104, in the opening initial of Matthew, the symbols of the four evangelists (see fig. 7).

As in late-medieval Latin Bibles, in the Earlier Version of the Wycliffite Bible the letters of the Hebrew alphabet, which are integral to the structure of three portions of Hebrew scripture – Psalm 118, Proverbs 31 and the

[38] *Later Gothic Manuscripts, 1390–1490*, vol. I, (*A Survey of Manuscripts Illuminated in the British Isles*, ed. J. J. G. Alexander, vol. VI), (London: Harvey Miller, 1996) pp. 35, 43–7. As Scott points out, there are pictures of the evangelists in two MSS of the *Glossed Gospels*; there are some masks, grotesques and the like in *G*IY, and at the opening of Genesis in R there are seven roundels portraying the Creation and Crucifixion (fol.1r): *Later Gothic Manuscripts*, I.70. Creation-roundels are frequent in late-medieval Latin Bibles; cf. Lambeth Palace 1364, Bodl. Lat. bibl. f. 3, Laud Lat. 13 and Lyell 7.

[39] The miniatures in W_o resemble those in the *Glossed Gospels*: see Doyle, 'English Books In and Out of Court', p. 168, and De Hamel, *Book*, pp. 173–5, and fig. 122.

Figure 7. The Four Evangelists, British Library Arundel 104, fol. 251r. London (?), c. 1430.

first four chapters of the Lamentations of Jeremiah – are rubricated in the text. The rubric at the opening of Lamentations (translated from the Latin) reads 'Her gynneþ þe Lamentacioun of Jeremye þat is in title Cenoth [*qīnot*, laments] wiþ þe soylinge out of Ebru lettris [key provided by the Hebrew letters]'.[40] The Later Version of the Wycliffite Bible omits this rubric, and omits the Hebrew letters in all three portions of scripture where they occur, although a gloss at the beginning of Lamentations in eight manuscripts points out that 'lettris of Ebru ben set in þe bigynnyng of versus in þe Latyn translacioun, for in Ebru þe versis bigynnen bi lettris of þe abice [abc], Lire here'.[41] Lyra denies, however, that the Hebrew letters provide a key to the interpretation of Lamentations. The Earlier Version, but not

40 *WB*, III.472 (*C*); 'quod est in titulo Cynoth absolutio litterarum hebraicarum'; for 'soylinge out' meaning 'exposition, setting forth', see *MED*, *soilen*, v. (4), ger. (b). In *Y*, there is a direction that the Hebrew letters 'schul be writen wit rede ynke', fol. 116r.

41 Marg. CGKPQU text EY, cf. *WB*, III.472. The only LV MS including the Hebrew letters is X (and, in Lamentations only, A).

the Later Version, includes the rubrics written within the text of the Song of Songs in many Latin Bibles, identifying who is speaking to whom at each point (see fig. 8).[42] All in all, the Wycliffites who were responsible for organizing the copying of the translation evidently wanted the first English Bible to look as much like a Latin Bible as possible, pictorial imagery excepted, and were able to make their wishes known in highly specific terms to the producers of the manuscripts.

In copying the order of the Old Testament books in Latin Bibles written in France after 1200, the order derived from the Septuagint, the Wycliffite translators were accepting a particular version of the biblical canon. Built into the alternative order, derived from the Hebrew scriptures, is Jerome's conviction that the books of the Old Testament which the Jews accept have more authority than the books the Jews do not accept. This conviction also resonates through Jerome's prologues, particularly the prologues to 1 Kings and to Proverbs, and it is therefore written into the Earlier Version of the Wycliffite Bible, which contains these prologues. The Later Version does not contain them, or any of the Latin Bible prologues to books of the Old Testament (with the exception of the prologue to Baruch, as we shall see in a moment); but the first chapter of the English Prologue to the Wycliffite Bible discusses the biblical canon, and, as Hudson says, 'explains at its outset the difference between the apocrypha and the canonical books in terms that not even Arundel could have found offensive'.[43]

In the Prologue, the twenty-five books of the Hebrew scriptures that for Christians 'ben bookis of feiþ and fulli bookis of holy writ' are named in the 'Paris Bible' order: Genesis, Exodus, Leviticus, Numbers, Deuteronomy, Joshua, Judges (including Ruth), 1–4 Kings, 1–2 Chronicles, 1–2 Ezra (counted as one book), Esther, Job, Psalms, Proverbs, Ecclesiasticus, Song of Songs, Isaiah, Jeremiah, Ezekiel, Daniel and Hosea–Malachi (counted as one book).[44] Then the Prologue-writer names the books that are 'set among apocrifa, þat is wiþouten autorite of bileue' (that is, that cannot be used to determine doctrine): Wisdom, Ecclesiasticus, Judith, Tobit and the Maccabees. The writer claims as his authority Jerome's 'prologe on the first book of Kyngis', which Jerome says serves as 'quasi galeatum principium omnibus libris quos de hebraeo vertimus in latinum' (translated in the Earlier Version of the Wycliffite Bible 'as an helmyd [helmeted] bigynnynge to

[42] These rubrics, deriving from Bede's commentary on the Song of Songs, are included in e.g. BL Royal I. B. XII (Salisbury, 1254), BL Royal I. E. IX (English, s. xiv ex), Bodl. Lat. bibl. e. 7 (English, s. xiii in), and Bodl. Lat. bibl. f. 3 (English? 1254). In LV, the rubrics are included in X only; see Appendix 4 and pp. 150–1, below.

[43] *PR*, p. 230.

[44] *WB*, I.1/1–16; quot. at 1.

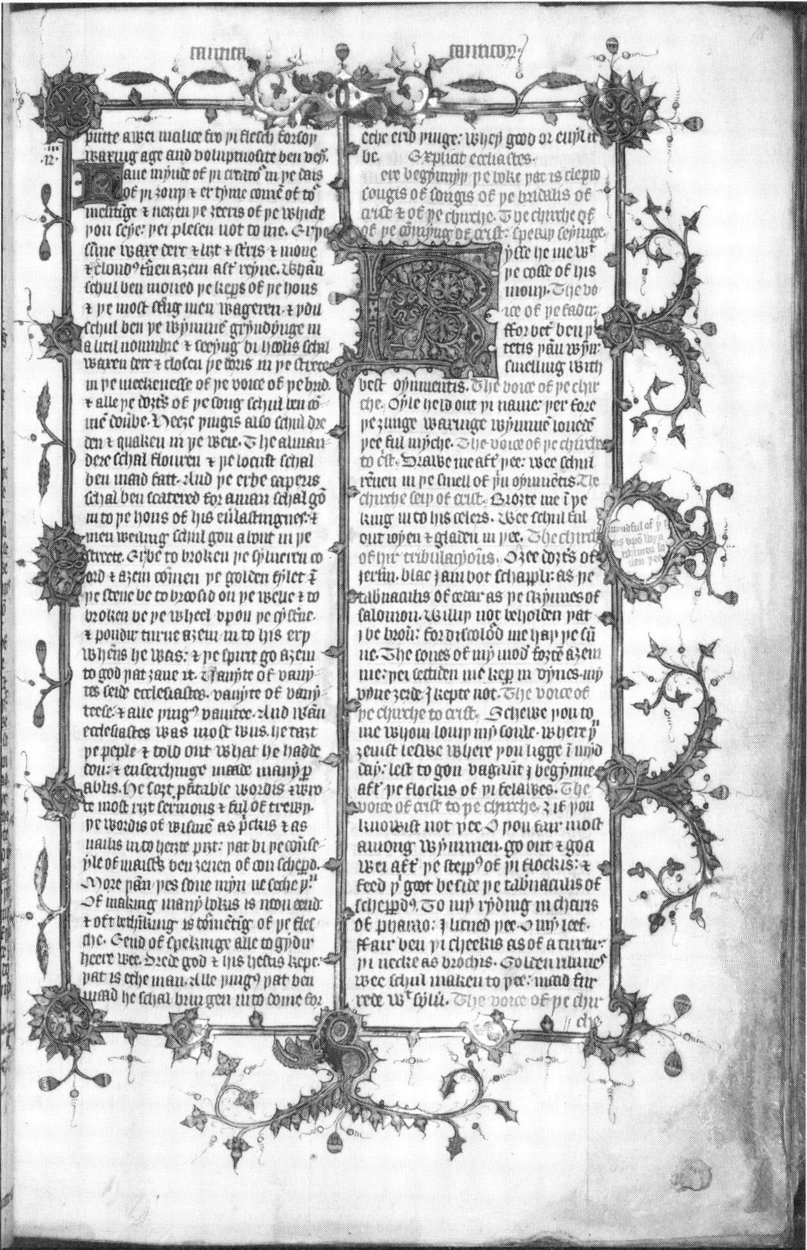

Figure 8. The Song of Songs, with speaker-rubrics, British Library Egerton 617, fol. 18r. London (?), before 1397.

alle þe bookes þe whiche fro Ebru wee han turned in to Latyn'), aggressively facing down the apocryphal books.[45] The number of canonical books is then recalculated as twenty-three, according to Jewish tradition,[46] and as twenty-seven, counting Ezra and Nehemiah separately and adding Judith as a book 'of bileue', on the authority of the Synod of Nicaea (325 AD) and of Jerome's prologue on Judith.[47] Then the apocryphal books are listed once more, including Judith, this time from Jerome's 'prologe on Prouerbis' (or rather on the Books of Solomon).[48] The church, says Jerome, reads these books for edification, but does not receive them 'inter canonicas scripturas', translated in the Earlier Version, which includes this prologue, as 'among þe rewler [canonical] scriptures'.[49]

Before discussing the New Testament canon, the writer of the Prologue explains that the word 'apocrifa' is used in two ways. Used of the Old Testament books already named, it means that 'þe autor is vnknowen and þe treuþe þerof is opyn [uncertain]', but the church acknowledges these books 'to lernyng of vertues', as providing moral teaching.[50] Used of the books which are not acknowledged by the church as part of the New Testament, apocryphal means that one 'doutiþ of þe treuþe þerof': the examples given are the [gospel of] the Infancy of the Saviour and 'þe book of þe takyng up of þe body of Seynt Marie to heuen' (the *Transitus Mariae*).[51] There is no suggestion of a blurring of the boundaries between these categories, as there is in the discussion of the New Testament apocrypha in *De Veritate Sacrae Scripturae*.[52] In the Prologue to the Wycliffite Bible, the books of the New Testament that are 'fulli of autorite of bileue' are the Gospels, twelve

45 Lindberg, *EV*, III.63/73–4 (*E*), *RBMA*, no.323; included in EV MSS + C_U_6680KOX, see Appendix 1; the apocryphal books of the OT are named at *EV*, III.63/77–81. Quotations from Jerome's prologues are from Robert Weber, *Biblia Sacra Iuxta Vulgatam Versionem* (Stuttgart: Deutsche Bibelgesellschaft, 1969).

46 *WB*, I.1/21 to 2/1. Jerome gives the books in the Hebrew order and according to the Hebrew divisions in the *Prologus Galeatus*: Lindberg, *EV*, III.62/32–62; *WB*, II.2/33 to 3/36.

47 *WB*, I.2/3–7; *RBMA*, no.335, included in EV MSS + aKO (see Appendix 1); Lindberg, *EV*, IV.97; *WB*, II.602.

48 *WB*, I.2/13; *RBMA*, no.457, included in EV MSS + aK, and in a revised version in R, Lindberg (see Appendix 1); Lindberg, *EV*, IV.246–7; *WB*, III.1–2.

49 Lindberg, *EV*, IV.247/27 (*E*), cf. *WB*, III.2/1; 'rewler' derives from Med. Lat. *regularis*, 'regular, canonical'.

50 *WB*, II.2/21–24.

51 Ibid., II.2/25–28. As his authority, Purvey cites *Catholicon*, the twelfth-century dictionary composed by Johannes Balbus of Genoa: *WB*, I.2/21, 28. On the gospel of the Infancy of the Saviour (the Infancy Gospel of Thomas), see J. K. Elliott, in Barton and Muddiman, eds., *The Oxford Bible Commentary*, pp. 1319–20, and on the *Transitus Mariae*, see Michael O'Carroll, 'Assumption Apocrypha', in *Theokotos* (Dublin: Dominican Publications, 1982), pp. 58–61.

52 See p. 30, above.

Epistles of Paul, seven 'smale pistils' (the Catholic Epistles), the 'Dedis of Apostlis' and the 'Apocalips'.[53]

The first chapter of the Prologue therefore establishes which biblical books are 'rewler' and which are not. The non-canonical status of Wisdom, Ecclesiasticus, Judith, Tobit and the Maccabees is written into the Wycliffite Bible in this chapter of the Prologue and in the prologues of Jerome defining the canon included in Old Testaments in the Earlier Version. Hudson, following Netter, makes the point that there would seem to be 'a logical inconsistency' here, since the selection of canonical texts depended upon the church's authority, an authority which the Wycliffites disputed.[54] Yet Wycliffites were apparently happy to abide by the church's lectionary for all the masses of the year, and what is most evident in the first chapter of the Prologue is the great esteem in which the writer holds one early Christian scholar and translator, Jerome. Because Jerome takes Hebrew scripture as the 'reule' of the Christian Old Testament, the Wycliffite translators (in the person of the writer of the Prologue) also elevate Hebrew scriptural tradition above the Septuagint. At Nicaea, the church's authority declared Judith canonical, but on Jerome's authority Judith is deemed apocryphal. The Wycliffite translators might hypothetically have decided to adopt the Old Testament canon of Augustine and Cassiodorus, based on the Septuagint and accepting Wisdom, Ecclesiasticus, Tobit, Judith and Maccabees 'inter canonicas scripturas'.[55] Instead, along with the whole of the western medieval church, they accepted Jerome's canon, thereby conceding that the apocryphal books and parts of books could not be determinative for Christian doctrine.

Nevertheless, these apocryphal texts were included in Latin Bibles and in the Wycliffite Bible, and fifteen of the twenty-seven manuscripts containing the whole or a substantial part of the Old Testament in the Later Version contain neither the Prologue to the Wycliffite Bible nor Jerome's

[53] *WB*, I.2/29–31. The number of Pauline Epistles is usually given as fourteen (or eleven, if 1–2 Cor., 1–2 Thess. and 1–2 Tim. are counted as one each), but they are listed as twelve in *A*, fol. 6v (see Appendix 4, below). The writer cannot intend to include Laodiceans: it is included in twelve late MSS of WB, between Colossians and 1 Thess. (see Appendix 3), but its prologue makes it clear that it was not originally part of WB: 'þis pistil is not in comyn Latyn bookis and þerfor it was but late translatid into Englisch tunge' (*WB*, IV.438/5–6). The translation was probably made after 1425.

[54] *PR*, p. 230; *Doctrinale*, 2, xx, ed. Blanciotti, I.343–8. Netter counters Wyclif's claim that the church has made additions to God's law (p. 346).

[55] On Augustine, see n. 16 above; Cassiodorus names the books of the Old Testament in *Magni Avrelii Cassiodori Senatoris Institutionis Divinarum Lectionum*, XIV (Antwerp, 1566), pp. 44–6. See also Martin Goodman, in Barton and Muddiman, eds., *The Oxford Bible Commentary*, pp. 617–26.

prologues on Kings and on the Books of Solomon.[56] Does the Wycliffite Bible in any way question or modify Jerome's position on the Old Testament apocrypha? The prologue to Wisdom in the Latin Bible explains the christological significance of the title: 'it is clepid þe book of Wisdom for in it þe comyng of Crist, which is þe Wisdom of þe Fader, and his passioun opinli ben schewid'.[57] While the synopsis of Wisdom in chapter eleven of the Prologue to the Wycliffite Bible opens with a reminder to the reader that this book is not 'of bileeue', the book is commended for praising wisdom and justice, for rebuking 'fleschly men for hire false bileeue and yuel lyuynge', for dealing in depth with Christ's incarnation ('manheed and godheed togidere'), and for harshly condemning idolatry.[58] Lincoln College Oxford Latin 119, a complete Bible in the Later Version, attaches the relevant sections of the Prologue to the individual books of the Old Testament, but it omits the Prologue's reference to Wisdom's non-canonical status, beginning instead with the positive statement that 'Þe book of Wisdom teechiþ myche riȝtfulnesse'.[59] The brief prologue to Wisdom in Queen's College Oxford 388 emphasizes and accounts for the book's place in the liturgy: '[Wisdom] is red in holi cherche in lessouns of the masse for þe mater þerof is goostli [spiritual] and profecie of þingis to comynge [to come]'.[60]

These two Bibles, Lincoln College Oxford Latin 119 and Queen's College Oxford 388, likewise omit any reference to the non-canonical status of Ecclesiasticus. The Lincoln College Bible again adapts the opening of the synopsis in the Prologue, so that its prologue begins 'Þe book of Ecclesiastici teechiþ myche wisdom', and the Queen's College Bible says that Ecclesiasticus 'tretiþ of wisdom and prudence in many degrees of þe world', summarizing the synopsis of Ecclesiasticus in the Prologue, and concluding that this book 'is profitable boþe to goostly gouernours and bodily lordis and iustisis and comyns also'.[61] The prologue of Jesus son of Sirach, who represents himself as having translated and completed the writings of his grandfather Jesus, warns the reader that the translation of the book from his grandfather's original Hebrew into Greek has led the writer to 'lack in composicioun of wordis' (lack appropriate equivalents for some words).[62]

[56] The fifteen MSS without them are BCDEFHLMNPR_91UVWY; AGIP_SSQ include ch.1 of the Prologue, and C U 6680KOPX contain one or both of Jerome's prologues, see Appendix 1.

[57] *RBMA*, no.468, included in EV MSS + aC_J_E_14 and in a rev. version in R, quot. *WB*, III.85/5–8 (R), cf. Lindberg, *EV*, IV.291 (*E*). The opening of the prologue derives from Jerome's prologue on the Books of Solomon (see n. 48, above).

[58] *WB*, I.41/25–29. On the synopsis of the OT, see pp. 122–9, below.

[59] Ibid., I.41/24–25, with 'þouȝ it be not a book of bileeue' omitted.

[60] Ibid., III.84; see p. 62, above.

[61] Ibid., III.122; *WB*, I.41/29, 36–7.

[62] Ibid., III.123/21–22 (R), cf. Lindberg, *EV*, IV.311 (*E*). *WB* misreads R's text as 'lackide compassioun of wordis', see Appendix 2.

Although this prologue is an integral part of the book of Ecclesiasticus, in all but two manuscripts of the Later Version it is omitted, presumably because it was thought to be one of the Old Testament prologues the translators had decided to omit.[63]

The fifteen manuscripts in the Later Version that lack the Prologue to the Wycliffite Bible and the Old Testament prologues make no reference to the fact that Wisdom and Ecclesiasticus are canonically inferior to Proverbs, Ecclesiastes and the Song of Songs. Jerome thought highly of these two books, but not of the non-canonical Tobit. His prologue to Tobit expresses polite surprise that bishops Cromatius and Heliodorus should desire him to translate from 'Caldee sermoun' into Latin a fable that the Jews themselves sever from 'Goddis scripturis'.[64] The Later Version of the Wycliffite Bible counters Jerome's low opinion of Tobit with a marginal gloss on Tobit 1:1, in effect a mini-prologue, offering readers the conclusion of Lyra's careful consideration of the question of the book's factuality: 'Þis storie of Tobie bifelde in þe sixte ȝeer of king Ezechie, Lire here'.[65] The Prologue to the Wycliffite Bible says nothing about this, and prefaces its discussion of the book with a reminder that Tobit is 'not of bileeue', but recommends it extremely highly to simple men, as teaching them

> to do werkis of mercy and teche wel hire children and to take wyues in þe drede of God, for loue of children and not al for foul lust of body, neiþer for coueitise of goodis of þis world; and also children moun lerne heere bi ȝunge Tobie to be meke and obedient and redi to serue fadir and modir in her nede; þerfore amonge alle þe bookis of þe elde testament symple men of wit schulden rede and here ofte þis book of Tobie.[66]

This astonishingly high view of Tobit demonstrates that unambiguous moral lessons about marriage and familial relations were what 'symple men of wit' were supposed to need above all. Such people were not necessarily without means; the scribe of British Library Harley 3903, containing Tobit and Job in the Later Version, notes that it cost a mark.[67] One de-luxe copy of Tobit alone, surely commissioned by a wealthy layperson, calls Tobit a 'blessid book'. The initial 'T' in this manuscript, Bodleian Douce 36,

[63] It is included in K (in EV) and R; see Appendix 1.

[64] *RBMA*, no.332, included in EV MSS + KO; Lindberg, *EV*, IV.84 (*E*). See Joseph A. Fitzmyer, in Barton and Muddiman, eds., *The Oxford Bible Commentary*, pp. 626–7.

[65] GPP_SQ add 'kyng of Juda' after 'Ezechie'; the gloss is included in AbCEGHKLPP_SQ; *WB*, II.577 (*WB* does not record the MSS). N has the rubric 'Tobie is a storie of an hooly man þat bifelde in þe first [sic] ȝeer of Ezechie king of Juda' (not recorded in *WB*).

[66] *WB*, I.35/31–7; G omits 'not of bileeue', beginning 'Þe book of Tobie is ful deuout'.

[67] 'þe priis of þis book is vi.s and viij. pence', fol. 46v, s.xv. in.

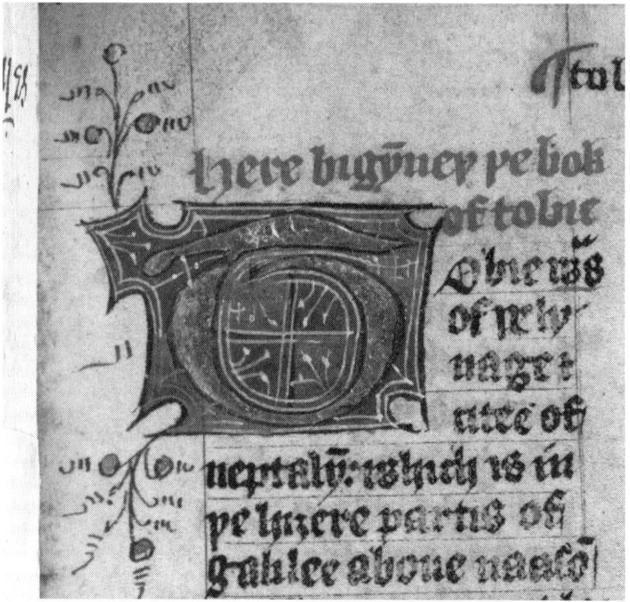

Figure 9. Initial at the opening of Tobit, Bodleian Douce 36, fol. 11r. London (?), c. 1410–20.

is a particularly good example of the kind of initial commonly found in Wycliffite Bible manuscripts (see fig. 9).

In terms of canonical status, Judith ought to fall into the same category as Tobit given that, as the Prologue to the Wycliffite Bible says, the Jews do not regard the book as authoritative, 'as Jerom witnessiþ'.[68] Yet the Synod of Nicaea included Judith in the canon.[69] The Prologue is here offering a partial translation of the first prologue to Judith in the Latin Bible and in the Earlier Version.[70] Judith is a far more problematic text for the writer of the Prologue than Tobit is, because the moral lessons are ambiguous. Judith is an uncomfortable hero, a woman who reproves priests (although the writer concedes that 'goode prestis tooken meekly þis repreuyng of a womman') and who is 'medelid wiþ manye synnes', especially that of lying

[68] *WB*, I.35/42–3. On the origins of Judith, see Amy-Jill Levine, in Barton and Muddiman, eds., *The Oxford Bible Commentary*, p. 633. The text was almost certainly originally Hebrew (as the evidence of the Dead Sea Scrolls attests).

[69] *WB*, I.35/39–41, repeating I.2/5–6.

[70] *RBMA*, no.335, included in EV MSS + aKO (see Appendix 1); Lindberg, *EV*, IV.97; *WB*, II.602. Jerome's second prologue, *RBMA*, no. 336, also included in EV + aKO, establishes the historicity of Judith as well as presenting Judith slaying Holofernes as a figure of the church cutting off the devil's head. G begins 'þe book of Judith comendiþ chastite', *WB*, II.35/44.

to Holofernes.[71] What the Prologue says about Judith's lying is a confused précis of Lyra on the subject: 'vs nediþ not to excuse Judith fro lesingis [lies] and tresoun to Olofernes, but we moun [must] fauourably excuse hir fro deedly synne'.[72] Her sins, in other words, were not mortal but venial, and it is unnecessary to make excuses for her, says Lyra, because even the apostles after the coming of the Holy Spirit were not immune from venial sin.

Four of the five books of the Old Testament which are not 'of bileeue', Wisdom, Ecclesiasticus, Tobit and Judith, have their special status recognized in the synopsis of the Old Testament in the Prologue to the Wycliffite Bible as well as in the discussion of the canon in the first chapter. Only Maccabees lacks such a reminder. The brief prologue in Queen's College Oxford 388 borrows from the Prologue to the Wycliffite Bible the message that Maccabees teaches its readers 'to stonde in tyme of persecucioun stifli bi þe lawe of God', 'to þe deeþ' if need be, reminding us that the concluding books of the Old Testament were regarded as a source of comfort and consolation by those who were persecuted as Wycliffites but called themselves 'trewe men'.[73]

After naming the five Old Testament books the church reads for edification but does not regard as authoritative, the first chapter of the Prologue to the Wycliffite Bible turns its attention to the Greek appendices to Jeremiah known as the book of Baruch and the Epistle of Jeremiah (Baruch 6), the Prayer of Manasseh (2 Chron. 37) and the non-Hebrew portions of Esther and Daniel.[74] The prologue to Baruch in the Latin Bible, the only Old Testament prologue included in all manuscripts of the Wycliffite Bible containing this book, in the Earlier and Later Versions, notes that Baruch and the Epistle of Jeremiah are not 'in þe canoun eþer auþorite of Ebreu', but that they are worthy of their place in the Christian scriptures because they 'schewen many þingis of Crist and of þe laste tymes'.[75] A gloss in some manuscripts of the Earlier Version notes that the 'preyere of Manasses is not in Ebreu';[76] in the Later Version, only British Library Cotton Claudius

[71] *WB*, I.36/6, 18.

[72] *WB*, I.36/8–10; cf. '[her lying] non est mortale peccatum sed veniale tamen, a quo non oportet excusare Iudith quia nec apostoli longe perfectiores et maxime post receptionem spiritus sancti non dicuntur immunes a peccato veniali', Lyra, and the marginal gloss in C, *WB*, II.622 (this gloss is also in B).

[73] *WB*, III.778/2, 7. The glosses on the titles of Ps. 43, 52 and 122, derived from Lyra, relate these psalms to the persecution of the Jews in Macc., and a marginal gloss at Is. 6:12 explains '[þe lond] þat was forsakun' as relating to 'þe tyme of Macabeys, Lire here', C, *WB*, III.218.

[74] *WB*, I.1/21–25.

[75] *RBMA*, no. 491, *WB*, III.484/5, 7–8 in LV ('canoun eþer' *om.* A), cf. Lindberg, *EV*, V.245 (*E*), and *Baruch*, pp. 54–7. This early ninth-century prologue is relatively rare before 1200, see n. 22, above.

[76] Within the text (not underlined) in *A*, as a rubric in L_o, and in the margin in *EH*, see Appendix 2.

E. II has a gloss to the same effect, derived from Lyra.[77] On the other hand, all manuscripts of Wycliffite Esther and Daniel include Jerome's rubrics specifying which parts of the text are not in Hebrew. In Esther, British Library Cotton Claudius E. II and Royal 1. C. IX sometimes point out to the reader that Jerome's words are rubrics, but no manuscript makes use of the 'spite' or 'spere' mentioned as a textual marker in the rubric at Esther 10:3.[78]

Jerome's prologue to Esther comments on the corrupt nature of the text known to him, and he prides himself on his success in re-ordering and restoring the story 'as it is had in Ebrue'.[79] The canonicity of the Hebrew Esther is made explicit in the Later Version in an intratextual gloss from Lyra at Esther 9:32: Esther and Mardocheus (Mordecai) wrote to the Jews ordaining 'þat þei schulden resseyue among hooli bookis' the contents of the book of Esther.[80] In contrast, neither the summary of the content of Esther in the Prologue to the Wycliffite Bible nor the short prologue to Esther in Queen's College Oxford 388 make any mention of canonical questions.[81] They concern themselves only with the moral sense: 'God helpiþ hem þat tristen in him and lyuen iustli in þe drede of him', and 'tirauntis schulden be aferd to conspire aȝens Goddis seruauntis leest God take veniaunce on hem'.[82] The prologue to Daniel in Cambridge University Library Dd. 1. 27 and Queen's College Oxford 388 concerns itself solely with Daniel as a seer and interpreter of visions, in particular visions of the last things.[83]

The chapter on the canon in the Prologue to the Wycliffite Bible concludes its discussion of the Old Testament with the third and fourth books of Ezra; 1 and 2 Ezra (Ezra and Nehemiah) have already been named as canonical,[84] whereas 3 and 4 Ezra are vehemently rejected by Jerome in his first prologue to Ezra.[85] The Prologue to the Wycliffite Bible translates the

77 'Þis is þe preyere of Manasses but it is not in Ebreu neþer it is of þe text, Lire here', C, *WB*, II.475.

78 *WB*, II.658. At Esth.11:1 and 13:7 B includes 'þis is a rubrich' in the rubric text; at 13:7 C notes 'a rubrich' in the margin.

79 *RBMA*, no. 341, included in EV MSS + aKO (see Appendix 1); Lindberg, *EV*, IV.114 (*E*). Jerome says he indicates the Septuagint order by means of an 'abece of red colour vnto þe eiȝþe letter' (*WB*, II.636/20, cf. *EV*, IV.114/18–19), but no MS reproduces this.

80 *WB*, II.658, *om.* I. This is reduplicated in BC in a marginal gloss at Esther 9:30, 'and resseyue þe treuþe of þis book among hooly bokis, Lire here', see p. 164, below.

81 *WB*, I.36/20–46; M, *WB*, II.636.

82 M, *WB*, II.636/4–5; *WB*, I.36/42–3.

83 *WB*, III.621.

84 *WB*, I.1/6–7. The synopsis of 1–2 Ezra in ch.11 of the Prologue regards them as one book, since it concludes with a moralization of both together: 'Þis process of Esdras and of Neemye schulde styre vs to be bisy to biylde vertues in oure soule', *WB*, I.35/26–27. The second prologue to 1 Ezra, *RBMA*, no. 329, included in EV MSS + KO asserts, translating Jerome, that 'Esdras and Neemye . . . in oon volume ben drawyn': Lindberg, *EV*, IV.33 (*E*). 2 Ezra is named 'Neemye' in the Prologue (*WB*, I.34/41), and the running-head is 'Neemie' in X. M has short but distinct prologues to the two books.

85 *RBMA*, no. 330, included in EV MSS + KO; Lindberg, *EV*, IV.32–3 (*E*).

relevant portion, again providing a partial Later Version of a Latin Bible prologue: Jerome 'biddeþ þat no man delite in þe dremis of þe iij. and iiij. Book of Esdre þat ben apocrifa, þat is not of autorite of bileue . . . þe bookis of þe olde testament þat ben not anentis Ebreies [are not accepted by the Jews] and ben not of þe noumbre of holy writ owen to be cast fer awey'.[86] Yet in fact the *somnia* of 3 Ezra are there in all Old Testaments in the Earlier Version for the reader to delight in, and 3 Ezra is found in a revised version in Bodley 277 (this Bible does not contain Jerome's prologue to Ezra, but it does contain the first chapter of the Prologue). The writer of the Prologue states that at Jerome's bidding 'Y translatide not þe þridde neiþer þe fourþe book of Esdre'.[87] Since the Earlier Version habitually contains 3 Ezra and the Later Version does not, an editorial decision to omit it must have been made during the production of the Later Version, and before the writing of the first chapter of the Prologue. It follows that the unique 3 Ezra in Bodley 277, c. 1425–35, must be the work of an independent reviser (it is only lightly revised).[88] Lindberg dates the revision to the 1390s, and associates it with Purvey; he regards the manuscript as a whole as a revision of the Later Version.[89] We shall find in chapter 6 that Bodley 277 is one revision among others, and that there was a continuous process of textual revision,[90] although the component parts of the Earlier and Later Versions remained stable.

For a reader of the Wycliffite Bible wishing to be sure which Old Testament books the church reads as authoritative and which for edification, the Earlier Version provides the relevant material from Jerome's writings in full, in the prologues to individual books and in rubrics within them, and in the more extensive discussions prefixed to Kings and the Books of Solomon. Manuscripts of the Later Version containing the Prologue to the Wycliffite Bible provide this same material in summary form, with some verbatim extracts. Rubrics in all manuscripts show the reader which parts of canonical books are without canonical authority. Because the Prologue was not normally included, the decision to omit the Old Testament prologues from the Later Version, with the exception of the prologue to Baruch, had

[86] *WB*, I.2/14–18, cf. Lindberg, *EV*, IV.32 (*E*). [87] *WB*, I.2/18–19.

[88] See Fristedt, *WB*, *I*.137 and the description of I in Appendix 4. The textual glosses in 3 Ezra are shared with LV in other OT books: 1:2 stolis (EV), *or longe cloþis* (I), cf. Is. 63:1 (LV); 1:30 children (EV), *or seruauntes* (I), cf. 4 Kings 5:23 (LV); 4:45 termes (EV), *or marchis* (I), cf. Prov. 22:28 (LV); 7:13 gentiles (EV), *or heþen folk* (I), cf. Lev. 26:33 (LV). There are no marginal glosses, and there is no indication that Lyra has been consulted; see also *WB*, I.xxxii.

[89] *KHB*, I.47. Lindberg is following Forshall and Madden, who place I 'within a few years after the completion of the later version', i.e., in the 1390s, *WB*, I.xxxi. See further pp. 150–2, below.

[90] As Ernest W. Talbert first realized, 'A Note on the Wyclyfite Bible Translation', *Texas Studies in English* 20 (1940), 29–38; see Hudson, *PR*, p. 243.

the effect of leaving many readers to discover for themselves, or not discover at all, what authority the church attributed to the books categorized as apocryphal. The translators did not in any way question the authority of Jerome, or indeed of the late-medieval church, on these matters, but the fact that they chose to translate the late-medieval Latin Bible in its entirety suggests that the editor of the Lincoln College Oxford Bible was working within the spirit of the Wycliffite Bible enterprise in electing to omit all references to canonicity. On the other hand, the translators did not choose to leave the canonical scriptures to speak for themselves, and the subject of the next chapter is the interpretive guidance provided in the prologues written for the first English Bible.

CHAPTER 5

The English prologues

Interpretation of the Latin Bible in the late Middle Ages was guided by Jerome's Prefatory Epistles and by the prologues of Jerome and others to sections of the Bible and individual books. How much guidance Jerome's prologues provided to an English reader encountering these highly wrought and deeply self-conscious (sometimes frankly self-indulgent) texts, in a very literal translation, is questionable. The translation of extracts from Jerome's prologues in the Prologue to the Wycliffite Bible and in the tract 'First seiþ Bois' is more idiomatic, and the extracts are carefully contextualized.[1] Nevertheless, the Earlier Version of the Old Testament habitually contains the Latin Bible prologues – only, however, as far as the book of Baruch. There is good evidence that there was a hiatus in the translation at Baruch 3:20. Bodley 959 breaks off at the beginning of that verse ('exsurrexerunt/ v. 20/ iuvenes', 'risen / þe ȝunge'); the first part of Bodleian Douce 369 ends at exactly the same point, with a colophon in a different but contemporary hand, 'Explicit translacioun Nicholay de herford', and a rubric in the same place in Cambridge University Library Ee. 1. 10 records 'Here endiþ þe translacioun of N and now bigynneþ þe translacioun of J. and of oþere men'.[2] The formula is the same as that for the ending of one book and the beginning of another. Josiah Forshall and Frederic Madden, Carl Lindberg and Harumi Tanabe identify linguistic changes supporting the manuscript evidence of a break in the translation in the middle of Baruch.[3] The colophon naming Hereford (and adding corrections and

[1] See Bühler, 'A Lollard Tract', p. 177/249 to p. 178/276, and pp. 33–4, above.

[2] *E*, fol. 332r; *C*, fol. 250r; Z, fol. 61v; Henry Hargreaves, 'The Vernacular Scriptures: the Wycliffite Versions', *CBH*, II.400–2; De Hamel, *Book*, pp. 170–3 and figs. 119–21.

[3] E.g., *ambulare* is translated 'gon' at Bar. 1:18 and 3:13 (Lindberg, *EV*, V.246, 248) but 'walke' at Bar. 4:2, 13 and 26 (Lindberg, *EV*, VI.73–4), 'The Break at Baruch 3:20 in the Middle English Bible', *English Studies* 60 (1979), 106–10, detail at 109; see also Lindberg, *MSS*, 345; *WB*, I.xviii, and Harumi Tanabe, 'On Some English Readings in the Vocabulary of the Wycliffite Bible', in Kinshiro Oshitari *et al.*, eds., *Philologia Anglica: Essays Presented to Professor Yoshio Terasawa on the Occasion of his Sixtieth Birthday* (Tokyo: Kenkyusha, 1988), pp. 392–3; see further pp. 154–5, below.

chapter numbers throughout) may, Christopher de Hamel thinks, be the same hand as the final hand of Bodley 959, and may perhaps be the hand of Hereford himself.[4]

Forshall and Madden account for the break by supposing that 'the writer was suddenly stopped in the execution of his work', and think it a not unreasonable conjecture 'that the cause of the interruption was the summons which Hereford received to appear before the synod [the Blackfriars Council] in 1382'.[5] Hereford's personal fortunes may not, however, have had much or anything to do with the break in production of the translation. Supposing that the work of translation was organized by Wyclif and centred in Oxford, Wyclif's withdrawal to Lutterworth in the late autumn of 1381 must have caused serious disruption and involved a raft of decisions. Fristedt thinks Wyclif continued to superintend the work, in Leicestershire, which would have entailed moving some translators and material resources there.[6] We simply do not know. In any case, when the translation of the Old Testament in the Earlier Version was probably nearly complete (since Baruch is five-sixths of the way through the Old Testament), a decision was made not to translate any more of the Latin Bible prologues.[7]

The scribe writing British Library Additional 15580 left space for the expected prologue to Ezechiel, the book following Baruch, before realizing there was none:[8] the short prologue to Baruch is the last Old Testament prologue in the Earlier Version.[9] Intriguingly, it is also the only prologue from the Latin Bible preserved in the Old Testament in the Later Version; all manuscripts containing Baruch include it. Perhaps it survived because it was understood to be a rubric rather than a prologue, and was therefore written into the biblical text, whereas the prologues apparently circulated independently (the scribe of British Library Additional 15580 evidently expected to receive the prologue to Ezechiel as a separate text). It looks as though the translators were already at work on the revision of the Earlier Version, and had reached 1 Chronicles, about a third of the way through

4 Forshall and Madden say that the third of the three hands in *C* (Esth. 2:5 to Bar. 3:20) is the same as the final hand of *E* (Ecclus 48:6 to Bar. 3:20, fols. 288r–332r, see Appendix 4), *WB*, I.l, but De Hamel doubts this (*Books*, p. 172), as does the present writer.

5 *WB*, I.xvii.

6 See Fristedt, *WB*, *I*, pp. 115–17. Fristedt assumes Hereford continued to work on OT in EV at Lutterworth; cf. Lindberg, *EV*, IV.30–1.

7 Forshall and Madden rightly point to the absence of prologues as one of the characteristics of the continuation of EV after the break at Bar. 3:20, and also identify translational changes, *WB*, I.xvii–xviii.

8 *Y*, fols. 122v–123r. L_o leaves space for the prologues to Ezek., Dan. and all the Minor Prophets, see Appendix 4, below.

9 *RBMA*, no. 491; see p. 99, above. *H* has an incipit (but no text) for 'þe prologe in Amos' (fol. 329r).

the Old Testament (since the prologue to that book is the last surviving prologue in a revised version),[10] when they reached the conclusion that the Latin Bible prologues, even when revised to make their syntax more reader-friendly, would be of little use. The translators cannot at that stage have expected or desired that the Earlier Version would continue to be copied with the Latin Bible prologues intact as far as Baruch and lacking thereafter; the decision must have been meant to apply to the Wycliffite Old Testament as a whole.

Many Wycliffite New Testaments in the Earlier Version lack some or all of the Latin Bible prologues. No Bible in the Earlier Version has all the New Testament prologues: Longleat 3 (c. 1390–1400) and Corpus Christi College Oxford 4 (c. 1400–10) lack all of them; Christ Church Oxford 145 (c. 1390–1400) has prologues to the Gospels but no other New Testament prologues, and Thomas of Gloucester's Bible lacks the prologues to Matthew, Mark, Acts, the Catholic Epistles, the Pauline Epistles (except Philemon) and the Apocalypse, but the scribe leaves space for 'The prologe of Poulis Pistle to Romayns', and prologues to the rest of the Pauline Epistles and the Apocalypse.[11] British Library Royal 1. B. VI, a New Testament c. 1390–1400, and John Rylands Library Eng. 81, a New Testament c. 1400, lack all prologues. On the other hand, New York Public Library 67, a New Testament c. 1390, includes the whole set of prologues. A generation later, Trinity College Dublin 75, the manuscript with the 'Peruie' monogram (probably c. 1425), contains the New Testament in the Earlier Version, with prologues to Matthew and Galatians in the Earlier Version and prologues to the other Pauline Epistles, Acts and the Catholic Epistles in the Later Version. There is no prologue to Romans, and the prologues to Mark, Luke, John and the Apocalypse in the Later Version precede the New Testament. This mix of Earlier and Later Version prologues doubtless looks more chaotic to us than it would have done to scribes and early readers, since they would not have been able to identify the versions nearly as readily as we can.[12]

[10] *RBMA*, no. 328. C_U_6680 opens with a set of revised EV prologues: Jerome's Prefatory Epistles, fols. 1r–3v; the prologue to Joshua, fols.3v–4r; the prologue to Kings, fols. 4r–5r, and the prologue to 1 Chron., fol. 5r. X opens (after the Lectionary) with the same set: Prefatory Epistles, fols. 10r–12v, Joshua, fols. 12v–13r, Kings, fols. 13r–v, and 1 Chron., fols. 13v–14r. See Appendix 1 and 4, below. Lindberg argues that work on EV and LV proceeded simultaneously: 'The Language of the Wyclif Bible', p. 105.

[11] See the descriptions of L_o, *A*, *X* and *G* in Appendix 4.

[12] Cf. *O*, in which the prologues to Matt., Mark and Luke are in EV and the rest (incl. prologues) is in LV; and *U*, in which Matt.–Luke 19:13 and the prologues to Matt. and Luke are in EV and the rest (incl. prologues) is in LV. In C, Luke 19:12 to 20:10, and Philemon, are in EV, and the rest of the Bible is in LV.

All one can deduce with confidence from the manuscript evidence is that the New Testament prologues in the Earlier Version usually circulated separately from the biblical books, and that they were often unavailable to scribes. A large part of the prologue to Romans is inserted in the prologue to Luke's Gospel in four manuscripts, including Thomas of Gloucester's Bible; evidently a leaf of the set of prologues had been misplaced in the common exemplar.[13] The manuscript evidence also suggests that the decision not to translate the Old Testament prologues from Ezekiel onwards may have been intended to apply to the New Testament as well, but that the forces of custom and expectation led to their being translated not long after the text of the New Testament had been completed in the Earlier Version. In Wycliffite New Testaments in the Later Version the full set of prologues is habitually included, with the exception of the first, long prologue to the Pauline Epistles, which may have been omitted accidentally.[14] The translators chose to combine the two post-1200 prologues to Matthew (where the Earlier Version has the pre-1200 prologue only),[15] and to replace the pre-1200 Apocalypse prologue with the 'Paris Bible' prologue associated with Gilbert de la Porrée.[16] It is easy to see why this prologue appealed to the Wycliffite translators: it focusses on the persecution suffered by Christ's true followers, the consolation John's visions offer them, and the need for patience in adversity, 'for þe traueile is schort, and þe meede grete' (IV.640/9). This is the only Apocalypse prologue found in Later Version manuscripts.

Surprisingly, when the translators revising the Earlier Version reached the beginning of Isaiah, having omitted all prefatory materials to that point, they decided to include a new prologue in English, to be prefixed to that book and to serve as 'a general prolog for alle þe bokis of profetis suynge'.[17] This prologue accompanies the text of Isaiah in the Later Version in all twenty-one manuscripts containing that book,[18] and is the only Wycliffite

[13] MSS *GKQY*; see *WB*, I.xvi and IV.141.

[14] *RBMA*, no.669, included in I only. Ten late LV MSS add the prologue 'Romayns ben þei þat of Jewis and of heþene men gaderid', *RBMA*, no.674; *WB*, IV.301–3; see Appendix 1.

[15] The opening of *RBMA*, no. 590, is followed by *RBMA*, no. 589; in CdPU, the prologue concludes 'Jerom in hise tweie prologis on Matheu seiþ pleynli þus', cf. Q; *WB*, IV.2.

[16] *RBMA*, no. 839; *WB*, IV.638–40.

[17] This title, in EPY, derives from the Prologue to WB, *WB*, I.41/36–7.

[18] ACC_U_668oEFGHIKMNPP_SQRR_91SUVXY. It replaces Jerome's prologue to Isaiah (*RBMA*, no. 482) even in those LV MSS which otherwise contain EV or rev. versions of Jerome's prologues. It is not displaced in K, *pace WB*, I.xlviii; the heading 'anoþer prolog on Isayee and oþere profetis' is inaccurate, as there is only one prologue to Isaiah, fol. 223r.

prologue fully integrated into the Wycliffite Bible. It was written before the Prologue to the Wycliffite Bible, for the writer of the Prologue mentions it when he comes to Isaiah in his synopsis of the Old Testament: 'þe Prophetis han a general prologe for alle'.[19] Although the writer does not explicitly state that he wrote the prologue to the Prophets, in that prologue he says 'of þese foure vndurstondyngis [literal, allegoric, moral, anagogic] schal be seid pleynlier, if God wole, on þe bigynnyng of Genesis'.[20] This must refer to chapters twelve to fourteen of the Prologue, which means that at the time the prologue to the Prophets was written the intention to write a Prologue prefixed to Genesis had already been formed, and part of its content had already been planned. Further evidence of the close relation between the two prologues is the fact that in the prologue to the Prophets the writer says he expects before long to finish his gloss on the Minor Prophets, and quotes from Jerome's 'prologe on þe Twelue Profetis',[21] while in the passage of chapter thirteen of the Prologue bewailing the sins of the clerical estate in England, and in particular in the University of Oxford, he is evidently writing with Jerome's commentary on the minor prophet Amos in front of him and in the forefront of his mind.

The commination in the Prologue is structured around Jerome's exposition of Amos 1:3, where 'God seiþ bi Amos "on þre greete trespasis of Damask and on þe iiij., I schal not conuerte him"' ('haec dicit dominus super tribus sceleribus Damasci et super quattuor non convertam eum').[22] The writer of the Prologue summarizes Jerome's discussion of the four stages of sin and translates the etymology of the name 'Damascus', 'drinkynge blood eiþer birling [pouring out] blood'.[23] He asks those who know to judge whether Oxford is not another Damascus 'bi sleeinge of quyke men and bi doinge of sodomye, in leesinge [losing] a part of mannis blood [that is, semen] wherbi a chiild myȝte be fourmed' (I.51/22–23). Contrasting the glories of Oxford's past with the shamefulness of its present, the writer lists the members of the university from the least to the greatest: 'children' (boys

19 *WB*, I.41/36. Isaiah and Baruch are the only prophetic books with prologues in G (which attaches the relevant portions of the Prologue to individual books), whereas M has a unique prologue to Jeremiah and prologues to Ezekiel and Daniel shared with R.

20 *WB*, III.226/24–5.

21 *RBMA*, no. 500, which 'is sette in þe bigynnyng of Osee [Hosea]', *WB*, III.225/30. This prologue is not included in WB.

22 *WB*, I.51/17–18; 'hym', Lindberg *EV*, VI.190 (*E*), becomes 'it' in LV, *WB*, III.693. The Hebrew text means 'I shall not reverse it' (i.e., the punishment due).

23 WB, I.51/18–21; *In Amos*, I, i, 231–5, 237–8; ed. M. Adriaen, *S. Hieronymi Presbyteri Opera: Commentarii in Prophetas Minores*, CCSL LXXVI, pars 1, vol. 6 (Turnhout: Brepols, 1969), p. 219.

below the age of fourteen), young men studying Arts, civil lawyers, canon lawyers and 'dyuynys' (theologians); once all were devout, chaste and studious, like angels, or if the lawyers were not exactly like angels they were 'so bisy on her lernyng þat þey tooken ful litil reste of bed' (I.27–31). Now, 'men seyn', the university is riddled from top to toe with every kind of sin and vice. Last-mentioned, and worst, is that theologians 'maaken leesingis [lies] in preching, to eschewe bodyly persecuscioun and to gete benefices' (I.51/31–7).

Like Damascus, Oxford commits four great sins, and the sins of the *clerkis* are listed in ascending order of abomination. The first sin, worldliness, 'is generaly in þe vniuersite, as men dreden and seen at iʒe [see with horror with their own eyes]'. The second sin is

> sodomy and strong mayntenaunce þereof, as it is knowen to many persones of þe reume and at þe laste parlement. Alas! dyuynys, þat schulden passe [surpass] oþer men in clennesse and hoolynesse, as aungels of heuene passen freel [frail] men in vertues, ben most sclaundrid of þis cursid synne aʒens kynde. (I.51/37–41)

The third sin is simony, spiritual prostitution, which is 'myche worse and more abomynable þan bodily sodomye', as Wyclif and the thirteenth-century Dominican William Peraldus also say, for if sodomy spills the seed that might have created a human being, 'in illa simonia semen verbi dei deicitur, per quod in Christo Iesu spiritualis generacio crearetur' ('in the act of simony the seed of the word of God, through which a spiritual creature might be born in Christ Jesus, is spilled').[24]

If these three sins were all, says the writer of the Prologue, 'God wolde graciously conuerte clerkis, if þei wolden do very penaunce' and amend their lives, but the fourth sin cries out for vengeance:[25]

> On þe iiij. most [the fourth and greatest] abomynacoun purposid now to letten cristen men, ʒhe prestis and curatis, to lerne freely goddis lawe til þei han spendid ix. ʒeer eiþer x. at art [Arts], þat comprehendiþ many strong errouris of heþene men aʒens cristen bileeue, it seemiþ wel þat God wil not ceese of veniaunce til it and oþere ben punschid soore; for it seemiþ þat worldli clerkis and feyned [hypocritical] relygiouse [members of religious orders] don þis þat symple men of wit and of fynding [men with limited intellectual and financial resources] knowe not goddis lawe to preche it generaly aʒens synnes in þe reume. (I.52/1–6)

24 *WB*, I.51/42–5; Wyclif, *De Simonia*, ed. Sigmund Herzburg-Fränkel and M. H. Dziewicki (London: Wyclif Society, 1898), p. 8; Peraldus, *Summae Virtutum ac Vitiorum*, 'De Avaritia', 7; vol. II (Antwerp, 1571), p. 51r; see Carolyn Dinshaw, *Getting Medieval: Sexualities and Communities, Pre-Modern and Postmodern* (Durham, N.C.: Duke University Press, 1999), pp. 62, 241–2. Wyclif, following Peraldus, adds that sodomy is an act against the law of nature, simony against the law of grace, citing Matt. 10:15.

25 *WB*, I.51/45 to 52/1.

Addressing those who are responsible for this decision, the writer says this greatest of abominations is nevertheless of little importance:

wite (know) ȝe . . . þat God boþe can and may, if it lykiþ hym, speede symple men out of þe vniuersitee as myche to kunne hooly writ as maistris in þe vniuersitee; and þerfore no gret charge [matter] þouȝ neuer man of good wille be poisend wiþ heþen mennis errouris ix. ȝer eiþer ten, but euere lyue wel and stodie hooly writ bi elde doctouris and newe, and preche treuly and freely aȝens opin synnes, to his deþ. (I.52/7–11)

As Henry Wharton thought when he read the Prologue at the end of the seventeenth century, this sounds like someone with no respect at all for the Oxford curriculum, someone who is proud of having avoided imbibing heathen men's heresies (not, therefore, Wyclif, or an Oxford *maistir* or doctor, but possibly Purvey).[26] Rita Copeland argues that in claiming that 'ten years of university schooling are ten years of poisoning' the writer 'challenges the symbolic power of . . . "duration", the idea that real knowledge is produced through prolonged institutional mentoring'.[27] He also, however, challenges the specific content of that mentoring. The traditional justification of the curriculum was that the liberal arts enabled 'divine eloquence [the Bible] to be better understood': 'God has provided this worldly knowledge (*saecularem scientiam*) as a step', says Gregory the Great, 'to raise us up to the lofty height of divine scripture.'[28] The writer of the Prologue, in contrast, associates worldly knowledge with worldliness, a cast of mind that makes it impossible to interpret scripture accurately.

With savage irony, the writer warns worldly *clerkis* to amend their lives lest they (rather than, we understand him to say, the Wycliffites they are persecuting) prove themselves to be 'eretikis þat seruen þe wombe and glotonye', in accordance with Jerome's tropological reading of the 'fat cows' of Amos 4:1 ('ȝe fatte kien þat ben in þe hille of Samarie, here þis word').[29] This identification leads Jerome, and, following him, the writer of the Prologue, to consider the senses of scripture, the topic from which the passage on the *clerkis* was a digression. The Prologue-writer translates Jerome precisely: 'we owen vndirstonde [scripture] bi þe lettre [literally] and do alle þingis þat ben comaundid to vs þerinne [that is, morally]; þe ij. tyme bi allegorie, þat

[26] *Auctarium Historiae Dogmaticae Jacobi Usserii*, pp. 424–5; see p. 73, above. There is no evidence of Purvey matriculating at either university; see Hudson, 'John Purvey', p. 86.

[27] *Pedagogy, Intellectuals and Dissent*, pp. 124–5. Ian C. Levy points out that Wyclif associates sophistry with the Arts faculty; *John Wyclif*, pp. 102–5.

[28] P. Verbraken, ed., *Gregorius Magnus: In Librum Primum Regum Expositio*, CCSL CXLIV (Turnhout: Brepols, 1963), pp. 471–2.

[29] *WB*, I.52/19–20; *WB*, III.697; Jerome, *In Amos*, II, iv, 59–61, pp. 257–8.

is goostly vndirstonding, and in þe iij. tyme bi blisse of þingis to comynge [that is, anagogically]'.[30] Then, a copy of Lyra's *Postilla* having recently arrived, he turns to Lyra's much more extended discussion of the senses of scripture, which we shall look at later in this chapter.

This passage from chapter thirteen of the Prologue to the Wycliffite Bible happens to contain all three pieces of evidence that have been used to date this text: the 'sleeinge of quyke men' in Oxford, the 'sodomy and strong mayntenaunce þereof' practised in the university, and the intention to enforce a university statute which had been on the books since 1253, requiring students to become regents in Arts before beginning the study of Divinity.[31] If Lindberg is right that this passage is a later addition to the Prologue, the date of the former does not date the Prologue as a whole, and some part of it could have been written by Wyclif (as Lindberg believes to be the case).[32] There is no evidence, however, that this passage is an addition. The intention to enforce the 1253 statute must be dated 1387, since on 17 March and 1 August of that year Richard II, responding to complaints from graduands in religious orders, instructed the university authorities not to proceed with their intention.[33] The 'killing of live men' may possibly refer to a riot that took place in Oxford in April 1388, but the reference is very imprecise.[34]

With regard to the practice of sodomy at Oxford being made known 'to many people in the kingdom, and at the last parliament', Margaret Deanesly, following John Lewis, claims the writer must be referring to *The Twelve Conclusions of the Lollards* affixed to the doors of Westminster Hall during the parliament of 1395, and (according to Thomas Walsingham) on the doors of St Paul's.[35] Deanesly therefore dates the Prologue

[30] 'Debemus enim scripturam sanctam primum secundum litteram intellegere, facientes in ethica quaecumque praecepta sunt. Secundo iuxta allegoriam, id est, intellegentiam spiritalem. Tertio secundum futurorum beatitudinem': *In Amos*, II, iv, 196–9, pp. 261–2; *WB*, I.52/21–24.

[31] See Strickland Gibson, *Statuta Antiqua Universitatis Oxoniensis* (Oxford: Clarendon Press, 1931), pp.xliv, 49.

[32] Lindberg also believes the larger part of ch. 10 (*WB*, I.29/44 to 34/31, missing in two MSS, see n. 80 below), and the end of ch. 15, are additions: 'Literary Aspects of the Wyclif Bible', 85; also Lindberg, 'Who Wrote Wiclif's Bible?', p. 134.

[33] Anthony à Wood, *The History and Antiquities of the University of Oxford*, trans. John Gutch, vol. I (Oxford: Clarendon Press, 1792), p. 517, and see *WB*, I.xxiv. Deanesly refers to the statute as an 'anti-Lollard measure', *LB*, p. 257, but it was primarily anti-fraternal. Urban V had intervened on behalf of the mendicants in 1365; see Gibson, *Statuta Antiqua*, p. cxiv.

[34] Wood, *The History and Antiquities of the University of Oxford*, p. 518; the date is accepted in *WB*, I.xxiv, but, as Deanesly says, it 'might refer to any brawl' (*LB*, p. 257).

[35] Lewis, *NT*, p. 9; Deanesly, *LB*, p. 257; on the circumstances of the posting of *The Twelve Conclusions of the Lollards*, see Wendy Scase, 'The Audience and Framers of the *Twelve Conclusions*', in Barr and Hutchison, eds., *Text and Controversy*, pp. 283–301 (on Walsingham's evidence, p. 286).

after the parliament of January–February 1395 and before the parliament of January–February 1397.[36] The posting of *The Twelve Conclusions* at Westminster, as Wendy Scase says, 'has become an event of iconic significance for the founding of an English literature of dissent',[37] and the desire to associate the Prologue with that event is understandable. The accusations of sodomy in the *Conclusions* seem to have been read as a crucial element of the text: a stanza that circulated with the Latin text of the *Conclusions* begins 'Plangunt Anglorum gentes crimen sodomorum' ('the people of England bewail the sin of the Sodomites'). The stanza associates the evils of sodomy and simony with idolatry (on the authority of Romans 1:23–7), and locates all these sins within the hierarchy of the church, while a second stanza turns the accusations back on the Lollards, advocating death by burning.[38]

When translating 'Plangunt Anglorum' John Foxe does not name sodomy,[39] and Wanley, cataloguing Robert Harley's copy of the Prologue to the Wycliffite Bible in around 1720, is appalled by its 'horrid imputations' on the University of Oxford, and replaces the word 'sodomy' with a dash to spare the reader's blushes.[40] He misses the writer's point. Sodomy is only the second of four great sins; the culminating abomination is the intended enforcement of the statute insisting on Arts preceding Theology. In her edition of the final chapter of the Prologue, Hudson points out that 'the terms of [the third of the twelve conclusions] are less specific than the reference in the Prologue would lead one to expect'.[41] The English text declares that 'þe lawe of continence [chastity] annexyd to presthod . . . inducith sodomie in al holy chirche', and that sodomites can be recognized by their 'lik[ing] non wymmen'.[42] There is no reference to Oxford, and the test by which one may know sodomitical clergy implies that the framers

36 See Hudson, *PR*, p. 247; this date is also accepted by Fristedt, *WB, I*, pp. 10, 145 and *WB, II*.lxiv.

37 'The Audience and Framers of the *Twelve Conclusions*', p. 300.

38 Dinshaw, *Getting Medieval*, pp. 59–68; Scase, 'The Audience and Framers of the *Twelve Conclusions*', pp. 291–6. Scase thinks both stanzas may date from c. 1395, since (as she demonstrates, pp. 286–90) judicial execution of relapsed heretics was being considered at that time.

39 *Acts and Monuments*, ed. Cattley and Pratt, III.206. Nor is the accusation named in Article XII brought against Richard Hunne, which summarizes this passage of the Prologue; see ibid., IV.186, and p. 126, below.

40 BL Harley 1666; Wanley, Casley and Hocker, eds., *A Catalogue of the Harleian Manuscripts*, II.169.

41 Hudson, *SEWW*, p. 174; cf. Forshall and Madden's observation that 'the terms used [in the Prologue] imply specific charges or proceedings, rather than such a general allegation of the evils arising from vows of chastity as the third of the Lollard conclusions exhibits' (*WB*, I.xxiv).

42 *SEWW*, p. 25/5–7, 30–1. The English text of *The Twelve Conclusions* derives from Roger Dymmock's *Liber Contra Duodecim Errores et Hereses Lollardorum*, ed. H. S. Cronin (London: Wyclif Society, 1922).

of *The Twelve Conclusions* are thinking of a non-university context. The wording of the Prologue does not invite us to suppose that it was the writer or those associated with him who made the facts about sodomy in Oxford known. Forshall and Madden follow Waterland in giving more weight to the Prologue's reference to the intended enforcement, in 1387, of the statute of 1253; as Waterland rightly says, this 'would have been very impertinent so late as 1396'.[43] I think the Prologue was probably written in 1387, and the prologue to the Prophets in 1386–7.

What, then, does 'as it is knowen to many persones of þe reume and at þe laste parlement' refer to? The *Historia Vitae et Regni Ricardi Secundi*, written at Evesham Abbey, suggests an answer, although not one that at first meets the eye. This chronicle records that:

> In hoc parliamento [the parliament of Jan.–Feb. 1395] accusatus est publice quidam Iohannes Bloxham, custos collegii Mertoni Oxon', doctor theologie, per duos socios dicti collegii, de crimine pessimo, non nominando; qui, ut dicebatur, per plures dominos parliamenti confortati et instigati fuerunt.[44]

> (In this parliament, one John Bloxham, Warden of Merton College Oxford, Doctor of Theology, was accused publicly by two Fellows of that college of the worst of crimes, not to be named. It was said that they were incited and encouraged by many of the lords at the parliament.)

Bloxham denied the charge, and no judicial proceedings were (or could in that arena be) entered into; but King Richard was furious that the accusation had been made, doubtless perceiving it as an attack on the good name of the church. Dinshaw suggests that the chronicler of the second part of the *Historia Vitae et Regni Ricardi Secundi* associated this event with the parliament of 1395 because of the furore about sodomy created by the posting of *The Twelve Conclusions*; be that as it may, the chronicler has misplaced the event, since the Bloxham who was Warden of Merton, and who was a member of the Blackfriars Council, was dead by July 1387.[45] The latest parliament at which Bloxham could have been accused of sodomy was the 'Wonderful Parliament' of October–November 1386, a parliament which, apart from the account in Knighton's Chronicle, is particularly poorly

[43] Letter of 19 Oct. 1729, *The Works of Daniel Waterland*, vol. X, p. 385. Forshall and Madden date the Prologue 1388 (*WB*, I.xxiv).

[44] George B. Stow, ed., *Historia Vitae et Regni Ricardi Secundi* (Philadelphia: University of Pennsylvania Press, 1977), p. 135/3011–3019.

[45] *Getting Medieval*, p. 248; on John [aka Geffrei] Bloxham, see *BRUO*, I.204 (he was not technically a 'doctor', since he did not incept). Stow observes that after 1390 the dating of the chronicle is 'hopelessly confused': *Historia Vitae et Regni Ricardi Secundi*, p. 1.

documented.[46] The highly specific association the writer of the Prologue makes between Oxford divines and sodomy should possibly be associated with accusations made against the Warden of Merton in the mid-1380s.

THE PROLOGUE TO THE PROPHETS

The prologue to the Prophets was the translators' first attempt at writing a prologue to an Old Testament book, although some of the prologues to the *Glossed Gospels* may have been written earlier.[47] As a declaration of the principles the translators believe should govern interpretation of scripture, this is one of the most significant hermeneutic documents of the Wycliffite movement. What persuaded the translators to insert themselves into the biblical text at this point? I suspect they were influenced by Jerome's version (in his *Epistola LIII* ad *Paulinum*, the first Prefatory Epistle) of the story of the Ethiopian eunuch who read Isaiah uncomprehendingly until the apostle Philip preached him the gospel (Acts 8:35). Philip's preaching to the eunuch is the culminating example in Jerome's argument that 'þou maist not entre in hooly scripturis withoute a forgoere [herald] and shewynge þe weie þerof'.[48] Philip, says Jerome, showed the eunuch Jesus, 'qui clausus latebat in littera' ('þe whiche restide pryuely closed in þe lettre', that is, in the text of Isaiah).[49] The translators had trusted readers to make their way through the Old Testament in the Later Version without any herald showing the way, as far as Ecclesiasticus, but the felt need for a prologue to Isaiah opened up an opportunity to alert the reader with little or no formal education to the way scripture should be read, and, more particularly, to the way in which it should *not* be read.

The belief that the 'simple man of wit' should have access to the whole Bible is not quite the same as a belief that the whole Bible is accessible. It is consonant with the first of the two main hermeneutic systems Kantik Ghosh identifies in the English Wycliffite Sermons, that which 'postulat[es] an "open", anti-hierarchical and accessible [biblical] text'.[50] Uneducated

46 See Nigel Saul, *Richard II* (New Haven: Yale University Press, 1997), p. 157; Knighton's account is ed. Martin, *Knighton's Chronicle*, pp. 394–8.

47 On the prologues to the *Glossed Gospels*, see Copeland, *Pedagogy, Intellectuals and Dissent*, pp. 131–9.

48 'In scripturis sanctis sine praevio et monstrante semitam non posse ingredi'; Lindberg, *PE*, p. 95; *WB*, I.66/36–8 (O).

49 Ibid., p. 93; WB, I.66/28–29 (O). The lengthy prologue to the Prophets in Petrus Aureoli's highly influential *Compendium Litteralis*, pp. 113–17, may also have contributed to the sense that a prologue to Isaiah was particularly necessary; cf. Wyclif's lengthy prologue to Isaiah in his *Postilla in totam Bibliam*, see pp. 26–7, above.

50 Ghosh, *WH*, p. 134.

readers have as much access to the Bible as *clerici* do, once they can read it in their own language; this is what Knighton believed. There is, however, a second hermeneutic system Ghosh identifies in the Wycliffite Sermons, which acknowledges that 'the often obscure scriptures require "myche special declaryng [precise elucidation]"'.[51] Ghosh argues that the Wycliffite Sermons 'vacillate between [these] two hermeneutic systems'. The authorship, purpose and audience of these sermons are obscure,[52] but a similar tension between the assertion of accessibility and the felt need for guiding interpretation is found in the two English prologues included in the Wycliffite Bible. Easy as it would be to read this as a straightforward tension between Lollard clerical radicalism and Lollard clerical conservatism ('give the literate laity the Bible in their own language, but teach them how to read it'),[53] these two prologues suggest that the relationship between guiding interpretation and the idea of an 'opin' text is much more sinuous and subtle than that. Exegetical and political dimensions are inseparably intertwined.

The first words of the prologue to the Prophets, 'As seynt Jerom seiþ', and its last words, 'as seynt Austyn seiþ', seem to wrap the new text in unassailable authority. In the Latin Bible and in the Earlier Version of the Wycliffite Bible the authority lying behind the 'I' of this and other prologues is unspecified. Turning Jerome's first-person text into reported speech implies that the prologue to the Prophets will be another translation of Jerome's prologue, but straightaway we find that the prologue-writer cannot accept Jerome's praise of Isaiah's elegant and urbane Hebrew rhetoric, calculated to appeal to the educated but bound to suffer particularly badly in translation, translated in the Earlier Version as 'in his sermoun he is wijs [*disertus* properly means 'skilled'], forsoþe as a noble man and of curteys fair speche, ne any þing is mengd of chirlhed in his faire speche, wherfore it falleþ þat þe translacioun shal not mown kepen þe flour of his sermoun beforn oþere'.[54] Wyclif had countered Jerome, in the prologue to Isaiah in his *Postilla super totam Bibliam*, insisting that biblical rhetoric is different in kind from pagan rhetoric.[55] Nicholas of Lyra claims in his prologue to Isaiah that the book's

[51] The Middle English phrase comes from Anne Hudson and Pamela Gradon, eds., *English Wycliffite Sermons*, vol. I (Oxford. Clarendon Press, 1983), p. 521/14–15.

[52] Ghosh, *WH*, p. 112, and Hudson and Gradon, *English Wycliffite Sermons*, vol. IV (1996), pp. 20–36.

[53] I am not suggesting that Ghosh reads the vacillation between the two hermeneutic systems in the sermons in this way. His conclusion is that the homilists were 'trapped' by their attempt to find certitude via a dialogic discourse dependent upon rhetorical persuasion: *WH*, pp. 144–6.

[54] Lindberg, *EV*, V.103 (*E*); 'In sermone suo disertus sit, quippe ut vir nobilis et urbanae elegantiae nec habens quicquam in eloquio rusticitatis admixtum, unde accidit ut prae ceteris florem sermonis eius translatio non potuerit conseruare.'

[55] See Benrath, *Wyclifs Bibelkommentar*, pp. 64–5, and p. 26, above.

forma tractandi is 'lucidus et ornatus', both clear and rhetorically ornate.[56] The prologue to the Prophets rather awkwardly mingles Lyra's text with Jerome's: 'Isaie is ful witti and ful opyn in his writyng in Ebreu, þouȝ þe translacioun in to Lateyn miȝte not kepe þe fairnesse of speche'.[57] Impliedly, a translation *can* retain Isaiah's openness.

The English prologue again terms Isaiah's writing 'opyn' in translating Jerome's claim (also made in the *Epistola LIII ad Paulinum*) that Isaiah is not so much a prophet as an evangelist: Isaiah is 'a gospellere, for he declariþ so opynli [*ad liquidum*] þe mysteries of Crist and of hooli chirche'.[58] Isaiah is an Old Testament gospel, in which, *pace* Jerome's letter to Paulinus, no secret meanings lie enclosed within the words. Here, as Copeland so well argues in relation to Wycliffite writings more generally, '"open" also takes on its political inflection of public rights and common accessibility . . . "Simple men's wit" becomes the abiding standard, the "open" measure, for who should be allowed to read Scripture.'[59] In declaring the openness of Isaiah, its accessibility to all, this prologue openly deconstructs itself, transforming the genre of *accessus* into praise of the book to which no prologue needs to be attached.

After his introduction, the writer modulates from the first hermeneutic system described by Ghosh to the second system, with elucidation of the historical context of Isaiah. He translates Jerome's prologue to the effect that Isaiah began to prophesy in Jerusalem before the Israelites were deported by the Assyrians (732 BCE), and prophesied both this disaster, the Babylonian captivity (cf. 4 Kings:16–19), and the return from exile (Isaiah 40). According to a postill on Jerome's prologue, Isaiah was still prophesying in the reign of Manasseh (696–641 BCE), the figure of the exemplary tyrant in the Prologue to the Wycliffite Bible.[60] The prologue to the Prophets also reports what the Jews say, according to Lyra's postill on the first verse of Isaiah, about Isaiah's miraculous escape from torture and death at Manasseh's hands. This subject-matter, unproblematic for the writer because part of the *sensus historialis* has been definitively sorted out by Lyra, is dealt with briskly.

For the translators, as for Lyra, the historical sense is not synonymous with the literal sense, as it had typically been for earlier medieval exegetes.

[56] Quotations from Lyra are from *Biblia Latin cum Postillis Nicolai de Lyra*. [57] *WB*, III.225/7–9.

[58] *WB*, III.225/10–11; 'Ita enim uniuersa Christi ecclesiaeque mysteria ad liquidum persecutus est ut non eum putes de futuro vaticinari sed de praeteritis historiam texere'. Lindberg, *PE*, p. 129/158–9. In EV, 'ad liquidum' is translated 'to cleer, *or cleerli*': ibid., V.103/13–14 (*E*).

[59] 'Rhetoric and the Politics of the Literal Sense', p. 20; also *Pedagogy, Intellectuals and Dissent*, pp. 123–7.

[60] On Manasseh, see p. 125, below.

Sensus historialis is only an aspect or dimension of *sensus litteralis*.[61] The terms could still be used as synonyms in the late fourteenth century, as they are in William Woodford's anti-Wycliffite *Quattuor Determinationes* (1389–90),[62] but for the Wycliffite writer, following Lyra, the author's 'entent' (intention) is also an essential aspect of the literal sense. He has it on Jerome's authority that whatever the historical circumstances in which or about which Isaiah was prophesying, 'neþeles al his bisynesse [*cura*], þat is principal entent, is of þe clepyng [summoning] of heþene men and of þe comyng of Crist'.[63] The summoning of the gentiles and the advent of Christ is therefore the principal literal sense of Isaiah's book. As Copeland puts it, what the author intended 'is the essence, in Wycliffite thought and its scholastic antecedents, of the literal sense'.[64]

Moving on from Isaiah to the prophetic books in general, the English prologue takes from Jerome's prologue to Hosea in the Latin Bible the reassuring point, as far as the historical sense is concerned, that where the context in which a prophet prophesied is not 'teld opynli' in the biblical text it can be assumed to be the same as that of the previous prophet.[65] As far as the literal sense of the prophetic books is concerned, the prologue to the Prophets goes on to proffer three rules guiding interpretation by which 'þe derk places of þe profetis moun be vndurstondun liȝtli' (*WB*, III.225/30–1). The hermeneutic system postulating an accessible and historically determinable text is momentarily challenged here, as the writer admits the idea that some parts of the prophetic books are indeed obscure; but readerly alarm is averted through the play on 'derk' and 'liȝt' and the equivocation on 'liȝtli', both lightly and easily. The first rule is 'þat þe principal entent of þe profetis', as of Isaiah, 'is to declare þe mysterie' of Christ and the church; the second rule is that the intention of the Prophets is to 'warnen þe puple of Jewis of her grete synnes' and incite them to do penance rather than suffer tribulation and eternal torment.[66] The third rule is that the Prophets rehearse the benefits God has given the Jews in order to encourage them to believe in the good things promised in their books of prophecy, expounded wherever possible in relation to the historical books of the Old Testament, and otherwise in relation to the New Testament – in relation to the New

61 See Ocker, *Biblical Poetics before Humanism and Reformation*, pp. 179–83.
62 See Ghosh, *WH*, p. 68.
63 'tamen omnis ei cura de vocatione gentium et de adventu Christi est'; *WB*, III.225/17–18.
64 *Pedagogy, Intellectuals and Dissent*, p. 132.
65 Or the most recent prophet in the Hebrew order (which is different from the Septuagint order) for whom the title does provide historical information: *RBMA*, no. 500; *WB*, III.225/21–5.
66 *WB*, III.225/31 to 226/2.

Testament, however, only as a last resort, for from the time of Abelard onwards it had been accepted that 'The New Testament is inadmissible as evidence in the context of a Jewish–Christian debate.'[67]

These three rules for interpreting the obscure parts of the Prophets are rules *contra Judeos*, intended to turn around Jewish interpretation of Hebrew prophecies. They are rooted in the Lyran assumption that the Jews would understand the christological content of their own scriptures if only they would read them literally. The traditional Christian complaint was that the Jews were blinded by reading their scriptures too literally and failing to recognize spiritual senses. As Bartholomew of Exeter puts it in his *Dialogue against the Jews* (c. 1170–80), 'The chief cause of disagreement between ourselves and the Jews seems to be this: they take all the Old Testament literally . . . They will never accept allegory, except when they have no other way out.'[68] Lyra, on the other hand, held that the Jews were blinded by failing to read literally enough, for, as Frans von Liere argues, Lyra was convinced that 'if correctly interpreted, everything in the Old Testament pointed irrefutably to Christ', and not only the Old Testament but the Talmud and the Targumim as well.[69]

Providing guidelines for interpreting the Prophets literally, that is christologically, leads the English writer into an emphatic assertion of the centrality of the literal sense:

Þe literal vndurstondyng of hooli scripture is þe ground of al gostli vndurstondyng þerof, þat is of allegorik, of moral and of anagogik. No goostli vndurstondyng is autentik,[70] no but [unless] it be groundid in þe text opynli, eþer in opyn resoun suynge of [following from] principlis eþer reulis of feiþ, as seynt Austin witnessiþ opynli

in his epistle to Vincent the Donatist.[71] This privileging of the literal sense derives from the second prologue to Lyra's *Postilla*.[72] Any sense other than the literal must be plainly, clearly, evidently warranted by the text itself or by 'opyn' (not subtle or sophistical) reason, on the authority of

[67] Theresa Gross-Diaz, 'What's A Good Soldier To Do? Scholarship and Revelation in the Postills on the Psalms', in Krey and Smith, eds., *Nicholas of Lyra*, p. 127; see also Daniel J. Lasker, *Jewish Philosophical Polemics Against Christianity in the Middle Ages* (New York: Ktav, 1977), pp. 4–6.

[68] Bodl. 482, fol. 1v; quoted from Smalley, *The Study of the Bible in the Middle Ages*, 3rd edn, pp. 170–1.

[69] 'The Literal Sense of the Books of Samuel and Kings: from Andrew of St Victor to Nicholas of Lyra', in Krey and Smith, eds., *Nicholas of Lyra*, pp. 80–1.

[70] 'Autentik' is glossed 'eþer preuable', within the text, in EPY.

[71] *WB*, III.226/9–12; Augustine, *Epistola XCIII*, VIII, 24; ed. A. Goldbacher, CSEL XXXIV (Vienna: Tempsky, 1898), pp. 469–70.

[72] Trans. Minnis and Scott, eds., *Medieval Literary Theory and Criticism*, p. 268.

Augustine, Jerome's commentary on Jonah (in the commentary on the Minor Prophets), Lyra and 'Ardmakan', Richard FitzRalph, 'in his book of Questiouns of Armenyes' (III.226/13–15). *Summa in Questionibus Armenorum*, a favourite Wycliffite text, developed Lyra's ideas on authorial intention and the literal sense.[73]

A prologue to the short gloss on Matthew in the *Glossed Gospels* also gives a significant place to reason in interpretation of the literal sense of scripture and in formation of ecclesiastical tradition: 'in þis schort exposicioun is set oneli þe text of holy writ wiþ opyn sentensis of elde holi doctours and appreuyd of hol chirche, and summe lawis of þe chirche groundid in Goddis lawe and resoun'.[74] Ghosh argues that the Wycliffite emphasis on reason as a hermeneutic tool 'points towards the positivist vision of scriptural meaning as accessible and determinate', not subject to 'ymaginacioun' (idiosyncratic and self-interested interpretation).[75] The writer of the prologue to the Prophets finds an authentic Wycliffite voice as he warns the reader against the dangers of a spiritual sense rooted not in the words of scripture or in 'opyn resoun' but in 'fantasye'. Provocatively, spiritual interpretation is glossed moral make-believe:

> Men moten seke þe treuþe of þe text and be war of goostli vndurstondynge eþer moral fantasye, and ȝyue not ful credence þerto, no but it be groundid opynly in þe text of hooli writ in o place or oþer, eþer in opyn resoun þat may not be avoided, for ellis it wole as likyngli be applied to falsnesse as to treuþe, and it haþ disseyued grete men in oure daies bi ouer greet trist to her fantasies. (III.226/15–20)

At the climax of his argument, the writer acknowledges the reader as his contemporary, inviting him or her to agree that powerful men have been deceived by preferring the delusions of their imagination to the open sense of the Bible – have been deceived, the reader understands him to say, into persecuting the Wycliffites, who, impliedly, never swerve from the open literal sense. The subtext careers towards the same 'ideological *impasse*' Ghosh identifies in the English Wycliffite Sermons: 'the conviction of a direct access to God can result only in a critique of other ideologies, not one's own'.[76]

[73] On the importance of FitzRalph to the Lollards, see Minnis, '"Authorial Intention" and "Literal Sense"', pp. 5–10.

[74] BL Add. 41175, fol. 1v; see Copeland, *Pedagogy, Intellectuals and Dissent*, pp. 132–3. On the role of reason in interpretation, see also Wyclif, *Tractatus de Potestate Papae* (1379), ed. Johann Loserth (London: Wyclif Society, 1907), p. 51, and Ghosh, *WH*, pp. 68–9.

[75] *WH*, p. 140; cf. his account of Nicholas Love's 'resonable ymaginacioun', pp. 163–4.

[76] Ghosh, *WH*, p. 138.

Who the 'grete men' are, and what the consequences of their self-deception are, is too dangerous to be written, but this clause reveals that the writer understands that the debate about biblical interpretation is a debate about the exercise of control in church and state, about power and persecution.[77] In what for the Wycliffites are dark days, the open Lollard sense turns both writer and implied reader into potential victims. Retreating into circumspection, the prologue proceeds to name the four senses of scripture, promising to give a fuller account prefaced to Genesis, 'if God wole', a phrase that catches resonance in context (III.226/20–5). The prologue to the Prophets ends with a few lines of guidance, ultimately derived from Augustine's *De Doctrina Christiana*, for understanding the Prophets' use of figurative language – part of the literal sense, according to Aquinas, Lyra, FitzRalph and the translators, but liable to misprision because in one place a metaphor may signify a vice and in another place the same metaphor may signify a virtue. For example, 'men ben clepid culuueris [doves] sum time for madnesse and sum tyme for innocence, symplenesse and charite'.[78] A much fuller account of figurative language, as we shall see, is given in the Prologue to the Wycliffite Bible. At all events, if 'þe sentence takun of þe text be trewe and acorde wiþ charite . . . þan it is þe sentence of þe Hooly Goost, as seynt Austyn seiþ'.[79]

The prologue to the Prophets ends, as it begins, unexceptionably. Yet the deference to Augustine and Jerome in which it is wrapped is blatantly at odds with its tendentious and politically reckless claim about the dangers of spiritual interpretation 'eþer moral fantasye' on the part of 'grete men'. The 'opin', literal sense is accessible to everyone, lay or not, educated or not, male or not, but those who persecute the known followers of Wyclif choose to deceive themselves by inventing false spiritual senses. Because they call themselves Christians, their present and future state is far worse than that of the Jews who are blind to the true literal sense of their own prophetic books. If we ask again what persuaded the translators to insert themselves into the biblical text by including a prologue to the Prophets, I think the answer is that they could not resist incorporating their own historical moment: translator and reader *contra mundum*, or rather against the powers of this world. The writer promises the reader more of the same, anticipating that he has created an appetite for this new genre.

77 Cf. Copeland, *Pedagogy, Intellectuals and Dissent*, pp. 138–9.

78 *WB*, III.226/32–3; cf. Augustine, *DDC*, III, xxv, 36/14–23.

79 *WB*, III.226/35–7; *DDC*, I, xxxvi, 40/1–7. CR_91 include a full reference to Augustine (not noted in *WB*).

THE PROLOGUE TO THE WYCLIFFITE BIBLE[80]

Contents of the Prologue to the Wycliffite Bible:

chapter 1[81]	The canon and the apocrypha
chapter 2	The old law and its supersession
chapter 3	Synopsis of the Pentateuch
chapter 4	Synopsis of Joshua – 2 Kings
chapter 5	Synopsis of 3 Kings
chapter 6	Synopsis of 4 Kings 1–18
chapter 7	Synopsis of 4 Kings 19–25
chapter 8	Synopsis of 1 Chronicles and 2 Chronicles 1–24
chapter 9	Synopsis of 2 Chronicles 24–36
chapter 10	Coda to synopsis of Chronicles
chapter 11[82]	Synopsis of Ezra – Maccabees (not including the Prophets)
chapter 12[83]	The four senses of scripture
	Abridgment of part of Augustine, *DDC*
chapter 13	Abridgment of part of Augustine, *DDC*
	Commination against the university of Oxford
	Translation of part of first prologue to Lyra's *Postilla*
chapter 14	Translation of part of second prologue to Lyra's *Postilla*
chapter 15	Description of the process of production of WB
	Arguments for an English translation

[80] Complete texts of the Prologue are included in the following five MSS: β, fols. 1r–94r; P_S, fols. 1r–17r; Q, fols. 275r–290v; S, fols. 1r–8r and *T*, fols. 218r–251r. G includes chs. 1, 2 and the opening of ch. 3 as a prologue to Genesis, written at the end of the OT, fols. 279r–v; the synopses of individual OT books are extracted as prologues to those books, with slight adaptations (see pp. 96, 97 and 98, above) It lacks most of ch. 10 ('but alas alas', *WB*, I.21/35, to 'for þese opyn synnes and many moo', I.29/44), chs.12–15, and *WB*, I.40/3–8 (see p. 123, below). Like all other LV MSS, this MS contains the prologue to the Prophets.

α, fols. 1r–111v, lacks the larger part of ch.15 (from 'dispisen and stoppen', *WB*, I.57/3, to 60/14).

ι, fols. 1r–29r, like G, lacks the larger part of ch. 10 ('but alas alas', *WB*, I.21/35, to 'for þese opyn synnes and many moo', I.29/44).

For MSS of fragments of the Prologue to WB, see the following three notes. There are also two early printed editions: John Gough, ed., *The Dore of Holy Scripture* (London, 1536) (STC 25587.5), and Robert Crowley, ed., *The Pathwaye to Perfect Knowledge*, STC 25588 (London, 1550). An edition is being prepared by the present writer.

[81] This chapter only is included in A, fols. 1r–v, and I, fol. 1r.

[82] Keio University Lib. 170 X 9. 6 (formerly part of Huntington Lib. 501) includes part of chs. 11–15 (*WB*, I.41/8 to 57/28, illegible in many places). The section on Psalms only (*WB*, I.37/35 to 40/2) is included in D_72, fols. 96r–v, and Huntington Lib. 501, fols. 22r–v. The section on Psalms–Ecclus only (*WB*, I.37/35 to 41/37) is included in BL Add. 31044, fols. 7r–9r, and Worcester Cath. Lib. F. 172., fols. 167r–168r.

[83] The opening of this chapter only (*WB*, I.43/22-'haue in heuene' 30) is included in i, fol. 4v, and Huntington Lib. 501, fol. 24r.

By the time the final chapter of the Prologue was written, the text of the Wycliffite Bible, in its revised version, was apparently complete, for the writer speaks of the text of 'þis English Bible late [newly/recently] translatid' as being freer from errors than 'comune Latyn Biblis' (I.58/3–4). This has been taken to be a reference to the Earlier Version,[84] but the writer is advertising the achievement of the translators and there is no evidence in the Prologue to suggest that he regarded the Earlier Version as a separate English Bible in its own right.[85] He mentions the prologue to the Prophets when he comes to Isaiah in the synopsis of the Old Testament which occupies chapters three to eleven of the Prologue: 'þe prophetis han a general prologe for alle' (I.41/37–8). Forshall and Madden think he should have reserved the earlier prologue for the appropriate place in chapter eleven of the synopsis, which would have been neat.[86] The fact that he did not indicates that the synopsis had not been planned at the time the prologue to the Prophets was written, and the lack of a synopsis of the Prophets in the Prologue indicates that this was not a freestanding treatise, adapted to serve as a Prologue to the Wycliffite Bible.

The prologue to the Prophets suggests that the translators envisaged the Prologue on the beginning of Genesis as a guide to the interpretation of the senses of scripture, and perhaps that would have been its entire content if copies of the text needed for this purpose had been available when work on the Prologue began. It seems they were not, for in chapter eleven the writer says he does not at present have Isidore's *De Summo Bono*, or the prologues to Lyra's *Postilla Litteralis*, or Richard FitzRalph's *Summa in Questionibus Armenorum* (I.48/21–26). In the following chapter he says 'Lyre cam late to me' ('Lyra's *Postilla* has recently arrived'), and at once he launches into what Lyra says about the senses of scripture.[87] The difficulty in obtaining books was to make a carefully structured argument about the senses of scripture impossible. The synopsis of the Old Testament was perhaps conceived and executed while the writer was waiting for copies of the texts he needed. For such a synopsis, only the biblical text (including the Latin Bible prologues) was required, although a few details derive from Lyra: for example, that Judith's sins were venial rather than mortal.[88] The clumsiness at this point suggests that he did not have the Latin in front of him.

[84] Deanesly, *LB*, p. 280; Hargreaves, 'The Vernacular Scriptures: the Wycliffite Versions', *CHB*, II.410, and De Hamel, *Book*, p. 175. Deanesly assumes that LV was complete when the Prologue was written (*LB*, p. 281; cf. Hudson, *PR*, p. 247).

[85] See further pp. 139–42, below.

[86] *WB*, I.xxviii.

[87] *WB*, I.52/24–25, see pp. 133–4, below.

[88] See p. 99, above.

The synopsis of the Old Testament follows the Wycliffite Bible order. Beginning with the claim that 'symple men of wit moun be edified mych to heuenly lyuyng bi redyng and knowyng of þe olde testament' (I.3/33–4), for each book in turn the writer summarizes the content, more and more fully as he progresses through the historical books from Genesis to Chronicles (as is clear from the table of contents at the beginning of this section). At the end of each book, he provides an all-encompassing *moralitas*: 'Al þis proces [series of events] of Genesis', for example, 'shulde stire cristen men to be feiþful and for to drede and loue God and in alle þingis to do his wille' (I.4/3–4). 'Proces' is the word almost invariably used in the Prologue for Old Testament narratives, doubtless to avoid any connotation of the fictional. The elucidation of the moral sense of Jewish scripture in the Prologue's synopsis of the historical books of the Old Testament takes it for granted that the summary of each book's literal content can be seamlessly matched with a Christian moral sense. Only very occasionally does the writer interrupt his synopsis to warn against the simple literal sense; when, for instance, he points out that the husband's legal right to give his wife a bill of divorcement (Deut. 24:1) is 'forbedun of Crist in þe Gospel of Matt. 5[:32] and 19[:6–9]', reminding the reader that this is one of the Mosaic judgments which, as he explained in chapter two, 'was ended in þe tyme of Cristis passioun'.[89] For the Prologue-writer, as for Jerome in his commentary on the Minor Prophets, the moral sense of scripture is a dimension of the literal sense.

After the very expansive treatment of the books of Kings and Chronicles, occupying nearly six chapters (although the first book of Chronicles is summarized in one sentence, I.21/31–5), the rest of the Old Testament, nearly two-thirds of the whole, is dealt with much more compendiously, in one chapter (see the table of contents). In spite of the Prologue's high view of Tobit, there is no synopsis of the book's narrative; no mention of the demon, the fish or the proverbially unnamed dog, only the impeccable tropological sense.[90] The writer presumably realized that if he continued at the same leisurely pace his vigorous, idiomatic narrative would become an alternative Old Testament for 'symple men of wit': another of the many biblical paraphrases available to laypeople in lieu of the very words of scripture, rather than a guide to interpretation. Were that to happen, the whole purpose of the translation project would be frustrated; and indeed

[89] *WB*, I.7/14; I.3/11–12.

[90] See p. 97, above. On the unnamed dog, see the sermon for Trinity V in *English Wycliffite Sermons*, ed. Gradon and Hudson, vol. I (1983), p. 241: 'Hit is no nede to depen vs in þis story more þan þe gospel telliþ, as hit is no nede to busyen vs to wyte what hiȝte Tobies hownd.'

the Prologue may sometimes have been read in this way, since the Prologue survives without the Old Testament in four manuscripts.[91] In any case, although Ezra, Tobit, Judith, Esther, Job and Maccabees are narratives, the Psalms, the five Sapiential books and the Prophets are not, so that narrative summary followed by a concluding *moralitas* was not an option for these books.

In the case of the books of Solomon, the simple moral sense is given first, for all three: 'lyue iustly to God and man' (Proverbs); 'forsake and sette at nouȝt alle goodis in þe world . . . drede God and kepe his heestis' (Ecclesiastes);

> þe Songis[92] of Songis techen men to sette al hire herte in þe loue of God and of hire neiȝeboris, and to do al hire besynesse to bringe men to charite and saluacioun bi good ensample and trewe preching and wilful [willing] suffring of peyne and deþ, if nede be.[93]

The men to whom the morality of the Song of Songs is addressed seem to be imagined as Wycliffite priests, potential victims of persecution who share the writer's clerical estate and convictions. The hierarchy of moral perfection ascending from Proverbs to the Song of Songs is mirrored in a hierarchy of readership, from 'simple men of wit' to *clerkis*. Guidance to the moral interpretation of each of the three books is followed by guidance to the literal interpretation, offered with warnings against the dangers of misprision. The Jews did not allow anyone under thirty years of age to study the Song of Songs,[94] because it is 'sotil to vndirstonde', and some of the book 'seemiþ to fleschly men to sounne [signify] vnclene loue of leccherie, where it telliþ hiȝ [noble] goostly loue and greet preuytees of Crist and of his chirche, and þerfore men moten be ful wel war to conseyue wel [be extremely careful to comprehend accurately] þe wordis of þe Holy Goost in þis book' (I.41/16–20). A summary of Lyra's postill on the Song of Songs hints at how to identify the speakers accurately: 'Þe Songis of Songis touchen derkly [are a figurative account of] Þe staat of þe synagoge, fro þe gooing out of Egipt til to Cristis incarnacioun and passioun, and þanne þo

91 MSS αβ1*T*; see n. 80, above, and Index of MSS.

92 In the later Middle Ages, the Latin title of the Song of Songs is normally 'Cantica Canticorum' rather than 'Canticum Canticorum', the earlier and more accurate title. It is called 'Songis of Songis' in EV + EGKNPY and 'Book of Songis' in FRU.

93 *WB*, I.40/3, 4–5, 5–8. This material is omitted in G, presumably because the scribe could not readily prefix it to any individual book. Instead, he prefixes to each of the books of Solomon the more detailed descriptions that follow.

94 Or the beginning of Genesis or the beginning and end of Ezechiel: see Jerome, *Tractatus in Marci Euangelium* (14:5), ed. D. Germanus Morin, CCSL LXXVIII (Turnhout: Brepols, 1958), p. 500.

Songis touchen þe staat of Cristis chirche, and of þe synagoge in þe ende of þe world' (I.41/12–15).[95]

After the intricacies involved in guiding his readers through the books of Solomon, Wisdom and Ecclesiasticus (his efforts were valued, since two manuscripts extract this material as a prologue to these five books),[96] the writer must have arrived with relief at Isaiah, for 'þe prophetis han a general prologe for alle', even though nothing is said in the prologue to the Prophets about the specific content of Jeremiah, Lamentations, Baruch, Ezekiel, Daniel or any of the Minor Prophets. Another reason the writer gives for passing over the Prophets without tarrying is that he has already 'declaride sumdel þe Grete Profetis and in party þe Litil Prophetis, and þenke[þ] soone to make an ende wiþ Goddis help of þe glos on þe Smale Prophetis'.[97] Hudson conjectures that there may have been a *Glossed Prophets* 'parallel to the *Glossed Gospels*'.[98] Glosses on the biblical text are, however, specifically mentioned in association with the verb 'declarid' in the synopsis of the book of Job: 'I haue declarid in party in þe glos hou þe harde sentensis of Job schulen be vndirstonden' (I.37/1–2). Whatever mode of clarification the writer has in mind (we shall consider this further in relation to the glosses in the Wycliffite Bible as a whole),[99] he is conceding that the 'ful opyn' Isaiah proclaimed in the prologue to the Prophets needs some opening up in order to be understood.

The writer by no means limits his commentary to the interests or comprehension of readers of relatively humble estate who will be challenged by any text more demanding than Tobit. The first book of Kings 'schulde stire prestis to be not necligent in her offis, neiþer to be coueytous, and styre seculer lordis to be meke and iust to God and men' (I.10/3–5). If 'kingis and lordis', he says at the end of the synopsis of Chronicles, were to know no more holy scripture than the stories of the good kings Jehoshaphat, Hezekiah and Josiah, 'þei myȝte lerne sufficiently to lyue wel and gouerne wel hire puple bi Goddis lawe, and eschewe al pride and ydolatrie and coueitise and oþer synnes' (I.29/40–44). At this point, after two chapters on Chronicles, we expect the writer to move on to the first book of Ezra. Instead, the cry 'But alas, alas, alas' heralds a 3000-word coda to the synopsis of Chronicles,[100] arguing that Christian lords 'now in Engelond', 'cristene

[95] On Lyra's postill, see Dove, 'Literal Senses in the Song of Songs', in Krey and Smith, eds., *Nicholas of Lyra*, pp. 129–46.

[96] BL Add. 31044 and Worcester Cathedral F. 172; see n. 82, above.

[97] *WB*, I.41/38–9. These words are lacking in Gough's edition of the Prologue, see n. 80, above.

[98] *PR*, p. 236. Some notes on the Major and Minor Prophets survive in F: see Oliver S. Pickering and V. M. O'Mara, *The Index of Middle English Prose, Handlist XIII: Manuscripts in Lambeth Palace Library, Including Those Formerly in Sion College Library* (Cambridge: Brewer, 1999), p. 79.

[99] See pp. 152–72, below.

[100] *WB*, I.29/10–11; this coda is lacking in G1, see n. 80, above.

lordis in name', that is, 'and heþene in condisciouns [characteristics]', do the opposite of the exemplary deeds of the good kings Jehoshaphat, Hezekiah and Josiah, preferring to take their (im)moral lesson from the wicked king Manasseh, whose perfidy is detailed in chapter nine of the Prologue.[101] Rather than following Jehoshaphat's example by ensuring that God's law is taught 'opinly' to the people, they are complicit in the offering of worthless pardons;[102] rather than following Hezekiah's example by purifying God's house, they 'bringin in symonient [simoniac] clerkis . . . to stoppe Goddis lawe', and employ priests in worldly, temporal offices;[103] rather than following Josiah's example by casting out idols from the temple, they praise and glorify not the Lord but the letters of friars, 'ful of disceit and leesingis'. They cruelly persecute those 'þat wolden teche treuly and freely þe lawe of God', and maintain those who preach 'fablis' and 'synful mennis tradiciouns, eiþer statutis' while inhibiting scripture from being preached, known and observed.[104]

Like Manasseh, kings and lords are idolaters, worshipping mortal sins in their heart and placing 'idolis in Goddis hous, whanne þei maken vnworþi prelatis eiþer curatis in þe chirche'; witness the words of God 'to an vnable prelat: "A þou schepherde and idole, forsakinge þe floc"'(Zech. 11:17).[105] A marginal gloss included in ten Wycliffite Bible manuscripts identifies the shepherd as 'Antecrist', following Lyra,[106] but here the 'ordinary' parabolic literal sense, shepherd as metaphor for prelate, suits the writer's argument better. Lords and prelates, the coda to Chronicles continues, swear by the limbs of God and Christ and by the saints whom they make into idols, slander good men 'and clepen hem lollardis, eretikis and riseris of debate and of tresoun aȝens þe king', over-tax, extort, and shed blood both in war and by refusing alms to the poor.[107] Manasseh in the end repented, according to 2 Chronicles 33:12–16;[108] he does not, however, repent in the account of his reign in 4 Kings 1–18, and perhaps the idea for the frame of chapter ten of the Prologue occurred to the writer when he arrived at Manasseh's repentance in his synopsis of 2 Chronicles. He prays that God may stir lords and prelates who sin openly, as Manasseh did, to repent, as he did.[109]

In his strictures on unworthy prelates, the heart of chapter ten, the writer cites eight *capitula* from the 'Rosarie', the *Rosarium super Decreto*

101 *WB*, I.33/36; I.30/11; I.27/33–39, 2 Chron. 33:2–9.

102 *WB*, I.30/1–5, cf. I.23/1–4, 2 Chron. 17:7–9.

103 *WB*, I.30/8–16, cf. I.26/19–28, 2 Chron. 30:13–20. See also the sixth of the *Twelve Conclusions of the Lollards*, ed. Hudson, *SEWW*, p. 26/62–72 and p. 152.

104 *WB*, I.30/16–23, cf. I.28/12–18, 2 Chron.34:3–5.

105 *WB*, I.30/43–44; I.31/1–4.

106 'scheepherde, *þat is antecrist*, Lire here' (CEFINPQR_91UY), *WB*, III.760 (at Zech. 11:16).

107 *WB*, I.33/9–14, 36–7.

108 See *WB*, I.27/42 to 28/3.

109 *WB*, I.34/30–1.

of the canon lawyer 'Erchedekene', Guido de Baysio (c. 1250–1313).[110] Evidently he had a copy of this book. He also cites Gregory the Great's *Regula Pastoralis*, Gratian's *Decretum* and two favourite Lollard authorities, Grosseteste and 'Parisience', Peraldus.[111] The Prologue gestures towards the reader ignorant of canon law, explaining that Guido de Baysio is 'oon of þe famouseste doctouris of þe popis lawe' (I.31/4–5), but in this passionate indictment of church and state he is writing as a schoolman to schoolmen.

This chapter of the Prologue was the source of eight of the thirteen articles produced by Dr Thomas Head, commissary of Richard Fitzjames, Bishop of London, 'out of the prologue of [Richard Hunne's] English Bible', according to John Foxe, and brought against Hunne at St Paul's Cross in 1514.[112] This Bible may actually have been owned not by Hunne but by one Thomas Downe, since a witness at Hunne's posthumous trial deposed 'that he heard one Roger, the parish clerk of St Botolph's, say that the English Bible which Hunne had [in his cell] was one Thomas Downe's . . . and that the said book was wont to lie in St Margaret's church in Bridge Street sometimes a month together when he was clerk there'.[113] Even in the context of the Reformation, John Gough felt an apology for the potentially offensive material in chapter ten was appropriate. In the preface to his edition of the Prologue to the Wycliffite Bible he says:

> moste gentyl christen Reader. I humbly requyre you in case ye fynde ony thyng in this boke that shall offend you in the .x. chapiter or in the .xiii. I praye you blame not me though I haue folowed myne orygynall and olde copy in worde and sentence.[114]

[110] Archdeacon of Bologna and archchancellor of the university. The *capitula* are *sunt in ecclesia* (*WB*, I.31/9–10; *Rosarium*, Venice, 1495, fol. t7r, i); *nichil* (I.31/11; *Rosarium*, fol. k6r, ii); *qui nec* (I.31/12; *Rosarium*, fol. p8v, i); *non omnes* (I.31/13–15; *Rosarium*, fol. p9r, i); *in mandatis* (I.31/15; *Rosarium*, fol. f4v, ii); *quoniam regula* (I.31/17; *Rosarium*, fol. f8r, ii); *ecclesie epulas* (I.31/23; *Rosarium*, fol. e6r, i), and *sit rector* (I.31/24 to 32/4; *Rosarium*, fols. f4r, ii–f4v, i). The Prologue provides full references to *causae*, *questiones* and *distinctiones*.

[111] *Regula Pastoralis*, *WB*, I.32/10–12 and 33/36, ed. H. R. Bramley (Oxford, 1874), 12, 82; *Decretum*, *WB*, I.33/18–20, ed. Richter and Friedberg, *Corpus Iuris Canonici*, I.863, 861; Grosseteste, *WB*, I.32/14–37, Thomson, *The Writings of Robert Grosseteste*, *Premonitus a Venerabili Patre* (pp. 173–4), *Dominus Noster Jesus Cristus* (p. 171), and *Scriptum Est de Leuitis* (p. 176); Peraldus, *WB*, I.32/43–4, *Summa de Vitiis*, IV, *De Avaritia*.

[112] Articles III–X, *Acts and Monuments*, ed. Cattley and Pratt, IV.186. Only five of the thirteen articles correspond with the notes written by Bishop Geoffrey Blyth in the Prologue to WB in S (see Appendix 4), and there is no reason to associate Hunne with S.

[113] W. R. Cooper, 'Richard Hunne', *Reformation* 1 (1996), 229. The WB MS now associated with Downe, owned by Dr Steve Sohmer, is an NT without any prologues: see De Hamel, *Book*, fig. 132, p. 186 and p. 336, and Index of MSS.

[114] Fol. Avi[r]; see n. 80, above. No doubt Gough is thinking of the material about sodomy in ch. 13. His 'orygynall' was probably Q; see p. 43, above.

Chapter ten is outdone in political recklessness (*per impossibile*) at the end of the synopsis of the Old Testament. After detailing the violent acts perpetrated in 2 Maccabees, the writer himself advocates violence, suggesting that God's law might be best maintained in Richard II's England by knights wielding their swords against lords and priests 'þat wolen compelle men, for drede of prisoun and deþ, to forsake þe treuþe and fredom of Cristis gospel' (I.43/18–19).

Why did the writer include such outrageously controversial passages? If the translators had discussed the content of the Prologue together, perhaps they would have concluded that overtly controversial material was likely to jeopardize the success of their project. Perhaps the writer of the Prologue was over-influenced by the late writings of Wyclif, in which no polemical holds are barred. It was almost certainly because of its controversial content that the Prologue failed to become the standard preface. Only four of the fifteen surviving Wycliffite Bibles in the Later Version contain the whole of most of it, and one of these, Lincoln College Oxford Lat. 119 (along with a copy of the Prologue prefixed to a New Testament), omits the coda to Chronicles and chapters twelve to fifteen.[115] The decisions to place the first three chapters of the Prologue at the end of the Old Testament, in the Lincoln College Bible, and to place the whole Prologue between the Old and New Testaments, in Cambridge University Library Mm. 2. 15, were presumably taken to ensure that a quick look at the Bible would not identify it as containing the Wycliffite Prologue. The fact that the first chapter only is included in two other Bibles implies that the editors made a choice not to include the rest of the Prologue.[116] A Wycliffite Old Testament, St John's College Oxford 7, almost certainly originally contained the complete Prologue, in all likelihood detached during the fifteenth century.[117]

The writer was certainly not naïve. The Prologue is ever acutely aware of who wields political power, how that power is likely to be exercised and what the consequences will be for the Wycliffite Bible. After contrasting the wicked actions of contemporary lords with the actions of Jehoshaphat,

[115] GP_SQS, see n. 80 above. G is exceptional because of the way in which the Prologue is divided up; ı also omits the coda to Chron., see n. 80, above. For complete WBs in LV, see the Index of MSS and pp. 17–18, above.

[116] AI, see n. 81, above.

[117] Ralph Hanna's collation of N shows that two quires are lacking at the beginning: *A Descriptive Catalogue of the Western Medieval Manuscripts of St John's College Oxford*, p. 9. There is a reference to 'þe prolog' in the list of books in C, fols. 351v–352r, but the collation shows that this MS did not contain the Prologue at the time it was bound (only two fols. are missing at the opening, and these must have contained Gen. 1–9:23). M lacks one fol. at the beginning, incl. Gen. 1:1–20, and possibly ch. 1 of the Prologue? For further details of CM, see Appendix 4.

Hezekiah and Josiah, the writer contrasts the hundreds of false prophets who counselled King Ahab with the prophets Elijah and Micaiah who were in sole possession of the truth.[118] He likens the translators' predicament to theirs: 'so now a fewe pore men and idiotis, in comparisoun of [contrast with] clerkis of scole, mown haue þe treuþe of holy scripture aȝens many þousinde prelatis and religiouse þat ben ȝouen to worldly pride and coueitise, symonie, ypocrisie and oþer fleschly synnes' (I.30/27–30). Experiencing persecution as a known Wycliffite, the writer chooses to make capital out of the role of outsider, taking up what Fiona Somerset has identified as the 'extraclergial' position characteristic of Lollard writers, a position they adopt in spite of the fact that they are 'if anything more ostentatiously learned than the typical clerical writer'.[119]

Determined to place as wide a gap as possible between true lovers of scripture on the one hand and schoolmen, ecclesiastics and those in religious orders on the other, the writer associates himself and the translators with the all-but-unteachable kind of *illiterati*, the 'lewed pepel þat ben iclepid ydiotis' who can be taught only the bare elements of Christianity, according to the tract on biblical translation 'Alle cristine peple stant in þre maner of folke'.[120] In the final chapter of the Prologue he refers to himself as a 'symple creature', and imagines 'worldli clerkis' sneeringly asking 'what spiryt makiþ idiotis hardi to translate now þe Bible into English?'[121] The implied answer is, of course, the Holy Spirit, and the conviction that the Holy Spirit enables the translators to 'haue þe treuþe of holy scripture' emboldens the writer to speak out against the Wycliffites' persecutors. If 'idiotis' translate scripture into English and understand the meaning of scripture in English better than worldly priests, prelates, lords and schoolmen understand it in Latin, God's grace is all the more evident and the English Bible is all the more transparently the word of God.

However certain the writer may be that the Holy Spirit is with the translators, the Prologue, as well as voicing the ascetic Augustinian principle that understanding the truth of scripture goes hand-in-hand with holy living and devout religious practice, fully acknowledges how hard it is to interpret scripture. In his introduction to Psalms, included as a prologue to

118 *WB*, I.30/23–7, cf. 3 Kings 18, 22.

119 *Clerical Discourse and Lay Audience*, p. 13; also Gloria Cigman, '*Luceat Lux Vestra*: The Lollard Preacher as Truth and Light', *Review of English Studies* 40 (1989), 484, Peikola, *Congregation of the Elect*, esp. 120–2, 167–8, 293–4, and Anne Karin Ro, '"Symple men" and "worldli clerkis": Lollard sentiments in the General Prologue to the Wycliffite Bible', in Leiv E. Breivik *et al.*, eds., '*These Things Write I vnto thee . . .*': *Essays in Honour of Bjørg Bækken* (Oslo: Novus Press, 2006), pp. 227–39.

120 Ed. Hunt, *TFST*, II.265/249; see pp. 20–1, above.

121 *WB*, I.57/6; 59/3–4.

Psalms in four Wycliffite Bible manuscripts,[122] the writer points out that the study of this book involves exceptional textual difficulties, with the result that 'many doctouris' have renounced literal in favour of spiritual interpretation – a dangerous move, as the prologue to the Prophets indicates.[123] Some Latin Bibles include parallel Hebrew and Gallican Psalters; the Wycliffite Bible does not, but the writer of the Prologue claims that he has recorded 'what þe Ebru haþ' in the margin, because the Psalms 'of alle oure [Latin] bokis discordiþ most fro Ebreu'.[124] 'Wel were him', he exclaims, 'þat koude wel vndirstonde þe Sautir and kepe it in his lyuyng and seie it deuoutly and conuicte [persuade] Jewis þerbi'; persuade Jews, that is, to understand that the literal meaning of the Psalms points to Christ (the brief prologue to Psalms in one Wycliffite Bible, Queen's College Oxford 388, emphasizes their christological content).[125] Certainly for the writer of the Prologue the christological meaning is a dimension of the literal meaning, but it does not override local textual questions. Reading literally is something fervently to be desired but extremely hard to accomplish in practice.

When the Prologue at last turns to address exegetical issues at the level of theory, the writer envisages himself translating his sources, as he translates the Bible and composes the synopsis of the Old Testament, for 'symple men of wit', in spite of the fact that he is translating and abridging texts written for men schooled in Latin. He begins with a thoroughly traditional sketch of the four senses and what they teach, illustrated by the four meanings of the word 'Jerusalem'.[126] There follows an assertion of the centrality of the literal sense very similar to that in the prologue to the Prophets,[127] with the addition that allegorical interpretation of the Old Testament is confirmed as an appropriate mode of reading since it occurs within the New Testament, as in the well-known example of Paul's allegory of the wife and handmaiden of Abraham (Gal. 4:22–31).[128] But there is no warning here, as there is in the prologue to the Prophets, of the dangers of spiritual interpretation;

[122] D_72, BL Add. 31044, San Marino Huntington Lib. 501 and Worcester Cath. F. 172; see n. 82, above.

[123] *WB*, I.38/5.

[124] *WB*, I.58/5–7; see ch. 4, n. 20, above, and pp. 160–1, below.

[125] *WB*, I.38/5 to 39/2; *WB*, II.736.

[126] Two WB MSS, i and Huntington Lib. 501, excerpt the sketch of the four senses, *WB*, I.43/22–30, see n. 83, above. The choice of the word 'Jerusalem' to illustrate the four senses goes back to John Cassian, but here probably derives from the *Glossa Ordinaria* and from the first prologue to Lyra's *Postilla* (cf. also *WB*, I.52/43 to 53/9).

[127] *WB*, I.43/35–7, cf. III.226/9–11, 17–18.

[128] *WB*, I.43/37–43. Wyclif, however, argues that Gal. 4 reads Gen. 17 *ad litteram*: see *De Veritate Sacre Scripture*, I, 6; ed. Buddensieg, I.121/16–20, also Ghosh, *WH*, p. 36, and p. 27, above. Wyclif's reasoning here is the same as that of Lyra on the third rule of Tyconius, see pp. 134–5, below.

the writer moves smoothly into an abridgment of Augustine's rules, in *De Doctrina Christiana*, for recognizing spiritual senses.

Throughout most of chapter twelve of the Prologue,[129] this abridgment is very similar to that in one of the prologues prefixed to Matthew in the *Glossed Gospels* in terms of the extracts chosen from *De Doctrina Christiana*, although there are significant differences in the translation.[130] This Matthew prologue is included in three Wycliffite Bible manuscripts.[131] Although the abridgment of *De Doctrina Christiana* in the Matthew prologue is more abbreviated than that in the Prologue to the Wycliffite Bible, it contains some material not in the latter.[132] The writer of the Prologue apparently has a copy of *De Doctrina Christiana*, or a fuller version of the abridgement, for he continues his abridgment after the point where the Matthew prologue ends, choosing material that suits his purposes.[133] He also inserts into the material from *De Doctrina Christiana* some material from a sermon of Augustine 'of þe preysing of charite'.[134] The biblical quotations in the extracts from *De Doctrina Christiana* in the Matthew prologue resemble the Earlier Version; in the Prologue to the Wycliffite Bible, the biblical quotations resemble the Later Version, and sometimes quote it directly.[135] Deanesly, assuming Purvey to be the author of both prologues, thought Purvey expanded and revised his own earlier abridgment of *De Doctrina Christiana* in chapter twelve of the Prologue to the Wycliffite Bible.[136] Hunt argues persuasively that both abridgments 'are independently derived from some longer source' with the extracts in the same order.[137] It looks as though Wycliffites made a digest of the teaching about biblical interpretation in *De Doctrina Christiana*, just as they made a digest (I shall argue) of Lyra, and both the compilers of the *Glossed Gospels* and the translators of the Wycliffite Bible made use of it; even if there was no overlap between the two groups, they must surely have communicated with each other.

[129] *WB*, I.44/3 to 49/1.

[130] Inc. 'Seynt Austyn saiþ in þe secounde book of Cristen Docctryne', ed. Hunt, *TFST*, II.370–82, also *WB*, I.44–9. Hunt calls this the 'intermediate' Matthew prologue.

[131] D_76, R_77 and Dresden Sächsische Landesbibl. Od. 83; see Appendix 1, and p. 52, above.

[132] The additional material is Hunt, *TFST*, II.370/21–22, 'figuratyf' (*DDC*, III, x, 14/3–4); II.370/27 to 371/2 (*DDC*, III, x, 14/10–12); II.371/34, 'bifore-tellynge' to 35, 'present' (*DDC*, III, x, 15/27–8). At II.372/75–6, 'of his body' (*DDC*, III, xxxi, 44/1) is correct, where the Prologue's 'of his holy spirit' (*WB*, I.46/14) is an error. The Matthew prologue also includes some glosses on the biblical text not included in *DDC* or the Prologue to WB.

[133] *WB*, I.49/1, at *DDC*, IV, viii, 22/11.

[134] *WB*, I.45/26 to 46/15; cf. I.2/34–7; Augustine, Sermo CCCL, 'De Charitate' II, PL XXXIX.1533–35.

[135] In the Matthew prologue see in particular *TFST*, II.371/52–4; and in the Prologue to WB see in particular I.49/16–18. As in other Wycliffite writings, however, the translation often seems to be made directly from the Latin of the original.

[136] Deanesly, *LB*, pp. 281, 456–7.

[137] Hunt, *TFST*, I.192–6, quot. at 196.

The Prologue, then, explains to its reader that, according to Augustine, 'holy scripture haþ many figuratif spechis [*tropos*]',[138] so that 'It is to be war in þe bigynnyng þat we take not to þe lettre a figuratif speche [that we do not take tropes literally] for þanne, as Poul seiþ, þe lettre sleeþ, but þe spirit, þat is goostly vndirstonding, qwykeneþ' (2 Cor. 3:6).[139] The gloss on 'spirit', spiritual interpretation, is not in Augustine's text but is entirely traditional; Palmer cites this same verse from Corinthians against the translators, arguing that the higher, spiritual senses are reserved for those who read the Bible in Latin.[140] The writer of the Prologue, on the other hand, is confident that a reader with little or no formal education is competent to understand a literal translation of Augustine's guide to interpretation of figurative language. He therefore translates for such readers Augustine's golden rule that scriptural language that is literally consonant with charity is never figurative and should never be interpreted spiritually, whereas language that seems to advocate evil action or evil ends is always figurative and should always be interpreted spiritually.[141]

In accordance with this rule, Christ's commandment that the disciples should eat the flesh of the Son of Man and drink his blood (John 6:54) 'semiþ to comaunde wickidnesse eiþer cruelte, þerfore it is a figuratif speche and comaundiþ men to comune wiþ Cristis passioun and to kepe in mynde sweetly and profitably þat Cristis flesch was woundid and crucified for vs'.[142] The writer surely translated this decision of Augustine with glee, since it accords with Wycliffite but not with orthodox late-medieval belief about the eucharist.[143] These lines from the Prologue are the basis of the eleventh article brought against Hunne; intending to condemn Lollardy, his accusers found themselves condemning Augustine.[144] Augustine's 'sermoun of þe preysing of charite' confirms that 'þe ende of lawe, þat is þe perfeccioun eiþer filling [fulfilment] of þe law, is charite' (Gal. 5:14),[145] and therefore love of God and neighbour (Matt. 22:37–40) is a necessary condition for interpreting both the 'opin' parts of scripture, those consonant with charity, and the 'hid' parts of scripture, those consonant with charity only if they are understood spiritually.[146]

Now follows some more intellectually demanding material from *De Doctrina Christiana*, an abridgment of Augustine's version of the *Book of Rules* of

[138] *WB*, I.43/43 to 44/1; *DDC*, III, xxix, 40/1. [139] *WB*, I.44/3–5; *DDC*, III, v, 9/3–5.
[140] See pp. 11–12, above. [141] *WB*, I.44/26 to 45/1; *DDC*, III, xvi, 24/1–4.
[142] *WB*, I.45/1–5; *DDC*, III, xvi, 24/3–9.
[143] On Wyclif's opinions about the eucharist, see Levy, *John Wyclif*, pp. 217–319.
[144] *Acts and Monuments*, ed. Cattley and Pratt, IV.186; see p. 126, above.
[145] *WB*, I.45/30 to 46/1; the translational gloss is added. [146] *WB*, I.46/1–14.

his contemporary Tyconius the Donatist, interpreting 'many derke þingis of hooly scripturis'.[147] What Augustine says of the second of Tyconius' seven rules, that it 'axiþ [requires] a waking eiþer diligent redere [*lectorem uigilantem*]',[148] might well be said of all. Tyconius's identification of seven types of scriptural trope, often with a metonymic relation between vehicle and tenor, is rhetorically and theologically impressive, but hardly a layman's guide to figurative language and its spiritual senses.[149] Augustine admires Tyconius because he demonstrates that scriptural tropes are more pervasive and subtle than the average grammarian supposes,[150] but the Prologue-writer concedes the obscurity of Augustine on Tyconius when, at the end of his abridgment of the rules, he expresses the wish that he had Isidore's *De Summo Bono*, which condenses them, or Lyra's (second) prologue which 'touchiþ more opinly þese reulis' (I.48/21–23).

He turns to the fourth book of *De Doctrina Christiana*, Augustine's praise of the eloquence of scripture and consolation for the difficulties of interpreting figurative language. Scripture's 'preuyteis' (*mysteria*) keep 'vnfeiþful' readers at bay but confer on good men the grace that results from the exercise of interpreting it well.[151] Turning back to the conclusion of the second book, the climax of Augustine's praise of scripture, everything found in the wisdom of philosophers is also found in scripture; many things are found in 'þe wondirful hiȝnesse [*altitudo*] and in þe wondirful meeknesse of hooly scripturis', and nowhere else.[152] In case the reader should wonder how this might be, the writer translates Grosseteste's explanation, in his sermon *Premonitus a Venerabili Patre*, that scripture contains everything profitable to be known 'preuyly in þe vertu of wittis eiþer vndirstondingis, as wynes ben conteyned in grapis, as ripe corn is conteyned in þe sede, as bowis [boughs] ben conteyned in þe rootis and as trees ben conteyned in þe kernels'.[153]

With the topic still the inferiority of philosophy to scripture, the writer translates Augustine on sophistry, anathema to Wyclif and his followers:[154] 'hooly scripture wlatiþ [loathes] sofymys' – witness Ecclesiasticus 37:23 on the hatefulness of speaking sophistically – and the writer supplies the Later Version of the Wycliffite Bible's translation of this verse, 'he þat spekiþ

147 *WB*, I.46/15–16. 148 *WB*, I.47/2–3; *DDC*, III, xxxii, 45/9–10; the translational gloss is added.

149 See Pamela Bright, *The Book of Rules of Tyconius: Its Purpose and Inner Logic* (Indiana: University of Notre Dame Press, 1988).

150 *DDC*, III, xxix, 40/3–4; cf. *WB*, I.44/1–3.

151 *WB*, I.48/26 to 49/1; *DDC*, IV, vi, 9 /6–7; vii, 11–21 (summarized); viii, 22/ 4–11 (abbreviated).

152 *WB*, I.49/2–10; *DDC*, II, xlii, 63/1–12.

153 *WB*, I.49/11–15; Thomson, *The Writings of Robert Grosseteste*, p. 173.

154 See Levy, *John Wyclif*, pp. 102–5, and Ghosh, *WH*, p. 52.

sofisticaly, *eiþer bi sofymys*, schal be hatful and he schal be defraudid in ech þing'.[155] Any wisdom or benefit the writings of philosophers contain properly derives from God, and is the rightful property of his people.[156] 'Bi þese reulis of Austin,' says the writer, as if reassuring himself at the end of chapter twelve that his guide to the senses of scripture will achieve its purpose, 'and bi foure vndirstondingis of hooly scripture and bi wijs knowing of figuratiif spechis, wiþ good luyunge and meeknesse and stodyinge of þe Bible, symple men moun sumdel [well] vndirstonde þe text of holy writ' (I.49/26–28). Then he turns to address his intended readers, as if suddenly realizing that if they really follow the programme he has outlined for them, and attain true understanding of scripture, they will be putting themselves in the same sort of danger he himself is in: 'for Goddis loue, ȝe symple men, be war of pride and veyn iangling and chyding in wordis aȝens proude clerkis of scole and veyn religious . . . and if eny man in erþe, eiþer aungel of heuene, techiþ ȝou þe contrarie of holy writ . . . fle fro him in þat as fro þe foul deuel of helle'.[157]

Still lacking other books, the writer of the Prologue perseveres with the second book of *De Doctrina Christiana*, opening chapter thirteen with Augustine's seven steps to true knowledge and love of God as revealed in scripture.[158] In his translation these *gradus*, steps, become 'degres', which put him in mind of academic degrees, and of the 'fleschly apis and worldly moldewerpis [moles]' who profess to study and teach the Bible but actually, through their pride and greed, 'maken omage to Satanas' (I.50/41–4). Once more speaking in the role of simple man, he reminds 'worldly foolis' that Christ says that 'þe fadir of heuene hijdiþ the preuytees of hooly scripture fro wijse men and prudent, þat is wijse men and prudent to þe world and in her owne siȝt, and schewiþ þo [preuytees] to meke men' (Matt 11:25; Luke 10:21).[159] This makes him think of the statute preventing students from studying divinity until they have completed the Arts curriculum and been Master of Arts for two years (I.51/12–13). The commination on the university of Oxford, structured around Jerome's exposition of Amos 1:3, ends with Jerome's three senses of scripture (literal and moral combined, allegorical and anagogical), and then, Lyra having just arrived, the writer seizes upon extracts concerning the senses of scripture from Lyra's second

155 *WB*, I.49/15–17, cf. *WB*, III.195 (see apparatus); *DDC*, II, xxxi, 48/16–17.

156 *WB*, I.49/17–25; *DDC*, II, xxxi, 48 /16–17; xl, 60 /1–4, 6–16 (summarized), 17–20; xl, 61/30–3.

157 *WB*, I.49/29–30, 34–6.

158 *WB*, I.50/1–32; in order, *DDC*, II, vi, 8 /32–42; vii, 9 /1–2, 7–10; vii, 10/13–17, 25–32; vii, 11/38–48, 53–61.

159 *WB*, I.51/2–4. The gloss is added by the translator. The reading 'meke men' (*BS* reads 'parvulis', children) derives from the *Glossa Ordinaria* and Lyra.

prologue and then from Lyra's first prologue, largely repeating material from the beginning of chapter twelve.[160] While waiting for Lyra he has apparently not planned how he will incorporate Lyra on the senses of scripture into his Prologue, or considered how he might avoid repetition; he is simply anxious to get down to translating the words of the authority he regards most highly.

He translates Lyra's second prologue *in extenso* in chapter fourteen, beginning with the assertion that the literal sense is like the foundation of a building and the only sense from which proofs can be derived, according to Augustine's epistle to Vincent the Donatist (points included in the prologue to the Prophets).[161] At the end of the chapter, he translates Lyra's warnings against apparently literal readings which are actually hyper-literal to the point of being sophistical and contrary to open reason ('be war of folydoom', says a marginal note beside this passage in Harley 1666). For instance, scripture sometimes 'rehersiþ þe comune opynyoun of men and affermeþ not þat it was so in dede' (I.56/13–14). But the greater part of chapter fourteen is a translation of Lyra's version of the rules of Tyconius for interpreting figurative language. Had the writer received Lyra earlier, presumably he would have omitted Augustine's version of the rules of Tyconius in chapter twelve. In the event, even the reader without Latin can test the writer's claim that Lyra 'countriþ [contradicts] not Austin but declariþ him ful mychel to symple mennis witt' (I.55/44–5).

The most interesting case is the third rule, which according to Augustine concerns the law and the promises, or the letter and the spirit, or commandment and grace (the relationship, that is, between the old and new covenants). The only comment Augustine makes about the rule is on a point of doctrine where Tyconius was in error.[162] Lyra says that this same rule is commonly taken to mean that a passage of scripture can have both a literal and a spiritual sense, but he prefers to say that a passage sometimes has a *duplex sensus litteralis*, which the writer translates as a 'double literal sense'.[163] Lyra's example, which is repeated by Wyclif,[164] is that God says in Chronicles concerning Solomon 'I schal be to him into a fadir, and he schal be to me into a sone' (1 Chron. 17:13).[165] This is said literally of Solomon, son of God by grace (in his youth, at any rate); but the same verse is cited in Hebrews 1:5 as said literally of Christ, where it is a proof-text for Christ

[160] *WB*, I.52/24–29 to 53/9 (52/41ff. repeats 43/22–34). [161] *WB*, I.53/1–8, cf. III.226/9–13.

[162] 'Tyconie erride in seyinge þat werkis ben ʒouen of God to vs for meryt of feiþ, but feiþ it silf is so of vs þat it is not of God to vs', *WB*, I.47/10–12; *DDC*, III, xxxiii, 46/5, 1–4, 8–10. Augustine has simply 'Tyconius said', but points out that what he says is a heresy, 46/12. Augustine cites the proof-texts against Tyconius; they are omitted in the translation.

[163] *WB*, I.54/12, see p. 27, above. [164] In his postill on the Prophets; see p. 27, above.

[165] *WB*, I.54/13–14.

being higher than the angels. Proof cannot be based on a spiritual sense, as Augustine says in his epistle to Vincent the Donatist; *ergo* both the Old Testament verse and the New Testament verse are 'outtirly' literal – but yet the verse from Hebrews is 'goostly and preuy in sum maner, in as myche as Salamon was þe figure of Crist'.[166] Wyclif, following Lyra but avoiding any suggestion of a 'goostly' sense, argues that the literal sense of the verse from Hebrews is *principalior*, although the literal sense according to which the son is Solomon is still a principal sense.[167] Utterly literal and also somehow spiritual and secret: 'symple mennis witt' might well deem Lyra's conclusion determined to have its cake and eat it, but Lyra's enlargement of the domain of the literal sense to include all manner of figurative senses, including prefiguration, was of the utmost importance to the translators. It enabled them to claim that the meaning of scripture is 'opin', and therefore not confined to the clerical class, educated in biblical interpretation.

The Prologue-writer's claim that Lyra's version of the rules of Tyconius is implicit in Augustine's is his only theoretical contribution to the Prologue's discussion of the senses of scripture. It would have been truer to make the broader claim that Lyra's discussion of the literal sense is implicit in Augustine's *De Doctrina Christiana*, in particular in his perception, translated (unusually awkwardly) in book twelve, that the same words of scripture may have two or more meanings, and that although the human author may have been unaware of the full significance of what he wrote, the Holy Spirit intended all meanings that are consonant with truth.[168] In any case, the writer evidently wishes his discussion of the senses of scripture to be seen to be thoroughly traditional. He has retreated from the controversial position on spiritual interpretation and its dangers that he took up in the prologue to the Prophets. If he had been in possession of the books he wanted, and planned his discussion in advance, possibly the Prologue might have been a blandly uncontroversial text, routinely prefixed to copies of the Wycliffite Bible.

In the final chapter of the Prologue, the writer discusses the formation of the English Bible in some detail, but what he chooses to tell his readers is largely determined by his agenda, which is to argue the case for the Bible in English, with 'þe English Bible late translatid' (I.58/3) as a case in point. Whether the other translators had any input into the contents of the

166 *WB*, I.54/14–24; see also Minnis, '"Authorial Intention" and "Literal Sense"', pp. 8, 30. Minnis is mistaken in thinking (p. 29) that ch. 12 is 'an amalgam of certain ideas of Lyre, FitzRalph and Wyclif'; Augustine is in fact the sole source.

167 See p. 27, above.

168 *WB*, I.45/16–26; *DDC*, III, xxvii, 38/1–5, 10–18. The translation in the 'intermediate' Matthew prologue is much clearer; Hunt, *TFST*, II.60–71.

Prologue or not, he blows the trumpet for the 'trewe and hool translacioun' (I.58/36) he claims has been achieved by the hard work of them all. He opens with a global perspective: Christ, in the Gospels, and David, in the Psalms (as interpreted by Jerome), proclaim that the word of the Lord (the scriptures written 'by autorite and confermynge of þe Hooly Goost', an authority given to nobody, however holy, since the apostles) shall be preached throughout the world.[169]

Specifically, the desire of the English people for holy writ is written into Luke's Gospel, where Jesus says that the stones of the temple would cry out 'Hosanna' if the Jews failed so to do (Luke 19:40). 'We Englische men', says the Prologue-writer, asking his readers to focus on their national identity and national language, should identify with the stones of the temple, stones being 'heþen men þat worshipiden stoonis for her goddis', and the ancestors of the English being heathens.[170] Englishmen should, that is, 'crie hooly writ', since Jews, whose name means 'confession' and signifies 'clerkis', fail to acknowledge their sins and 'dispisen and stoppen holi writ as mych as þei moun'.[171] Therefore, 'wiþ comune charite to saue alle men in our rewme whiche God wole haue sauid, a symple creature haþ translatid þe Bible out of Latyn into English'.[172] The nature of the text of the translation will be the subject of the next chapter.

169 *WB*, I.56/31–40. The writer cites Matt. 24:14, Ps. 18:4, Ps. 86:6 (Gallican Psalter, which differs markedly from the Hebrew Psalter in this verse), and Jerome on Ps. 86:6, PL XXVI.1084.

170 *WB*, I.56/40–4. Cf. Bede's comment on Luke 19:40, PL XCII.570, and Hudson, *SEWW*, p. 174.

171 *WB*, I.56/44 to 57/4.

172 *WB*, I.57/5–7. In *WB*, there is a comma after 'rewme', in error; Christina von Nolcken comments on the theological implications in 'Lay Literacy, the Democratization of God's Law and the Lollards', p. 181.

CHAPTER 6

The text

TRANSLATION AND REVISION

Conrad Lindberg has recently claimed that the text of the first English Bible began as a 'slavish imitation of the Latin',[1] and he previously argued that the first 'turning', not yet a translation, was interlinear, a word for word rendering without respect for English grammar or syntax.[2] Some English translations of Latin texts apparently began in that way,[3] and textual corrections to the Latin Bible from which the translation was made may well have been made between the lines of the Latin text; but, if the English Bible began with a phase of 'slavish imitation', the surviving manuscripts provide no evidence of this. Fully aware of the dissimilarities between Latin and English, the Wycliffite translators must have been highly conscious of the difficulty of producing a literal translation, 'a strictly true and faithful rendering which omits nothing and adds only what is necessary', as Lindberg puts it.[4] From the first, they will have wanted to make Latin English rather than mimic Latin in English.

The first verse of Genesis, 'In principio creavit deus caelum et terram', is translated in Christ Church Oxford 145 (a complete Bible in the Earlier Version) 'In þe firste made God of [from] noȝt heuen and erþe'.[5] The translation of this verse is stable across manuscripts of the Earlier Version. In the context of God's creation, *creare* was understood to mean 'make from nothing'; the verb *create* is first recorded in the last two decades of the fourteenth century,[6] but 'made of nouȝt' survives into the Later

[1] 'The Alpha and Omega of the Middle English Bible', in Barr and Hutchison, eds., *Text and Controversy*, p. 195; cf. *EV*, V.93.
[2] *EV*, VIII.71 and *Judges*, p. 74, see p. 79, above.
[3] See Fristedt, *WB*, *II*, where the Latin text of *De Salutaribus Documentis* is printed with interlinear English glosses and interlinear corrections of the Latin text.
[4] *EV*, V.93.
[5] *X*, cf. Lindberg, *EV*, I.37 (*E*), *WB*, I.79 (*A*). The first entry in the Latin–English glossary in BL Add. 34305 is 'Creauit made of nowȝt', see Index of MSS.
[6] Chaucer uses 'create' of God's creation in the *Tale of Melibee*, B.2293, and in the Parson's Tale, I.218, both written c. 1390–95; see *MED*.

Version of the Wycliffite Bible. There is 'substantial lexical innovation' in the Wycliffite Bible, as David Crystal says,[7] but the translators did not borrow words indiscriminately. In the Later Version, 'firste', the superlative used substantively not necessarily implying 'first in time', and therefore less 'opin' than it might be, is replaced with 'bigynnyng', and 'made God' becomes 'God made': 'In þe bigynnyng God made of nouȝt heuene and erþe'.[8] There is no manuscript that reads, as an interlinear translation would read, 'made of nouȝt God'; the translators were writing English, albeit, in the Earlier Version, what seems to us extremely Latinate English. If any interlinear translations were made, no evidence survives.

The opening words of Genesis were a simple proposition compared with the suave opening of Jerome's *Epistola LIII ad Paulinum*, the first Prefatory Epistle:

> Frater Ambrosius tua mihi munuscula perferens detulit simul et suavissimas litteras, quae a principio amicitiarum fidem iam probatae fidei et veteris amicitiae nova praeferebant.

The Christ Church Bible reads:

> Broþer Ambrose to me þi litle ȝiftes parfitly berende haþ broȝt wiþ and riȝt swete lettris, þe whiche han shewed soþfastnesse of now proued feiþ fro þe beginnynge of frenshepis and newe þingis of old frenshepe.[9]

In the four Later Version manuscripts which include a revised version of this Prefatory Epistle the word-order of 'to me þi litle ȝiftes parfitly berende' (indirect object: direct object: adverb: participle) is reversed: 'bryngynge fully þi litil ȝiftis to me'; the conjunction 'wiþ and' becomes 'also'; 'now proued feiþ' becomes 'feiþ þat is now preued', and 'newe þingis of old frenshepe' turn into 'newe tidyngis of olde frenschip'.[10] These revisions undoubtedly bring the sentence stylistically somewhat closer to Jerome's smooth elegance, but in the Earlier Version only 'wiþ and' could be said to be so un-English as to be virtually unintelligible.[11] Again, there is no evidence for any earlier stage of the translation than that preserved in the Earlier Version.

[7] *The Stories of English*, p. 240. WB supplies the first recorded usages of more than 1,100 words in the OED.

[8] *WB*, I.79, see Lindberg, *EV*, V.74–5. The LV reading is likewise stable across LV MSS.

[9] *X*, cf. Lindberg, *EV*, I.26 (*E*). For 'berende' (East Midland pres. part.), most MSS have 'beringe'.

[10] C_U_6680FOX (see Appendix 1), Lindberg, *PE*, p. 60 (Lindberg does not, however, use C_U_6680 for his edition).

[11] Cf. Lindberg's account of the differences between the EV and LV versions of the second Prefatory Epistle, *RBMA*, no. 285, 'From Jerome to Wyclif, an Experiment in Translation: the First Prologue', *Studia Neophilologica* 63 (1991), 143–5.

In some respects, the translation of Psalms to Baruch 3:20 in the Earlier Version is even closer to the Latin than the translation of Genesis to Job. As Harumi Tanabe's statistical analysis has shown, composite Latin verbs are more precisely rendered in this part of the Bible than elsewhere.[12] The fourth psalm, for example, begins 'Whan I inwardli clepede, fulout herde me þe God of my riȝtwisnesse' ('Invocante me, exaudi me deus iustitiae meae').[13] 'Inwardli clepen' is the normal translation of *invocare*, in the Earlier Version, from Genesis to Ezekiel (from Daniel to the Apocalypse the normal translation is 'ynclepen'), but *exaudire* is normally translated simply 'heren', as against '(ful) out heren', from Genesis to Job and from Ezekiel onwards.[14] In the first verse of the fourth psalm, the Later Version retains 'inwardli clepede' but deletes 'fulout' (except for Bodley 277, which restores the Earlier Version reading).[15] 'Fulout herde' is etymologically closer to the Latin than 'herde', but not in fact a more literal, in the sense of more meaningful, rendering.

The fact that some books of the Earlier Version are closer to the Latin in particular details than others suggests that different parts of the Bible were apportioned to different translators. There was presumably some discussion, however general, of overall methodology, but the translators would inevitably have made diverse choices in individual instances. They were, in any case, expecting their work to be corrected and revised. Josiah Forshall and Frederic Madden were confident that the Later Version 'caused the earlier translation to fall into disuse',[16] and it is true that Later Version manuscripts outnumber Earlier Version manuscripts by more than five to one: only thirty-six Wycliffite Bible manuscripts are wholly in the Earlier Version.[17] On the other hand, Forshall and Madden's wording implies that Wyclif and the translators expected the Earlier Version to be copied for the use of English readers until the revised version became available. But is this what they expected? It seems much more likely that they expected that their English Bible would begin to be copied and circulated only when the translation had been corrected and revised. Copying of the revised translation could perhaps have begun when a substantial portion was finished

[12] 'On Some English Readings in the Vocabulary of the Wycliffite Bible', in Oshitari *et al.*, eds., *Philologia Anglica*, pp. 395–8, and Fristedt, *WB*, *I*.76.

[13] *X*, cf. Lindberg, *EV*, IV.169 (*E*), and *WB*, III.740 (*C*).

[14] Tanabe, 'On Some English Readings in the Vocabulary of the Wycliffite Bible', pp. 392, 397. *Exaudire* and *invocare* occur sufficiently frequently throughout the Bible to make statistical study meaningful.

[15] *WB*, III.740. I reads 'full out herde', Lindberg, *KHB*, II.455.

[16] *WB*, I.xxxii; cf. Hudson, 'it seems reasonable to think that, once produced, [LV] superseded [EV]', *PR*, p. 239.

[17] Nine MSS are partially in EV, and six MSS have EV readings in a lectionary only.

(Genesis to Job or Psalms, for example), but the fact that the writer of the prologue to the Prophets says that he intends to write a prologue to be prefixed to Genesis indicates that copying of the revised translation had not yet begun, and that he is confident that he is in control of the project. At that point, however, he and his fellow-translators seem not to have been in control of the text we call the Earlier Version.

As long as the first translation was perceived to be only a stage in a process, editorial decisions about the content of the English Bible (however informally these decisions were arrived at) necessarily affected Earlier and Later Versions alike. This was still the case when the decision was taken to omit the Latin Bible prologues from Ezekiel onwards: both Earlier and Later Versions lack all Old Testament prologues after Baruch. Apparently, however, the translators did not expect at that stage that the Earlier Version would have an independent manuscript existence, since the decision did not (or could not) extend to the deletion of the Old Testament prologues already translated in the Earlier Version. The same can be said of the translation of 3 Ezra. The decision not to revise it but to omit it, on the authority of Jerome, did not (or could not) extend to the deletion of the Earlier Version of 3 Ezra, which survives in all Earlier Version manuscripts containing this part of the Old Testament.[18]

The Wycliffites who organized the production of manuscripts of the Wycliffite Bible in the Earlier Version were able, as we have already observed, to make their wishes known in quite specific terms (probably via stationers) to the professional scribes who wrote the manuscripts and the craftsmen who decorated them. If they were not the translators themselves, they must have been in close contact with the translators. Yet they seem to have taken no account of any decisions made after the decision to omit the prologues from Ezekiel onwards. None of the distinctive features of the content of the Later Version are found in Earlier Version manuscripts, although some Later Version manuscripts have a few of the features of the content of the Earlier Version, and some manuscripts, as far as their text is concerned, are in a mix of Earlier and Later Versions.[19]

To recapitulate: all Wycliffite Bibles and Old Testaments in the Earlier Version contain 3 Ezra, but in the Later Version only Bodley 277 contains this book, in a lightly revised version.[20] All Wycliffite Bibles and Old

[18] The decision to omit 3 Ezra may have been made about the same time as the decision to omit the Latin Bible prologues, if that decision was indeed made after the revisers had reached Chronicles (see pp. 104–5, above), since the books of Ezra immediately follow Chronicles.

[19] In U, the Pentateuch is in EV (opening with the Prefatory Epistles) and the rest of the Bible is in LV, see Appendix 4. For other MSS in a mixture of EV and LV, see Index of MSS.

[20] See p. 101, above.

Testaments in the Earlier Version contain translations of Latin Bible prologues as far as Baruch; nine Later Version manuscripts contain revised or unrevised versions of some of these prologues, but most omit them altogether.[21] Wycliffite Bibles and New Testaments in the Earlier Version, insofar as they contain prologues at all, contain the prologue to Matthew beginning 'Mathew of Jewerye born, as he is putt first in ordre' and the prologue to the Apocalypse found in pre-1200 Latin Bibles (neither of which occurs in manuscripts of the Later Version), and also a long prologue to Romans, contained in just one Later Version manuscript, Bodley 277.[22] Wycliffite Bibles and Old Testaments in the Earlier Version, following Latin Bibles, include letters of the Hebrew alphabet in Psalm 118, Proverbs 31 and Lamentations; in the Later Version, only Hereford Cathedral O. VII. 1 includes them in all three texts, and British Library Royal 1. C. VIII in Lamentations 1–4.[23] Wycliffite Bibles and Old Testaments in the Earlier Version include a translation of the Latin Bible rubrics specifying who is speaking to whom throughout the Song of Songs; in the Later Version, only Hereford Cathedral O. VII. 1 includes them.[24]

At the time the Prologue to the Wycliffite Bible was written, the writer anticipated that it would normally be prefaced to Wycliffite Bibles in the Later Version but in most copies it was not, and, except for those manuscripts containing it, or containing revised or unrevised Earlier Version prologues, the only prologues in Wycliffite Bibles and Old Testaments in the Later Version are the English prologue to the Prophets and the accidentally preserved Latin-Bible prologue to Baruch.[25] Neither of the two English prologues is ever found in Earlier Version manuscripts. Wycliffite Bibles and New Testaments in the Later Version contain a composite prologue to Matthew and the 'Paris Bible' prologue to the Apocalypse, neither of which is found in manuscripts of the Earlier Version.[26]

Among surviving Earlier Version manuscripts, at least Thomas of Gloucester's Bible (British Library Egerton 617/618), Bodley 959 (Genesis to Baruch 3:20), the first part of Bodleian Douce 369 (Numbers 20:2 to Baruch 3:20), Bodleian Douce 370 (Genesis to 2 Chronicles) and New York Public Library 67 (a New Testament autographed by Richard of Gloucester before he became king) may have been written in the 1380s.[27] In Thomas

[21] MSS adC_J_E_14C_U_6680FKORX; see Appendix 1, and pp. 104–5, above.

[22] *RBMA*, nos. 590, 834 and 669; see Appendix 1, and pp. 105–6, above.

[23] See Appendix 4, and pp. 90–1, above.

[24] See Appendix 4, and pp. 91–2, above.

[25] *RBMA*, no. 491; see Appendix 1, ch. 5, nn. 80–3, and pp. 106, 104, above.

[26] *RBMA*, nos. 590+589 and 839; see Appendix 1, and pp. 43, 106, above.

[27] See the descriptions in Appendix 4, and the Index of MSS. According to De Hamel, Richard's signature in *S* is not an owner-inscription (as has been supposed) but an autograph written in a volume the owner prized particularly highly: *Book*, pp. 188–9.

of Gloucester's Bible, rubrics at the beginnings and endings of New Testament lections specify at which masses they are to be read, and the lectionary which follows the New Testament, with cues both in Latin and in the Earlier Version, is a natural supplement. The decision to compile the lectionary must have been made not long after copying of the Earlier Version began.[28]

In the final chapter of the Prologue to the Wycliffite Bible, the writer's advocacy of the complete and accurate new English Bible precludes any mention of the existence of another version of the translation. He, and the men working closely with him, seem not to have recognized the Earlier Version as a translation in its own right, but we can hardly avoid the conclusion that some of the translators, or Wycliffites close to them, did regard the Earlier Version in this way. This is underlined by the fact that the compilers of the *Glossed Gospels* used the Earlier Version of the Gospels as their biblical text.[29] Some of the component parts of the *Glossed Gospels* are in a revised form of the Earlier Version, and the text of the lemmata (biblical cues) in the commentary also contains elements that are intermediate between the Earlier Version and the Later Version.[30] As Lindberg's edition of the New Testament in the Earlier Version has made clear, a significant number of manuscripts contain elements of a partially revised translation, sometimes coinciding with the Later Version.[31] This indicates that at least some of the translators working on the Earlier Version were familiar with the practices of the translators producing the Later Version, but it also suggests that the Earlier Version, in the New Testament at any rate, was revised independently of the production of the Later Version. The compilation of the *Glossed Gospels* undoubtedly required the resources of an academic centre, most likely Oxford; if work on the Earlier Version continued there, the Later Version was possibly being produced elsewhere (Lutterworth?).

Textual revision, in any case, seems to have been an ongoing process throughout the Wycliffite Bible project. Although the Earlier Version was copied independently of the Later Version, inconsistencies within the

[28] *S* also contains part of a lectionary in EV.

[29] See Hargreaves, 'Popularising Biblical Scholarship: the Role of the Wycliffite *Glossed Gospels*', pp. 171–6. P_P*UV* borrow Luke 1:1–4, missing in all other WB MSS, from Glossed Luke; see Lindberg, *EV*, VII.114, *WB*, I.xvii, and Appendix 1, 3. On other corrections in these MSS, see pp. 179–80, below.

[30] 'Popularising Biblical Scholarship', pp. 175–6. The lemmata in the glosses on the Wycliffite NT in e*V* are also in a partially revised version of EV, although e is in LV; see further below.

[31] Lindberg, *EV*, VII.19–25. His arrangement of EV MSS 'according to the degree of later revision' [in NT] is: *X* – *SY* – *A* | Durham UL Cosin V. v. 1 | *GMPQ* – R_81*WW*_o – C_U_6682 | Columbia UL New York Plimpton 308 | Bodl. Hatton 111 | BL Royal 17. A. XXVI | *N* | Queen's Coll. Oxf. 369 | *T* D_74D_76 – Tokyo, Takamiya 28 | *CK*L_oP_P*UV*; *EV*, VII.24. Huntington HM 134 also has a revised text from Matt. 4:20–13:33, see Hargreaves, 'The Vernacular Scriptures: the Wycliffite Versions', *CHB*, II.406–7, and Talbert, 'A Note on the Wyclyfite Bible Translation', 29–38.

surviving manuscripts may derive from the original translators or from revisers of their work, and only the composite and heavily corrected Bodley 959 (c. 1380–90) is likely to represent the translators' earliest attempts other than sporadically. Forshall and Madden were confident that Bodley 959 was 'the original copy of the translator, from which the other copies were made',[32] and it is certainly a working copy, with corrections and revisions made both between the lines and in the margins while the leaves were unbound (see fig. 10).[33] That the four (or five) scribes who wrote it thought of it as a 'good' copy is suggested by the fact that it has speaker-rubrics in the Song of Songs, aleph-bet rubrics in Psalm 118, Proverbs 31 and Lamentations, and other decorative features characteristic of manuscript bibles.[34] It cannot be the translators' original: Lindberg points to the moment in the parable of the trees of the forest choosing a king (a *locus classicus* for the parabolic literal sense) where the thorn says that if the other trees do not want to rest beneath its shade, let fire go out from it and devour 'þe seedis of Liban' ('cedros Libani', Judg. 9:15), 'seedis' being corrected 'see \ d/res' only in the Longleat Bible.[35] On the other hand, Lindberg believes (as I do) that Bodley 959 was probably copied directly from the original.[36] It notoriously includes some egregious mistranslations, which must surely belong to the translators' earliest attempts: 'misericordia uberi' ('in abundant mercy', Ps. 91:11) is translated 'in þe mercy of þe tete'.[37]

The Christ Church Bible has the most conservative text of the Earlier Version, with the fewest textual glosses and with some extreme literalisms, such as 'I ȝaf ȝow in to eggyng of teeþ' ('dedi vobis stuporem dentium', Amos 4:6), elsewhere in the Earlier Version 'I ȝaf to ȝou eggyng of teeþ'.[38] Unfortunately, Forshall and Madden do not make use of the Christ Church Bible in the Old Testament. Forshall was to blame for this: after visiting Oxford to locate bibles in the Earlier Version, he reported that Christ Church had none. Madden later notes: 'This was a fatal mistake'.[39] Lindberg warns, however, against supposing that this Bible is close to the

32 *WB*, I.xlvii. Madden suspected that *E* was the earliest text of EV when he first saw it in May 1830, Bodl. Engl. hist. c. 147, fol. 169r.

33 As Hudson points out (*PR*, p. 279), and see Appendix 4.

34 See pp. 90–2, above, and Appendix 4.

35 *Judges*, pp. 72, 242–3; corrected 'cedris' LV, *WB*, I.640. On the parabolic literal sense, see p. 27, above. On L_o, see Appendix 4.

36 Lindberg critiques many of Fristedt's points of detail (*WB*, *I*.60–78), while agreeing with him that *E* cannot be the translators' original: *EV*, I.21–3.

37 Mistaking *uber*, adj., for *uber*, third-declension noun: Lindberg, *EV*, IV.218, *corr. al. m.* 'plenteous mercy'. See Fristedt, *WB*, *I*.54 for this and other examples, and p. 175, below.

38 Lindberg, *EV*, VI.192, the alternative reading is in *AGHK*L_oW_o*Y*; 'I ȝaf to ȝou astonying of teeþ', LV, *WB*, III.697.

39 2 Jan. 1830, Bodl. Engl. hist. c. 147, fol. 139r.

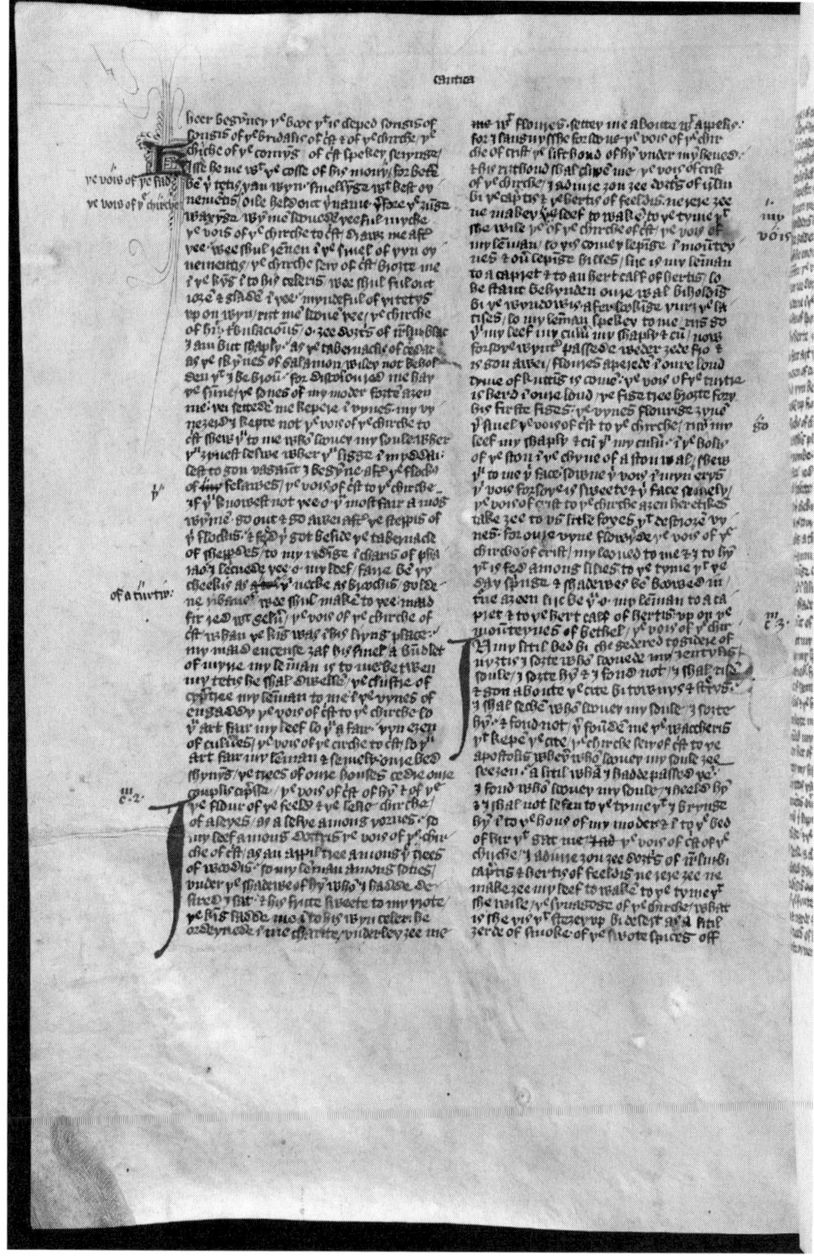

Figure 10. Corrections in Bodley 959, fol. 269v. Oxford (?), c. 1380–90.

translators' original; the fact that its text is conservative, highly literal and free from glosses, 'does not mean . . . that it is free from revision and correction'.[40] In Genesis and Exodus, three marginal glosses from the Later Version are written in the scribal hand.[41]

In the final chapter of the Prologue to the Wycliffite Bible, the writer gives an account of ways in which translation practices adopted during the first stage of production were modified when the translation was revised. Speaking from experience, but at the same time echoing Jerome's experience of biblical translation, he says that in translating from Latin to English a sense-for-sense rather than word-for-word translation is best, if the meaning of the text is to be 'as opin eiþer openere in English as in Latyn, and go not fer fro þe lettre [while staying close to the Latin text]'.[42] If it is not possible to stay close to the Latin text, the translator should ensure that the meaning is 'hool and open', for otherwise the English words will be 'superflu [superfluous] eiþer false'.[43] He proceeds to detail six ways in which Latin constructions may be made 'open' in English, providing, as J. D. Burnley says, 'the first extensively-reasoned account of the methods of formal translation in English'.[44] The writer assumes his reader will be familiar with the grammatical terminology associated with the study of Latin; in any event, he provides examples. It has to be said, however, that further examples would have strengthened this passage, which gives the impression of having been hastily put together.

First, Latin constructions involving verbal participles taking the place of temporal verbs ('absolute' participial constructions) may be 'resoluid [made clear]' in English, the writer says, by turning the participle into a temporal verb and adding an appropriate conjunction.[45] As Hudson points out, this will usually involve the translator in interpreting the relationship between the two resulting verbs.[46] 'Whan I inwardli clepede, fulout herde me' (Ps. 4:1), translating 'Invocante me, exaudi me', is an example in the

[40] For examples, see Lindberg, *EV*, VII.24. On *X*, See Hargreaves, 'The Vernacular Scriptures: the Wycliffite Versions'; Lindberg, *EV*, VI.43, and Appendix 4.

[41] See Appendix 4.

[42] *WB*, I.57/15–17; cf. Jerome, *Epistola LVII ad Pammachium*, V, ed. Bartelink, *Liber de Optimo Genere Interpretandi*, pp. 43–63. 'Opin' means clear / not obscure, cf. Lyra's use of the verb *pateo* (e.g., 'patet sententia', Prov. 6:11); on the misunderstanding that it refers to a mode of translation, see J. D. Burnley, 'Late Medieval English Translation: Types and Reflections', in Roger Ellis, ed., *The Medieval Translator: the Theory and Practice of Translation in the Middle Ages*, vol. I (Cambridge University Press, 1989), p. 50, and Hudson, *SEWW*, pp. 174–5.

[43] *WB*, I.57/17–20; cf. the point about the difficulty of achieving a full translation in the seventh article of Arundel's *Constitutions*, see pp. 35–6, above. On the implications of this for Wycliffite understanding of the 'naked' text, see Andrew Cole, 'Chaucer's English Lesson', pp. 1135–6, 1152–3.

[44] 'Late Medieval English Translation', p. 50.

[45] *WB*, I.57/20–28.

[46] Hudson, *SEWW*, p. 175.

Earlier Version. When Joseph visits his ailing father, the Latin Bible reads 'et ingresso ad se Ioseph' (Gen. 48:3), which Bodley 959, before correction, translates as '[and?] Joseph commen [past participle] inne to hym', and the Later Version as 'and whanne Joseph entride to hym'.[47] The strategy does not always deliver good sense: when the Latin Bible says that Haman (the villain of the book of Esther), angered by Mordecai, returned to his home 'dissimulata ira' (Esther 5:10), the Earlier Version translates this as 'þe wrathe feyned, turned aȝeen in to his hous', and the Later Version, trying to follow the recommended strategy, 'whanne þe ire was dissymelid, he turnede aȝen in to his hows'.[48] Two manuscripts offer a much better revised reading: 'Aaman feynyde him as not wrooþ herfore, and turnyde aȝen in to his hous'.[49]

The second, closely associated strategy the Prologue-writer recommends is that all kinds of verbal participles may be translated by a clause with a temporal verb. This will often make the English 'open', he promises, where a word for word rendering would be 'derk and douteful'.[50] For example (again, not the writer's example), in the book of Numbers, where the Lord sends a glut of quails to the Israelites in the desert, the Latin Bible reads 'ventus . . . arreptas trans mare coturnices detulit' (Num. 11:31). The Earlier Version translates this, obscurely enough by any standards, as 'a wynde . . . brouȝte cauȝt coorluwys ouer see', whereas the Later Version, adopting the recommended strategy, has 'a wynde . . . took curlewis and bar ouer þe see'.[51] The strategy is not always necessary, however, as Lilo Moessner points out.[52] The Latin Bible's 'odientes me disperdisti' (Ps. 17:41) becomes, in the Earlier Version, 'þe hatende me þou scateredist', and, in the Later Version, 'þou hast distried men hatynge me', which is perfectly clear.[53] Nevertheless,

[47] Lindberg, *EV*, I.97; *WB*, I.186. 'Ioseph' is an addition to the Latin text; see Lindberg, *EV*, I.19–20, 168, and Appendix 3. The 'corrected' text of *E* and other EV MSS (incl. *X*) have the inaccurate 'and to Joseph comun in to him' [and to *sup. ras. pr. m. E*].

[48] *X*, cf. Lindberg, *EV*, IV.120 (*E*); *WB*, II.648.

[49] Lindberg, *KHB*, II.404 (IS). For other examples of absolute participial constructions, see Joseph Carr, *Über das Verhältnis der Wiclifitischen und der Purvey'schen Bibelübersetzung zur Vulgata und zu einander* (Leipzig, 1902), p. 92, *WB*, I.xxii, and Hudson, *SEWW*, p. 175. For examples from I, Lindberg, *KHB*, I.42–3, II.38–9.

[50] *WB*, I.57/28–30. Again, the contrast is between 'opin' and 'derk', not between idiomatic and literal translation.

[51] *X*, cf. Lindberg, *EV*, II.89 (*E*); *WB*, I.398. On the use of 'curlew' to translate *coturnix*, see OED (the translators are probably following Rolle's *Psalter* here).

[52] The strategy applies only to participles that are denotationally ambiguous, not to persons, and it 'proved irrelevant for the real translation problems': 'Translation Strategies in Middle English: The Case of the Wycliffite Bible', *Poetica: An International Journal of Linguistic–Literary Studies*, 55 (2001), 143. Moessner's study is based on Ps. 1–50 only.

[53] *X*, cf. Lindberg, *EV*, IV.176 (*E*); *WB*, II.754.

in the revised Later Version in Bodley 277 the recommended strategy gives 'þou hast distried hem þat hatiden me'.[54]

The Prologue-writer recommends, thirdly, that the Latin relative, when used as a resumptive subject [or object], should be translated by repeating the antecedent and adding 'and': his example is that 'qui occurrit' may be translated not as 'which renneþ' (as it would be in the Earlier Version), but as 'and he renneþ'.[55] After the Levite's concubine, in Judges 19, has been raped and killed by the men of Gibeah, and the Levite has found her in the morning dead in the doorway, the Latin says he went back into his house, and 'quam cum esset ingressus', when he had gone in, 'arripuit gladium', he snatched up a sword (to cut her into twelve pieces, Judg. 19:29). In the Earlier Version, this is translated word for word, 'þe whiche whanne he was gon in he cawȝte a swerd', but in the Later Version the Prologue-writer's strategy is adopted: 'and whanne he entride in to þat hows he took a swerd'.[56] This is fully 'opin', but the advantage of the Latin construction is that the syntactical focus of attention is the action 'arripuit'.

A word may be repeated, says the writer, as often as necessary in English without becoming 'superflu', even though it may appear only once in Latin.[57] At the beginning of the eighth chapter of the book of Wisdom, in which wisdom is figured as the supremely desirable object of love, the Earlier Version has 'þis I louede and soȝte it [wisdom] out fro my ȝouþe' (Wisd. 8:2), referring back to the subject of the previous chapter, but the Later Version reads 'I louede þis *wisdom maad*' (that is, created wisdom, not the second person of the Trinity), a clarification included in Lyra's *Postilla* on this book.[58] These resumptive repetitions are usually underlined in Later Version manuscripts, presumably because they are (strictly speaking) like glosses, additions to the text.

The Prologue-writer's fifth comment about translation practice is that words like *autem* and *vero* should be translated according to the context, not by fixed equivalents[59] – as *autem*, for example, is consistently and awkwardly translated 'forsoþe' in the genealogy in the first chapter of Matthew's Gospel in the Earlier Version, but by a range of constructions in the Later Version.[60]

54 Lindberg, *KHB*, II.462. For other examples, see *WB*, I.xxii, Hudson, SEWW, p. 175, and Lindberg, *KHB*, I.43–4, II.39–41.

55 *WB*, I.57/32–4 (the Latin is not given). For examples, see *WB*, I.xxii and Hudson, *SEWW*, p. 175.

56 Lindberg, *EV*, III.52 (*E*), also *X*; *WB*, I.669.

57 *WB*, I.57/34–5.

58 Lindberg, *EV*, IV.298 (*E*), also *X*; *WB*, III.98. For other examples, see *WB*, I.xxiii and Hudson, *SEWW*, p. 175.

59 *WB*, I.57/35–9, elaborated at 60/5–11.

60 Lindberg, *EV*, VII.27 (*X*); contrast LV, *WB*, IV.2–3. For other examples, see *WB*, I.xxiii and Hudson, *SEWW*, p. 175.

Last, but certainly not least, the writer recognizes that the word-order of the Latin sometimes makes a word-for-word translation impossible, because English, a less inflected language than Latin, cannot normally tolerate the reversal of subject and object. Palmer makes the relative lack of inflections in English an argument against translation of the Bible into such a barbarous language, but Ullerston maintains that the grammar of English follows its own rules, and that faithful translation is possible as long as the translator understands the grammatical rules of both languages.[61] The writer of the Prologue says that where word-for-word translation does not make sense, natural English word-order should be followed.[62] In accordance with this, the translators alter the Earlier Version's confusing 'Two folkus hateþ my soule' ('duas gentes [object] odit anima mea [subject]', Ecclus 50:25)' to 'My soule hatiþ twei folkis'.[63]

Apart from marginal glosses (which will be discussed later in this chapter), the manuscripts of the Later Version generally present a more uniform text than the manuscripts of the Earlier Version. The dialectal differences are much slighter, with the language of almost all manuscripts (and of all copies of the Prologue to the Wycliffite Bible) being identifiable as Central Midlands, South-East Midlands or a mix of the two, whereas, among early manuscripts of the Earlier Version, hands A and B of Bodley 959 manifest characteristically West Midland features, the other hands of the same manuscript manifest characteristically East Midland features and the hand of the first part of Bodleian Douce 369 is characterized by North Midland features.[64] In the early part of Bodley 959, some attempt has been made to alter West Midland forms to what are now classified as 'standard' (that is, Central or South-East) Midland forms.[65] While this desire for dialectal homogeneity on the part of at least one of the translators is not quite the same as awareness of an emerging standard, we can see how the concern that the Bible in English should be as 'opin' as possible might, during the life of the translation project, have evolved into a shared awareness that the dialect of the Central and South-East Midlands was the most widely comprehensible kind of English.

[61] Deanesly, *LB*, pp. 426–7; Ullerston, Vienna, Österreichische Nationalbibl. 4133, fol. 204r.

[62] *WB*, I.57/37–41. The writer's example is 1 Kings 2:10; see Hudson's comment, and her example from Is. 53:1, *SEWW*, p. 175; also Carr, *Über das Verhältnis der Wiclifitischen und der Purvey'schen Bibelübersetzung*, pp. 96–101, and *WB*, I.xxii. Moessner says that EV preserves the OS word-order of the Latin in 21 out of 32 cases in Ps. 1–50, and that LV changes all OS word-orders into SVO: 'Translation Strategies in Middle English', pp. 144–5, 147.

[63] *X*, cf. Lindberg, *EV*, V.101 (*E*); *WB*, III.220.

[64] See Lindberg, *Judges*, pp. 68–73, *EV*, I–VIII, and Appendix 4 and the Index of MSS for the dialect characteristics of individual MSS.

[65] See Lindberg, *EV*, I.18–19, and n. 221, below.

There are some inconsistencies in the vocabulary of the Later Version that suggest that the text may originally have been divided between different translators; in particular, and predictably, that the Old Testament may have been assigned to one group of translators and the New Testament to another.[66] Any such inconsistencies may, of course, reflect inconsistencies in the Earlier Version not noticed or not resolved in the revision process. There are, however, indications that there was a change of translators in the latter part of the Old Testament, somewhere between Baruch and Amos.[67] At the same time, the Earlier Version seems to have been less intensively revised in the latter part of the Old Testament. Sven Fristedt notes that in the Later Version 'non est qui' ('there is no one who') is translated 'noon is þat' as far as Amos 5:2, but that from Amos 5:6 onwards the Later Version has the same translation as the Earlier Version (and Bodley 277), 'þer is not þat'.[68] The Earlier Version's 'þe Lord God swoor in his hoely' ('iuravit dominus deus in sancto suo', Amos 4:2) is left unrevised, where we should have expected 'in his hooli dwellyng'.[69]

Early in Amos, there are some strong revisions. 'ȝee ȝeuen wyn to naȝareis' (to men pledged to abstain from drink, 2:12) becomes 'ȝe birliden [poured out] wyn to naȝareis', reminding us of the etymology of the name Damascus ('drinkynge blood eiþer birling blood'), in the Prologue's excursus on Amos 1:3.[70] The Lord's threat to the sons of Israel 'I shal soune strongli [*stridebo*] vnder ȝou as a wayn chargid [wagon loaded] wiþ hei souneþ strongly' (Amos 2:13, in the Earlier Version) becomes, far more effectively, 'Y schal gnast eþer charke' as a hay-wagon 'charkiþ'.[71] Later in Amos, however, the same Latin verb, used of the hinges of the temple, is translated 'gretly sounen' in both versions (8:3).[72] The natural explanation for this, and for the lack of revisions the earlier part of the Later Version has led us to expect, is haste on the revisers' part. This is borne out, as we shall see, by textual inaccuracies in the Later Version from Ecclesiasticus onwards, but neither lack of stylistic revision nor inaccuracy is evidenced in the New Testament in the Later Version. If the latter part of the Old Testament was the last portion of the Later Version of the Wycliffite Bible

66 Tanabe, 'On Some English Readings in the Vocabulary of the Wycliffite Bible', pp. 398–9.
67 Ibid., pp. 399–401.
68 Fristedt, *WB*, *I*.26, see also *WB*, *II*.xl; e.g. Gen. 40:8, Lindberg *EV*, I.86, *WB*, I.165, Lindberg, *KHB*, I.29, 95. For the change in Amos 5, see Lindberg, *EV*, VI.193, *WB*, III.582.
69 Ibid., VI.192 (*X*); *WB*, III.697.
70 Ibid., IV.191 (*X*); *WB*, III.695 (I = LV). On the etymology of 'Damascus', see p. 107, above.
71 Ibid., IV.191 (*X*); *WB*, III.694 (C). A has 'charke' only, but CC_U_6680EFGHIKMNPP_SQRSUXY have both alternatives.
72 Ibid., IV.195 (*X*); *WB*, III.703 (I = LV).

to be completed, the decision to include a prologue to the Prophets was made during the final stage of the revision process, and this would make sense, since the writer was already planning the prologue to be prefixed to Genesis.

Work on the text of the Later Version did not stop when the English Bible began to be copied, c. 1390. Forshall and Madden's base text, Royal 1. C. VIII (c. 1400–10), is slightly revised from Genesis to Numbers 20 and from Psalms to the end of the Old Testament.[73] Lindberg's edition of Bodley 277 (c. 1425–35) makes clear for the first time the extent of the revisions in this manuscript, throughout the Bible.[74] These revisions are often in the direction of vernacular idiom, sometimes following the strategies recommended in the Prologue where the Later Version does not do so. To the examples already given, we can add Ruth and Orpah's reaction to Naomi's farewell, 'whiche [the daughters-in-law] bigunnen to wepe with vois reisid' ('quae elevata voce flere coeperunt', Ruth 1:9). Bodley 277 resolves the relative just as the Prologue suggests, 'and þei bigunnen to wepe wiþ hiȝe voice'.[75] Another characteristic of Bodley 277's revisions is the addition of existential 'þer', especially before the verb 'to be', so that in John's Gospel the story of the healing of the nobleman of Capernaum's son is introduced with the words 'And þer was a litil kyng' ('Et erat quidam regulus', John 4:46), where the Later Version has 'and a litil kyng was'.[76] In the Song of Songs, the lover's 'no wem [*macula*] is in þee' (4:7 in the Later Version) becomes, in Bodley 277, 'þer is no wem in þee'.[77]

More surprisingly, Bodley 277 also reverts to Earlier Version readings (as in the example from the fourth psalm already noted). Throughout the Song of Songs the male lover calls the female beloved 'leef', as he does in the Earlier Version, where the Later Version has the female-specific 'frendesse', a word found only there and once in Proverbs, 'clepe þou prudence þi frendesse' (7:4).[78] I have argued elsewhere that when the Wycliffite translators realized that the authority of Lyra undermined the accuracy of the Bedan rubrics which identified the speakers throughout the Song of Songs, and are included in the Earlier Version of the Song of Songs (see figs. 8, 10),

[73] As is P_S from Ps. to the end of OT; see Appendix 2 and p. 155, below.

[74] Lindberg, *KHB*, I–IV, I also includes 3 Ezra and the EV long prologue to Romans. It shares many readings and glosses with S in Gen. –Joshua and 1 Chron.–Job, and with N in 1 Chron.–2 Ezra, see Lindberg, *KHB*, II.49.

[75] *WB*, I.679; Lindberg, *KHB*, I.28, 377.

[76] Ibid., IV.16, 146; *WB*, IV.246; 'sum lityl king was', Lindberg, *EV*, IV.173 (*E*); 'litil kyng' is a literal rendering of *regulus*, diminutive of *rex*. See also Lindberg, *KHB*, III.40.

[77] *WB*, III.77; Lindberg, *KHB*, III.43, 89. Another characteristic of I's revisions is the addition of an object pronoun, e.g. 'þei feliden *it* noȝt' (Bar. 6:19), *KHB*, III.41, 313.

[78] *WB*, III.11; Lindberg, *EV*, IV.252 (*E*).

they decided they had to omit them.[79] In the absence of the rubrics, they chose to write into the text wherever possible indications of whether the speaker is male or female, that is, divine or human. In the Later Version of the Song of Songs, the translators consistently use a female form of the noun spouse, 'spousesse', as the equivalent of *sponsa*, bride.[80] 'Derlyng' is consistently gendered male, as in 'Mi derlyng come in to his gardyn to ete þe fruyt of hise applis' (5:1), words which are quoted in the fourth tract in favour of biblical translation in Cambridge University Library Ii. 6. 26.[81] These gender-specific choices on the part of the translators, in defiance of normal English usage as represented in the Earlier Version, map the hierarchy of divine and human love onto a hierarchy of male and female love-language. Although Bodley 277 reverts to the Earlier Version's 'leef', it retains the other gender-specific choices of the Later Version, and coins some further female-specific nouns, such as 'techestere' (Wisd. 8:4) and 'weilsteris [female wailers]' (Jer. 9:17).[82]

The word-order in Bodley 277 can be unexpectedly Latinate: participial adjectives, for example, follow their nouns, so that the *repudiatam* whom the Levites of the New Temple are warned against marrying is 'a womman forsakun' (Ezek. 44:22), where other Later Version manuscripts read 'a forsakun womman'.[83] The second of the good servants in the parable of the talents is rewarded, in the Earlier and the Later Versions, with the command 'be þou on fyue citees' ('tu esto super quinque civitates', Luke 19:19); in reverting to the Latin word-order here, 'þou be on fyue citees', Bodley 277 disguises the imperative and is less 'opin' than earlier translations.[84] Lindberg tentatively suggests that this revision was completed between 1390 and 1400 under the direction of the writer of the Prologue to the Wycliffite Bible,[85] but it seems most unlikely that the Prologue-writer would have reversed his decision to exclude 3 Ezra, or concurred with the inclusion of chapter one of his Prologue only. The examples Lindberg gives of 'þe correcting of þe translacioun' (*WB*, I.57/14–15), which he envisages as a

79 Dove, 'Love *ad litteram*: the Lollard Translations of the Song of Songs', *Reformation* 9 (2004), 1–23.

80 In C, *spousesse* is written *sup. ras.* at 2:7, at the first occurrence. Cf. 'He þat haþ þe spousesse is þe spouse' (John 3:29, *X*)'; 'he þat haþ a spouse, *or wyf*' (*GMNPQTWY* Queen's College Oxford 369 *sup. ras. A*); 'he þat haþ a spousesse, *or wyf*', *WB*, IV.242 (*K*). *X*'s reading is probably later than that of *G*, etc.

81 *WB*, III.78; fol. 27r, 'come doun', confuses 'uenit' (Song 5:1) with 'descendit' (6:1). See Dove, 'Love *ad litteram*', 1.

82 Lindberg, *KHB*, III.12, 98, 'techeresse' *WB*, III.98 (EV LV); *KHB*, III.240, 'weileressis' LV, 'wymmen þat weilen' A, *WB*, III.365. I's words are not recorded in OED or *MED*.

83 Lindberg, *KHB*, III.43, 375; *WB*, III.608.

84 *WB*, IV.211 (*K*, A); Lindberg, *KHB*, IV.15, 130.

85 *KHB*, I.47. In *KHB*, II–IV, Lindberg does not repeat his suggestion about the origins of I, but talks of 'several stages of revisions': *KHB*, IV.34.

separate, fifth stage of the translation project, after the Later Version had been completed, are examples of stylistic revision rather than correction.[86]

The unrevised Later Version, as represented in a good manuscript like Lincoln College Oxford Latin 119 or Cambridge University Library Mm. 2. 15, is, in my view, the end of the line as far as the project described in the Prologue is concerned. Stylistic revision, textual correction and further glossing occurred more or less sporadically during the copying process, and the decision to translate the epistle to the Laodiceans was probably made in the second quarter of the fifteenth century.[87] The revisions in Bodley 277 are, however, by far the most thoroughgoing. The reviser evidently had copies of the Bible in both the Earlier and the Later Versions, and was familiar with the content and the translation practices of both. It is likely that he had been one of the translators (working in Oxford?), and certainly either he himself or those who had access to his revised text were in a position to have it copied by master-craftsmen, perhaps for a royal owner.

TRANSLATION AND INTERPRETATION

Lindberg speaks of the translators of the Earlier Version adding 'only what is necessary'. The writer of the Prologue to the Wycliffite Bible warns against including elements in the translation that are 'superflu' or 'fals', and John Colop's common-profit book includes a tract warning against adding to God's law or abridging, contradicting or changing it. Unquestionably the Wycliffite translators intended to give English readers access to the naked, literal text of scripture. Wyclif and the Wycliffites' profound unease with glossing, which they associate above all with the friars, might lead us to expect the translators to forgo glosses entirely.[88] The suspicion that glossing was characteristically tendentious and without any authoritative textual basis is inscribed in the Middle English verb 'glosen', meaning 'to interpret', but also having the pejorative sense 'to entice, deceive'. The Earlier Version uses it in this sense when translating Paul's words 'sermo meus et praedicatio mea non in persuasibilibus sapientiae verbis' (1 Cor. 2:4), 'my wrd and my preching not in persuable *or sutyl glosing* wrdis of manes wisdam'.[89]

[86] Ibid., III.47. [87] Only twelve late MSS include it; see Appendix 3 and p. 95, above.

[88] See Ralph Hanna, 'The Difficulty of Ricardian Prose Translation, esp. p. 337; also Mary Dove, 'Chaucer and the Translation of the Jewish Scriptures', in Sheila Delany, ed., *Chaucer and the Jews: Sources, Contexts, Meanings* (New York: Routledge), pp. 97–8, and Ghosh, *WH*, 120–1, 150–1.

[89] Lindberg, EV, VIII.96 (*X*). *V* reads, with LV, 'sutel sturyng wordis', *WB*, IV.341. 'Persuable' should read 'persuasible', as in the Northern Pauline Epistles, ed. M. J. Powell, EETS e.s. 116 (London, 1916), p. 55; see *MED*.

On the other hand, Wyclif had no compunction about using glosses for his own ends, as David Aers has established.[90] The prologue to the Prophets makes it clear that the glosses which trouble the Wycliffites are those that distort the text for worldly purposes, replacing the open, literal meaning with a 'goostli' interpretation at odds with it. There is no reason to suppose that the translators were suspicious of glosses introduced in order to make the text 'opin' and intelligible; after all, the Latin Bible itself includes glosses of this kind, such as 'vocatumque est nomen eius Horma, id est anathema', 'and þe name of þe cite was cleped Horma, þat is corsynge' (Judg. 1:17).[91] When the translators borrow a Latin word, as it is often convenient or necessary for them to do, it makes sense for them to define the borrowed word for English readers. Although the word *incestus* is defined by its context in the purity laws in Leviticus, ten manuscripts in the Later Version include a gloss explaining 'incest, *þat is leccherie of kynesmen and wymmen*' (Lev. 18:17).[92]

Whatever the translators may have anticipated in advance, in practice they discovered that there is no hard and fast line between literal translation and supplementary explanation. Where the Latin Bible has God commanding the waters to bring forth 'reptile animae viventis' (Gen. 1:20), the Earlier Version has 'þe crepende kinde of þe lyuende soule', simultaneously a name and a description.[93] In the dietary laws in Leviticus, the unclean ibis, in the corrected Earlier Version in Bodley 959, is described as 'þe vnclene water foul þat wiþ his bile puttynge water in to his ars purgeþ hymself' (Lev. 11:17),[94] and the characteristics of the equally unclean *brucus*, *attacus*, and other creatures named in this chapter are all supplied in the corrected Earlier Version and remain in the Later Version, although the first hand of Bodley 959, before correction, simply gives the names ('bruk', 'athachus', and so on), without explanation.[95] It looks as though in this chapter Bodley 959 preserves a first, literal and unglossed translation, later expanded by way of material derived from Isidore of Seville's *Etymologiae*.

90 'John Wyclif's Understanding of Christian Discipleship', in *Faith, Ethics and Church Writing in England, 1360–1409* (Cambridge University Press, 2000), pp 119–48.

91 Lindberg, *EV*, II.206 (*E*).

92 In the margin in BCGKLPQ *sim.* I and within the text in N *sim.* S; *WB*, I.336. As usual, *WB* does not provide full details.

93 *X*, cf. Lindberg, EV, I.37 (*E*).

94 Ibid., II.44–5; the gloss is written *sup. ras. al. m.* and continued in the margin (but not italicized in *WB*, I.316). *X* includes this gloss.

95 The creatures whose characteristics are described are the 'ophiomachus' (11:22), 'corcodillus' (11:29), 'migale', 'cameleon', 'stelio' and 'lacerta' (11:30); Lindberg, *EV*, II.44–5; *WB*, I.316 (*A* in EV, A in LV); the glosses are supplied, with sigla, in the margin *al. m.* in *E* (but not italicized in *WB*). *X* includes these glosses.

A 'strictly true and faithful rendering' of the Latin original ran the risk of being unintentionally cryptic and of causing problems at the revision stage. The programme of research outlined in the final chapter of the Prologue to the Wycliffite Bible suggests that the translators were aware that material not in the Latin text, or only implied in the Latin text, would need to be added if their translation were to be 'opin' enough for the reader who could not read, or did not have at hand, books interpreting 'harde wordis', and commentaries and postills interpreting the biblical text. All Earlier Version manuscripts, including the Christ Church Bible, have the following explanatory glosses: the measure by which the manna in the desert is weighed is a 'gomor, *þat is of þrettene pound wiþ þe tenþe part of two pond*' (Exd. 16:18);[96] at the placing of the ark of the Lord in the tabernacle in Jerusalem, priests 'sungen cynychyon, *þat is to þe God ouercomere victorie and preysyng*' (1 Chron.15:21);[97] in the epistle of Jeremiah, a satire on idolatry, it is explained that the 'kukumeris', the scarecrow, uselessly protects 'ben bitter erbis' which nobody would want to harvest (and idols are similarly otiose, Bar. 6:69);[98] in Ezekiel's vision of the north gate of the temple, there were 'wymmen moornende *a maumet* [idol] *of leccherie þat is clepid* Adonydes' (Ezek. 8:14).[99] Explanatory glosses in the Earlier Version become much more common after Baruch 3:20, one of the several pieces of evidence suggesting a hiatus in the translation at or near that point, followed by a reconsideration of translation practice. In the New Testament, glosses are frequent.

When Forshall and Madden say there are no textual glosses in the Earlier Version as far as Baruch 3:20 they are thinking not of explanatory glosses but of variant translations, which are not really glosses at all.[100] These 'synonymous variants', to use Lindberg's term, are common throughout the text of the Later Version.[101] The first, at the beginning of the narrative of the Flood, is 'ech fleisch *eþer man* hadde corrupt his weie' (Gen. 6:12), written within the text in all Later Version copies of Genesis.[102] Here, the translators rightly take *caro* ('fleisch') to be a metonym, and the non-figurative 'man' is offered as a more 'opin' alternative. The extent of these

96 Lindberg, *EV*, I.123 (*E*), 'þrettene' *sup. ras.*; 'þrettenþe' (*ABDEFH*), *WB*, I.230. LV has a different gloss at Exd. 16:16: 'gomor, *þat is conteynynge a qwart and half*, Lire here (marg. BDGKQSTP_SXX text LNR), *þat is oþer half quart* (text IS). *X* has the LV gloss in the margin at 16:16 as well as the EV gloss in the text at 16:18.

97 Cynychyon, *var.* epynychion > Greek ἐπινιχιον; Lindberg, *EV*, III.246 (*E*); *WB*, II.351 (*B*).

98 *EV*, VI.78 (*X*); *WB*, III.500 (*K*).

99 Lindberg, *EV*, VI.88 (*X*); *WB*, III.516 (*A*).

100 'Hereford . . . never introduces textual glosses', *WB*, I.xvii.

101 Lindberg, 'The Alpha and Omega of the Middle English Bible', p. 195.

102 *WB*, I.89; 'or man' (ELP).

variant translations is obscured in Forshall and Madden's edition, since their base text of the Later Version, British Library Royal 1. C. VIII, is a revised text that typically chooses one or other of the alternatives (or occasionally a new term altogether), from Genesis to Numbers 20 and from Psalms to the end of the Old Testament. 'Fallyng *eþer deþ*' (*ruina* in the Gallican Psalter and *plaga* in the Hebrew Psalter, Ps. 105:29) becomes 'fallyng' (the figurative alternative) in the Royal manuscript, but in William H. Scheide 12, another Bible in the Later Version that sometimes chooses between synonymous variants from Psalms to the end of the Old Testament, the alternative chosen is 'deþ'.[103] Variant translations are also characteristic of the Earlier Version, but only after the hiatus at Baruch 3:20. The first of many which the versions have in common in the latter part of the Old Testament comes in the stringent directions on household management in the book of Ecclesiasticus (42:7): 'discriue *or wrijt*' / 'discryue þou *eþer write*' details of gifts received.[104]

Another kind of gloss, easily confused with a synonymous variant, offers alternative meanings, the translators not having been able to decide between them. There are two examples in Amos in the Earlier Version, the 'plage [region] *or wound* of þe litil bed' (the Latin *plaga* having these two distinct meanings, 3:12), and, in the vision of the locusts easting the grass of the land, 'after þe clipper of floc *or kyng*' (*gregis* being a variant of *regis*, 7:1).[105] In both cases the Later Version makes – as was surely intended – a choice between the two, in the first case selecting the appropriate in-context meaning, 'cuntrei of bed', and in the second selecting the better reading, 'þe clippere of þe kyng', although Bodley 277 changes 'kyng' to the inferior 'flocke'.[106] At least one correctorial variant remains in the Later Version: 'An herte þat entriþ bi tweie weies', that knows what is good but does not act accordingly, 'schal not haue prosperitees *eþer reste*' (*requiem* being a variant of *successus*, Ecclus 3:28).[107] In this case, the Earlier Version was already correct: a divided heart 'shal not han welsum chaunces'.[108] The revisers should have decided between 'prosperitees' and 'reste', but perhaps failed to register that these are

[103] *WB*, II.847. Readings from P_S are not recorded in *WB*. In *WB*, variant translations are recorded in the *apparatus criticus* from Ps. to 2 Macc. For other examples, see Ps. 106:29, Ps. 113:14 and Ps. 118:15 in Appendix 2, below.

[104] Lindberg, *EV*, IV.356 (marg. *al. m. E, om. CX*); *WB*, III.205.

[105] Lindberg, *EV*, VI.191 (gloss in *AKGHL*_oW_o*Y*); Lindberg, *EV*, VI.195 (gloss in *AGHL*_oW_o*YZ*); see Appendix 3.

[106] *WB*, III.696, 701; Lindberg, *KHB*, III.426 (*sup. ras.*), cf. III.46. For another example, see 2 Tim. 4:13, Appendix 3.

[107] *WB*, III.129; see Appendix 3. A marginal gloss explains 'þat is, þat haþ þe knowing of good in vndurstondyng, and malice in wille, Lire here' (C).

[108] Lindberg, *EV*, IV.315 (*E*).

variants; another piece of evidence that the revisers were less than thorough in the latter part of the Old Testament.

When the translators revising the Earlier Version revisited Genesis, they kept the translation of *reptile* as 'a crepynge beeste [kinde EV]' (1:20, *WB*, I.80). Five manuscripts, however, borrow the Latin word and add a variant, 'a reptile *eþer a crepinge beeste*'; three of them have this gloss in the margin, but two, Bodley 277 and another partial revision of the Later Version, St John's College Oxford 7, incorporate this reading into the text.[109] This is the first of a series of glosses on the Pentateuch, at least some of which are included in all Later Version manuscripts including these books except Cambridge University Library Additional 6680 (a complete Bible).[110] The last of this series of Pentateuch glosses, which are more often written in the margin than in the text, is 'þe ȝok of hem, *þat is þe lordschip of Moabitis*' (Num. 21:30).[111] Another series of glosses, included in some Later Version manuscripts and not in others, but written in the margin in all manuscripts that include them, runs from 1 Chronicles 3:5 to 2 Chronicles 3:3.[112] A third series, included in some Later Version manuscripts and not in others, usually written in the margin but in some manuscripts in the text, runs throughout 1–2 Maccabees.[113]

The majority of Later Version manuscripts include glosses at the beginning of many of the psalms, in effect mini-prologues, as far as Psalm 72 (and a few include such glosses for later psalms).[114] In Proverbs, five Later Version manuscripts share a number of glosses.[115] In the Prophets, a few manuscripts include glosses too sporadic to be called a series, but more frequent, and occasionally very lengthy, in Daniel.[116] As well, there are some three dozen glosses included in most Old Testaments in the Later Version, including British Library Royal 1. A. VIII: among these are six glosses in 3–4 Kings, mini-prologues to Tobit and Job, twelve glosses in Isaiah (clustered in Isaiah 33–5) and four in Jeremiah.[117] In Bodley 277, Corpus Christi College

109 Marg. BdP_S; Lindberg, *KHB*, I.48 (I). The first recorded use of *reptile* in *MED* is in Gower's *Confessio Amantis*, VII.1011, and there are no citations from WB; see Lindberg, 'The Alpha and Omega of the Middle English Bible', p. 195.

110 ABCDdEFGILMNOPP_SQRSTX include Pentateuch glosses. BCGOQX include most of them, and DFMT relatively few; A includes the glosses at Exd. 23:28 and 30:13 only.

111 Marg. BdGKQX text CN; *WB*, I.424.

112 BbCEGKLPQSU include many of these glosses.

113 CEeIKNPQUY include many of these glosses and AH some of them.

114 KORSUV include some glosses after Ps. 72, and B_554 includes glosses on all psalms, as well as extensive glosses throughout the text of Psalms (not recorded in *WB*); see further below.

115 CKNR_91.

116 CGQU include most of these glosses, and KLPP_S some. R_89 has some unique glosses in Dan., see Appendix 2. There are lengthy glosses at Dan. 2:1, 4:3, 7:1, 11:36–45 and 12:11.

117 3 Kings 4:22, 7:26, 8:2, 12:11 and 15:13 and 4 Kings 18:4; Is. 13:21, 17:6, 18:2, 28:25, 29:1, 33:4, 34:11, 34:14 (3), 35:4, 45:8 and 60:15; Jer. 8:22, 20:14, 32:9 and 51:27. See also Exd. 23:28 and 30:13, Prov. 6:34, Ecclus 28:26 and Zech. 11:16.

Cambridge Parker 147 and St John's College Oxford 7, there are numerous moral glosses from Genesis to Job, especially in Deuteronomy and Numbers.[118] Over and above all of these glosses, throughout the Old Testament explanatory and interpretive glosses (as well as variant translations) are incorporated into the text of all manuscripts of the Later Version.[119]

Many of the glosses end with the words 'Lire here', that is, Lyra says this when commenting on these words in his *Postilla* on the whole Bible. If the Wycliffite translators were to depend particularly heavily on the authority of any one biblical commentator, Lyra, who was familiar with the *hebraica veritas* of the Old Testament, and who had (unusually) commented on the literal and moral meaning of every book of the biblical canon, was the obvious choice. Wyclif's commentary on the Bible owed a great deal to Lyra. None of the translators would have doubted the wisdom of making use of Lyra's commentary in order to establish an accurate biblical text and in order to reach a fuller and more precise understanding of what the biblical text meant, before translating the 'sentence' from Latin into English as openly and truly as possible.

In the Song of Songs, the 'spousesse', in the Later Version, says 'Y schal *cleue by loue* to my derlyng' (7:10), incorporating Lyra's gloss 'per amorem inhaereo' within the 'ego dilecto meo' of the Latin Bible.[120] When Joshua puts Amalech and his people to flight 'in ore gladii' (Exd. 17:13), the Later Version, incorporating Lyra's clarification of the metaphor, translates 'in þe mouþ of swerd, *þat is bi þe scharpnesse of þe swerd*' ('id est, acie vel acumine gladii').[121] In the Song of Moses, the Lord is said to have found the children of Israel 'in terra deserta' (Deut. 32:10), and, following Lyra, 'id est, privata dei cultura', a textual gloss explains 'þat is, priued [deprived] of goddis religioun'.[122] When Gideon asks the men of Succoth for bread, so that he and his people can pursue Zebah and Zalmunna, kings of Midian, 'þe princes of Socoth answeriden, *in scorne*, "in hap [perhaps] þe pawmes of þe hondis of Zebee and Salmana ben in þin hond, and þerfor þou axist þat we ȝyue looues to þin oost"' (Judg. 8:6).[123] Lyra often, as here, alerts the reader to the tone in which words are spoken (in this case 'negative et derisorie'). When the psalmist asks that those who 'dicunt mihi "euge euge"' (Ps. 39:16) may be confounded, the Later Version translates '[those] þat seien to me "wel wel", *in despijt, þat is in scorn*', Lyra explaining that

118 See the descriptions in Appendix 4 and the Index of MSS.

119 The first of these common textual glosses is 'delium [*bdellium*, var. *dellium*], *þat is a tree of spicerie*' (Gen. 2:12), *WB*, I.82; 'arbor est aromaticus', Lyra.

120 *WB*, III.82; EV reads 'I to my leef', Lindberg, *EV*, IV.290.

121 *WB*, I.233; in B (only) the gloss is in the margin. In IS, the text of the gloss continues 'Josue killide þe stronge men of Amelech', incorporating part of the marginal gloss on Exd. 17:13 in CGQX.

122 *WB*, I.546, *om.* I.

123 *WB*, I.636; in I (only) the gloss is in the margin.

'euge' is an 'interiectio exultationis', an exultant cry which may convey rejoicing or derision, and in this case the latter.[124]

Rewriting direct speech to show that what is said is true, although apparently, literally, it is not, is another characteristic of Lyra that endears him to Wyclif and to the translators. One of the series of glosses in the Pentateuch, in the margin in seven manuscripts, comments on God's words to Moses concerning the rebellious Israelites, 'Y schal waste hem' (Num. 14:12): 'þouȝ gode dide not þis, neþeles he seide soþ, for he spak bi þe yuele disseruyingis of hem, as if he seide [*quasi diceret*] "þey disserueden þat Y schulde do þis to hem", Lire here'.[125] The concomitant promise God makes to Moses, 'Y schal make þee prince on a greet folk', is conditional, Lyra says, on God's destruction of the Israelites (and will not, therefore, come to pass). A marginal gloss in five manuscripts reads 'þis is vndirstondun in a condicioun, Lire here' ('hoc autem intelligitur conditionaliter, id est, si facerem primum facerem et istud secundum').[126] These kinds of comments did not, of course, lend themselves to being integrated into the biblical text.

The translators intended that all additions to the Latin text, including all intratextual glosses, would be underlined in red, and often they are, but equally often the underlining is in brown ink, even in exceptionally high-quality Wycliffite Bibles like Bodley 277 and, in the Earlier Version, like British Library Egerton 617/618. In most manuscripts the underlining is sporadic. Additions are therefore not always as obvious to the eye as they might be, but there is another kind of gloss in the Later Version that cannot be visually indicated because it is completely integrated into the text. According to the Latin Bible, for example, David assembles the leaders of Israel 'filiosque suos cum eunuchis' (1 Chron. 28:1), which the Earlier Version translates as 'and her [their] sones with þe geldyngis'.[127] The revisers correct 'her sones' to 'his sones' (that is, David's), and translate 'and hise sones wiþ nurchis [tutors]'.[128] A marginal gloss in six manuscripts, one of the series of glosses in Chronicles, explains that the eunuchs are not literally eunuchs: 'þe Latyn word here *eunuchis* is propirly geldingis, but here it is takun for nurscheris and techeris, þat ben seid geldingis for þey weren chast and onest, Lire here'.[129] Lyra's interpretation is incorporated

[124] The words 'in despijt' are in C_U_6680DKMP_SQS only, and follow 'þat is in scorn' in W; see Appendix 2.

[125] Marg. BCdGKQX; *WB*, I.403.

[126] Marg. CdKQX; *WB*, I.403.

[127] Lindberg, *EV*, III.261 (*E*).

[128] *WB*, II.378. *MED*, 'norice', 1 (b), cites WB for the first recorded use of this word to mean 'tutor'.

[129] Marg. bCGKQU, 'þe [þis G]'; *WB*, II.378. Cf. Lyra's gloss on Acts 8:27, explaining that the Ethiopian is not a eunuch 'ex precisione membrorum genitalium, sed a castitate et honestate morum'.

into the text of the Later Version. This happens most often in Psalms, as Hargreaves has shown.[130] 'In voce cataractarum tuarum' (Ps. 41:8), for example, is translated 'in þe vois of þi gooteris' in the Earlier Version, but 'in þe vois of þi wyndows' in the Later Version, following Lyra's comment 'cataractae dei dicuntur fenestrae caeli [windows of Heaven]'.[131]

There is very little at stake here, or in translating *eunuchis* 'nurchis', but there is also a very fine line between a gloss that helps the reader to understand the literal sense of the biblical text and a gloss that interprets the literal sense of the biblical text, and the translators sometimes overstep the mark. The most striking example (not noted by Hargreaves) is the translation of the words 'speciosus forma prae filiis hominum' (Ps. 44:3), in the Earlier Version translated word for word, 'fair in forme befor þe sones of men', but in the Later Version '*Crist*, þou art fairer in schap þan þe sones of men'.[132] After all, the Lyran gloss on the title of this psalm, included in most manuscripts of the Later Version, states that 'þis salm is seid of Crist and of hooli chirche modir and virgyn, for Poul in [Hebr. 1: 8–9] aleggiþ þis salm seid of Crist to þe lettre [*ad litteram*]'.[133] Here, the literal sense of the words is overridden by what Karlfried Froehlich calls their 'true literal sense', encompassing all the figurative senses intended by the writer and all the christological significations the Holy Spirit has inscribed within the text.[134] This is the way in which Lyra and the writer of the Prologue to the Wycliffite Bible (translating Lyra) understand 'literal', and the divine authorial intention could not – in the eyes of the Wycliffite translators, and of late-medieval scholars more generally – be clearer than it is in this psalm. On the authority of Paul in the Epistle to the Hebrews, it is Christ of whom the psalmist is speaking. Yet Christ is not named in the text of the psalm, and, even where underlining draws the reader's attention to the fact that 'Crist' is an addition, '*Crist*, þou art fairer in schap þan þe sones of men' is an interpretation rather than a translation of the Latin.

Glossing in the margins was a far less problematic method of interpretation than glossing within the text. It is, however, very difficult to determine which marginal glosses should be regarded as an integral part of the Later

130 'The Latin Text of Purvey's Psalter', pp. 76–8, 80–3.

131 Lindberg, *EV*, IV.189; *WB*, II.778; Hargreaves, 'The Latin Text of Purvey's Psalter', pp. 76, 81; see also Hargreaves, 'The Vernacular Scriptures: The Wycliffite Versions', p. 413.

132 Lindberg, *EV*, IV.191; *WB*, II.781.

133 Gloss in AB_554bCD_T_72EGiLPQSUX *al. m. X sim.* K; *WB*, II.781. On Lyra's christological reading of the Psalms see Gross-Diaz, 'What's a Good Soldier to Do?', pp. 126–8.

134 '"Always to Keep the Literal Sense in Holy Scripture Means to Kill One's Soul": The State of Biblical Hermeneutics at the Beginning of the Fifteenth Century', in Karl Miner, ed., *Literary Uses of Typology from the Late Middle Ages to the Present* (Princeton University Press, 1977), p. 47.

Version. Hudson asks whether 'any form of marginal glossing was ever put out with any authority', observing that Forshall and Madden's edition of the glosses is an inadequate basis for an answer,[135] but since the writer of the Prologue, in the course of his discussion of the text of the English Bible, says 'where þe Ebru, bi witnesse of Jerom, of Lire, and oþere expositouris discordiþ fro oure Latyn Bibles, I haue set in þe margyn bi maner of a glose what þe Ebru haþ . . . and I dide þis most in þe Sauter, þat of alle oure bokis discordiþ most fro Ebru',[136] it seems reasonable to suppose that at least those glosses that comment on the difference between the Hebrew original and the text of the Latin Bible were written by the translators to supplement the text of the Later Version.

The series of glosses in the Pentateuch and in Chronicles, and the more sporadic glosses in the Prophets, include many matching this description. 'Sauyour of þe world', for example, the translation of the Egyptian name given to Joseph by the pharaoh, is glossed in the margin in three manuscripts 'in Ebrew it is schewinge priuitees, as Jerom and Lire here seyen' (Gen. 41:45).[137] 'Þei [the spies sent by Moses into Canaan] camen into Ebron' is glossed in five manuscripts 'in Ebru it is, he cam in to Ebron, for Caleph [Caleb] aloone ȝede þidir, as Rabi Salomon [Rashi] seiþ' (Num. 13:23): this gloss names Lyra's main source for the *hebraica veritas*.[138] Lyra explains, in a gloss in eleven manuscripts, that the 'litle goldun liouns' ('leunculos aureos') made from the gold David gave to Solomon to adorn the temple, are, in the Hebrew text, 'goldun clensyng vessels, þat is goldun basyns in which þe blood was borun in to þe hooly of hooli þingis in day of clensing' (1 Chron. 28:17).[139] A gloss on 'daemoni' and 'onocentauri' (Is. 34:14) comments, following Lyra, that 'Ebreis seien martynapis and wielde cattis; martinapis ben liyk apis and ben tailid'; this gloss is included in ten manuscripts.[140]

Although the Prologue-writer claims to have glossed the Psalms especially intensively because of the great disparities between the text of the Gallican Psalter and the text of the Hebrew Psalter, there is only a smattering of glosses of this kind in two or three manuscripts. 'In imagine pertransit homo'

135 *PR*, pp 235–6. Lindberg omits marginal glosses in his editions of Baruch and Judges, as he says in *Judges*, p. 77, but he includes them in *KHB*.

136 *WB*, I.58/4–7. On the writer's low opinion of the Gallican Psalter, which he thinks was translated by men who 'hadden myche lasse kunnyng and holynesse þan Jerom hadde' (58/9), see Hudson, *SEWW*, p. 176.

137 CGQ, *WB*, I.169; 'occultum reuelans', Lyra; C. R. T. Hayward, *Saint Jerome's Hebrew Questions on Genesis* (Oxford: Clarendon Press, 1995), pp. 78, 226–7. The Egyptian name probably means 'the god speaks and he lives'.

138 Marg. dGKQX; *WB*, I.401.

139 Marg. BbCEGKLPQSU; *WB*, II.380.

140 Marg. CEGKPQSU text NY; *WB*, III.284.

(Ps. 38:7), for example, in three manuscripts is glossed 'a man passiþ in ymage, *þat is derknesse*', following Lyra, 'in hebraeo habetur in obscuritate'.[141] The glosses at the beginning of psalms often comment on the difference between the Hebrew title and Jerome's title: the title of Psalm 35 in the Later Version is 'to victorie to Dauiþ þe seruaunt of þe lord', and three manuscripts preface this title with 'in Ebrew þus', and add 'Jerom seiþ þus, *for þe victorie of Dauiþ þe seruaunt of þe lord*'.[142] All such glosses, and all textual and marginal glosses in the Psalms in Wycliffite Bible manuscripts, are included in Bodley 554, a Glossed Psalter with the Psalms in the Later Version, c. 1400.[143] In this volume, however, comments on readings from the Hebrew Psalter occur in the context of very extensive glossing from Lyra, Augustine and other authorities, and the gloss is as much concerned with moral and spiritual as with literal interpretation of Psalms.[144] Bodley 554 may incorporate some or all of the translators' marginal glosses on the Hebrew Psalter, but its text is probably not very close to the glossed Psalms the writer describes in the Prologue.

When he claims he has 'declarid in party in þe glos hou þe harde sentensis of Job schulen be vndirstonden', and has also 'declaride sumdel þe Grete Profetis and in party þe Litil Prophetis', the writer of the Prologue certainly seems to be referring to broadly interpretive rather than narrowly textual glossing, but the reference must surely be to glossing which is part of the English Bible rather than to a separate enterprise, the compilation of a *Glossed Prophets* or a *Glossed Job*.[145] No doubt he has in mind the work involved in interpreting the biblical text, and elucidating 'harde wordis and harde sentencis', as well as the provision of glosses resulting from that preparatory work; but the glosses in Job and the Prophets elucidate only a small selection of the outstandingly 'derke' words and utterances. Supposing that the series of glosses in the Pentateuch, Chronicles and Maccabees were compiled by the translators, they surely cannot have expected or wanted the English Bible to be copied with these books of the Old Testament substantially glossed and the other books only very sporadically glossed. Either the translators did not have time to compile marginal glosses on

141 Marg. B_554V text K; *WB*, II.776. For other examples, see Appendix 2.

142 B_554iV, see Appendix 2.

143 The reading of K can be corrected from B_554 at e.g. Ps. 113 (title), 'eche synnere þat haþ gete [B_554 greet K *WB*, II.855] merci'; for futher details, see Appendix 2.

144 Jerome and Cassiodorus are also cited, often by way of Lyra; the glosses from Augustine are not as extensive as Forshall and Madden suggest, *WB*, I.xlviii. Lyra is the only source for the glosses on the canticles 'Confitebor tibi' (Is. 12), fol. 81v, and 'Ego dixi' (Is. 38:10–20), fols. 81v–82r. Michael Kuczynski is preparing an edition entitled *A Glossed Lollard Psalter: MS Bodley 554*.

145 *WB*, I.37/1–2, 41/37–8; see Hudson, *PR*, p. 236, and p. 124, above.

the other books before the English Bible began to be copied, or the glosses on the other books have not survived. Since the first and last books of the Old Testament are glossed, and since the writer of the Prologue specifically mentions marginal glosses in Psalms, the likelihood must be that many more marginal glosses in the Old Testament were produced than have survived in the manuscript tradition.

Although glosses within the text can be problematic, they have the advantage that they cannot be accidentally or deliberately omitted, or misplaced. Cambridge University Library Additional 6680, a Bible with no marginal glosses at all, includes all the Later Version's textual glosses, among them, in Isaiah, 'Tophet, *that is helle*' (Is. 30:33, *WB*, III.279). In contrast, the marginal gloss 'pryde, *þat is glorie and onour*' (Is. 60:15), warning the reader against taking pride in the usual, negative sense in the promise 'I shal putte þee in to pride of worldis' ('ponam te in superbiam saeculorum'), is written in the margin in seven manuscripts, written in the text in three, and omitted in the eleven other manuscripts containing Isaiah in the Later Version.[146] Yet without this warning the reader is very likely to misunderstand 'pryde', and fail to read the text literally.

A rubric at the end of the prologue to the Prophets in Lambeth Palace 1033 (2 Chronicles–Baruch, c. 1410–20) asks for the distinction between text and gloss to be absolutely clear: 'here bigynneþ þe text of Isaye, wiþ a short glose on þe derke wordis, and loke ech man þat he wryte þe text hool bi itself and þe glose in þe margyn, eþer leue it al out'.[147] The writer of this rubric probably knew that confusion was resulting from scribes attempting to incorporate marginal glosses in their exemplar into the text. In Trinity College Dublin 67 (Proverbs–2 Maccabees), three of the glosses in Isaiah are completely disarranged, the gloss alone being written in the text and the words being glossed omitted and supplied in the margin.[148] At Isaiah 35:4, the gloss on God, 'þat is Crist', is written first: '*þat is Crist* God'[149] There are several cases of the same practice in British Library Arundel 104, including '*þat is an horned eddre* cerastes' (Gen. 49:17), and '*þat is power* fyngur' (Exd. 8:19).[150] Both the Trinity and the Arundel manuscripts, in Maccabees, write glosses

[146] Marg. CGIPQSU text ENY ('superbia non sonat hic in vitium sed in honoris excessum', Lyra); *WB*, III.331. This gloss is lacking in AC_U_6680 FHKMP_SRR_91VX.

[147] See Hargreaves, 'The Vernacular Scriptures: The Wycliffite Versions', p. 413. As Hargreaves says, there are no marginal glosses in Isaiah in this MS; it does, however, include the textual glosses, underlined in red.

[148] At Is. 17:6, 28:15 and 29:1; see Index of MSS.

[149] Marg. ACGKPQSU text NY; *WB*, III.285. See also the gloss at Jer. 14:20, below.

[150] Marg. BCGKPP_SQT text DELRS, *WB*, I.189; marg. BCGKPQX text EL; *WB*, I.209; see the description of E in Appendix 4, and the gloss at Jer. 14:20, below.

in the text in a miniature gloss-hand, either before the words glossed or at the end of the verse, sometimes including lemmata and usually attributing them 'Lire here', so that these glosses are effectively marginalized, in spite of being written in the text.[151] Certainly they fail to meet Hargreaves's definition of a textual gloss, 'a gloss included in the appropriate place in the same handwriting as the rest of the text and distinguished from it, if at all, only by underlining'.[152]

Very few of the 'derke' words and utterances in Jeremiah are elucidated in marginal glosses, but nine manuscripts include a gloss explaining that when Jeremiah says 'cursid be þe dai where ynne Y was borun' (14:20):

þese ben not wordis of Jeremie vnpacient and dispeiringe, but in þis he declareþ þe hidousnesse of sensualite [absence of reason] in comparisoun of euil neiȝinge, which euil, þat is peyne, þe resoun suffrede pacientli, as seint Joob, ensaumpler of pacience, seide *þe dai pershe in which I was born* [Job 3:2], and þis is þe sentence, *cursid be þe dai*, etc., þat is, if I suede þe hidousnesse of sensualite I shulde curse þe time of my birþe, Lire here.[153]

Two further manuscripts include only the last part of this gloss, summarizing the 'sentence'.[154] The whole gloss is a summary of Lyra's scholium on Job 3:2, refuting Gregory, who says that Job's words should not be taken literally, and refuting Thomas Aquinas, who takes Job's words at their face value. Lyra's gloss is included in the margin in two manuscripts, British Library Cotton Claudius E. II (a complete Bible, c. 1410) and Royal 1. C. IX (the first volume of a three-volume Bible, c. 1400–10).[155]

In these two Wycliffite Bibles, there are extensive and almost identical marginal glosses from Lyra throughout Job. Genesis to Esther and Proverbs to Isaiah 8:4 are also glossed in the Cotton Bible, 1–4 Kings and the five Sapiential books exceptionally heavily. The Royal Bible is glossed from Genesis to Esther, sharing most of its glosses with the Cotton Bible (and with other manuscripts that have the series of glosses in the Pentateuch and Chronicles), but including a number of unique glosses, especially in 4

151 On E, see further Appendix 4. N attributes its glosses 'Lire here', written in the text, throughout Proverbs.

152 Hargreaves, 'The Marginal Glosses to the Wycliffite New Testament', *Studia Neophilologica* 33 (1961), 285–300, esp. 290.

153 Marg. GHKLPQU text EY (in EY, the gloss is written before the words being glossed); *WB*, III.388. At Job 3:2, LV has 'perische þe dai in which Y was borun'; the gloss is probably translating Lyra without reference to WB. 'Exemplar patientie' is the opening of a Latin Bible prologue on Job, *RBMA*, no. 350.

154 Glossing the words 'be not blessid', marg. M text N.

155 *WB*, II.676. See the descriptions of BC in Appendix 4.

Kings 22–5, in 2 Chronicles 20–5 and in Job.[156] Many leaves of these two Bible have glosses crammed into every inch of every margin.[157] Hargreaves thinks that the writer of the Prologue is referring to the glosses in these manuscripts when he says he has elucidated Job and the Prophets, and that the rest of an equally extensive gloss on the Prophets has been lost.[158] Yet if the revisers had intended to gloss as extensively as this the English Bible would have needed a *mise-en-page* like that of the *Glossa Ordinaria*, where a short portion of biblical text is surrounded by wide columns for glosses, or like that of the *Glossed Gospels*, where a short portion of biblical text is followed, in the same column, by extensive commentary. There is no manuscript evidence for such formats: the provision for glosses is typically an outer column less than half the width of one of the two columns of text. Many manuscripts have no ruled margin for glosses at all.

The text of the glosses in the Cotton and Royal Bibles is very likely to be the work of the translators, since there is evidence to suggest that one or more of them produced an abbreviated translation of Lyra, supplemented by material from the *Glossa Ordinaria*, the set of marginal and interlinear glosses on all the books of the Bible to which the later Middle Ages assigned especial authority.[159] The fact that marginal glosses in the Cotton and Royal Bibles sometimes replicate intratextual glosses in the Later Version suggests that the function of this translation was to assist with the process of correcting and revising, including the provision of glosses. For example, the canonicity of the Hebrew Esther is made explicit when Esther and Mordecai write to the Jews ordaining 'þat þei schulden resseyue [this story] among hooli bookis' (intratextual gloss in the Later Version, Esth. 9:32), but the Cotton and Royal Bibles also include a marginal gloss to the same effect with very similar wording, 'and resseyue þe treuþe of þis book among hooly bokis, Lire here'.[160] The translation of Lyra, supplemented with material from the *Glossa Ordinaria*, also supplied intratextual glosses in the New Testament in the Earlier Version, such as 'vncoruptible, þat may not deie

156 From Joshua onwards, the presence of glosses in B is not recorded in *WB*. For the text of the unique glosses, see Appendix 2.

157 See Appendix 4. In B, the glosses also intrude into the biblical text columns throughout Job, fols. 220v–233r

158 'The Vernacular Scriptures: The Wycliffite Versions', p. 412. Hargreaves, however, is not aware of the extensive glosses in Job in B. Is. 5:1–7 (only) is extensively glossed, within the text, in BL Lansdowne 455.

159 A number of scholars were involved, including Anselm of Laon, working in various Northern French schools and religious houses between c. 1090 and c. 1140; see Beryl Smalley, '*Glossa ordinaria*', *Theologische Realencyclopëdie* XIII (1984), 452–7, and Margaret T. Gibson, 'The Glossed Bible', in *Biblia Latina cum Glossa Ordinaria*, facsimile reprint, vol. I (Turnhout: Brepols, 1992), pp. vii–xi.

160 *WB*, II.658, *om.* I; see p. 100, above.

ne be peirid [damaged]' (Rom. 1:23), which is identical in wording to a marginal gloss in British Library Harley 5017 (part of the same Bible as Royal 1. C. IX), 'þat is, þat may not die ne be peirid, Lyre here'.[161] The Later Version has no intratextual gloss at this point.

The marginal glosses from Romans 1:20 to Apocalypse 1 in Harley 5017 clearly derive from the same document as the marginal glosses from 1 Corinthians 6:4 to Jude in New College Oxford 67, a New Testament in a much-revised Earlier Version. The lemmata in the glosses in both manuscripts are predominantly in a revised form of the Earlier Version similar to that in New College Oxford 67, as Hargreaves demonstrates, but it does not necessarily follow that the glosses were written in order to accompany a New Testament with a text of this kind.[162] The gloss-text may already have existed, and the lemmata may have been adapted. In the Old Testament marginal glosses, the lemmata are usually in the Later Version, and sometimes incorporate a textual gloss, as in 'manly *eþer curteis* [in hauynge compassioun on oure defautis]' (Wisd. 7:23).[163] Sometimes, however, the lemmata are in the Earlier Version, particularly in the Cotton Bible glosses in the Sapiential books: 'a serchere of maieste', for example, who pries too curiously into divine secrets, 'schal be oppressid of glorie' (Earlier Version), where the Later Version reads 'schal be put doun fro glorie' (Prov. 25:27).[164]

The translators presumably made their version of Lyra as and when they could, and used whatever manuscripts of the biblical translation happened to be at hand at the time. Both in the Old and the New Testament glosses the biblical text is sometimes translated directly from Lyra, and resembles neither the Earlier nor the Later Versions.[165] In the gloss in Proverbs on the four things whose ways are unknowable, Lyra (translated in the Cotton Bible) interprets the way of an eagle in the air as 'Crist in his assencioun', the way of a serpent on a rock as 'Crist in his rising aȝen', the way of a ship in the middle of the sea as 'Crist in his conuersacioun in þe world', and the way of a man 'Crist parfit man in kunnyng and vertues, in a ȝong wexinge womman

161 Lindberg, *EV*, VIII.76 (*om.* X); *WB*, IV.305. K has an abbreviated version of the same gloss, 'eþer þat mai not dye'.

162 Hargreaves, 'The Marginal Glosses to the Wycliffite New Testament', 284–300.

163 *WB*, III.97, gloss in C; 'manly eþer curteis' LV, 'curteis' A. At Eccl. 7:30, the lemma of C's gloss is the LV textual gloss, 'eþer expownyng of a word', *WB*, III.43.

164 Lindberg, *EV*, IV.269 (*E*); *WB*, III.41; the biblical text in C reads as LV. See also 'woundis of þe louyere' (EV) in the gloss on Prov. 27:5, *WB*, III.43, Lindberg, *EV*, IV.270; 'and Y knew not þe kunnyng of seyntis' (EV) in the gloss on Prov. 30:3, *WB*, III.48, Lindberg, *EV*, IV.273.

165 For example, 'preie not for it [for it is not to preie for hem þat ben dampned]' (marg. e*V*) [Lyra] (1 John 5:16); 'not for it Y seie þat ony man preie' EV LV; *WB*, IV.629. See also Job 3:2, above.

[*adolescentula*], þat is in þe blessid virgyn' (Prov. 30:19).[166] The Later Version follows the reading of the Latin Bible, 'þe weie of a man in ȝong wexinge age' ('viam viri in adulescentia'),[167] but Lyra knows that the Hebrew text means 'the way of a man in/with a young woman', and that, since the whole verse is christological, the text must literally be referring to Mary: 'hec est vera littera quia sic est in hebraeo, et dicit hic *adolescentula* beata virgo Maria'. To us, textual and interpretive kinds of knowing seem very different; Lyra, however, was as confident of the latter as he was of the former.

Here, the text of the English Bible is not revised in accordance with Lyra's commentary. The translators no doubt regarded this as a case of the Hebrew text being at variance with the Latin, and in such cases their usual practice was to translate the text of the Latin Bible and record the Hebrew in the margin – although not, on the evidence of the surviving manuscripts, by any means consistently. Where, on the other hand, Lyra comments that emended Latin Bibles have one reading and unemended Bibles have another, the Later Version typically corrects the Earlier Version in line with what Lyra determines to be the correct reading.[168] Lyra's *Postilla* is simultaneously an interpretive commentary and a *correctorium*, a textual commentary, and many of the glosses in the Later Version are correctorial comments, often giving Lyra's authority for corrections the revisers have already made.[169] A gloss in the Cotton Bible on God hurling 'gloriouse men fro hir bed' ('de lecto suo', Ecclus 48:6) comments on the variant 'for her trespas' (delicto suo), although the Earlier and Later Versions both have the correct reading here.[170] Conversely, there are many correctorial glosses that are not matched by an emended text: a marginal gloss in the Cotton Bible and six other manuscripts at Numbers 11:4 reads 'desire of fleischis [*carnium*], *þis word*, of fleischis, *is not in Ebreu neþer in bokis amendid, for þei* [the Israelites in the desert] *desiriden fleischis and fischis and oþere þingis as it is seid wiþynne*, Lire here', but all Wycliffite Bible manuscripts nevertheless preserve the interpolation.[171]

The text of 1–4 Kings includes many interpolations, a good number of which are preserved in the Later Version in spite of correctorial glosses in

166 C, *WB*, III.49.
167 EV, similarly, reads 'þe weye of a man in his waxynge ȝouþe', Lindberg, *EV*, IV.274 (*E*). No Latin Bible reads *adulescentia*, but *BS* restores this reading on the authority of the Masoretic text.
168 See Appendix 3, and pp. 180–2, below.
169 For example at Deut. 33:23 (C, *WB*, I.551), 2 Kings 24:24 (BC, *WB*, II.157), Is. 26:1, 'Sion' (K, *WB*, III.268), 2 Macc. 3:1 (U, *WB*, III.852), 2 Macc. 11:18, 'he grauntide' (PEUY, *WB*, III.881) Apoc. 14:18 (*V*, *WB*, IV.665), Apoc. 22:14 (*V*, *WB*, IV.681).
170 *WB*, III.216; Lindberg, *EV*, V.99 ('his' *corr.* 'þeir', *al. m. E*).
171 Marg. CdGKQX; *WB*, I.395; see Appendix 3.

Lyra, but at one point the translators intended to remove an interpolation and instead preserved the interpolation and removed a part of the text. 'And Dauid brak togidre his men wiþ þes wordis and suffride hem not þat þei rysen into Saul' (1 Kings 24:8, EV) is omitted in the Later Version, in line with the correctorial gloss in the Cotton Bible, 'Crist of þe lord ['christum domini', the last words of the interpolation in 1 Kings 24:7], *in summe bokis it sueþ*, and Dauyþ brak hise men bi siche wordis and suffride not hem þat þey risiden aȝenus Saul, *but þis lettre is not in Ebreu neþer in bokis amendid*, Lire here' [see fig. 11].[172] What Lyra says, however, is 'Vivit deus [the first words of the interpolation in 1 Kings 24:7] usque ibi exclusive Et confregit Dauid ['and Dauyþ brak', 24:8] non est in hebreo nec in libris correctis.'[173] A translator misreads Lyra and wrongly identifies the interpolation; the revisers delete the wrong part of the text, making the Later Version an unholy mess at this point. The coincidence of the error in the gloss in the Cotton Bible and the error in the text of the Later Version implies a common English original.

The glosses in the Cotton Bible are so similar to the glosses it shares with British Library Royal 1. C. IX that both sets of glosses undoubtedly derive from the same original.[174] In Kings, however, the glosses in the Royal Bible are often abbreviated. The gloss on the death of Achitophel reads, in the Royal Bible, 'he perischide bi hangyng, *þat is hangide him silf*' (2 Kings 17:23), but the Cotton Bible has a more extended gloss, explaining the reasons for Achitophel's suicide:

> He hangide him silf for indignacioun þat his councel was not doon, and for bi þe foly of Absolon and of his puple he perseyuede and helde for certeyn þat Dauyþ schulde haue þe maistry and turne aȝen in to þe rewme, wherfor he dredde to be slayn of him bi foul deþ and peyneful, and þerfor he wolde haste his deþ bi an oþer weye, Lire here.[175]

Commenting on the literal meaning of the biblical text involves commenting on the literary as well, and Lyra is at his literary-critical best here, thinking through Achitophel's motives in the context of the narrative as a whole.

[172] *WB*, II.71; Lindberg, *EV*, III.98 (*E*); see Appendix 3.

[173] The text of the interpolation in LV is 'Þe lord lyueþ, for no but þe lord smyte him, eþer his dai come þat he die, eþer he go soun in to batel and perische, þe lord be merciful to me, þat Y sende not myn hond in to þe crist of þe lord'. This text, as the *correctoria* point out (see Appendix 3), belongs at 1 Kings 26:10–11.

[174] The only hint of independent translation of Lyra is 'þe laste men [*novissimi*], *þat is of vile persoones*' ('de vilibus personis', Lyra, 4 Kings 17:32) (C), *WB*, II.286, '*þat is of þe fouliste men*' (B); see Appendix 2.

[175] *WB*, II.134.

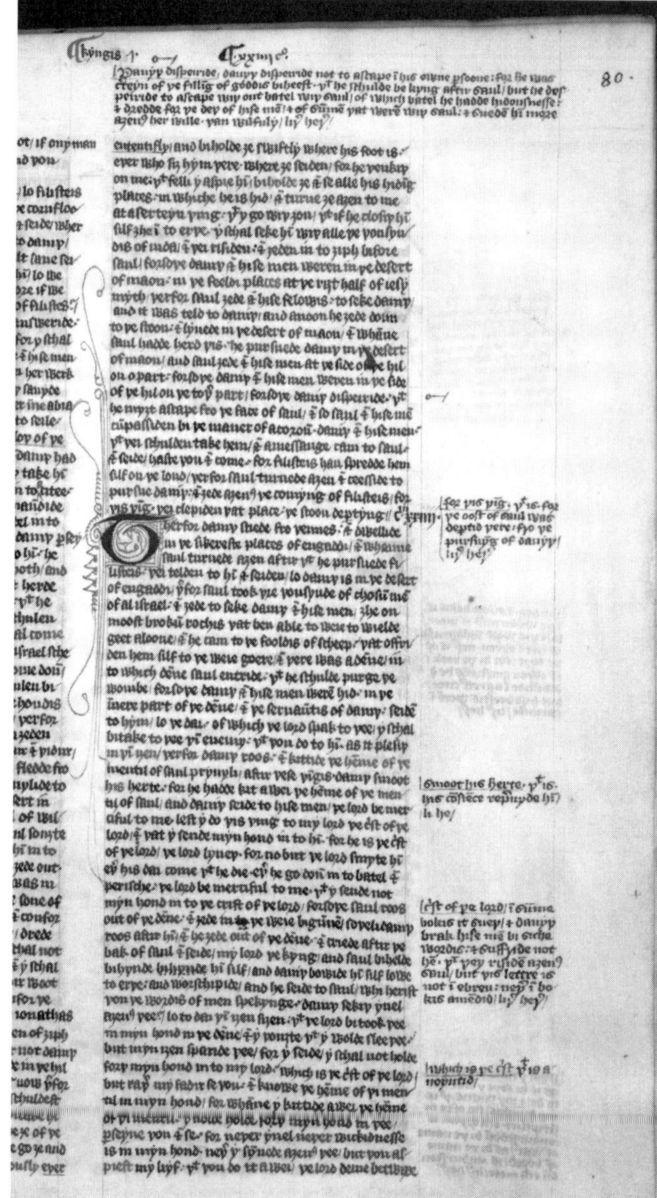

Figure 11. Marginal glosses in British Library Cotton Claudius E. II, fol. 80r. London (?), c. 1410. Reproduced by permission of the British Library Board.

Where the glosses in the Cotton Bible are fuller than those in the Royal Bible, the Cotton Bible is likely to be closer to the original text. Hargreaves makes the same point about the relationship between the New Testament glosses in New College Oxford 67 and British Library Harley 5017, where the latter often omits or summarizes material in the former.[176] It may be that the same original text, a translation of Lyra with supplementary material from the *Glossa Ordinaria*, lies behind both the Old and the New Testament glosses, but, if so, the text of the New Testament glosses seems to have derived far more material from the Gloss than the Old Testament glosses do, and to have been far more scrupulous than the Old Testament glosses are about naming the authorities cited in the Gloss. The Old Testament glosses sometimes make a distinction between marginal and 'enterlinarie' glosses in the *Glossa Ordinaria*, but only very occasionally name their authors. In the gloss on God's 'sorewe of herte' (Gen. 6:6), for example, Lyra's comment, 'for he hadde him silf at þe maner of a man sorowinge in doynge awey man whom he had formed to his ymage', is followed by a comment on predestination, attributed simply to 'þe glos here', and then by 'God semeþ to repente while he chaungiþ þe werk, neþeles his wil and ordinaunce dwelliþ vnchaungeable', attributed to 'þe glose enterlinarie here'.[177]

In contrast, in the composite gloss on 'temptacioun take ȝou not, no but manes [temptacioun]'[178] ('temptatio vos non adprehendat nisi humana', 1 Cor. 10:13), the first interpretation, that 'human temptation' refers to 'venial synne', is attributed to 'Lyre here and þe Glos in sentence [in agreement]'; the second interpretation, that 'human temptation' refers to seeking man's help and despairing of God's, rather than suffering with Christ-like fortitude, is attributed to 'þe Glose here rehersinge Ambrose', and the third, that it refers to human frailty, or self-righteousness, or 'enuie to beter men', leading to 'discencioun and þe sacrilegie of eresie', is attributed to 'þe Glose here rehersinge Austin in his book of þe lordis sermoun in þe hill [*De Sermone Dei in Monte*] and in his book of baptism [*De Baptismo contra Donastistas*]'.[179] It is possible, of course, that the translators' text of the *Glossa Ordinaria* named its authorities more fully in the New Testament volumes than in the Old,[180] and it also possible that the labour was divided

176 Hargreaves, 'The Marginal Glosses to the Wycliffite New Testament', 290–1.

177 Marg. BFGKP_SQUX, *WB*, I.89. Only P_S has 'þe glos here' at the right place; the other MSS (and *WB*), place the attribution after 'þe werk'. A gloss at 2 Kings 24:1 cites Gregory in the Gloss (C), *WB*, II.154–5, and a gloss at Is. 1:23 cites Jerome in the *Glossa Ordinaria* (C), *WB*, III.229.

178 Lindberg, *EV*, VIII.106 (*X*); the lemma is 'no but mannus temptacioun', *V*, VIII.105.

179 e*V*, *WB*, IV.356–7. The gloss in e ends (due to lack of space) at 'Austin'.

180 In the first printed edition of the *Glossa Ordinaria*, Augustine is named in the glosses on 1 Cor. 10:13, but not Ambrose, and the works of Augustine from which the material is derived are not named; Margaret Gibson and Karlfried Froehlich, eds., *Biblia Latina cum Glossa Ordinaria*, 4 vols. (Turnhout: Brepols, 1992).

among different translators, who followed different practices in this respect. The relative lack of material from the Gloss in the Old Testament glosses, and the ubiquity of Lyra, is not surprising; the emphasis of the Gloss is on spiritual rather than literal interpretation, and the translators perceived questions concerning the letter of the text, Lyra's speciality, to be far more significant in the Hebrew scriptures than in the Greek. The text of the marginal glosses as preserved in the Cotton Bible and British Library Royal 1. C. IX often includes Lyra's citations of other authorities, especially Augustine, Gregory and Jerome but also Aristotle, Aquinas and Comestor, and it sometimes names the source-texts as well – Jerome's *Quaestiones Hebraicae* at least seven times.[181] Such details occur only occasionally in the series of glosses in the Pentateuch, Chronicles and Maccabees, which present Lyra's own interpretation.

Hargreaves presumes that the very few marginal glosses in the New Testament included in manuscripts other than New College Oxford 67 and British Library Harley 5017 derive from the same text that was the source of the extensive glosses in those manuscripts.[182] Similarly, I presume that all the marginal glosses in the Old Testament, with the exception of the moral glosses in Bodley 277 and the two revised manuscripts related to it, derive from the same text that was the source of the extensive glosses in the Cotton Bible and in British Library Royal 1. C. IX. This text was also, I think, the source of the Lyran glosses in the Glossed Psalter, Bodley 554. The degree to which the source-text is abbreviated differs from manuscript to manuscript, and from book to book within the same manuscript. Bodleian Fairfax 2, which includes a greater number of glosses than any manuscript except the Cotton and Royal Bibles, characteristically cuts the glosses to their essence in Job, Psalms and Proverbs, but not elsewhere. Abbreviation can lead to muddle: the Glossed Psalter's gloss on 'lownesse, *bi which a man is maad low bi tribulacioun*, Austin, *in Ebreu it is*, on my turment, Lire here' (Ps. 118:50) is cut to the nonsensical 'lownesse, *maad bi turment*' in the Fairfax Bible.[183]

All the glosses in the Wycliffite Bible, marginal and textual, derive from the writings of biblical commentators who were highly esteemed by

[181] For example, Augustine *ad Simplicianum* is cited in the gloss on 1 Kg. 28:14 (C), *WB*, II.82, and *De Civitate Dei* and Gregory, *Homiliae in Evangelia*, on Esth. 3:2 (BC), *WB*, II.643. *Quaestiones Hebraicae* are cited at Gen. 41:45 (CGQ), *WB*, I.169, 1 Kings 3:2 (C), *WB*, II.12, 1 Kings 6:13 (C), *WB*, II.46, 1 Kings 25:2 (C), *WB*, II.73, 2 Kings 15:7 (C), *WB*, II.127, 2 Kings 24:1 (C), *WB*, II.154–5 and Job 1:1 (A BbEGHIKLNOPP_SQU), *WB*, II.672.

[182] Hargreaves, 'The Marginal Glosses to the Wycliffite New Testament', 291. Hargreaves does not mention the gloss at 1 Cor. 16:15, for which see Appendix 2.

[183] Text K, 'þat is maad bi turment', marg. V, *WB*, II.862; see Appendix 2.

late-medieval scholars in general, not just by the translators, and all the glosses are designed to make the 'sentence' of the English Bible as 'opin' as that of the Latin Bible – 'eiþer', as the writer of the Prologue says, 'openere in English as in Latyn'. When he says he has 'set in þe margyn bi maner of a glose what þe Ebru haþ', he is assuring the reader that the glosses in the English Bible are a necessary adjunct to understanding the literal sense of God's law; they are not glosses supplying spiritual senses at the expense of the literal sense, or making polemical points. Nevertheless, it is not entirely true that they are as 'free of partisanship as the text itself', as Hargreaves claims.[184] Where Lyra makes points that are particularly congenial to the translators, the Wycliffite translation of Lyra seems to have included some elaboration of its source.

Translating Lyra, a marginal gloss in the Cotton Bible explains why Hezekiah was justified in breaking the gates of the temple and seizing its riches to pay off Sennacherib, King of Assyria:

> Ezechie [Hezekiah] wiste þe puple suget to him and Achaz his fadir hadde offendid God in many maneris, and þerfor he dredde skilefuly lest for veniaunce of þe forseid yuels þe king of Assiriens schulde be suffrid to come on his rewme, and þerfor to kepe þe citee of Jerusalem where goddis worschip was in strengþe, and þe puple as myche as he myȝte fro distriyng [being destroyed], he spendide þe riches of þe temple and of þe king as þe text here seiþ, *brak þe ȝatis of þe temple*, in whiche myche gold was fastned bi kyngis biforgoinge, and bi him, to fairnesse and worschip; and bi nede he was compellid to do þis, for he hadde noon oþer þing wherof he myȝte paie so greet a summe. Of þis is had an argument, eþer preef, þat princes in nede moun take of þe tresours of þe chirche for þe sauyng of þe comyn puple, Lire here
> (4 Kings 18:16, *WB*, II.289–90)

The argument that the church could be deprived of its property in time of necessity was one with which Wyclif and the Wycliffites were profoundly in sympathy, and the translator of this gloss shows that he endorses Lyra's argument by providing details of authorities supporting it, with full references: 'Ambrose and *Decrees* . . . and Gregorie in his *Registre* . . . witnessen this pleynly.[185] And king Richard [I] dide þis in dede, as Sistrense [Higden] seiþ'. According to Higden, the money for Richard's ransom, a hundred

[184] 'The Vernacular Scriptures: The Wycliffite Versions', *CHB*, II.413. Hargreaves is contrasting the glosses in WB with Tyndale's tendentious glosses. There is one such gloss in S, at Exd. 6: 11, 'þus þe peple fariþ now for fere of þe prelatis more and lesse' (see *WB*, I.lvi) and another at Rom. 16:17, 'Loo how opinli cristen men ben forbeden to comoun not wiþ vicious prestis, þat for her coueitiise lustis disturblen þe chirche', *WB*, IV.336 (MS unidentified; not G).

[185] Ambrose, *De Officiis*, II.28, cited in *Decretum*, pars 2 causa xii quest. ii, ed. Richter and Friedberg, I .710; Gregory, *Registrum Epistularum*, VII, 13, 33, IX, 19, ed. Dag Norberg, CCSL CXL (Turnhout: Brepols, 1982), pp. 462–3, 506–7; CXL A, 579.

thousand pounds of silver, was extorted from the church, from regular and secular clerics alike.[186] The Wycliffite glossator cannot be accused of being controversial, but neither can there be any doubt that he believes Richard I's exactions were justified, and that Richard II would do well to take heed of his predecessor's example.

TRANSLATION AND TEXTUAL CRITICISM

The writer of the Prologue tells us that the translators intended 'to make þe sentence as trewe and open in English as it is in Latyn, eiþer more trewe and more open þan it is in Latyn' (*WB*, I.57/42–3). How open, we were considering in the previous section; now we investigate how 'trewe' the first English Bible is. Thomas More believed that the translation of the Bible by Wyclif, in his view a notorious heretic, must have 'purposely corrupted that holy texte, malycyously plantyng therein suche wordys as myght in the reders erys serue to the profe of suche heresyes as he went about to sow'.[187] In fact, the only textual evidence that has been adduced in support of purposeful corruption on the translators' part is the Wycliffite Bible's mistranslation of two words in the Gospels, 'pauperes evangelizantur' (Matt. 11:5; Luke 7:22), which the gospellers regard as one of the signs that Christ fulfils Isaiah's prophecies about the Messiah. The Earlier Version in the Christ Church Bible translates these words accurately, though gnomically, 'pore men ben preched' (Matt. 11:5),[188] but most other manuscripts of the Earlier Version read 'pore men ben taken to prechynge of þe gospel, or ben maad keepers of þe gospel'.[189] The Later Version selects the first alternative, 'pore men ben taken to prechyng of þe gospel'.[190] Herbert Workman suspects that the translators were falsifying the text 'in favour of Poor Priests', and this is one of the reasons why he 'regret[s] that Wyclif did not abandon his polemics, and devote himself to the supreme task of doing the Bible into the vernacular instead of handing it over to his assistants'.[191]

186 'Relaxatus est rex Ricardus pro centum millibus librarum argenti . . . extorta est tota lana alborum monachorum et canonicorum, quin etiam praelatorum anuli, vasa, cruces, calices, cum auro de feretris sanctorum abraso, sunt conflata': Higden, *Polychronicon*, VII, xxviii, ed. Lumby and Babington, *Polychronicon Ranulphi Higden*, VIII.128.

187 *A Dialogue Concerning Heresies*, ed. Lawler *et al.*, VI.314/28–31. See p. 39, above.

188 Lindberg, *EV*, VII.42 (*X*); this reading is recorded in the *apparatus criticus*, *WB*, IV. 27. At Luke 7:22 *X* reads as EV, Lindberg, *EV*, VII.128.

189 *WB*, IV.27, 167 (*K*). At Matt. 11:5, *OP*_P*U* Tokyo, Takamiya 28 read 'maad keperis of þe gospel', Lindberg, *EV*, VII.42. The alternative translation is omitted in L_o*OQ* at Luke 7:22, Lindberg, *EV*, VII.128.

190 *WB*, IV.27, 167.

191 *John Wyclif*: *A Study of the English Medieval Church*, II.176. The chief reason for his regret is that Wyclif, in his view, was a better stylist.

The Wycliffite translators were not alone, however, in having problems with 'pauperes evangelizantur'. In the English Wycliffite Sermons, the words are translated 'poore men ben preysud of God' (Matt. 11:5),[192] and the thirteenth-century French Bible has the poor being raised up, 'les povres sont eslevez', suggesting that the translators' Latin Bible may erroneously have read 'elevantur'.[193] Workman's suspicion is as unfounded as More's conviction that the translators 'purposely corrupted that holy texte'. The text of the Wycliffite Bible, as Deanesly says, is 'a remarkable attempt to produce a scholarly and accurate translation'.[194] The truth of scripture was central to Wyclif's thought and the topic of one of his most important works, and the translators aimed to make that truth transparent throughout the text of the first English Bible. No word of the translation was to be 'superflu eiþer false', even when words needed to be added to make the sense 'hool and open' (I.57/18–20).

Absolute accuracy was, of course, unachievable, but the Prologue-writer, offering the new English Bible as the common-profit book *par excellence*, 'for charite and for comoun profyt of cristene soulis', invites any wise man to 'sette in þe trewe sentence' where the translators have erred.[195] First, however, he should 'examyne truli his Latyn Bible, for no doute he shal fynde ful manye Bibles in Latyn ful false if he loke manie, nameli [especially] newe, and þe comune Latyn Biblis han more nede to be corrected, as manie as I haue seen in my lif, þan haþ þe English Bible late translatid'.[196] This boast that the newly translated English Bible is superior to most Latin Bibles is directed at enemies of biblical translation who were arguing, as Butler was to do in 1401, that a Bible in English would introduce and multiply error.[197] Even Ullerston, who determines that the benefits of translation outweigh the dangers, concedes that an English Bible is likely to disseminate errors characteristic of late-medieval Latin Bibles.[198]

The writer of the Prologue says that the corrupt state of the text in most books of the Latin Bible (predominantly in the Hebrew books of the Old Testament) can be estimated by the differences between the text of the Latin

[192] Except in Pembroke Coll. Camb. 237, where 'preysud' is *corr.* 'prechud': Gradon and Hudson, eds., *English Wycliffite Sermons*, vol. I (1983), p. 336/22, but at Luke 7: 22 the words are translated 'pore men ben / prechid gode': Pamela Gradon, ed., *English Wycliffite Sermons*, vol. III (1990), p. 17/19 to p. 18/1.

[193] Clive R. Sneddon, 'A Critical Edition of the Four Gospels in the Thirteenth-Century Old French Translation of the Bible', D.Phil. Dissertation, vol. II (Oxford, 1978), p. 32. Sneddon's base text is Rouen, Bibl. mun. A. 211. The variant 'elevantur' is not recorded in *BS*.

[194] *LB*, p. 231. [195] *WB*, I.57/43–5. [196] *WB*, I.57/45 to 58/3.

[197] Deanesly, *LB*, p. 401/6–7; see p. 21, above.

[198] Vienna, Österreichische Nationalbibl. 4133, fol. 195v; see p. 22, above.

Bible and the 'propre origynals' preserved in Jerome's commentaries.[199] He assumes, in other words, that an authoritative text of Jerome's translation of a biblical book can be extrapolated from his verse-by-verse analysis, which is true to a limited extent. No doubt the Prologue-writer had observed for himself the differences he mentions, although the many allusions in the marginal glosses to Jerome's Latin text, and to Jerome's comments on textual questions, almost without exception derive from Lyra. At all events, the final chapter of the Prologue claims that the first stage in the translation process was the establishing of a corrected, authoritative text of the Latin Bible from which to translate: 'þis symple creature hadde myche trauaile wiþ diuerse felawis and helperis to gedere manie elde Biblis, and oþere doctouris and comune glosis, and to make oo Latyn Bible sumdel [very] trewe'.[200]

One could wish that the writer had described the translators' procedure in greater detail. 'Assembling many old Bibles' sounds somewhat haphazard: presumably the translators sought out Bibles written before the thirteenth century, although they could have been sure of this only in the relatively rare cases where a Bible had a recorded history. Perhaps they sought out the 'great Bibles' typical of twelfth-century Bible production throughout Europe,[201] physically so different from the handy-sized Bibles produced in Paris from the early thirteenth century onwards. Conceivably they borrowed Bibles from great monastic libraries like that of Christ Church Priory, Canterbury, closely associated with Canterbury College, Oxford, of which Wyclif was warden from 1365 (although he was displaced by the Benedictine Henry Wodehull two years later, in acrimonious circumstances).[202] In any case, their criteria for distinguishing between biblical-textual traditions were rudimentary, and in establishing a 'correct' text of the Latin Bible from which to translate they certainly depended far more on the writings of 'doctouris', above all Jerome and Lyra, than on their own first-hand comparisons between the texts of Latin Bibles. They probably made such comparisons largely in order to confirm what the authorities said about the 'trewe' biblical text.

Surprisingly, there are no contemporary comments on the accuracy of the translation. The earliest comment is also one of the earliest references in Wycliffite Bible manuscripts to Wyclif as translator. A marginal note in Corpus Christi College Cambridge Parker 147, probably in the hand of Blyth,

[199] *WB*, I.58/9–11; see Hudson, *SEWW*, p. 176.
[200] *WB*, I.57/7–9. For 'sumdel' meaning 'very', see *MED som-del*, (c).
[201] See Walter Cahn, *Romanesque Bible Illumination* (Ithaca: Cornell University Press, 1982), and De Hamel, *Book*, pp. 78–91.
[202] See Larsen, 'John Wyclif, c. 1331–1384', in Levy, ed., *A Companion to John Wyclif*, p. 14.

who annotated the Prologue in this Bible, accuses Wyclif of being ignorant of Latin because he translates 'erodii domus dux est eorum' (Ps.103:17 in the Gallican Psalter) as 'þe hous of þe gerfaukun [gerfalcon] is þe leader of þo', although *erodius* means 'stork'.[203] The Wycliffite translators were perhaps following Rolle, in whose *Psalter* the words are translated 'hous of þe gerfawkyn is leder of þaim'.[204] By any standards 'gerfaukun' is a minor error: the bird named in this verse in the Psalter *Iuxta Hebraicum* is *milvus*, 'bird of prey' (although the Hebrew word means 'stork'), and the reading in Augustine's commentary on Psalms is 'fulicae domus dux est eorum', a *fulica* being, says Augustine, a 'marina auis', sea-bird.[205] In one thirteenth-century French Bible, a scribe feels it necessary to add a gloss explaining that an 'erodion' is a kind of bird: 'la mesniee d'erodion, *ce est de cel oisel qui a non herodion*, est leur conduiz'.[206] Whoever wrote the finicky note in the Corpus Christi Cambridge Bible was clutching at anti-Wycliffite straws, and the translators would not have worried unduly about such comments.

Enemies of Wyclif could, however, have identified gaffes if they had looked carefully. Egregious errors in the earliest stages of the translation were usually corrected during the process of revision, as one would expect, but anyone happening to look at Bodley 959 with the intention of finding fault could have seen that 'misericordia uberi' (Ps. 91:11) had been translated 'in þe mercy of þe tete', before this was crossed through and corrected 'plenteous mercy',[207] or that 'adoravit rex in lectulo suo' (3 Kings 1:47) had been translated 'kyng Dauiþ smellede in his bed', before this was crossed through and corrected 'honouride'.[208] Hereford has been blamed for these and several other howlers in the Old Testament before Baruch 3:20, but more than one translator may well have been involved.[209] Occasionally, an error in the Earlier Version which is simply the result of mistranslation survives in Bodley 959 and all other manuscripts. In the phrase 'in medio tui Hierusalem' (Ps. 115:19), 'tui' is ambiguous: the translators of the Earlier Version read it as a possessive, 'in þe myddel of þi Jerusalem', but the revisers, during the production of the Later Version, realized that it was

203 Fol. 227v, *WB*, II.842; see Appendix 4. On the note, see *WB*, I.xlvi (but the biblical ref. there is incorrect, and the note is now in the gutter in V). EV also reads 'jerfacoun', Lindberg, *EV*, IV.223.

204 Ed. Bramley, *The Psalter or Psalms of David*, p. 363.

205 *Enarrationes in Psalmos* [Ps.103:17]; ed. Dekkers and Fraipont, CCSL XL.1513–14. On the Masoretic reading, 'the stork has her home in the junipers', see Emmanuel Tov, *Textual Criticism of the Hebrew Bible*, 2nd edn (Minneapolis: Fortress Press, 1992), p. 132.

206 BL Harley 616, fol. 307v.

207 *Marg. al. m.*, see Lindberg, *EV*, IV.218, and p. 143, above.

208 *Marg. al. m.*, see ibid., III.146, 319. Perhaps the Latin text read 'odoravit', but, if so, the translator should have realized that this was a copyist's mistake.

209 For other examples, see Fristedt, *WB*, *I*.54, Hargreaves, 'The Vernacular Scriptures: The Wycliffite Versions', *CHB*, II.401–2, and Lindberg, *EV*, V.91.

a pronoun and accordingly translated 'in þe myd of þee, Jerusalem'.[210] In fairness to the translators producing the Earlier Version, they anticipated that their work was going to be corrected, and it is only by chance that a record of gross and of more excusable mistakes survives in Bodley 959.

Given his insistence on the accuracy of the text of the English Bible, the writer of the Prologue would have been less than happy to know that in the judgment of Lindberg and Raphael Loewe the text of the Earlier Version of the Wycliffite Bible derives from a manuscript like Bibliothèque nationale lat. 15467, written in the Sorbonne in the early thirteenth century and manifesting the errors typical of Latin Bibles of this date.[211] In this manuscript, for example, and in Bodley 959 before correction, Lamech lived for five hundred and eight-five years (Gen. 5:30), but 'eyȝty' is corrected to 'nynti' over an erasure in Bodley 959, and all Wycliffite Bible manuscripts have the correct reading.[212] The same correction is made in Bodleian Laud Lat. 113, a Latin Bible written in Oxford, c. 1240–50, and illuminated by William de Brailes, whose workshop was in Catte Street; this manuscript includes a *correctorium*.[213] The Latin text of Genesis 5:30 and the English translation of it were corrected during the production of the Earlier Version, as they were also in the account of the death of Terah, father of Abraham. Bodley 959 reads 'þe days of Thare ben made' ('facti sunt dies Thare', Gen. 11:32), but before correction it read 'þe days ben made', *Thare* presumably lacking in the translator's original at that point, as it is, before correction, in Bibliothèque nationale Mazarin lat. 5, another manuscript with characteristic thirteenth-century errors.[214] In the Song of Songs, before correction Bodley 959 translates 'pulchrae sunt genae tuae sicut turturis' (1:9) as 'faire ben þy cheekis as a tour', the Latin text from which the translation was made evidently reading 'turris' ('of a tower'), as does Bodleian Canon Bib. Lat. 47, a Latin Bible written in Paris c. 1240–50.[215] 'As a tour' is

[210] Ibid., IV.231 (*E*); *WB*, II.857; see Hargreaves, 'The Latin Text of Purvey's Psalter', 75.

[211] Lindberg, *EV*, I.19 (Lindberg is referring specifically to *E*); Loewe, 'The Medieval History of the Latin Vulgate', *CHB*, II.104–5. In *BS*, BN lat. 15467 has the siglum Ω^{S}, Ω being the siglum for the archetype of the 'Paris' text: *BS*, I.xxxvii, xl–xli, but see p. 24, above.

[212] Lindberg, *EV*, I.42; *WB*, I.88; see Appendix 3.

[213] On this MS, see J. J. G. Alexander, 'English or French? Thirteenth-century Bibles', in *Manuscripts at Oxford: An Exhibition in Honour of Richard William Hunt*, ed. A. C. de la Mare and B. C. Barker-Benfield (Oxford: Bodleian Library, 1980), p. 71, fig. 46, and O. Pächt and J. J. G. Alexander, *Illuminated Manuscripts in the Bodleian Library*, vol. III (Oxford: Clarendon Press, 1973), no.435, pl.xxxvii.

[214] 'of Thare' inserted *al. m.*, see Lindberg, *EV*, I.19, 48; Ω^{M} in *BS*, I.xxxviii. None of the Latin Bibles selected for this study, all written in France or England in the thirteenth or fourteenth centuries, has this reading; see Appendix 3.

[215] Lindberg, *EV*, IV.286, 379; see further Appendix 3. On the Bodleian MS, see Pächt and Alexander, *Illuminated Manuscripts in the Bodleian Library*, vol. I (1966), no. 562. In Bodl. Lyell 7, 'turris' is *corr.* 'turturis'. For other examples of correction of *E pr. m.*, see Lindberg, *EV*, I.19–20.

crossed through, and 'of a turtir [turtle-dove]' substituted in the margin (see fig. 10).

The translators would not have expected their work in progress to be available for scrutiny by later generations. The corrections do, however, reveal, as Lindberg demonstrates, that the text of Bodley 959 before correction is based on a Latin Bible with a text of the 'Parisian' (early thirteenth-century) type. To complicate matters, some of the 'corrections' also derive from a text of the same type. Where the lover in the Song of Songs, for example, commands his friends 'ne makeþ þe leef to wake' ('neque evigilare faciatis dilectam', 2:7), 'þe' is crossed through, expuncted and corrected 'my' in the same hand (see fig. 10), and all other Earlier Version manuscripts read 'my leef', but 'meam' is an interpolation characteristic of late-medieval Latin Bibles (albeit a very natural one in context). The Later Version, correcting the Earlier Version and altering the ungendered 'leef', reads 'neþer make to awake þe dereworþe spousesse'.[216] Another miscorrection in Bodley 959 occurs in the genealogy of the kings of Edom, descendents of Esau, where Anah is described in the Latin Bible as 'that Anah who found hot springs in the wilderness when he was feeding the asses [*cum pasceret asinos*] of his father, Zibeon' (Gen. 36:24). Before correction, Bodley 959 translates 'whenne he fed þe asseȝ', but 'asseȝ' is altered to 'she asseȝ', *asinas* (fem.) being a well-established variant; it occurs, for example, in a tenth-century Bible from León.[217] The Later Version corrects the text once again, following Lyra and restoring the better reading ('whanne he kepte þe assis').[218]

Whether Anah's asses were male or female is a minor detail, but the translators were concerned enough with accuracy to revise the reading twice (at least), the first time supposing that the accurate text from which they were translating was in error because its reading differed from that of most late-medieval Latin Bibles, and the second time realizing that the reading of the majority of late-medieval Latin Bibles was inferior. It looks as though the Latin Bible from which parts of the earliest translation were made happened to have an unusually good text, but that the translators only became aware of this after they had worked for some time on the text of the Latin Bible.[219] The fact that what at first appeared to be errors were (mis)corrected during the production of the Earlier Version shows that work on the text of the Latin Bible was proceeding at the same time as work on the

216 Ibid., IV.379 (*E*); *WB*, III.75; BXIII also reads 'm'amie'; see further Appendix 3.

217 Add. marg. *al. m.*, see Lindberg, *EV*, I.81 ('she asses' also in *X*); Colegiata de San Isidoro, Cod. 2 (960 CE); see further Appendix 3.

218 *WB*, I.156, see *WB*, I.xxii. For other examples, see Lindberg, *EV*, III.28–33 (etc.).

219 Some readings of *E pr. m.* before correction are better than either EV or LV, e.g. Song of Songs 2:13; see Lindberg, *EV*, IV.379, and Appendix 3.

translation. As we have noted before, work on all the stages of the translation process described in the Prologue must have proceeded simultaneously.[220] As work progressed, and the translators made more systematic use of Lyra, they realized that the translation required a considerable amount of textual revision, as well as the stylistic revision already envisaged.

Nevertheless, the readings of the Earlier Version are sometimes better than the readings of the Later Version. In the second verse of Genesis, for instance, the Earlier Version reads 'þe spirite of God was (y)born vp on þe waters' ('spiritus dei [elohim] ferebatur super aquas', Gen. 1:2).[221] The revised translation in the Later Version reads 'þe spiryt of þe lord was borun on þe watris' (*WB*, I.78), the translators adopting the reading 'spiritus domini' not recorded before the twelfth century. 'Spiritus domini' is the reading in two great Spanish Bibles, the Codex Burgensis, written in San Pedro de Cardeña in the twelfth century, and the Codex Historialis, written in San Millán de la Cogolla, Castile, at the beginning of the thirteenth century.[222] It is also found in Latin Bibles written in France and England in the thirteenth and fourteenth centuries (including the Bible made for Robert de Bello (Abbot of St Augustine's Canterbury, 1230–40), in early printed editions of the Vulgate and in the first printed edition of the Gloss.[223]

In this case, the Latin Bible from which Genesis in the Earlier Version was translated had the correct reading, as does the Anglo-Norman translation of Genesis to Tobit made in Reading Abbey in the late fourteenth century ('l'esprit de nostre pere').[224] The prologue to Genesis in the thirteenth-century French Bible comments that Isidore identifies 'li esperiz damedieu' as the Holy Spirit.[225] The reading in Lyra's *Postilla* is 'spiritus dei'. If the Wycliffite translators had consulted Bodleian Laud Lat. 13, the Oxford Bible illuminated by De Brailes, they would have seen that the original

[220] Hudson, *PR*, p. 243; see p. 101, above.

[221] Lindberg, *EV*, I.37 (*E*); the Southern participial prefix 'y-' is erased, in line with usual practice in the Prefatory Epistles and Genesis in *E*, see *EV*, I.18–19.

[222] Burgos, Biblioteca Provincial cod. 846; Madrid, Bibl. de la Real Acad. de la Hist. 2–3; on the Burgos Bible, see Cahn, *Romanesque Bible Illumination*, pp. 289–90, and De Hamel, *Book*, p. 78, and on the Madrid Bible, see John J. Williams, 'A Castilian Tradition of Bible Illustration: The Romanesque Bible from San Millán', *Journal of the Warburg and Courtauld Institutes* 28 (1965), 66–85. The Bury Bible and the Winchester Bible both read 'spiritus dei'.

[223] See Dahan, 'La critique textuelle dans les correctoires de la Bible du XIIIe siècle', in De Libera *et al.*, eds., *Etudes de philosophie médiévale, langages et philosophie* (Paris: Vrin, 1997), p. 382. It is perhaps too recent an error to be picked up by the *correctoria*. For further details, see Appendix 3.

[224] BL Royal 1. C. III; see Berger, *La Bible française au Moyen Age*, pp. 231–7, 386, and p. 84, above.

[225] BL Harley 616, fol. 1v. The *Glossa Ordinaria* cites Jerome to the same effect. On the prologue to BXIII, see Clive R. Sneddon, 'Translation Technique and the *Old French Bible*', *Forum for Modern Language Studies* 35 (1999), 346.

reading, 'domini', is expuncted and corrected 'dei'. But, rather surprisingly, the translators revising the text of the Earlier Version determined that the 'trewe' reading in 'elde Biblis' was 'þe spiryt of þe lord', possibly because they interpreted the words as a reference to the presence of Christ with God before the Creation, in accordance with the opening words of John's Gospel. In the absence of a critical edition of the Latin Bible, Forshall and Madden thought the Later Version was correcting the Earlier Version here, but in this case the Earlier Version is more authoritative.[226]

In the New Testament, the Earlier Version has Jesus seeing Peter and Andrew 'sendende net in to þe se' ('mittentes rete in mare', Matt. 4:18), a better reading than the Later Version's 'nettis', although the reading 'retia' goes back to at least 800, and is found in the Oxford De Brailes Bible (where is it not corrected), and in the thirteenth-century French Bible.[227] The fifteenth-century Latin-English glossary, based on the Later Version of the Wycliffite Bible, corrects it here, reading 'rete, þe nett'.[228] In the Epistle to the Galatians, the Earlier Version correctly reads 'God sente þe Spirit of his Sone' ('misit deus spiritum filii sui', Gal. 4:6), where the Later Version has the inaccurate 'God sente his Spirit', which has no textual authority but is also found in the thirteenth-century French Bible.[229] The verse is an important locus for the doctine of the double procession of the Holy Spirit (Lyra comments here that 'the Holy Spirit is called the Spirit of the Son and of the Father, since the Holy Spirit proceeds from both'), which makes the translators' error puzzling.

Some manuscripts of the Earlier Version, in the New Testament only, share revisions with the Later Version. When Jesus reminds his disciples what 'alle profetes and lawe til Jon Baptist profecieden' (Matt. 11:13), the Later Version corrects 'til to Joon', and so do five Earlier Version manuscripts, including New College Oxford 67, the manuscript with extensive marginal glossing.[230] This glossed manuscript is extensively revised in line with the Later Version, even copying the Later Version's 'walke ȝe and stonde ȝe in þe feiþ' for 'wake ȝee' ('vigilate', 1 Cor. 16:13), which certainly

226 *WB*, I.xxii. EV is also correct at Song of Songs 7:13 and Ecclus 43:15, see Appendix 2.

227 Lindberg, *EV*, VII.31 (*X*); *WB*, IV.9; see Appendix 3. Again, Forshall and Madden think LV has the better reading, *WB*, I.xxii.

228 BL Add. 34305, fol. 104v.

229 Lindberg, *EV*, VIII.133 (*X*); *WB*, IV.403. Tertullian's Old Latin text may have read 'spiritum suum'; cf. *Adversus Marcionem*, PL II.476, but none of the selected Latin Bibles has this reading; see Appendix 3.

230 Lindberg, *EV*, VII.42–3 (*X*); *WB*, IV.27, see *WB*, I.xxii (none of the selected MSS reads 'usque ad Iohannem babtistam'). *NOP*_P*UV*[2] have the revised reading, cf. the revision in P_P*UV* at Mark 5:11; see Appendix 3.

derives from a scribal error in the archetype of the Later Version.[231] Among Later Version manuscripts, only Bodley 277 corrects this error.[232]

More surprisingly, some manuscripts of the Earlier Version, in the New Testament, have revised readings that are unrevised in the Later Version. The clearest example is in the parable of the royal wedding feast in Matthew's Gospel. In both Earlier and Later Versions, in the tract 'The holi prophete Dauid seiþ', and in the concordance to the New Testament, the king tells his guests 'my bolis [bulls] and my volatilis [winged creatures] ben slayne' (Matt. 22:4), although the Latin Bible reads 'tauri mei et altilia [beasts fattened for slaughter]', and no variant 'alati' has been recorded.[233] The thirteenth-century French Bible makes the same mistake, 'mes toreax et mes voleilles sont ocises'.[234] 'Volatilis' is, however, corrected to 'fatte beestis' in five manuscripts of the Earlier Version (including the glossed manuscript), indicating that this version was being corrected (in the Gospels, at least) independently of the Later Version, after the Later Version was complete.[235] This is consonant with the fact that three of these five manuscripts are the only Wycliffite Bible manuscripts to include the first four verses of Luke, borrowed from Glossed Luke in the *Glossed Gospels*.[236] That at least some parts of the production of the Later Version and some parts of the revision of the New Testament in the Earlier Version were carried out separately seems an inescapable conclusion.

Yet although some manuscripts of the Earlier Version have revised readings in the New Testament where the Later Version retains the earlier reading, and although the revisers producing the Later Version sometimes introduce an inferior reading, in numerous cases the Later Version corrects the text of the Earlier Version, where the text of the Earlier Version is based on an inferior or inaccurate reading in the Latin Bible(s) from which the translation was made. Often, the translators were alerted to such readings by their study of Lyra. In the Earlier Version, for example, Jacob, who has served seven years for Rachel and has been tricked into sleeping with her sister Leah, asks Laban 'why vnderputtis þou Lya to me?' ('why have you secretly brought Leah to me?'), whereas, in the Later Version, Jacob asks

231 Lindberg, *EV*, VIIII.115 (*X*); *WB*, IV.371. *V* shares LV's corrected reading at Apoc. 22:14, see Appendix 3.

232 'wa(l)ke', Lindberg, *KHB*, IV.205. The concordance to NT in WB has the correct reading, BL Royal 17. B. I, fol. 153v.

233 WB, IV.59; cf. Lindberg, *EV*, VII.63 (*X*); Deanesly, *LB*, p. 454; Royal 17. B. I, fol. 22r.

234 Sneddon, 'A Critical Edition of the Four Gospels', II.69.

235 *OP*_*PUV* Tokyo, Takamiya 28. See Lindberg, *EV*, VII.19–21.

236 P_*PUV*, Lindberg, *EV*, VII.113–14; see Appendix 3. Latin phrases from these verses are included in the Latin–English glossary, but the translation differs from that in Glossed Luke and is probably the glossator's own, BL Add. 34305, fol. 118v.

'whi hast þou disseyued me?' ('quare imposuisti mihi?', Gen. 29:25).[237] A marginal gloss in four manuscripts in the Later Version, one of the series of glosses in the Pentateuch, explains: 'þis [whi hast þou disseyued me] is þe verie lettre, as Lire seiþ here, but comyn Latyn bokis han þus, whi hast þou priuyly put Lya to me, but þis is fals lettre [*falsa est littera*], as Lire seiþ here'.[238] Both the *correctorium* of the Dominicans of St-Jacques, Paris, and the *correctorium* of Hugh of St Cher note that 'quare Lyam supposuisti me' is an incorrect reading, and it is underlined and corrected in the margin in the Oxford De Brailes Bible; but it is a common error in late-medieval Latin Bibles, and is also found in the thirteenth-century French Bible ('por quoi m'as tu baillie Lyam?'), and the Reading Abbey Anglo-Norman translation ('pur quei as tu mys a moy Lie?').[239]

Similarly, the revisers correct the Earlier Version's text of the blessing of Moses, at the end of the Pentateuch. In the Earlier Version, Moses blesses Naphtali and promises 'erly and mydday he shal weelde' (Deut. 33:23), reflecting the erroneous reading of the Codex Toletanus and a number of Latin Bibles of the thirteenth and fourteenth centuries, 'mane et meridiem possidebit'.[240] A marginal gloss in the Cotton Bible makes it clear that 'mane', a *lectio facilior*, should read 'mare [sea]': 'for þe see of Galile, as to þe souþ part þerof, felde in þe lot of Neptalym, Lire here' (*WB*, I.551). The Later Version restores the 'trewe' reading, 'he schal welde þe see and þe souþ'.[241] Translating the blessing of Moses on Israel, the Earlier Version reads 'þer ys noon oþer god as þe most riȝt god . . . þour [through] þe hydous doynge of hym to and fro rennyn þe cloudys' (Deut. 33:26).[242] The Later Version emends 'þe most riȝt god' to 'þe god of þe most riȝtful'; 'deus rectissimi', says Lyra, means 'the God of the people of Israel, who were governed by most righteous law'.[243] The Earlier Version's extraordinary 'þour þe hydous doynge of hym', perhaps the result of misreading 'magnificentia' as 'malificentia', is emended to 'cloudis rennen aboute bi þe glorie of hym' ('magnificentia eius discurrunt nubes').[244] The revisers did not need Lyra to see that the Earlier Version was in error here.

In the passage in praise of famous men in Ecclesiasticus, the Earlier Version has them 'in þer wisdam [*peritia*] sechende þe musyk maneris'

237 Lindberg, *EV*, I.71 (*E*); *WB*, I.138. 238 CGQX; *WB*, I.138. 239 See Appendix 3.

240 Lindberg, *EV*, II.171 (*E*); see Appendix 3.

241 *WB*, I.551, see *WB*, I.xxii. The *correctoria* of the Dominicans of St-Jacques and of Hugh of St Cher also correct 'mane'.

242 Lindberg, *EV*, II.171 (*E*).

243 *WB*, I.551; 'deus populi israel rectissima lege gubernati', Lyra; see Appendix 3. The Hebrew means 'O Jeshurun [Israel]'.

244 *WB*, I.551, see *WB*, I.xxii.

('requirentes modos musicos', Ecclus 44:5), but a Lyran gloss in the Cotton Bible reads 'bokis amendid han, in her childhed, þouȝ summe bokis han, in her kunnyng', and the Later Version accordingly reads 'in her childhod' ('like David', the *correctorium* of the Dominicans of St-Jacques points out).[245] 'The man who does not keep idols' (Bar. 6:72) is, illogically, a 'homo iniustus' in many late-medieval Bibles and 'vniust' in the Earlier Version, but 'iust' in the Later Version.[246] A telling instance in the New Testament shows the revisers restoring a reading for which Wyclif himself argues. In *De Veritate Sacrae Scripturae*, Wyclif says that 'in correctis codicibus' the reading of the words of Christ in John 10:35–6 is 'the scripture cannot be destroyed, whom [*quem*] the Father sanctified and sent into the world'; John is equating the text of the Bible (the word) with the human person of Christ (the incarnate Word).[247] This equation is central in Wyclif's writings.[248] Lyra's gloss on 'quem' is 'id est, meipsum' ('that is, myself'), and the Later Version rightly reads 'scripture may not be vndon, þilke þat [the one whom] þe fadir haþ halewid and haþ sent in to þe world', whereas the Earlier Version has the *lectio facilior* 'þe scripture whiche [*quam*] þe fader halewede'.[249]

Hargreaves's discussion of the Latin text from which the Later Version of the Wycliffite Psalter is translated includes several cases where the revisers correct in the Earlier Version an error or inferior reading characteristic of late-medieval Latin Bibles.[250] There are also places in the Psalms where errors characteristic of such Bibles find their way into Lyra's commentary and into the Later Version as a whole. One such place is 'effusa est contemptio super principes' ('contempt is poured out upon princes', Ps. 106:40), where both Wycliffite Versions read 'strijf' (*contentio*), in common with the first printed edition of the Gloss, Rolle's *Psalter*, the thirteenth-century French Bible, and Lyra, who provides a contemporary example of embattled princes, 'as we may see in the cities of Lombardy and elsewhere'.[251]

In places where the Later Version corrects the Earlier Version, all Later Version manuscripts normally have revisions in common. But this is not so in the translation of 'Sitivit anima mea ad Deum fortem vivum' (Ps. 41:3),

[245] *X*, cf. Lindberg, *EV*, IV.358 (*E*); *WB*, III.209; see Appendix 3.

[246] Lindberg, *EV*, VI.79 (*X*), *corr. al. m. K*; *WB*, III.500.

[247] *De Veritate*, I, 6; ed. Buddensieg, I.109/21 to 110/2.

[248] See Levy, *John Wyclif*, pp. 87–91, and Ghosh, *WH*, p. 55.

[249] *WB*, IV.267; Lindberg, *EV*, VII.185 (*X*).

[250] Hargreaves, 'The Latin Text of Purvey's Psalter', 74–5. At Ps. 17:13, LV follows Cassiodorus rather than Lyra: see Hargreaves, 'Latin Text', 86. For cases where LV incorporates Lyra into the translation, see p. 159, above.

[251] Lindberg, EV, IV.227 (*X*); *WB*, II.850; 'ut patet manifeste in ciuitatibus Lombardie et in aliis locis', Lyra; see Hargreaves, 'The Latin Text of Purvey's Psalter', 79, and Appendix 3.

where seven manuscripts read 'Mi soul þirstide to God, strong, quyk', and all others translate the longstanding, extremely common but erroneous reading 'fontem vivum', either retaining the Earlier Version's 'quik welle' (fifteen manuscripts, including most complete Bibles) or revising this to read 'welle of liyf' (eleven manuscripts, including five Psalters).[252] In Corpus Christi College Oxford 20, a manuscript with an excellent text (1 Ezra to the end of the Old Testament), 'strong quyk' is crossed through and 'welle of lijf' written above in the hand of a corrector; in British Library Royal 1. C. VIII (Forshall and Madden's base text), 'quik welle' is written over an erasure. Lyra comments that the *hebraica veritas* is 'fortem vivum', and that 'fontem vivum' is a scribal error, either a simple misreading or a 'correction' by association with 'fontes aquarum' (Ps. 43:1); this is summarized in a marginal gloss in the Glossed Wycliffite Psalter (one of the manuscripts reading 'strong quyk'): 'oure bookis han, welle, bi errour of writeris eþer of vnwise amenderis, Lire here'. Hargreaves may be right that the reading of the archetype of the Later Version was 'strong quyk', and that the more familiar reading was restored by later scribes; but another reading of the evidence is that the archetype of the Later Version had a lacuna at this point, and that one editor supplied the correct reading, while another took the easy way out by copying the reading of the Earlier Version.

For whatever reason, only a few manuscripts of the Later Version benefit from Lyra's textual commentary in this instance. In other instances, the translators apparently chose not to revise the Earlier Version, in spite of Lyra's textual commentary. Lyra's postill on Genesis, and the *correctoria* of the Dominicans of St-Jacques, of William de la Mare and of Bodleian Laud Lat. 13, all make it perfectly clear that the Hebrew text says that the Midianites sold Joseph for twenty pieces of silver, not thirty (Gen. 37:28), but the Wycliffite translators, along with many late-medieval Latin Bibles and the thirteenth-century French Bible, prefer the reading that links the sin of the Midianites with the sin of Judas.[253] Joseph was sold for 'þretti syluer pens' in the Earlier Version, and in the Later Version for 'þriȝtty platis of siluer'.[254] Less immediately explicably, the Later Version, like the Earlier Version, follows the text of the Latin Bible in the book of Esther when it states that the lot cast before Haman, who is plotting to destroy the Jews, 'hebraice dicitur *phur*': 'lot was sent in to a vessel, which lot is seid in

252 *WB*, II.778, and Hargreaves, 'The Latin Text of Purvey's Psalter', 87–9; Hargreaves's list of MSS is incomplete, see Appendix 3.

253 'Aliqui autem liber habent .xxx., sed falsa est littera', Lyra. For details, see Appendix 3.

254 Lindberg, *EV*, I.83 (*E*); *WB*, I.159–60.

Ebrew *phur*, bifor Aaman' (Esth. 3:7).[255] This is in spite of the fact that a gloss in the Cotton Bible quotes Lyra's comment that '*phur* is no word of Ebrew but of Persis [Persian], and þerfor in Ebreu it is seid, *phur* [that is] *goral*, so þat *goral* is an Ebreu word, and signefieþ lot'.[256]

The Wycliffite translators know that the Latin Bible's statement about the Hebrew word is inaccurate, but they also know that it is an authentic reading. Latin scholars without first-hand knowledge of the Hebrew text, they are translating the 'trewe' text of the Latin Bible, not the Hebrew scriptures. With this principle in mind, it is easier to see why the revisers decided to retain many of the readings Lyra's textual commentary defines as interpolations, lacking in the Hebrew text. One of the series of glosses in the Pentateuch quotes Lyra to the effect that when the Israelites were consumed with 'desire of fleischis [*carnium*, Num. 11:4], þis word, of fleischis, is not in Ebreu neþer in bokis amendid for þei desiriden fleischis and fischis and oþere þingis as it is seid wiþynne', but all Wycliffite Bible manuscripts preserve the interpolation.[257] 'Flagravit desiderio carnium' is the reading in Theodulf's recension, in the first printed edition of the Gloss, in the thirteenth-century French Bible and in the Reading Abbey Anglo-Norman Genesis to Tobit. In British Library Royal 1. B. XII, the Bible written by William de Hales in Salisbury in 1254, 'carnium' is inserted into the text in the scribal hand, and in the Oxford De Brailes Bible it is added in the margin to a text that originally (correctly) lacked it. It is not surprising that the Wycliffite translators determined that the word was an authentic part of the text, although lacking in Hebrew.

The rubric at the beginning of Genesis in two Wycliffite Bibles shows that at least one editor understood that the marginal glosses had a correctorial as well as an interpretive function; specifically, to alert the reader to material added to the biblical text: 'here biginneþ þe Bible playnly þe text, and where þat ony maner clause is set in þe text, and is not þerof, Lire certifieþ it plainly'.[258] The writer of the rubric was perhaps a Wycliffite who held that 'thu schuldest not adde ouȝt' to the law of God.[259] In principle, the translators would have agreed with him, but in practice the Later Version includes nearly all the interpolated text commonly included in medieval Latin Bibles, even in those with good texts. Understandably, the translators

[255] *WB*, II.644, cf. Lindberg, *EV*, IV.118 (*E*).

[256] The correctorial apparatus in Bodl. Laud Lat. 13 also points out that 'phur' is not in the Hebrew text; see Appendix 3.

[257] Lindberg, *EV*, II.88 ('desire of flesch' *E*); *WB*, I.395; marg. CdGKQX, see p. 166, above, and Appendix 3.

[258] B, fol. 1r; d, fol. 2r; see *WB*, I. 79 (where MSS are not specified).

[259] CUL Ff. 6. 31 (pt. 1), fol. 61r; see p. 51, above.

revising the Earlier Version seem to have been happier deleting short phrases they recognized as interpolations than deleting more substantial portions of text. In accordance with Lyra's textual commentary, for example, they delete the information, included in the Earlier Version, that 'þis [Doech of Ydumee] fedde þe mulys of Saul' (1 Kings 21:7), and a marginal gloss in the Cotton Bible comments that 'þis þat sueþ in summe bokis, and he kepte þe mulis of Saul, is not in Ebreu, neþer is of þe text, Lire here'. This gloss, deriving from the first-century CE Jewish scholar Josephus, is, however, restored in three late manuscripts of the Later Version.[260] A gloss written within the text in the Fairfax Bible comments that 'þe citee of oure strengþe' (Is.26:1) is unnamed: 'þis word, Sion, is neþer in Ebrew neþer in bokis amendid, Lire here'. The revisers delete the word.[261]

Even so, correctorial commentary in Lyra, and in the Later Version, is sporadic, in spite of the Wycliffite rubricator's assurances. Neither in the Hebrew scriptures nor in the Septuagint does David lament that he has loved Jonathan 'as a modir loueþ oon aloone sone' (2 Kings 1:26), but 'sicut mater unicum amat filium suum ita te diligebam' is included in nearly all medieval Latin Bibles, and although the *correctoria* point out that it is an interpolation (albeit an 'irreproachable' one, according to William de la Mare), Lyra does not say so, and the Later Version has no gloss to that effect.[262] The opening of David's lament is also an interpolation, 'And Dauid seyde: Israel, biholde þou, for þese men þat ben deed, woundid on þin hiȝe placis' ('et ait: considera israel pro his qui mortui sint super excelsa tua uulnerati', added after 'in libro Justorum', 2 Kings 1:18).[263] These words are glossed in the commentary of Rabanus Maurus on Kings, as the *correctorium* of William de la Mare points out, but have no textual authority. They are underlined as an interpolation in the Oxford De Brailes Bible, but Lyra makes no textual comment.

In medieval Latin Bibles, much of the 'interpolated' text in the Old Testament is translated from the Septuagint. Some books and portions of books of the Old Testament in the Septuagint have no equivalent in Hebrew and yet are customarily included in medieval Latin Bibles.[264] The Greek additions to the Hebrew text of the four books of Kings, Proverbs and Ecclesiastes, although on a smaller scale, should logically be regarded as being in the same category. Lyra, however, is firmly of the opinion that these

260 Lindberg, *EV*, III.94 (*E*); *WB*, II.64; see Appendix 3.
261 *WB*, III.268 (K), cf. Lindberg, *EV*, V.126 (*E*); see Appendix 3.
262 *WB*, II.92, cf. Lindberg, *EV*, III.109 (*E*); see Appendix 3.
263 *WB*, II.91–2, cf. Lindberg, *EV*, III.108 (*E*); see Appendix 3.
264 See Tov, *Textual Criticism of the Hebrew Bible*, pp. 142, 337, and pp. 95–102, above.

additions are 'not of þe text' because they are 'not in Ebreu', as a marginal gloss in the Cotton Bible says of the additional text at the end of the fourth chapter of Proverbs, 'For þe lord knowiþ þe weies þat ben at þe riȝt side, but þe weies ben weiward þat ben at þe leftside. Forsoþe he schal make þi goyngis riȝtful, and þi weies schulen be brouȝt forþ in pees.'[265] These words, translated from the Septuagint, are included in many early-medieval Latin Bibles, nearly all late-medieval Latin Bibles, the thirteenth-century French Bible and the *Bible historiale complétée*. In contrast, the additional text from the Septuagint at Proverbs 15:27 is signalled as such in the *correctoria* of the Dominicans of St-Jacques and of William de la Mare, and also in the corrected Oxford Bible, but Lyra does not make any textual comment and there is no gloss in the Wycliffite Bible.[266] Even if the revisers of the Earlier Version could identify 'interpolated' text, and in principle wished to delete it, they were right to be wary of deleting anything other than short phrases. We have seen how, in attempting to delete an interpolation, they instead erased part of the 'trewe' text of 1 Kings 24:8, on the authority of a mistranslation of Lyra.[267]

In respect of interpolated material, the text of the Later Version of the Wycliffite Bible is no worse than that of 'comune Latyn Biblis', but not significantly better, either. In respect of material omitted, accidentally or deliberately, the text of the Later Version is not as good as the text of the Earlier Version. Both versions, in common with a minority of late-medieval Latin Bibles, lack the first four verses of Luke's Gospel, Luke's preface to Theophilus, although they are restored, from Glossed Luke, in three manuscripts of the Earlier Version.[268] John Lewis excuses the translators for omitting this passage, as 'thro' want of Criticism' they thought it was an addition to Jerome's prologue, not the opening of the Gospel.[269] The Later Version also deletes the prologue of Jesus son of Sirach, an integral part of the book of Ecclesiasticus, since the revisers mistakenly regarded it as one of the Latin Bible prologues they had decided to omit.[270] Accidentally, the Later Version also omits part of a verse of Wisdom, 'eþer to distrie at oonys bi cruel beestis eþer bi an hard word' ('aut bestiis saevis aut verbo duro simul exterminare', Wisd. 12: 9),[271] a clause from Habakkuk, 'fro biginning' (Hab. 1:12),[272] and part of a verse of the Apocalypse, 'and anoþir booke is

[265] *WB*, III.8, cf. Lindberg, *EV*, IV.250 (*E*). [266] For details of Prov. 15:27, see Appendix 3.
[267] *WB*, II.71, see Appendix 3, and pp. 167–8, above.
[268] Bodl. Kennicott 15 also lacks Luke 1:1–4; P_*PUV* include it; see Appendix 1, 3, and p. 180, above.
[269] *NT*, p. 108.
[270] But it is included in K (in EV) and in R (in LV), see Appendix 1, 3, and pp. 96–7, above.
[271] *Add.* marg. AR_91, *WB*, III.105 (does not record R_91), cf. Lindberg, *EV*, IV.302 (*E*).
[272] *Add.* marg. I *sec. m.* A *sup. ras.* S, *WB*, III.731, cf. Lindberg, *EV*, VI.210 (*X*).

openid, whiche is þe boke of lijf' (Apoc. 20:12).[273] Scribes writing 'comune Latyn Biblis' also accidentally omit portions of text, of course, but the text is usually carefully revised, and omissions are supplied in the margin. This check on the completeness of the text seems not to have happened in the case of the archetype of the Later Version. If it had been read alongside the Earlier Version, or alongside the Latin Bible, the missing text would have been noticed.

In the latter stages of the production of the Later Version, we have noticed that the translators seem to have been in a hurry. The Earlier Version's 'þe lord god swoor in his hoely' (Amos 4:2) is left unrevised, an adjective with no noun,[274] and from Amos 5:6 onwards the Later Version ceases to revise the Earlier Version's translation of 'non est qui'.[275] Some surprising errors in translation, where the Earlier Version had translated accurately, tend to confirm that the revisers were working in haste. In what one Hebrew manuscript calls the 'Instruction about Shame',[276] in the book of Ecclesiasticus, 'vp on a shrewde woman good is a signe [seal]' ('super mulierem nequam bonum est signum', Ecclus 42:6) inexplicably becomes, in the Later Version, 'A seelyng, eþer closyng, is good on a wickid man'.[277] The gloss accords with Lyra's comment that 'signum' means 'clausura bene signata' ('a well-sealed enclosure'), but the change of gender must be a mistake.[278] An even less excusable mistake is the Later Version's translation of the Lord's prophecy in Amos 'pertransibo in medio tui' ('I shal passen bi þe myddel of þee', Amos 5:17, Earlier Version), as 'Y schal passe forþ in þe myddil of þe see'.[279] Again, if the complete text of the Later Version had been checked against the Earlier Version, or the Latin Bible, these readings would surely have been emended.

Circumstances apparently prevented the translators producing the Later Version from completing and revising the translation as thoroughly as they might have wished. The unexpected copying of the Earlier Version perhaps made them anxious for the revised translation to be available as soon as possible. But is the text of the Later Version, in spite of this, more accurate

273 *Add.* marg. in scribal hand A |BL Harl. 4890| *sec. m.* o |R| British and Foreign Bible Soc. Eng. 2, *WB*, IV.676, cf. Lindberg, *EV*, VIII.290 (*X*).

274 Lindberg, *EV*, VI.192 (*X*); *WB*, III.697; see p. 149, above.

275 From 'þer is not þat' to 'noon is þat', see p. 149, above.

276 See John J. Collins, 'Ecclesiasticus', in Barton and Muddiman, eds., *The Oxford Bible Commentary*, p. 693.

277 Lindberg, *EV*, IV.356 (*E*); *WB*, III.205 (C); A omits the translational variant. No Latin variants have been recorded.

278 *Corr.* marg. *al. m.* A *sup. ras. pr. m.* C.

279 Lindberg, *EV*, VI.193 (*X*); *WB*, III.699; *corr. sup. ras.* RU. See also Song of Songs 7:13 and Ecclus 43:15, Appendix 3.

than the text of the average Latin Bible, as the writer of the Prologue to the Wycliffite Bible boasts? Certainly the text of the Later Version is considerably freer from error, inaccuracy and inferior readings than the text of the Earlier Version, and the Wycliffites who decided to have the Earlier Version copied as a translation in its own right must have been close enough to the translators to know that they could not vouch for the accuracy of the Latin Bible(s) from which this translation was made. The revisers made considerable efforts to establish a text of the Latin Bible that was 'sumdel trewe', It certainly has fewer errors than the average Latin Bible written in France or England in the thirteenth or fourteenth century, and it is clearly superior to the text of the Latin Bible in the first printed edition of the *Glossa Ordinaria*.

CHAPTER 7

The effects

For Wyclif and his associates, establishing a 'trewe' text of the Latin Bible was a means to an end, not an end in itself. Eager to make the scriptures accessible in English, they began to translate before they had started serious study of the text of the Latin Bible, or at least before their studies of the Latin text were very far advanced. If they had known at the beginning of the translation project that what we call the Earlier Version would be copied and circulated as a translation in its own right, they might have devoted more of their resources and energies to establishing an accurate Latin text before beginning to translate. But they did not know, and one can understand their desire to start translating as soon as the project had been formulated, without waiting for 'elde Biblis', commentaries and glosses to be assembled and scrutinized verse by verse. They were, after all, biblical professionals.

In considering what the translators achieved, it is only fair to focus on the Later Version, the English Bible resulting from the processes described in the final chapter of the Prologue (although the Prologue-writer doubtless makes the processes sound more predetermined, regular and consistent than in practice they were). Opponents of translation had feared that an English Bible would introduce and multiply error, but although copies were made and circulated before the project was finished, and although the project was completed in haste, the translators were justly proud of having established a Latin text with a good degree of accuracy, and of having produced a translation that was as faithful to the original as was consonant with being able to be understood by readers with little or no knowledge of Latin, and that was as readily comprehensible as – in places more readily comprehensible than – the Latin Bible. The translators themselves must have found that the processes involved made them more sharply conscious of textual and interpretive issues, at the local level and more generally, and therefore made them better biblical scholars and better readers of the Bible.

Explanatory glosses within the text of the English Bible in many cases supplied guidance as to what the translators understood to be its literal meaning. Sometimes (especially in Psalms) glosses supplied guidance as to what the translators understood to be the text's literal meaning, as intended by the divine author but not immediately apparent in the unglossed words of the text. Neither Butler nor Palmer would have quarrelled with the content of the explanatory glosses, so far as it goes. Like the Wycliffite translators, these friars regarded Lyra, one of the most distinguished members of Butler's order, as an authority on the literal sense of scripture. On the other hand, both Palmer and Butler would surely have considered that the glosses they would have regarded as spiritual rather than literal, such as '*Crist*, þou art fairer in schap þan þe sones of men' (Ps. 44:3), constitute only a very rudimentary attempt to alert the English reader to the 'higher' senses of scripture. These two friars, is their contributions to the debate about biblical translation, claim that even if readers illiterate in Latin were to be able to read the text of the whole Bible in English they would not be able to understand what they were reading, and would therefore be likely to invent new heresies. They would have thought it doubly unnecessary to alert laypeople to differences between the text of the Hebrew scriptures and the Latin Bible, and to errors commonly found in Latin Bibles. The Wycliffite translators, on the other hand, wanted access to the Bible to mean equality of access.

The Victorian editors of the Wycliffite Bible, Forshall and Madden, were confident that the first English Bible was one of the principal causes of what for Butler and Palmer would have been an unimaginable heresy, England's rejection of the Roman Catholic Church:

> The effect of [the] circulation of scripture among the people in their own tongue was just what might have been expected. Men reading with their own eyes the words of the Saviour and of his apostles, found a marked contrast between the principles which they inculcated and many parts of the system upheld by the Romish church. Which of the two should be rejected could not be a matter of hesitation.

When the Reformation finally dawned, the Wycliffite Bible, according to Forshall and Madden, 'supplied an example and a model to those excellent men, who in like manner devoted themselves at the hazard of their lives to the translation of scripture, and to its publication among the people of the land'.[1]

The tone of this passage is unequivocally Protestant, and the publication of Forshall and Madden's edition was welcomed particularly warmly by Protestant reviewers because of the firm link it makes between the first

[1] *WB*, I.xxxiii–xxxiv.

English Bible and Wyclif. In its review of the edition, the Unitarian *Christian Examiner* calls Wyclif 'the pioneer and patriarch of Protestantism'.[2] Such language would not have appealed to the high-church element within the Church of England, but Anglican dignitaries had long felt that the first English Bible as a whole, not just the New Testament, should be available in a scholarly edition. The Bishop of Salisbury, Thomas Burgess, helped to get the editorial project off the ground in 1829,[3] and the Archbishop of Canterbury, William Howley (a supporter of the Oxford Movement), 'very handsomely subscribed for two copies of the Wycliffe, one largepaper, one small', as Madden records in his diary in January 1830.[4] When the edition was published twenty years later, the only discordant note was struck by Thomas Phillipps, bibliophile and friend of Madden, who sent Madden a message via his godson (Madden's third son, George), who was nine years old at the time: 'Will you tell your Papa, I congratulate him on finishing Wicliff, which was a waste of his labour.' 'Such is his opinion', exclaimed Madden, 'of the importance of publishing the earliest complete vernacular versions of the Scriptures! But what is his opinion worth? Just nothing!'[5] (Surprisingly, the friendship survived this event.)[6]

Madden's pride in his own and Forshall's achievement was abundantly justified, and their edition made it possible, for the first time, for the achievement of the Wycliffite translators to be recognized and evaluated. In 1850, it seemed obvious to the editors that medieval readers of the English Bible would be struck by the lack of fit between the biblical text and the institution that claimed to be founded upon it; once the Wycliffite Bible began to be copied, the English Reformation was a foregone conclusion.[7] A century and a half later, our evaluation of the achievement of the Wycliffite translators in terms of the effects of the translation must be far more cautious and provisional. The causes of the English Reformation are now understood to have been extraordinarily complex, a mix of the religious and the political, the long-standing and the aleatory, and while it would be a bold person who would claim that the Wycliffite Bible had no effect at all, determining the nature of its influence on events in the sixteenth century is well beyond the limits of this study.

[2] G. Livermore, 'John Wycliffe and the First English Bible', *The Christian Examiner* 51 (1851), 75. Livermore's only regret is that the edition does not include a biography of Wyclif, 63.

[3] See Madden's diary for 31 May 1829, Bodl. Engl. hist. c. 147, fol. 118r. Burgess was one of the founders of the Bible Society in 1804.

[4] 3 Jan. 1830, fol. 144r. Archbishop Sumner had succeeded Howley by the time the edition appeared.

[5] 21 Oct. 1850, Bodl. MS Engl. hist. c. 163, p. 350.

[6] But was terminated by Madden in 1866, when Phillipps offered him the post of librarian of his collections.

[7] Cf. Deanesly, *LB*, pp. 1–2.

In an article arguing the need for the King James Bible to be revised, Henry Bristow Wilson (one of the contributors to the notorious *Essays and Reviews* of 1860) denies any continuity between the medieval Bible and its successors in the Reformation. While he admires Forshall and Madden's industry, he comments that 'these old versions, however interesting as historical monuments, inasmuch as they are versions from a version, have no critical value; they can hardly be said to be the basis of the translations which we now have'.[8] It is no longer possible to be so dismissive. William Cooper is confident that when the lord in the parable of the talents says, in Miles Coverdale's Bible, 'enter thou in to the ioye of thy lorde' (Matt. 25:21), Coverdale is borrowing directly from the Wycliffite Bible (Tyndale has 'entre in in to thy masters ioye'), and while it seems likelier that Coverdale is translating directly from the Latin ('intra in gaudium domini tui'), there needs to be a 'thorough analysis of such apparent borrowings', as Daniell says, before the precise nature and extent of the effects of the first English Bible on sixteenth-century translations can be estimated.[9] Even if Tyndale and Coverdale did not have direct access to the Wycliffite Bible, it is possible, as Daniell suggests, that words or phrases from it had entered into common discourse.[10]

I suspect that the sixteenth-century translators were more influenced by the Wycliffite translators' discourse of interpretation, in the English prologues, than by the text of the Middle English translation itself, but investigation into such questions has a long way to go. In any case, *pace* Wilson, it was the Wycliffite translators and not their sixteenth-century successors who initiated a tradition of scholarly, textually respectable translation. Tyndale, of course, was translating from the originals and not from Latin, but in the Old Testament Coverdale sometimes reproduces inferior readings which had been present in the Earlier Version of the Wycliffite Bible and were corrected in the Later Version. In Amos's vision of the locusts eating the grass of the land, for example, the Earlier Version reads that the locusts ate the burgeoning grass 'aftir þe clippere of floc or kyng' (7:1), leaving the alternatives, 'post tonsorem gregis' and 'post tonsorem regis', open: Coverdale incorporates both into his translation 'after the kynge had clipte

[8] *The Westminster Review* 67 (1857), 135.

[9] *WB*, IV.70 (EV and LV); Cooper, *The Wycliffe New Testament, 1388, an Edition in Modern Spelling* (London: British Library, 2002), p. xi; Daniell, *The Bible in English*, p. 85. Coverdale's Bible was first published in Germany (Marburg?) in 1535; as he says in the preface, Coverdale made use of German translations.

[10] For some points of similarity and difference between WB NT in LV and Tyndale's NT, see Daniell, *The Bible in English*, pp. 85–8. On the influence of WB on English vocabulary, see Crystal, *The Stories of English*, p. 240.

his shepe'. The Great Bible (1540) and Matthew's Bible (1549) reproduce Coverdale's translation, which is not emended ('after the kinges mowing') until the Bishops' Bible (1568).[11] The Later Version, following Lyra, had already deleted the sheep.[12]

The new translations did not make the Wycliffite Bible redundant. Reformers associated it with 'the true relygion of the Ghospell of our Saviour Jesus Christ', as Richard Bowyer put it in his Wycliffite Bible, William H. Scheide 12.[13] Earlier and Later Versions were still read in the late sixteenth century. Avery Uvedale noted in his New Testament and lectionary (in the Earlier Version), in 1569, that 'this olde translacione is not so goode as the translacione at this daie',[14] but William Smith, servant in Queen Elizabeth's scullery, began to read Queen's College Oxford 388, a complete Bible in the Later Version, on 2 October 1561, and, having finished it on 10 June 1563, began to read it again two days later.[15] Henry Sayer, priest, read Cambridge University Library Additional 6680, a complete Bible in the Later Version, in twenty-six days in 1576.[16] There is a list of 'harde [Middle English] wordes', in a sixteenth-century hand, in Corpus Christi College Oxford 4, a complete Bible in the Earlier Version.[17]

Smith, Sayer and others probably felt that reading the Bible in Wyclif's English was an act of greater devotion than reading it in an English more readily understood. Presenting Queen Elizabeth I with a copy of the Wycliffite New Testament in the Later Version as a New Year's gift, John Bridges, one of her chaplains, wrote: 'if the reading of Gowers or Chawcers olde English geue [may give] so great a delectation for the antiquitie in profane matters, what greater reuerence and pleasure should it moue to read our auncient fathers English on the scripture?'[18] Even so, reading the Wycliffite Bible in under a month, as Sayer claims to have done, was certainly not something of which the Wycliffite translators would have approved. Attempting to ingest the entire biblical text in the minimum time suggests a commodification of scripture, a reduction to the absurd of the principle of *sola scriptura* – the principle that only the word of God speaks with the authority of revelation, and that ecclesiastical tradition does not partake,

[11] In the Bishops' Bible, a note on this verse reads 'After the publicke commaundement for mowing was geuen, or as some reade after the kinges sheepe were shorne.' For bibliographical details of all these Bibles, see Arthur Sumner Herbert, rev. T. H. Darlow and H. Moule, *Historical Catalogue of Printed Editions of the English Bible 1525–1961* (London: British and Foreign Bible Society, 1968).

[12] See ch. 6, n. 105, and Appendix 3. As Lyra says, the Latin should read 'tonsionem regis' rather than 'tonsorem regis', but the Wycliffite translators are faithful to the Latin.

[13] See p. 42, above. [14] *M*, fol. 242r. [15] Fol. 8v; see the description in Appendix 4.

[16] Fol. 404v; see the description in Appendix 4. [17] Fol. 6v; see the description in Appendix 4.

[18] BL Royal 1. A. XII, fol. 3r. Bridges (who became Dean of Salisbury in 1577 and Bishop of Oxford in 1604) says he does not know the identity of the translator.

either equally or similarly, of that authority. When Forshall and Madden claim that readers of the Wycliffite Bible had their eyes opened to the divergence between the principles advocated in scripture and those exemplified in the institutional church, their reasoning depends upon a further Protestant twist to the principle of *sola scriptura*, that Roman Catholic tradition not only lacks authority but also deliberately perverts the Bible's meaning.

The principle of *sola scriptura* has often been associated with Wyclif. The Carmelite Netter, one of Wyclif's foremost opponents, contended that Wyclif altogether rejected the authority of the church in his exegesis of scripture, and should logically have refused to accept the biblical canon, since the canon itself was determined by ecclesiastical tradition.[19] The high regard of Wyclif and the Wycliffites for the authority of Augustine and Jerome is, however, indisputable, and Heiko Oberman demonstrates that Wyclif fully accepted what he calls Tradition I, the ongoing interpretation of scripture by the church faithful to Christ.[20] What Wyclif rejected was Tradition II, extrascriptural tradition, which relies on human and not divine authority.

When Michael Hurley and Alastair Minnis argue that Wyclif set himself apart from church and tradition in his scriptural exegesis, they seem to me to place too much emphasis on the idiosyncracy of the ultra-Realist language of his arguments for the truth of holy scripture.[21] Wyclif believed that scripture's veracity, a crucial doctrine and a crucial component of tradition, was being betrayed and undermined by the sophistical relativism of his academic contemporaries. 'The decisive issue', as Levy well says, 'is not respect for tradition, but the assignation of authority in determining the nature of that tradition'.[22] For Wyclif, the church of Christ's faithful followers, which had overlapped with the visible church from the beginning, was the true custodian of the interpretation of scripture.

Wyclif and the Wycliffites' decision to translate the whole Bible for 'symple men of wit' might be taken as confirmation that he and they believed that the 'inspired reader'[23] could understand scripture on its own, without knowledge of the tradition of interpretation. Some assertions in the Prologue to the Wycliffite Bible suggest this: for example, that anyone who maintains meekness and charity truly understands 'al holi writ', and

[19] *Doctrinale*, 2, xx; ed. B. Blanciotti, I.343–8; see p. 95, above.

[20] *The Harvest of Medieval Theology: Gabriel Biel and Late Medieval Nominalism*, rev. edn (Grand Rapids: Eerdmans, 1967), pp. 371–8.

[21] Hurley, "'Scriptura sola': Wyclif and his Critics," *Traditio* 16 (1960), 275–352; Minnis, "'Authorial Intention' and 'Literal Sense'", 25–28.

[22] Levy, *John Wyclif*, p. 122, and on Wyclif and tradition, pp. 112–22.

[23] Minnis, "'Authorial Intention" and "Literal Sense"', 27.

that the 'simple man of wit' should not be too frightened to study it.[24] Augustine, who is being quoted here, is making the point that no amount of learning can compensate for lack of charity. Minnis points out that Pecock is responding to Lollard claims that meekness and holiness of life are the prerequisites for understanding scripture when he argues, in the *Repressor of Over Much Blaming of the Clergy* (c. 1449), that 'a viciose man' can understand the Bible as readily as 'a vertuose man' can, so long as he has at least as much natural intelligence.[25] Believing that Lollards are opposed to all glossing and commentary, Pecock presents them as adherents of the principle of *sola scriptura* in the sense of rejecting tradition altogether.[26] According to Pecock, they need to be persuaded that 'thei neden miche more to leerne and knowe . . . than what thei mowe leerne and knowe bi her reeding and studiyng in the Bible oonli'.[27] If they read more widely, they might even cease to blame the clergy for accepting extrascriptural traditions rooted in reason and 'kynde'.

Pecock writes as though all Lollards were laypeople, and he writes in the mother-tongue, he says, to enable them to read his *Repressor*, his *Just Apprising of Holi Scripture* and other works aimed at making up their deficiency in necessary knowledge.[28] They have been seduced by the honey-sweetness of reading scripture in their own language, but man cannot live on honey alone.[29] They should not boast of being 'leerned in the text of the Bible', but should take to heart Paul's warning to the Jews, who boasted of their knowledge of the scriptures and thereby condemned themselves. Pecock quotes the passage from Romans *in extenso*, from the Later Version of the Wycliffite Bible (Rom. 2:1–3, 11–23), adding a gloss on the words 'but if thou art a named Jew' (v. 17): 'or ellis for this present purpos for to seie thus: but if thou art a named knowun man [that is, a Lollard]'.[30] Pecock evidently has access to the Wycliffite Bible in the Later Version (the New Testament at least), but he does not use it consistently or faithfully.[31] The Jews of Paul's time, argues Pecock, 'magnifieden ouermiche the Oold Testament', and in his own day many Lollards make too much of the New Testament, or indeed 'dignifien ouermiche the writing of al the hool Bible', instead of

24 *WB*, I.2/36–8; see p. 18, above.

25 Ed. Babington, I.94/14–18; Minnis, '"Authorial Intention" and "Literal Sense"', 27.

26 *Repressor*, I.55; see p. 51, above. 27 Ibid., I.128/13–17.

28 Ibid., I.128/19–23; on the *Just Apprising*, now lost, see I.lxxvii.

29 Ibid., I.66–8. Pecock expects NT to be more widely available than OT, 66/1–3.

30 Ibid., I.63–4, quots. at 63/14 and 64/1–4 (WB not acknowledged); 'but if þou art named a Jew', *WB*, IV.307–8, EV and LV. See ibid. I.53 on Lollards as 'knowun men'; also Hudson, *PR*, p. 57.

31 For example, at 2 Cor. 4:3 *evangelium* is trans. 'gospel' in EV and LV, but Pecock prefers 'euangelie', *Repressor*, I.54/3; *WB*, IV.378.

allowing scripture to 'abide withinne his [its] owne termys and boundis'.[32] They should receive the first part of the *Repressor* and the *Just Apprising* as though they were the apostle James's 'graffid [grafted] word, which may saue [their] soulis' (Jas. 1:21, 'graffid' being a more exact translation of *insitum* than the Later Version's 'plauntid').[33]

Wyclif's horror at the concept of confining holy scripture within its proper limits and boundaries can well be imagined, but he would surely have regarded Pecock as a partner worth debating with, and Hudson aptly says that the Wycliffite translators or the compilers of the *Glossed Gospels* would have made more sense of Pecock than the Lollards of the 1440s are likely to have done,[34] however much they disagreed with him about the authority of extrascriptural tradition. Like Pecock, and like Augustine, the Wycliffite translators thought highly of reason.[35] The writer of 'The holi prophete Dauid seiþ', as well as citing Augustine on ethical prerequisites for understanding the meaning of holy writ, says it is necessary to study 'þe trewe and opyn exposicion of hooli doctours and oþere wise men', as well.[36] When the writer of the Prologue to the Wycliffite Bible warns that 'men moten be ful wel war to conseyue wel þe wordis of þe Holy Goost', he is referring specifically to the Song of Songs, which he thinks is especially liable to be misunderstood,[37] but evidently he believes that the words of the Holy Ghost require to be thoughtfully and knowledgably interpreted, not simply delighted in. Three chapters of the Prologue, after all, are devoted to rules for the interpretation of scripture, including rules which Augustine borrowed from Tyconius, and which Lyra expounded at greater length. Nobody who read the first English Bible with care could justly be called an 'ydiota circa scripturam'.

The English reader might not understand every word, but there was always the consolation that 'þe wysist clerk lyuynge vnderstondeþ not al þe Gospel, ne al þe Sauter, ne al holy write litterallich and spiritualiche', in the words of the tract in favour of translation 'Alle cristine peple stant in þre maner of folke'.[38] The writer of the prologues to the Prophets and to the Wycliffite Bible, echoing Lyra, stresses that the literal, 'opin' sense of scripture is the fundamental sense. Tyndale echoes both Lyra and the Prologue-writer when he says that the literal sense 'is the root and ground of all, and the anchor that never faileth'.[39] Yet the writer of the Prologue

32 Ibid., I.69/18–19, 30–1, I.70/16–17.

33 Ibid., I.68/32–3; *WB*, IV.597; 'in set' *X*, other EV MSS 'inset, or ioyned', Lindberg, *EV*, VIII.194–5.

34 *PR*, p. 442.

35 See pp. 117–18, above.

36 Deanesly, *LB*, p. 452/10–11; see p. 13, above.

37 *WB*, I.41/19–20; see p. 123, above.

38 CUL Ii. 6. 26, fol.7v; Hunt, *TFST*, II. 263/200–2; see p. 19, above.

39 Tyndale, *Obedience of a Christian Man*, ed. David Daniell (London: Penguin Books, 2000), p. 156.

would certainly have regarded Tyndale's assertion that 'Scripture hath but one sense, which is the literal sense' as a dangerous over-simplification. The first English Bible encourages its readers to engage with the full complexity of the biblical text, trusting them to work as hard at interpreting God's law as the faithful throughout the history of the church have worked on their behalf.

James Simpson contrasts evangelical and orthodox positions on the interpretation of the Bible, at the end of the Middle Ages in England, in terms of orthodox writers understanding that 'the text of the Bible is subject to material degradation across time', and that 'biblical meaning can only be persuasively elucidated by communal and temporally durable means', whereas for evangelical writers the 'plain, literal meaning' of the Bible 'is directly perceptible by divine inspiration'.[40] Evangelical writers, in other words, hold to the principle of *sola scriptura*. The Wycliffite translators do not fit into either of Simpson's categories. They hold that the open, literal sense of the Bible is perceptible to the reader who lives in charity with God and neighbour, but they also hold that some parts of scripture are 'derke', and that the reader should take advantage of every opportunity to study the authentic interpretive tradition. They hold that the text of the Bible is subject to corruption, and that its meaning is elucidated communally; but they also hold that it can be interpreted only within the church of the faithful, at one with Christ. In their view, the institutional church of the late fourteenth century was not a Christian community within which the meaning of scripture could readily become clear.

That Wyclif and his followers were perceived to be heretical was the principal reason why the Wycliffite Bible was censored in Arundel's *Constitutions*; but Simpson reminds us that the authorized publication of the Great Bible in 1539, a copy of which was ordered to be placed in every church in the land, was followed three years later by 'An Acte for th'advaucement of true Religion', made necessary by the activities of those who, the statute claims, 'subverte the veraye, true and perfecte exposicioun doctryne and declaracioun' of scripture 'after theyre pervers fantasies', a phrase that recalls the phrasing of the prologue to the Prophets.[41] The 1542 statute forbids copies of the 'craftye, false and untrue translacioun' of Tyndale to be kept or used, insists on the excision or erasure of unauthorized 'annotaciouns or preambles' (excepting *capitula*-lists) from copies of the Bible, on pain of a

[40] James Simpson, *The Oxford English Literary History*, Volume 2, *1350–1547: Reform and Cultural Revolution* (Oxford University Press, 2002), p. 475.

[41] Ibid., pp. 496–8; A. Luders *et al.*, eds., *Statutes of the Realm*, 34 Henry VIII, vol. III (London, 1817; Records Commission), p. 894.

fine of forty shillings, and prohibits public reading, preaching or teaching without a licence, although noblemen may read the Bible to their family in their home, or in their orchard or garden.[42] Chancellor More would have been happy with all these terms, if only the true doctrine the statute aimed to preserve had been the doctrine of the true church. Translation of the Bible into the vernacular, says Simpson, 'is a profoundly "democratizing" act, redistributing discursive power on a massive scale', and the institutional response was inevitably repressive, even when the state itself had authorized the translation.[43]

The Provincial Council did its legislative best to prevent the copying and reading of the Wycliffite Bible, or any part thereof, when it met in Oxford in 1407. By then, however, copies had been in circulation for some twenty years, and stationers knew how marketable English Bibles were, particularly New Testaments including a lectionary enabling owners to locate the epistles and gospels read at mass throughout the year. Most owners took the precaution of not signing their name in their copy, but perhaps the number of extant copies would not have been significantly greater had Arundel refrained from legislation against the Wycliffite Bible. More cheaply produced copies might have been made, but these would have been the copies least likely to have survived. The attempts at prohibition may have been, as Simpson suggests, inevitable, but they were nonethless gravely mistaken. Without formally approving the translation (and no previous translation had been formally approved) the ecclesiastical hierarchy could have enjoyed some of the credit for its success without relaxing their efforts to prevent the spread of what they regarded as dangerous errors and heresies. This is easier for us to see than it was for them, of course; not least because we know just how good a translation the first English Bible was.

[42] Ibid., III.894–6. [43] *Reform and Cultural Revolution*, p. 467.

APPENDIX I

Contents of the Wycliffite Bible

This Appendix lists the contents of the Wycliffite Bible in order, in the Earlier Version (**EV**) and in the Later Version (**LV**), with details of all prologues in extant MSS, and references to printed editions. Unless otherwise indicated:

The base MS in Lindberg, *EV*, from the beginning to Bar. 3:20 'risen' is *E*, and from Bar. 3:20 'þe ȝunge' to the end is *X*.

The base MS in *WB* in EV, from the beginning to 3 Kings is *A*; from 4 Kings to 2 Chron. is *B*, from 1 Ezra to Bar. 3:20 'risen' is *C*, from Bar. 3:20 'þe ȝunge' to Ezek. 1:26 is *K*, from Ezek. 1:27 to Ezek. 32:22 is *A*, from Ezek. 32:23 to Acts 28:15 'whanne' is *K*, from Acts 28:16 'Poul' to the end is *M*.

The base MS in *WB* in LV is A. Unless otherwise indicated, component parts are in both EV and LV.

PREFATORY MATERIAL

Jerome's prefatory epistles

(1) inc: Broþer Ambrose to me þi lytyll ȝiftis (**EV** MSS + K)
inc: Broþir Ambrose bryngynge fully þi litil ȝiftis to me (C_U_6680 FOX)
[Jerome, *Epistola* LIII *ad Paulinum*; *RBMA*, no. 284] *WB*, I.61–75 (*A*O); Lindberg, *EV*, I.26–35; Lindberg, *PE* (*X*O)

(2) inc: Ich haue (y)take desyrid epystles of my man Desiderye (**EV** MSS + K)
inc: I haue take þe epistlis myche desirid of my man Desiderye (C_U_6680FOX)
[Jerome, *Praefatio in Pentateucum ad Desiderium*; *RBMA*, no. 285] *WB*, I.75–8 (*A*O); Lindberg, *EV*, I.35–6; Lindberg, *PE* (*X*O)

Prologue to the Wycliffite Bible (General Prologue)
inc: Fyue and twenty bookis of þe olde testament ben bookis of feiþ (**LV**: for MSS, see ch. 5, nn. 80–3)
[English prologue written for WB] *WB*, I.1–60 (α to 'synnes and', ch.15, I.57/3, then Q)

OLD TESTAMENT

Genesis *WB*, I.61–192; Lindberg, *EV*, I.37–101
Exodus (Exodi) *WB*, I.193–292; Lindberg, *EV*, I.102–56
prol. inc: Þis book of Exodi þat is to seie of going out (M), *WB*, I.193
Leviticus (Leuitici) *WB*, I.293–363; Lindberg, *EV*, II.33–70
prol. inc: Þis book of Leuitici makiþ mencioun how God (M), *WB*, I.293
Numbers (Numeri) *WB*, I.364–463; Lindberg, *EV*, II.71–124
prol. inc: Þis book clepid Numeri þat is to seie þe book of Noumbre (M), *WB*, I.364
Deuteronomy *WB*, I.464–553; Lindberg, *EV*, II.125–71
prol. inc: In þis book of Deuteronomye ben contened þe wordis (M), *WB*, I.464
Joshua (Josue) *WB*, I.554–614; Lindberg, *EV*, II.172–205
prol. inc: At þe laste ended þe fyfe bokys of Moises (**EV** MSS + K)
inc: At þe last whanne þe fuye bookes (C_U_6680dOX)
[Jerome, *ad Eustochium*, *Prol. Iosue*; *RBMA*, no. 311] *WB*, I.554–6 (*A*O); Lindberg, *EV*, II.172–3
Judges (Judicum) *WB*, I.615–677; Lindberg, *EV*, II.206-III.61; Lindberg, *Judges* (*A*A)
prol. inc: Þis book of Judicum makiþ mencioun how þe sones of Israel (M), *WB*, I.615
Ruth *WB*, I.678–87; Lindberg, *EV*, III.57–61
prol. inc: Þis book of Ruth schewiþ þe feiþfulnesse and stidefast loue (M), *WB*, I.678
1 Kings (Regum) *WB*, II.1–89; Lindberg, *EV*, III.61–107
prol. inc: Þe tunge forsoþe of Syriis and of Caldeis (**EV** MSS + K)
inc: Þe langage of men of Sirus and of Caldeis (C_U_6680OX)
[Jerome, *Prologus galeatus in libros Regum ad Paulum et Eustochium*; *RBMA*, no. 323]
WB, II.1–5 (*A*O); Lindberg, *EV*, III.61–4
prol. inc: In þis book of Kingis þe first is contened how Anna (M), *WB*, II.1

2 Kings *WB*, II.90–157; Lindberg, *EV*, III.108–43
prol. inc: Þis secounde book of kingis (M), *WB*, II.90
3 Kings *WB*, II.158–235; Lindberg, *EV*, III.143–85
prol. inc: In þis þridde book of kingis (M), *WB*, II.158
4 Kings *WB*, II.236–312; Lindberg, *EV*, III.186–226
prol. inc: Þis fourthe book of kingis makiþ mencioun (M), *WB*, II.236
1 Chronicles (Paralipomenon) *WB*, II.313–84; Lindberg, *EV*, III.226–64
prol. inc: Iff þe making of þe seuenti remenouris abide stille pure (**EV** MSS + K)
inc: Iff þe makynge of þe seuenti interpretours dwelle (C_U_6680OX)
[Jerome, *Chromatio*; *RBMA*, no. 328] *WB*, II.313–5 (*B*O); Lindberg, *EV*, III.226–7
prol. inc: Þe booc of Paralipomenon þat is þe breggyng (**EV** MSS)
inc: Þe book of Paralipomenon þat is þe breggyng (KO)
[Jerome, *ad Paulinum*; *RBMA*, no. 326] *WB*, II.316 (*B*O); Lindberg, *EV*, III.227
prol. inc: Þis book of Paralipomenon þe firste bigynneþ at Adam (M), *WB*, II.313
2 Chronicles *WB*, II.385–477; Lindberg, *EV*, III.264–311
prol. inc: Eusebeus Jerome senden gretyng (**EV** MSS + O)
[Jerome, *Domnioni et Rogatiano*; Stegmüller, *RBMA*, no. 327] *WB*, II.385–6; Lindberg, *EV*, III.264–5
Prayer of Manasseh (= 2 Chron. 37) See Appendix 3.
1 Ezra (Esdras) *WB*, II.478–504; Lindberg, *EV*, IV.33–46
prol. inc: Wheþer it be hardere to don þat ȝee asken (**EV** MSS + KO)
[Jerome, *Domnioni et Rogatiano*; *RBMA*, no. 330] *WB*, II.478–9; Lindberg, *EV*, IV.32–3
prol. inc: Esdras and Neemye helpere (**EV** MSS + KO)
[Jerome, *ad Paulinum*; *RBMA*, no. 329] *WB*, II.479; Lindberg, *EV*, IV.33
'Þe comendacioun of Esdre', inc: Þis aftir Jude brend vp of þe Caldeys (**EV** MSS + KO), *WB*, II.479; Lindberg, *EV*, IV.33
prol. inc: Þis firste book of Esdre whiche was a wurþi man (M), *WB*, II.478
2 Ezra (Nehemiah) *WB*, II.505–41; Lindberg, *EV*, IV.47–65
prol. inc: In þis secounde book of Esdre (M), *WB*, II.505
3 Ezra (2 Esdras) (**EV** MSS + I) *WB*, II.542–75 (*C*I); Lindberg, *EV*, IV.65–84. See Appendix 3.
Tobit (Tobias) *WB*, II.576–601; Lindberg, *EV*, IV.84–97
prol. inc: To Cromacio and Eliodre bisshopis (**EV** MSS + KO)

[Jerome, *Chromatio et Heliodoro*; *RBMA*, no. 332] *WB*, II.576; Lindberg, *EV*, IV.84
prol. inc: In þis book of Tobie ben contened þe seuene dedis (M), *WB*, II.576

Judith *WB*, II.602–35; Lindberg, *EV*, IV.97–114
prol. inc: Anentis þe Ebrues þe boc of Judith is rad (**EV** MSS + aKO)
[Jerome, *Prol. Iudith*; *RBMA*, no.335] *WB*, II.602; Lindberg, *EV*, IV.97
prol. inc: Judith widewe þe doȝter of Merari (**EV** MSS + aKO)
[Jerome, *Prol. Iudith*; *RBMA*, no. 336] *WB*, II.602; Lindberg, *EV*, IV.97
prol. inc: Þis bok of Judiþ þe holi widewe (M), *WB*, II.602

Esther (Hester) *WB*, II.636–69; Lindberg, *EV*, IV.114–30
prol. inc: Þe booc of Ester to ben maad vicious (**EV** MSS + aKO)
[Jerome, *Prol. Esth.*; *RBMA*, nos. 341 + 343] *WB*, II.636; Lindberg, *EV*, IV.114
prol. inc: Þis book of Hester þe qween (M), *WB*, II.636

Job *WB*, II.670–735; Lindberg, *EV*, IV.130–65
prol. inc: I am constreyned bi alle þe bookis of Goddis scripture (**EV** MSS + KOR)
[Jerome, *Prol. Iob*; *RBMA*, no. 344] *WB*, II.670–1; Lindberg, *EV*, IV.130–2
prol. inc: Iff forsoþe a jonket wiþ resshe (**EV** MSS + KOR)
[Jerome, *Prol. Iob*; *RBMA*, no. 357] *WB*, II.671–2; Lindberg, *EV*, IV.132–3
prol. inc: In þis book of Joob is contened first (M), *WB*, II.670

Psalms (Psalter, Sauter) *WB*, II.736–888; Lindberg, *EV*, IV.165–246
prol. inc: Whan it is knowen alle þe prophetys to han spoken (**EV** MSS + KOR)
[Peter Lombard] *WB*, II.736–8 (*C*); *WB*, I.37–8 (*T*); Lindberg, *EV*, IV.165–7
prol. inc: Dauyd þe sone of Jesse whan he was in his rewme (**EV** MSS + KOR)
[Jerome, *RBMA*, no. 487] *WB*, II.738; Lindberg, *EV*, IV.167–8
prol. inc: Þis book Sauter is clepid þat is to seie þe book of songis of Dauiþ (M), *WB*, II.736
prol. inc: Greet abundaunce of gostly coumfort (*T* BL Add. 10046 BL_Add._31044 Worcs. Cath. F. 172) [prologue to Richard Rolle's *Psalter*, ed. Bramley, *The Psalter or Psalms of David*, pp. 3–5] *WB*, I.39–40 (*T*)

[**Canticles** in 7 LV MSS; see Index of MSS]

Proverbs (Parables) *WB*, III.1–52; Lindberg, *EV*, IV.246–75
prol. inc: To Cromacye and Eliodere bisshopis (**EV** MSS + aKR)

inc: Jerom sendeþ gretyng to Cromacye and Eliodore (aR)
[Jerome, *Chromatio et Heliodoro*; *RBMA*, no. 457] *WB*, III.1–2; Lindberg, *EV*, IV.246–7
prol. inc: In þese Prouerbis of Salomon is contened myche prudence (M), *WB*, III.1

Ecclesiastes *WB*, III.53–72; Lindberg, *EV*, IV.275–85
prol. inc: Þis almost þe fifte ȝer whan ȝit I was att Rome (**EV** MSS + aKR)
[Jerome, *Ad Paulam et Eustochium*; *RBMA*, no. 462] *WB*, III.53; Lindberg, *EV*, IV.275–6
prol: Here bigynneþ þe book of Ecclesiastes þat tretiþ also of wisdom and prudence and nediþ noon oþer prologe (M), *WB*, III.52

Song of Songs (title: Book of Songis FRU title: Songis of Songis EGKNPY)
WB, III.73–84; Lindberg, *EV*, IV.285–91

Wisdom (Sapience) *WB*, III.85–122; Lindberg, *EV*, IV.291–311
prol. inc: Þe booc of Wisdam anentis Ebrues nowher is (**EV** MSS + aC_J_E_14)
[Isidore, *RBMA*, no. 468] *WB*, III.85; Lindberg, *EV*, IV.291
prol. inc: Þe book of Wisdom is not hadde among Ebreuys (R), *WB*, III.85
prol: Here bigynneþ þe book of Wisdom which is red in holi cherche in lessouns of þe masse for þe mater þerof is goostli and profecie of þingis to comynge (M), *WB*, III.84

Ecclesiasticus *WB*, III.123–223; Lindberg, *EV*, IV.311–V.102
[prol.] inc: Off manye and grete bi þe lawe and profetes (**EV** MSS + K)
[authorial prologue of Jesus son of Sirach; an integral part of the biblical text] *WB*, III.123–4; Lindberg, *EV*, IV.311–12

Isaiah *WB*, III.224–341; Lindberg, *EV*, V.103–66
prol. inc: No man whan þe prophetis he shal seen (**EV** MSS)
[Jerome, *Ad Paulam et Eustochium*; *RBMA*, no. 482] *WB*, III.224–5; Lindberg, *EV*, V.103–4
prol. inc: As seynt Jerom seiþ in þe prolog of Ysaie (**LV** MSS)
[English prologue written for WB] *WB*, III.225–6

Jeremiah *WB*, III.342–471; Lindberg, *EV*, V.166–239
prol. inc: Jeremye þe prophete to whom þis prologe is ascriued (**EV** MSS)
[Jerome, *Ad Paulam et Eustochium*; *RBMA*, no. 487] *WB*, III.342; Lindberg, *EV*, V.166–7
prol. inc: God is redi to ȝyue good, to punshen a tariere (**EV** MSS)
WB, III.342–3; Lindberg, *EV*, V.167–8

prol. inc: Þis profete Jeremye tolde openli þingis to comynge (M), *WB*, III.342

Lamentations of Jeremiah *WB*, III.472–83; Lindberg, *EV*, V.239–245

Prayer of Jeremiah (= Lam.5)

Baruch *WB*, III.484–500; Lindberg, *EV*, V.245–VI.79; Lindberg, *Baruch* (*C*/*K*A)

prol. inc: Þis book þat Baruch bi name is befor-notid (**EV** MSS)

inc: Þis book which is titlid bi þe name of Baruk (**LV** MSS)

[*RBMA*, no. 491] *WB*, III.484; Lindberg, *EV*, V.245; Lindberg, *Baruch* (*C*A)

Epistle of Jeremiah (= Bar. 6)

Ezekiel *WB*, III.501–620; Lindberg, *EV*, VI.79–148

prol. inc: Þis profete Ezekiel seiȝ in visioun (MR), *WB*, III.501

Daniel *WB*, III.621–69; Lindberg, *EV*, VI.148–76

prol. inc: Þis profete Danyel was in þe transmygracioun of Babiloyne (MR), *WB*, III.621

Hosea (Osee) *WB*, III.670–85; Lindberg, *EV*, VI.176–86

Joel *WB*, III.686–92; Lindberg, *EV*, VI.186–9

Amos *WB*, III.693–706; Lindberg, *EV*, VI.189–97

Obadiah (Abdias) *WB*, III.707–9; Lindberg, *EV*, VI.197–8

Jonah *WB*, III.710–14; Lindberg, *EV*, VI.198–201

Micah *WB*, III.715–24; Lindberg, *EV*, VI.201–6

Nahum *WB*, III.725–9; Lindberg, *EV*, VI.207–9

Habakkuk (Abacuk) *WB*, III.730–5; Lindberg, *EV*, VI.209–12

Zephaniah (Sophonie) *WB*, III.736–41; Lindberg, *EV*, VI.212–15

Haggai (Aggei) *WB*, III.742–5; Lindberg, *EV*, VI.215–17

Zechariah (Sacarie) *WB*, III.746–66; Lindberg, *EV*, VI.217–28

Malachi *WB*, III.767–773; Lindberg, *EV*, VI.228–31

1 Maccabees (Machabeis) *WB*, III.774–845; Lindberg, *EV*, VI.232–71

prol. inc: Þis book of Machabeis techiþ alle men bi ensaumple (M), *WB*, III.774

2 Maccabees *WB*, III.846–97; Lindberg, *EV*, VI.271–300

NEW TESTAMENT

Matthew *WB*, IV.1–85; Lindberg, *EV*, VII.26–78

prol. inc: Mathew of Jewerie born, as he is put first in ordre (**EV** MSS; see p. 105, Appendix 4 and Index of MSS for further details of NT prols in EV MSS)

[*RBMA*, no. 590; WW, *NT*, 1.15–17] *WB*, IV.1; Lindberg, *EV*, VII.26–7

prol. inc: Matheu þat was of Judee, as he is set first in ordre (**LV** MSS)

[opening of *RBMA*, no. 590 + *RBMA*, no. 589] *WB*, IV.2
prol. inc: Þouȝ al holi writt is ful trewe nedeful and comfortable (p3), *WB*, IV.682[a] (p)
prol. inc: Siþþen aftir þe assencioun of Crist (y), *WB*, IV, 682[a]–[b]
prol. inc: Seynt Austyn saiþ in þe secounde book' (D–76R–77 Dresden Od. 83) ['intermediate Matthew prologue', *Glossed Gospels*, and prol. to *Oon of Foure*] Hunt, *TFST*, II.370–82
prol. inc: Oure lord Jesu Crist verry God and man (R_77 Dresden Od. 83) [prol. to *Oon of Foure*] *WB*, I.xiv–xv; Hunt, *TFST*, II.282–8

Mark *WB*, IV.86–140; Lindberg, *EV*, VII.79–112
prol. inc: Mark þe euangelist of God chosen and Petris sone in baptem (**EV** MSS)
inc: Mark þe gospeller was þe chosun seruaunt of God (**LV** MSS)
[*RBMA*, no. 607; WW, *NT*, 1.171–3] *WB*, IV.86–7; Lindberg, *EV*, VII.79–80
prol. inc: Siþ seint Mark so ful of þe Holi Goost (p), *WB*, IV.682[b]–3[b]
prol. inc: Þis gospeler Mark þe which was þe disciple of Petir (y), *WB*, IV.683[b]
prol. inc: Mark þe gospeller doynge þe office of preest to þe peple of Israel (P_P*U*)

Luke *WB*, IV.141–232; Lindberg, *EV*, VII.113–65
prol. inc: Luk of Antioche of Cire nacyoun in craft a leche (**EV** MSS)
inc: Luik was a man of Syrie bi nacioun and of Antiochie and was a leche (**LV** MSS)
[*RBMA*, no. 620; WW, *NT*, 1.269–71] *WB*, IV.141–2; Lindberg, *EV*, VII.113–14
prol. inc: Luk haþ manie special poyntis and nameli of oure ladi (p), *WB*, IV.684[b]
prol. inc: Whanne þe gospel was spred bi Matheu in þe Jewrie (y), *WB*, IV.684[b]

John *WB*, IV.233–97; Lindberg, *EV*, VII.166–203
prol. inc: Þis is John ewangelist, oen of disciplis off God (**EV** MSS)
inc: Þis is Joon euangelist, oon of þe disciplis of þe Lord (**LV** MSS)
[*RBMA*, no. 633; WW, *NT*, 1.485–7] *WB*, IV.233–4; Lindberg, *EV*, VII.166
prol. inc: Joon treetiþ moost of þe trynyte and of þe godhede and manhede (p), *WB*, IV.685[b]
prol. inc: Þis fourþe gospeller Joon þe apostil and þe euangelist whanne (y), *WB*, IV.685[b]
prol. inc: 'Oure lord Jesu Crist verry God and man' (D_76), see prologues to Matt., above

Romans *WB*, IV.298–337; Lindberg, *EV*, VIII.72–94
prol. inc: First vndirstonden vs bihoueþ to whom or whi þe apostil Powil (**EV** MSS + I)
[*RBMA*, no. 669; WW, *NT*, 2.5–7] *WB*, IV.298–300; Lindberg, *EV*, VIII.72–4 (*S*)
prol. inc: Romaynes þe whiche in þe cite of Rome leueden (**EV** MSS)
inc: Romayns ben in þe cuntree of Italye; þei weren disseyued (**LV** MSS)
[Marcion, *RBMA*, no. 677] *WB*, IV.303; Lindberg, *EV*, VIII.74–5 (*S*)
prol. inc: Romayns ben þei þat of Jewis and of heþene men gaderid (lmnopqr BL Lansdowne 455, Dresden Od. 83 *sim. U*) [*RBMA*, no. 674] *WB*, IV.301–3 (o)

1 Corinthians *WB*, IV.338–72; Lindberg, *EV*, VIII.95–115
prol. inc: Corintheis ben men of Achaie and þese also (**EV** MSS)
inc: Corinthies ben of Acaye and þei in lijk maner herden (**LV** MSS)
[Marcion, *RBMA*, no. 684; WW, *NT*, 2.153] *WB*, IV.338; Lindberg, *EV*, VIII.95 (*S*)
prol. inc: As þe apostil þat cowde alle langagis wroot þe pistil (p), *WB*, IV.686[b]
prol. inc: As þe apostil wroot þe pistil þat goiþ bifore to myȝti men (y), *WB*, IV.686[b]

2 Corinthians *WB*, IV.373–95; Lindberg, *EV*, VIII.116–29
prol. inc: Aftir penaunce don a counfortable epistil he wryteþ (**EV** MSS)
inc: After penaunce doon, Poul writiþ (**LV** MSS)
[Marcion, *RBMA*, no. 700; WW, *NT*, 2.279] *WB*, IV.373; Lindberg, *EV*, VIII.116 (*S*)
prol. inc: . . . stynatli þe pistil and magnified fals apostlis (frag. p), *WB*, IV.687[b]
prol. inc: In þe formere epistil þe apostil scharpli reproues hem (y), *WB*, IV.687[b]

Galatians (Galathies) *WB*, IV.396–407; Lindberg, *EV*, VIII.130–6
prol. inc: Galathiis ben Grekis. Þes þe wrd of treuþe (**EV** MSS)
inc: Galathies ben Grekis. Þei token first of þe postle (**LV** MSS)
[Marcion, *RBMA*, no. 707; WW, *NT*, 2.355] *WB*, IV.396; Lindberg, *EV*, VIII.130 (*S*)
prol. inc: And þouȝ Grekis ben of sharp wit (P_Sy *sim.* p) [WW, *NT*, 2.356] *WB*, IV.687[b]–8[b] (py)
prol. inc: Þe fynal conclusioun of þe postle in þis pistle (P_S) [WW, *NT*, 2.357] *WB*, IV.688[b]
prol. inc: In þe firste pistle þat is to Romayns Poul tretiþ of power (P_S), *WB*, IV.688[b]–9[b]

Ephesians *WB*, IV.408–19; Lindberg, *EV*, VIII.155–61
prol. inc: Ephecyes soþli ben Asianes (**EV** MSS)
inc: Effesians ben of Asie (**LV** MSS)
[Marcion, *RBMA*, no. 715; WW, *NT*, 2.406] *WB*, IV.408; Lindberg, *EV*, VIII.155 (*S*)
prol. inc: Effesies weren conuertid to cristen feiþ bifore þe comynge (py), *WB*, IV.689[b]
[Ephesians follows 2 Thess. in *X*]

Philippians (Philipensis, Filipenensis) *WB*, IV.420–8; Lindberg, *EV*, VIII.137–41
prol. inc: Philipenses ben men of Macedoyne (**EV** MSS)
inc: Philipensis ben of Macedoyne (**LV** MSS)
[Marcion, *RBMA*, no. 728; WW, *NT*, 2.455] *WB*, IV.420; Lindberg, *EV*, VIII.137 (*S*)
prol. inc: Þese Filipensis tooken of þe apostil þe word of prechynge (py), *WB*, IV.689[b]

Colossians (Colocensis) *WB*, IV.429–37; Lindberg, *EV*, VIII.142–6
prol. inc: Colocences also þese as Laodicensis (**EV** MSS)
inc: Colocensis ben also Laodicenses (**LV** MSS)
[Marcion, *RBMA*, no. 736; WW, *NT*, 2.491] *WB*, IV.429; Lindberg, *EV*, VIII.142 (*S*)
prol. inc: Poul wroot þis pistil to Colocensis to þe whiche him silf (py), *WB*, IV.689[b]–90[b]

[**Laodiceans** in 12 late LV MSS] *WB*, IV.438–9 (ow). See Appendix 3.

1 Thessalonians *WB*, IV.440–7; Lindberg, *EV*, VIII.147–51
prol. inc: Tessalonycenses ben men of Macedoyne (**EV** MSS)
inc: Thessalonicensis ben Macedonyes (**LV** MSS)
[Marcion, *RBMA*, no. 747; WW, *NT*, 2.525] *WB*, IV.440; Lindberg, *EV*, VIII.147 (*S*)
prol. inc: Þe apostil writiþ þis to Tessaloniensis (py), *WB*, IV.690[b]

2 Thessalonians *WB*, IV.448–52; Lindberg, *EV*, VIII.152–4
prol. inc: To Tessalonycensses þe apostil wrytiþ (**EV** MSS)
inc: Þe apostle writiþ þe secounde (**LV** MSS)
[Marcion, *RBMA*, no. 752; WW, *NT*, 2.555] *WB*, IV.448; Lindberg, *EV*, VIII.152 (*S*)
prol. inc: Þis epistil as þe toþer is departid into tweie partis (y), *WB*, IV.690[b]

1 Timothy *WB*, IV.453–63; Lindberg, *EV*, VIII.162–7
prol. inc: Tymothe þe apostil enfoormeþ and techeþ (**EV** MSS)
inc: He enformeþ and techiþ Tymothe (**LV** MSS)

[Marcion, *RBMA*, no. 765; WW, *NT*, 2.575] *WB*, IV.453; Lindberg, *EV*, VIII.162 (*S*)
prol. inc: Poul þe apostil writiþ þis epistil to Tymothe (p), *WB*, IV.690[b]–1[b]
prol. inc: Þe apostil writiþ fro Rome to Tymothe whom he ordeinede (y), *WB*, IV.691[b]

2 Timothy *WB*, IV.464–71; Lindberg, *EV*, VIII.168–72
prol. inc: Also he writiþ to Tymothe of þe exortacioun (**EV** MSS)
inc: He writiþ also to Tymothe of exortacioun (**LV** MSS)
[Marcion, *RBMA*, no. 772] *WB*, IV.464; Lindberg, *EV*, VIII.168 (*S*)
prol. inc: Poul þat schulde passe out of þis world (p), *WB*, IV.691[b]
prol. inc: Poul þe .ii. tyme whanne he was representid to Nero (y), *WB*, IV.691[b]

Titus *WB*, IV.472–6; Lindberg, *EV*, VIII.173–5
prol. inc: Tyte he counceiliþ and enformeþ (**EV** MSS)
inc: He warneþ Tite and enfourmeþ (**LV** MSS)
[Marcion, *RBMA*, no. 780] *WB*, IV.472; Lindberg, *EV*, VIII.173 (*S*)
prol. inc: Seint Poul ordeinede Tite erchebischop in Crete (p), *WB*, IV.691[b]
prol. inc: Poul bigat Tite in þe bileue of Crist and he ordeynede him (y), *WB*, IV. 691[b]–2[b]

Philemon *WB*, IV.477–9; Lindberg, *EV*, VIII.176–7
prol. inc: To Filomon he makiþ homly lettris (**EV** MSS)
inc: He makiþ famyliar or homeli lettris to Filemon (**LV** MSS)
[Marcion, *RBMA*, no. 783] *WB*, IV.477; Lindberg, *EV*, VIII.176 (*S*)
prol. inc: Þe apostil writiþ þis pistil to Filemon a man of Colosis (p), *WB*, IV.692[b]
prol. inc: Þe entent of þe apostle is to biseche forȝeuenesse of Filemon (y), *WB*, IV.692[b]

Hebrews (Ebrews) *WB*, IV.480–506; Lindberg, *EV*, VIII.178–93
prol. inc: In þe firste it is to seie whi þe apostil Powil (**EV** MSS)
inc: First it is to seye whi Poul þe apostle in þis epistle (**LV** MSS)
[Marcion, *RBMA*, no. 793; WW, *NT*, 2.679–80] *WB*, IV.480; Lindberg, *EV*, VIII.178 (*S*)
prol. inc: Poul wroot þis epistle more cleerli or exelently þan oþere (p), *WB*, IV.692[b]
inc: Þe apostil wroote to Ebrews þis pistil in Ebrew tunge (y), *WB*, IV.692[b]–3[b]

Acts of the Apostles (Deedis of Apostlis) *WB*, IV.507–93; Lindberg, *EV*, VIII.219–69

prol. inc: Luk of Sirie by nacioun whos preising in þe euangelie (**EV** MSS)
inc: Luk of Antioche of þe nacioun of Sirie whos preisyng (**LV** MSS)
[Hugh of St Cher, *RBMA*, no. 640; WW, *NT*, 3.1–2] *WB*, IV.507–8; Lindberg, *EV*, VIII.219 (*S*)
prol. inc: Þe principal conclusioun of þe Deedis of Apostlis is þis (py), *WB*, IV.693[b]
[Acts follows Catholic Epistles in *X*]

The Catholic Epistles, Canonical Epistles, Seuen Epistlis of Cristen Feiþ:

James *WB*, IV.594–604; Lindberg, *EV*, VIII.194–9
prol. inc: Not þe same ordre is at Greekis þat holly sauouren (**EV** MSS)
inc: Þe ordre of þe seuene epistlis whiche ben clepid canonysid (**LV** MSS)
[*RBMA*, no. 809; WW, *NT*, 3.230–1] *WB*, IV.594–5 (*S*A); Lindberg, *EV*, VIII.194 (*S*)
prol. inc: We reden þat whanne seynt Steuene was slayn (y frag. p), *WB*, IV.693[b]

1 Peter *WB*, IV.605–14; Lindberg, *EV*, VIII.200–5
prol. inc: In þis first pistil Petir tretiþ of moral vertues (y), *WB*, IV.694[b]

2 Peter *WB*, IV.615–21; Lindberg, *EV*, VIII.206–9
prol. inc: In þis secunde pistil first Petir telliþ þe giftis (y), *WB*, IV.694[b]

1 John *WB*, IV.622–30; Lindberg, *EV*, VIII.210–14
prol. inc: Seynt Joon þe euangelist hadde a special loue (py), p, *WB*, IV.694[b]

2 John *WB*, IV.631–2; Lindberg, *EV*, VIII.215

3 John *WB*, IV.633–4; Lindberg, *EV*, VIII.216

Jude *WB*, IV.635–7; Lindberg, *EV*, VIII.217–18
prol. inc: Judas þe broþir of James þe which also is clepid (frag. p), *WB*, IV.695[b]

Apocalypse (Reuelacioun of Seint Joon) *WB*, IV.638–81; Lindberg, *EV*, VIII.270–92
prol. inc: Jon þe apostil and euangelist of oure lord Jhesu Crist (**EV** MSS)
[Ps-Isidore, *RBMA*, no. 834; WW, *NT*, 3.407–8] *WB*, IV.638 (*S*); Lindberg, *EV*, VIII.270 (*S*)
prol. inc: Alle men þat wolen lyue mekeli in Crist as þe apostle seiþ (**LV** MSS)
[Gilbert de la Porrée?, *RBMA*, no. 839] *WB*.IV. 638–40
prol. inc: Þis is a prolog sett comynli in manie biblis (py), *WB*, IV.695[b]

APPENDIX 2

Additions and select emendations to Forshall and Madden's edition of the Wycliffite Bible

This appendix is a supplement and a preliminary *correctorium* to Forshall and Madden's edition of WB in LV. Nearly all the errors of transcription in their edition occur in the text of the glosses.

Unique readings in A: Forshall and Madden's base text of LV has some readings not found in any other MS yet included in *WB*'s text of LV. These are noted here alongside the reading of all other LV MSS.

Translational variants: A omits most translational variants from Gen. 1 to Num. 20 and from Psalms to the end of the OT, choosing one or other of the alternatives. In *WB*, the translational variants are recorded in the *apparatus criticus*. P_S, not collated for *WB*, also omits some translational variants, and its choices between alternatives are here supplied alongside those of A.

Glosses: *WB* omits some glosses found in LV MSS, and does not note any of the glosses in B after Deuteronomy. The text of all glosses omitted in *WB* is included here, and also the text of glosses in B which correct C (e.g., Job 30:21, below). The glosses in Psalms are compared with the equivalent glosses in the Glossed Psalter, B_554, not collated for *WB*. Unless otherwise stated, glosses are in the margin.

Gen. 30:37 dide awey, eþer shauede (K)

Exd. 30:18 wiþ his foundement, in Ebru it is, wiþ his seete [feet *WB*, I.266] [Lyra] (dGQX)

Judg. 12:3 and puttide my lijf, þat is, bi nede constreinynge [oft þinynge *WB*, I.649] (C)

Judg. 14:6 þe spirit, þat is, þe spirit of strengþe (B)

Ruth 3:11 drede, of matrimonye þat schal be to þee, Lire here (B)

1 Kings 17:18 ten litil, etc., þat is, x. litle chesis formed (BC) [*WB*, II.49 omits sigla]

1 Kings 24:7 crist, þat is, anoyntid (K)

2 Kings 13:19 coote to þe hele, in Ebrew it is, wiþ a coote of silk (B)
3 Kings 13:24 and killide, þis prophet was disceyued and sleyn iustly, for he had veyn glorie þat he vndirname stidefastly þe king, Gregorius, *Mor* [*alia in Iob*] (I)
3 Kings 19:21 killide hem, Helizee slewe hise oxen and fedde pore men of þat þat he hadde, þat he were not lett bi worldli hauing to sue þe prophet, Ambrose (I)
4 Kings 3:21 stoden in þe termes, þat is, in þe strayte places and harde, Lire here (B)
4 Kings 17:32 þe laste men, þat is, of þe fouliste men, Lire here (B) [cf. *WB*, II.286]
4 Kings 18:4 Noestam, eþer of copir, as if he seide no þing of godhed was in it, Lire here (B) [cf. *WB*, II.288]
4 Kings 21:16 to þe mouþ, þat is, as myche as it myȝte take, Lire here (B)
4 Kings 22:11 cloþis, in signe of sorowe for offensis passid (B)
4 Kings 22:14 þe prophetesse, oure doctouris seyen comounly þat Josias sente not to Jeremye for he was ȝonge þanne and was not in autorite, but semeþ not sooþ, for Jeremye hadde profecied þanne in fyue ȝeer at þe leeste, þerfor summe Ebreyes seyen þat he sente to a womman profetesse, for wommen ben wont to be moore mersiful þan men. Anoþer cause is þis, for Jeremye was goon þanne to teche bi word þe ten lynagis þat þei schulden not for ȝete þe lord in þe lond of her caytiftee, eþer to teche þo fewe þat werun left in þe lond of Israel, for þei werun not alle led in to caitifte bi Salmanasar, Lire here (B)
4 Kings 22:16 þese þingis, sey ȝe to þe man þat sente ȝou to me 'þe lord God of Israel seiþ þese þingis' (B)
4 Kings 22:17 quenchid, þat is, peyne determyned of me schal not be reuokid, and to þe lettre þe cytee of Jerusalem was brent of Caldeys in [4 Kings 25:9] wiþ ynne (B)
4 Kings 22:20 sepulcre in pees, þe contrarye semeþ, for he was slayn of þe king of Egipt. Þe soiling is, in pees, for þis distriyng of þe cytee and of þe temple bifelde not in hise daies, as þe lettre seiþ; eþer, in pees, for þei werun siker of her blis to comynge, and Josais was of þe noumbre of hem, Lire here (B)
4 Kings 23:3 þe grees, which king Salomon made in [2 Chron. 3:15–17] (B)
4 Kings 23:6 comyn puple, þat worschipide Baal (B)
4 Kings 23:7 men turnyd, þat is, of prestis of ydols þat werun geldid, litil howsis, Ebreys seyen here þe litil lynsis of munkis, of þe wode,

þat is, curteyns to make hore housis in þe wode when þe wommen diden horedam for þe onour of þe idol at þe teching of prestis, Lire here (B)

4 Kings 23:16 spak, in [3 Kings 13:2], Lire here (B)

4 Kings 23:18 Samarye, for Jewis of ten lynagis þat werun hid whanne oþere werun take prisoneris dwelliden aftirward in þo cytees, and þei obeyeden to Josias at þe manasing of Jeremye (B)

4 Kings 23:25 was lijk hym, þouȝ Dauiþ in summe þingis was deuouter, naþeles he was not moore innocent, for Josias dide not siche synnes as Dauiþ dide (B)

4 Kings 23:26 turned awei, for þe holynes of Josias clenside not þe malices of hise predecessouris, whiche malices werun ful grete as to þe greuousnesse of synnes and to lengþe of tymes (B)

4 Kings 23:29 Josias king, for þe king of Egipt ȝede by a part of þe rewme of Juda, and Josias nolde suffre þis and dredde leste þe king of Egipt þat entride in to his lond wolde take it eþer nome bi robberi, Lire here (B)

4 Kings 23:29 hadde seyn hym, þat is, hadde founde aȝenus him, Lire here (B)

4 Kings 23:32 hise fadris, þat is, Manasses and Achaz and oþere þat werun worste ydolatouris (B)

4 Kings 23:34 Eliachim, þe eldir sone of Josias, for þe puple of þe lond made king þe ȝongere sone, but Farao restoride þe rewme to þe eldir sone þat he schulde serue him moore feiþfuly, Lire here (B)

4 Kings 24:3 of Manasses, for þouȝ Manasses dide penaunce and was herd of God in his owne persone, as it is had in [2 Chron. 33:12–16], naþeles not as to þis þat þe puple schulde be delyuerid fro caytifte and þe cytee fro brennyng, for þe puple synnede as he dide and repentide not as he dide, and aftir Manasses alle þe kingis of Juda outake (except) Josias offendiden God, wherfore þe puple was maad caitif and þe cytee was distried, as in [4 Kings 25] suynge (B)

4 Kings 24:6 fadris, not þat he diede in pees, for Nabugodonosor killide him and made his bodi vnbiried to be cast forþ wiþ out þe ȝatis of Jerusalem, as Jeremye bifore seide in [Jer. 22:18–19], Lire here (B)

4 Kings 24:7 hys lond, þat is, aȝens þe kyng of Babiloyne, as Joachim lyþide (B)

4 Kings 24:12 ȝede out, he dide þis bi couceil of Jeremye, and ȝeldide him silf to Nabugodonosor leste þe cytee and þe temple were distried and al þe puple takun prisoneris for cause of him (B)

4 Kings 24:12 his rewme, þat is, of þe king of Babiloyne (B)

4 Kings 24:16 seuene þousind, iii. þousind werun of þe lynagis of Juda in þe laste chapitre of Jeremye, and þo ben not noumbrid here (B)

4 Kings 24:16 and crafti men, þat is crafti men, þis word, and, is set for, þat is (B)

4 Kings 24:17 Sedechie, [þat B] is interpretid þe riȝtfulnesse of þe lord (expl. C) for Nabugodonosor made him to swere bi God þat he schulde kepe feiþfulnesse to him, and ȝelde tribute to him in [2 Chron. 36:13], and herfor Nabugodonosor clepide him so þat he schulde be myndeful of þe ooþ which he made to him as it was iust, but he brak his ooþ and nolde bileeue to Jeremye in ony þing, Lire here (B)

4 Kings 25:24 swoor, þat is, boond of feiþfulnesse þat þei schulden dwelle pesibly in þe lond vndir þe seruage of þe king of Babiloyne (B)

4 Kings 25:25 ten men, but oþere mo werun hid wiþoutforþ, for ten men schulden not haue maad so greet slauȝter and haue take so greet prey as þis Ismael dide þenne, Lire here (B)

1 Chron. 2:24 fadir of pecue, þat is, lord of Techue (B)

1 Chron. 4:10 malice, þat is, but to lyue in contemplacioun (B)

1 Chron. 8:29 Abigabaon, in Ebreu it is, fadur of Gabaon (B)

1 Chron. 28:17 goldun lyouns, þat is, goldun basyns, siluerne lyouns, þat is, siluerne basyns, Lire here (B)

2 Chron. 18:11 stie þou, Mychee seyde þis by condicioun, þat is 'if þi profetis seyen soþ it schal be so as Y seie now'. Eþer he spak desiringe þat it schulde be so eþer deniynge þat it schulde be so, and þe kyng of Israel perseyuede þis bi summe signes, and þerfor he chargide Mychee to sey þe truþe in Goddis name, Lire here (B)

2 Chron. 19:6 but of þe lord, wherfor iugis þat holden þe place of God ben seid Goddis bi grace and office, Lire here (B)

2 Chron. 20:1 Ydumeys, in Ebreu it is, of Ammonytis. In truþe þei werun Ydumeys as þe text seiþ wiþ inne, but in Ebreu þei ben seid Ammonytis for þei token þe signes of Ammonytis and ioyneden hem to þe oost of Ammonytis as if þei werun of þe same puple, Lire here (B)

2 Chron. 20:32 hiȝe þingis (EV MSS + A) placis (all other LV MSS), þe contrarie semeþ in [2 Chron. 17:6]; þe soiling is þis [etc.] (B) [cf. C, *WB*, II. 430]

2 Chron. 21:16 spirit, þat is, wille and hardynes to assayle þe rewme of Joram, Lire here (B)

2 Chron. 21:19 brennyng, in brennynge swete smellinge spicis, Lire here (B)

2 Chron. 22:2 xlij. ȝeer, þis semeþ impossible, for it is seid in þe eende of þe chapitre biforegoing þat Joram his fadur was of xxxij. ȝeer whanne he bigan to regne and he regnede viij. ȝeer, wherof it sueþ þat Ocozie his sone was eldir þan his fadur bi ij. ȝeer. Jerom assoiliþ þus, þat Joram regnede xxviij. ȝeer and he regnede viij. ȝeer wel bifore þat he was drawen to idolatrie bi his wijf, and oonli þo viij. ȝeer ben rikened in his rewme. In þe oþere xx. ȝeer he regnede worst, and þerfor þo ben not rikened in his rewme, Lire here (B)

2 Chron. 24:6 Moyses, þat is, for ech heed half a sicle in [Exd. 30:12–16], Lire here (B)

2 Chron. 24:7 sones, þat is, prestis of Baal whiche sche noreschide, Lire here (B)

2 Chron. 24:14 vessels, þe contrarye semeþ in [4 Kings 12:13] where it is seid þus, vessels of þe temple werun not maad of þe same money. Þe soiling is þis, as longe as þe bilding of þe temple was in reparayling, vessels werun not maad of þat moneye and so spekiþ þat text, but aftir þat þe bilding of þe temple was fully reparailid vessels werun maad of þat moneye, and so spekiþ þis text, Lire here (B)

2 Chron. 24:17 worschipiden þe kyng, in ȝouynge to him Goddis onour, Lire here (B)

2 Chron. 25:13 fro Samarye, þis oost of Israel dyde noon harm til Amasye was rasid in to pride and worschipide þe goddis of Edom, þerfor by Goddis ordenaunce þei assailiden his rewme after þat þei werun comen to her lond, not in goinge to her lond. Þerfor it is seid, fro Samarye, etc., þat is, in comynge fro Samarye in to Bethoron. Forsoþe Samarye was in þe rewme of Israel and Bethoron in þe rewme of Juda, and þerfor if þei hadden do þis in goinge aȝen fro þe oost of Amasie þe scripture wolde haue seid in contrarye maner, þat is, fro Bethoron til to Samarie, Lire here (B)

2 Chron. 25:24 of ostagis, þese werun of princis of þe rewme of Juda, whiche þe kyng of Israel took in batel, and whanne he cam in to Jerusalem he changide and took þe sones for þe fadris, Lire here (B)

2 Chron. 36:10 cercle, not fro þe bigynnyng of his coronacioun, but þe cercle is seid here tyme able to go to batel, Lire here (B)

2 Chron. 37 lord God, þis preyere of Manasses is not in Ebreu (marg. *al. m. E* | *H* text *A*L_o) [*WB*, II.475 supplies the wrong sigla]

1 Ezra 3:10 hond, þat is, synginge þe song maad of Dauiþ, Lire here (B)

1 Ezra 7:6 lawe of Moises, þis is referrid to þe officis of prestis and dekenes in [Lev. 21], not to þe ordris of prestis and whilis of dekenes whiche Dauiþ ordeynede in [1 Chron. 6], Lire here (B)

2 Ezra 1:3 ȝatis, prestis schulden be cheef ȝatis of Goddis citee (I)
Tob. 2:8 þe comaundement of deeþ, þat is, deeþ comaundid to þee, Lire here (B)
Tob. 12:5 asidis half, eþer bi hem silf (text B)
Tob. 13:13 liȝt, þis liȝt was Crist offrid in þe temple, Lire here (B)
Judith 11:21 Holofernes seide þese þingis in gile (S)
Esth. 7:8 þey, þe ministris, eþer seruauntis (K)
Job 1:21 þidur, as a man comeþ in to þe world and is nakid of alle goodis, so he schal go nakid out of þe world, Lire here (B)
Job 2:3 in veyn, as to þi purpos, for he was not vnpacient neþer blasfemede God as þou purposidist, Lire here (B)
Job 3:9 abide it liȝt and se it not, Ebreis seyen þat þis is þe text, þat abiden to be maad wiþ out felowschip, for sum men anoyed of her liif abiden deeþ wiþ desier and coueiten to be departid fro her felowscipe, Lire here (B)
Job 3:26 dissymilide not, in not vengynge wrongis doon of oþere men to me, was not stille, in not answeringe schenschipis, restide not, in not disesinge oþere men, as if he seiþ 'ȝhis', and so he was innocent, Lire here (B)
Job 3:26 indignacioun, þat is, wretþid brouȝt in of God, which is þe signe of his indignacioun, Lire here (B)
Job 4:21 þis þat sueþ, fro hem, is not in Ebrew neþer is of þe text, Lire here (B)
Job 7:7 goodis, þat is, of þe present liif in fleschely liif, Lire here (B)
Job 8:16 schal go out, þat is, in þe rising of þe sunne it lesiþ þe vertu of seed (B)
Job 9:13 world, þat is, aungels, þat mynystren eþer rulyn ech bodily creature (B)
Job 9:17 [wiþ] out cause, þat is, knowen to me, þouȝ it be knowen to God (B)
Job 9:24 þat if he, þat is, Satan, is not, þe firste cause of þe forseid peynes, who is, as if he seye 'God suffriþ' (B)
Job 13:14 bere my lijf in myn hondis, þat is, Y recke not for to lese my liif for dispeir, come in his siȝt [16], þat is to resseyue heelþe, Lire here (*bis* B)
Job 14:20 wiþouten ende, þat is fro present lijf to deeþ wiþ outen comynge aȝen most, bi þe opynyoun of Joobis frendis denyinge þat ony þing of man dwelliþ after deeþ, Lire here (B)
Job 16:6 mouþ, þat is, ynduce ȝou to pacience, Lire here (B)

Job 17:13 helle, for, helle, is an Ebreu word þat signefieþ oþir [ofte WB, II.697] a diche oþir birying (BC) þat is biriyng wiþinne erþe (K)

Job 20:26 is not teendid, þat is, helle fier, not teendid by þe studye of man but of God (B)

Job 22:12 flowyng, þat is, strong and feers tribulacioun (B)

Job 23:8 apperiþ not, þat is, he is not knowen parfitly, Lire here (B)

Job 24:19 hellis, þat is, make þe synner to go doun to þe peyne of helle, be a worm [20], þat is, delitinge in synne schal be turnyd in to wormes, þat is gnawynge of conscience (B)

Job 26:4 made breþing, þat is, mannys soule (text B)

Job 26:10 liȝt and derknessis, þat is, day and nyȝt (text B)

Job 29:18 in my nest, þat is, my prosperyte goostli and temporaly (B)

Job 30:21 in to cruel, etc., þis is seid by þe comyn maner of speking of men, which maner Joob suede, þouȝ he helde stidefastly þat alle þingis [B lesingis C, *WB*, II.715] ben wrouȝt of God pitously and iustly, Lire here (BC)

Job 31:26 clereli, þat is, in doinge ydolatrie as heþen diden (B)

Job 33:16 [þe eeris] of men, þat is, þe vndirstonding of men, Lire here (B)]

Job 34:14 herte, þat is, wille (text B)

Job 35:11 þei, þat is, wickide men turmentid for her malice, Lire here (B)

Job 36:25 seen God, þat is, han knowyng of hym, Lire here (B)

Job 37:9 ynnere þingis, þat is, polus antarticus which is euer hid to us (B)

Job 42:8 riȝtful þing, þat is, verry techyng, Lire here (B)

Job 42:13 cassia, þat is a spice of swete smellinge spicerye (B)

Ps. 1:5 doom, þat is, to her [han *WB*, II. 739] saluacioun but to dampnacioun more (V), þat is, to þer saluacioun but more to þer dampnacioun (text K), þat is, to her saluacioun but more to dampnacioun of bodi and soule, Lire here (B$_{554}$)

Ps. 2 [title] þe secounde salm þat haþ [þouȝ it haue k] no title in Ebreu and in Jeromis translacioun was maad of Dauiþ as þe postlis witnessen in [Acts 4:25] [Lire here B$_{554}$] (B$_{554}$ C C$_{J\,E.14}$ D$_{T\,72}$ EIKkLPQSUX *al. m. X*)

þis secunde psalm is vndirstondun of Crist God and man (expl. V) to þe lettre, as Poul in [Hebr. 1:5] and þe postlis in [Acts 4:25] witnessen and þe eld doctours of Ebreis, forwhi preuyng bi gostli vndurstonding is not worþ but oneli of literal vndurstondynge, as Austin seiþ in his pistle aȝenus Vyncent Donatist, Lire here (B$_{554}$)

Ps. 7 [title] to God, þat is, for þe synne of ignoraunce of Dauiþ, by which he was occasioun of þe deeþ of prestis slayn of Saul and of Doech for þe helping of Dauiþ [Lire here B_554] (AbB_554C C_J_E.14 D_T_72EKiLPQSUX *X*) for þe synne þat was cause of deþ of prestis for loue of Dauiþ (V)

Ps. 7:10 reynes, þat is delitinges (marg. V text K), hertis and reynes, þat is þouȝtis and delitingis, Lire here (B_554) [cf. *WB*, II.743]

Ps. 19 [title] to gete victorie for his oost (V)

Ps. 19:8 þes, þat is [oure B_554] aduersaries tristen [Lire here B_554] (marg. B_554V text K) [cf. *WB*, II.756]

Ps. 25 [title] taking þe rewme aftir þe deeþ of Saul (k)

Ps. 26 [title] þat he made aftir Saulis deeþ bifore his anointing (V) aftir þe deeþ of Saul or he were anoyntid (k)

Ps. 27 [title] fleinge fro Jerusalem for drede of Absolon (k)

Ps. 35 [title] [in Ebrew þus B_554iV] to victorie to Dauiþ þe seruaunt of þe lord (LV) Jerom seiþ þus (in Jeroms translacioun þus B_554) for þe victorie of Dauiþ þe seruaunt of þe lord [Lyra] (B_554iV) aȝens þe persecucioun of Saul (kS)

Ps. 38:7 ymage, þat is derknesse (text K marg. V) in ebreu it is, in derknesse (marg. B_554) [cf. *WB*, II.776]

Ps. 39:16 wel wel, in despijt, þat is in scorn (text C_U_6680DKMP_SQS scorn, in despijt W) [cf. *WB*, II.777]

Ps. 48:6 heele, þat is, werk (text KV) þat is, werkis, Lire here (marg. B_554) [cf. *WB*, II.785]

Ps. 48:14 mouþ, þat is, bosting of lustful lijf (text K marg. V) for þei avaunten hem of sich lustful liyf as if þei han gete blis possible to man, Lire here (B_554) [cf. *WB*, II.785]

Ps. 50:19 troblid, þat is, sori for synne [Lire here B_554] (marg. B_554V text K) [cf. *WB*, II.788]

Ps. 54:20 chaungyng, þat is, fro synne to penaunce [Lire here B_554] (marg. B_554V text K) [cf. *WB*, II.791]

Ps. 58:5 dresside, my werkis [Lire here Q] (marg. bB_554OQ text AU) [cf. *WB*, II.795]

Ps. 58:7 cumpas, þat is, go a begging (K) Ps. 58:15 cumpas, þat is, gon a beggid (V) in sekinge liyflode bi beggynge, Lire here (B_554) [cf. *WB*, II.795]

Ps. 59:7 riȝt hond, þe puple of Israel [Lire here Q] (marg. B_554IQ text AU) [cf. *WB*, II.796]

Ps. 59:8 Siccimam, þat is, þe lond of Sichem [Lire here B_554] (marg. B_554V text K) [cf. *WB*, II.796]

Ps. 63:8 litle men, þat is, [of B_554] enuiouse men [Lire here B_554] (marg. B_554V text K) [cf. *WB*, II.799]

Ps. 64:12 coroun, eþer (þat is þe B_554) sercle [Lyra] (marg. B_554 text V) [cf. *WB*, II.800]

Ps. 65:20 remoued not my preyer and, took not awei [Lire here U] (marg. B_554 text AU) [cf. *WB*, II.802]

Ps. 71:5 moone, þat is, wiþoute bigynnyng and eende (text KV) longer extract from Lyra (B_554) [cf. *WB*, II.809]

Ps. 71:7 pees, þat is, gostli pees [Lire here B_554] (marg. B_554V text K) [cf. *WB*, II.809]

Ps. 72:8 wickidnesse, þat is, blasfemye [KV blasfemyng V *WB*, II. 810] aȝens God [Lire here B_554] (marg. B_554V text K) [cf. *WB*, II.810]

Ps. 72:11 an heiȝe, þat is, in [hiȝ B_554] heuene [Lire here B_554] (marg. B_554 text A), an hiȝ in heuene (D_T_70) [cf. *WB*, II.810]

Ps. 72:27 fer hem silf fro þee, [þat is V] bi deedli synne [Lire here B_554U] (marg. B_554V text U [cf. *WB*, II.811]

Ps. 75:6 sleep, þat is, weren deed [Lire B_554] (B_554V) [cf. *WB*, II.814]

Ps. 75:13 spirit, þat is, lif, Lire here (marg. B_554 text U) [cf. *WB*, II.814]

Ps. 76 [title gloss] Asaph bi þe spiritt of prophecie made þis salme of þe comyng of þe caitifte of Babilone and of þe ending þerof, Lire here (B_554K) [this gloss misplaced at Ps. 75 in K, cf. *WB*, II.813]

Ps. 76:9 ende, þat is, holliche, Lire here (marg. B_554 text U) [cf. *WB*, II.814]

Ps. 77:31 fatte, þat is [þe B_554] riche men [fillid wiþ richessis, Lire here B_554] (B_554V) [cf. *WB*, II.817]

Ps. 84:14 riȝtfulnesse, þat is, Johan Baptist [Lire here B_554] (marg. B_554V text K) [cf. *WB*, II.825]

Ps. 96:7 sculptilis, þat is, idols maad wiþ hondis [Lire here B_554] [Austin K] (B_554K), or grauen ymagis (BL Add. 31044) [cf. *WB*, II.836]

Ps. 98 [title] gloss misplaced at Ps. 97 K

Ps. 101:4 critons, [a gloos *X*] þat is, þat þat dwelliþ in þe panne of þe friyng [Lire here B_554] (bB_554CGQSX *al. m. X*), eþer leefing of frijng (text K) [cf. *WB*, II.839]

Ps. 101:24 it, þat is, þe chirche of Crist (text K), þat is, þe chirche answeride to Crist [etc.], Lire here (B_554) [cf. *WB*, II.840]

Ps. 103:11 þirst, þat is, to be filled [wiþ þo watris B_554] in her þirst [Lire here B_554] (marg. B_554 text K) [cf. *WB*, II.842]

Ps. 103:18 hiȝe hillis, ben refute (A), ben refuytis (all other LV MSS) [cf. *WB*, II.843]

Ps. 105:29 fallyng (A), deþ (P_S), fallyng, eþer deþ (all other LV MSS) [cf. *WB*, II.847]

Ps. 106:29 softe wynde (A), pesiblete (P_S), soft wynde, eþer pesiblete (all other LV MSS) [cf. *WB*, II.850]

Ps. 113 [title gloss] . . . goostli in þis salm eche synnere þat haþ gete (B_554 greet K, *WB*, II.855) merci is excited to herie God [Lire here B_554] (B_554K)

Ps. 113:14 encreesse (AP_S), adde, eþer encreese (all other LV MSS) [cf. *WB*, II.856]

Ps. 115:19 porchis (A), forȝerdis (all other LV MSS) [cf. *WB*, II.857]

Ps. 118:15 ocupied (AP_S), exercisid, eþer bisily ocupied (other LV MSS *om*. C_J_E.14S) [cf. *WB*, II.860]

Ps. 118:50 lownesse, [þat is V] maad bi turment (marg. V text K), bi which a man is maad low bi tribulacioun, Austin, in Ebreu it is, on my turment, Lire here (B_554) [cf. *WB*, II.862]

Ps. 118:70 cruddid, eþer maad hard [Austin here U] (text B_544UV) [cf. *WB*, II.862]

Ps. 118:158 meltid, eþer langwiȝsshede (K), þat is Y flowide out wiþ teeris, and þerfor in Jerom it is, and Y mournyde, Lire here (B_554) [cf. *WB*, II.867]

Ps. 119:7 aȝenseiden (AD_T_70), enpugneden (C_J_E.14P_S), enpugneden, eþer aȝenseiden (all other LV MSS) [cf. *WB*, II.868]

Ps. 128 [title] . . . for delyueraunse of þe puple of Israel fro her pursweris wiche is ofte red [offered *WB*, II.871 red ofte B_554] doon of God [Lire here B_554] (B_554K)

Ps. 131:6 Effrata, þat is in Silo [Lire here B_554U] (marg. B_554K text AI) [cf. *WB*, II.873)

Ps. 132:3 in to þe world, þat is wiþ outen end [Lire here B_554] (marg. B_554 text V) [cf. *WB*, II.874]

Ps. 134:13 memorial, or mynde (text I), þat is, þe mynde of þi benefice, Lire here (B_554) [cf. *WB*, II.875]

Ps. 135:2 God of goddis, þat is, of hooli aungelis [Lire here B_554] (B_554V) [cf. *WB*, II.875]

Ps. 138:16 þi book, þat is, in þi kunnyng [Lire here B_554] (marg. B_554 text IU) [cf. *WB*, II.878]

Ps. 138:21 failide, þat is, mournyde gretly [Lire here B_554] (marg. B_554 text IKUV) [cf. *WB*, II.878]

Ps. 138:24 wei (A), liyf (all other LV MSS) [cf. *WB*, II.879]

Ps. 140:10 aloone (A), syngulerli (all other LV MSS) [cf. *WB*, II.280], eþer aloone bi my silf [Lire here B_554] (marg. B_554 text UV)

Ps. 143:13 lambre (text A), eene (all other LV MSS) [cf. *WB*, II.883]

Prov. 3:8 in þi nawle, þat is, good disposicion of þe soule in prosperitees (K)

Prov. 3:8 boonys, þat is, stidefasnesse in aduersitees (K)

Prov. 19:2 he þat is hasti, þat is, doiþ heedliflij [heedli *WB*, III.30] hise werkis (K)

Prov. 29:12 alle mynystris vnfeiþful, for þey seken to plese him and serue [sue *WB*, III.47] (C)

Eccl. 11:9 good (AC_J_G.26H), goodnes (all other LV MSS) [cf. *WB*, III.70]

Song 4:6 schadewis . . . of which þo [þei *WB*, III.77] weren schadewe . . . (C)

Song 5:5 droppiden myrre, þat is Y dressede me to do werkis of penaunce [me to penaunce *WB*, III.79] (C)

Song 5:9 derlyng of þe louede (*sup. ras.* A), derlyng of a derlyng (all other LV MSS) [cf. *WB*, III.79]

Song 5:13 þe best myrre, eþir [þei *WB*, III.79] firste (X)

Song 5:15 hise hipis, etc. (*sup. ras.* in gloss lemma C)

Song 6:4 turne awey, þis is vndurtstondun bi þe contrarie, and þis is a maner of speking of louyeris to þe declaring of loue of ech to oþer [vndurstondun . . . to þe *om.* *WB*, III.80] (C)

Song 7:13 oure (AR_91) ȝoure (all other LV MSS) [*nostris BS* oure EV] [cf. *WB*, III.82]

Ecclus [prologue] lack in composicioun [lackide compassioun *WB*, III.123] of wordis (R)

Ecclus 21:10 treheurdis [*sup. ras.*], eþer bones (K)

Ecclus 39:17 odour of swetnesse, þat is, deuocioun, Lire here (C)

Ecclus 43:15 been (A) bees (all other LV MSS) [*aves BS* briddes EV] [cf. *WB*, III.207]

Is. 1:22 medlid wiþ watir . . . techeris worþi to ben blamed han no forhed [not forbed *WB*, III.229] to amende synneris, Lire here (C)

Jer. 9:17 wymmen þat weilen (A) weilsteris (I) weileressis (all other LV MSS) [cf. *WB*, III.365]

Lam. 1:21 weilyng, eþer sorowe (K)

Lam. 5:16 song (A), queer (P_S), queer, eþer song (all other LV MSS) [cf. *WB*, III.483]

Ezek. prologue: fals wurschiping in hiȝ [hid *WB*, III.510] places (MR)

Ezek. 1:10 face (A), cheer (P_S), cheer, eþer face (all other LV MSS) [cf. *WB*, III.502]

Ezek. 7:13 reuelacioun (A), visioun (P_S), visioun, or reuelacioun (all other LV MSS) [cf. *WB*, III.513]

Ezek. 33:6 aspiere (A), biholdere (P_S), lookere, eþer aspiere (all other LV MSS) [cf. *WB*, III.577]

Dan. 11:36 and þe king, þat is, Antecrist (marg. St John's Coll. Camb. Aa. 5. 1 text R_89)

Dan. 12:1 in þat tyme, þat is, of Antecrist (R_89)

Micah 4:3 picoisis, eþer mattokkis (K)

1 Cor. 8:1 we witen, þat of þo þingis geten [getende *WB*, IV.351] no filþe (e)

1 Cor. 16:15 Stheuene, þe womman (text CC_U_L_ 6683e | Bodl. Rawlinson c. 258), þis Stephan was a woman (AR_77R_78R_80 | BL Royal 1.A.XII, etc.), þat [þis E] was a womman (EK) [cf. *WB*, IV.371]

2 Cor. 5:21 God þe fadir made him þe synne for vs, þat is sacrifice for synne (marg. AaeIKPRR_76R_80*V* Emmanuel Coll. Camb. 34 BL Royal 1. A. IV BL Royal 1. A. XII text CER_75R_79, etc.), Austyn here (A, etc.) Lire here and þe Glose rehersinge Austyn (a*V* | Bodl. Laud Misc. 33), Lire and þe Glos here (R_76) [cf. *WB*, IV.381]

Acts 2:5 religiouse men, deuout in þe worschiping [worchyng *V*] of God (e*V*) [cf. *WB*, IV.511]

2 Pet. 2:10 more, God reserueth, hem, þat is, eretikis to be turmentid (*V*), þat is eretikis principaly (e) [cf. *WB*, IV.618]

1 John 1:1 Þat þing (LV MSS + *V*) [What *V*, *WB*, IV.627, but 'Wh' is illuminator's error]

APPENDIX 3

Textual scholarship: select readings

This appendix provides textual details relating to biblical books discussed in ch. 4 and details of the textual cruces discussed in ch. 6. As some indication of the commonness or otherwise of errors, inferior readings, interpolations or variants in post-1200 MSS, readings are provided here from thirteen selected Latin Bibles written in France or England in s.xiii or s.xiv, and from French and Anglo-Norman Bibles. In cases where errors, etc., occur in pre-1200 MSS, most of the information given here derives from *Biblia Sacra* and WW, *NT*, as do readings from Ω^{JMS} and comments from the *correctoria* of the Dominicans of St-Jacques, Hugh of St Cher and William de la Mare.

Selected Latin Bibles:

London: BL Add. 15253 (Paris, c. 1210–20) BL Royal 1. A. XI (England, s.xiii; lacks Ps.) BL Royal 1. B. XII (William de Hales, Salisbury, 1254) BL Royal 1. E. IX (England, s.xiv. ex) Lambeth Palace 1364 (Paris, s.xiii in)

Oxford: Bodl. Canon. Bib. Lat. 47 (Paris, c. 1240–50) Bodl. Canon. Bib. Lat. 52 (Paris, c. 1250) Bodl. Kennicott 15 (Paris, c. 1200–1210) Bodl. Lat. bib. f. 3 (England?, 1254) Bodl. Laud Lat. 11 (England, s.xiii) Bodl. Laud Lat. 13 (William de Brailes, Oxford, c. 1240–50; includes *correctorium*) Bodl. Lyell 7 (England, c. 1225–50) Wadham College A 12. 8 (Paris, 1244)

French Bibles:

BL Harley 616 (BXIII, Genesis-Psalms, France, s.xiii) BL Royal 1. A. XX (*Bible historiale*, Prov.-Apoc., France, 1312) BL Royal 1. C. III (Genesis-Tobit in Anglo-Norman, s.xiv ex) BL Royal 17. E. VII (*Bible historiale complétée*, France, 1356–7)

BS and WW, *NT* manuscript names and sigla:

Amiatinus Florence, Bibl. Mediceo-Laurenziana Amiatino 1 (Northumbria, c. 700) *Burgensis* Burgos, Biblioteca Provincial 846 (San Pedro de Cardeña, s.xii) *Cavensis* Cava, Archivio della Badia 1 (14) (Spain, s.ix ex) *Dublinensis* Book of Armagh, Trinity College Dublin (s.viii/ix) *Egertonensis* BL Egerton 609 (Tours, s.viii/ix) *Guill. correctorium* of William de la Mare, Vatican lat. 3466 (s.xiii) *Historialis* Madrid, Bibl. de la Real Academia de la Historia 2–3 (San Millán de la Cogolla, c. 1200–25) *Hubertianus* St Hubert's Bible (Theodulfian) BL Add. 24142 (s.ix/x) *Hug. correctorium* of Hugh of St Cher, Vatican Ottoben. 293 (s.xiii/xiv) *Iac. correctorium* of Dominicans of St-Jacques, Paris (in Ω^J) *Legionensis* León, Colegiata de San Isidoro 2 (960) *Lichfeldensis* Lichfield Gospels (Book of St Chad), Lichfield Cathedral (Northumbria, s.vii/viii) *Maurdramni* Amiens, Bibl. mun. 7–12 (Corbei, s.ix in) *Toletanus* Madrid, Bibl. Nac. Vitr.13–1 (Tol. 2–1) (Spain, s.x)

Ω^J Bn lat. 16719, 16720, 16721 and 16722, s.xiii, with marginal and interlinear corrections by the Dominicans of St-Jacques, Paris; see *BS*, I.xxxvii

Ω^M Bn Mazarin. lat. 5, s.xiv; see *BS*, I.xxxviii

Ω^S Bn lat. 15467, Sorbonne, Paris, s.xiii in; see *BS*, I.xxxvii

GENESIS

1:2 þe spiryt of God EV þe spiryt of þe lord LV

spiritus dei *BS* domini *Burgensis Historialis* BL Add. 15253 BL Burney 3 BL Royal 1. A. XI BL Royal 1. E. IX Bodl. Canon. Bibl. Lat. 52 Bodl. Lyell 7 Wadham Coll. Oxf. A 12. 8 *Glossa* 1480/1

li esperiz damedieu BL Harley 616 (BXIII French) lesprit de nostre pere BL Royal 1. C. III (Anglo-Norman)

dei *sup. ras.* Bodl. Laud Lat. 11 domini *expunct. corr.* dei Bodl. Laud Lat. 13 spiritus dei, Lyra

EV has the better reading here, *pace WB*, I.xxii.

5.30 Lameþ lyuid after þat he gete Noe fyue hundreþ and fyue and eyȝty (nynti *sup. ras. pr. m.*) wynter *E*

fyue hundrid and fyue and nynti ȝeer EV(*A*) fyue hundrid nynti and fyue ȝeer LV

vixitque Lamech postquam genuit Noe quingentos nonaginta quinque annos *BS* LXXXV Ω^S Lambeth Palace 1364 Bodl. Lat. bib. f. 3 Bodl. Lyell 7 Wadham Coll. Oxf. A 12. 8

dxcv (595) *sup. ras.* Bodl. Laud Lat. 13

E pr. m. corrected in *E* and all other MSS.

11:32 þe days ben mad *E* (d. of Thare inserted *al. m.*) þe daies of Thare ben maad EV(*A*) þe daies of Thare weren maad LV

facti sunt dies Thare *BS* Thare *om. corr. al. m.* Ω[M]

E pr. m. corrected in *E* and all other MSS.

29:25 why vnderputtis þou Lya to me EV whi hast þou disseyued me LV

disseyued me, þis is þe verie lettre as Lire seiþ here, but comyn latyn bokis han þus, whi hast þou priuyly put Lya to me, but þis is fals lettre, as Lire seiþ here (CGQX) (aliqui libri habent sic, quare Liam supposuisti mihi, sed falsa est littera, Lyra)

quare imposuisti mihi *BS* quare Lyam sub/pposuisti mihi *Historialis* Ω[S] BL Add. 15253 BL Royal 1. E. IX Lambeth Palace 1364 Bodl. Canon. Bibl. Lat. 52 Bodl. Kennicott 15 Bodl. Laud Lat. 11 Wadham Coll. Oxf. A. 12. 8 quare imposuisti mihi Liam Bodl. Lyell 7

pur quei as tu mys a moy Lie BL Royal 1. C. III (Anglo-Norman) por quoi mas tu baillie Lyam BL Harley 616 (BXIII French) BL Add. 40619 (BXIII French)

h[ebr.] et an[tiqui libri], quare inposuisti mihi Bodl. Laud Lat. 13 alii male habent, quare Liam supposuisti mihi *Hug.* alii, quare Lyam supposuisti mihi, sed non est vera littera sicut ant[iqui libri] et hebr. *Iac.*

EV corrected in LV.

36:24 whenn he [Ana] fed þe asseȝ *E pr. m.* whanne he fedde þe she assis EV(*A*) whanne he kepte þe assis LV cum pasceret asinos *BS* asinas *Legionensis* [et al.] Ω[S] BL Add. 15253 Lambeth Palace 1364 Bodl. Canon. Bib. Lat. 47 Bodl. Canon. Bibl. Lat. 52 Bodl. Kennicott 15 Bodl. Laud Lat. 11 Bodl. Laud Lat. 13 Bodl. Lyell 7 Wadham Coll. Oxf. A 12. 8 *Glossa* 1480/1

aliqui libri habent, asinas, sed falsa est littera, Lyra

E pr. m. and LV agree against EV; EV corrected in LV.

37:28 for þritty siluer pens EV for þriȝtti platis of siluer LV

viginti argenteis *BS* triginta *Historialis* [et al.] Ω[SM] BL Add. 15253 BL Royal 1. B. XII BL Royal 1. E. IX Lambeth Palace 1364 Bodl. Canon. Bibl. Lat. 52 Bodl. Lat. bib. f. 3 Bodl. Laud Lat. 11 Bodl. Lyell 7 Wadham Coll. Oxf. A 12. 8 *Glossa* 1480/1

pur trent peces dargent BL Royal 1. C. III (Anglo-Norman) xxx. deniers dargent BL Harley 616 (BXIII French) BL Add. 40619 (BXIII French)

xxx *corr. supra* xx Bodl. Kennicott 15 omnes antiqui libri et Ie[ronimus] et lxx [Septuagint] habent, viginti Bodl. Laud Lat. 13 omnes alicuius auctoritatis habent, viginti, hebr. graeci et latini *Guill.* glosa quaedam Ydisori [of Isidore] legit, triginta [all other authorities 20] *Iac.* aliqui autem libri habent, xxx, sed falsa est littera, Lyra

All WB MSS have inferior reading.

48:3 *& to* (*sup. ras. pr. m.*) Ioseph co(m)men inne to hym *E* and to Joseph comun in to him EV(*A*) and whanne Joseph entride to hym LV

et ingresso ad se *BS* ingresso + Ioseph Ω[S] Lambeth Palace 1364 Bodl. Canon. Bibl. Lat. 52 Bodl. Laud Lat. 11 Wadham Coll. Oxf. A 12. 8

E pr. m. and LV include interpolation, but are more accurate than EV.

NUMBERS

11:4 þe comun . . . brente wiþ desire of flesch EV + IS þe comyn puple . . . brent wiþ desire of fleischis LV *desire of fleischis*, þis word, of fleischis, is not in Ebreu neþer in bokis amendid for þei desiriden fleischis and fischis and oþere þingis as it is seid wiþynne, Lire here (CdGKQX) (carnium, non est in hebreo nec habetur in libris correctis, quia non solum desideravit carnes sed etiam pisces et alia, ut infra subditur, Lyra)

vulgus . . . flagravit desiderio *BS* + carnium *Hubertianus* (and other Theodulf Bibles) *Legionensis*[2] Ω BL Add. 15253 BL Royal 1. A. XI BL Royal 1. E. IX Lambeth Palace 1364 Bodl. Canon. Bib. Lat. 47 Bodl. Canon. Bibl. Lat. 52 Bodl. Kennicott 15 Bodl. Laud Lat. 11 Bodl. Lyell 7 Wadham Coll. Oxf. A 12. 8 *Glossa* 1480/1

add. in scribal hand BL Royal 1. B. XII *add.* marg. and *corr.* marg. Bodl. Laud Lat. 13

ardren desir des chars BL Royal 1. C. III (Anglo-Norman) desirrier de char BL Harley 616 (BXIII French)

All WB MSS include this interpolation.

DEUTERONOMY

33:23 erly and mydday he shal weelde EV he schal welde þe see and þe souþ LV

for þe see of Galile as to þe souþ part þerof felde in þe lot of Neptalym, Lire here (C) (quia mare Galilee quantum ad sui partem meridionalem cecidit in sortem Nephtali, Lyra)

mare et meridiem possidebit *BS* mane et meridiem *Maurdramni* [*et al.*] BL Add. 15253 BL Royal 1. A. XI BL Royal 1. B. XII Bodl. Canon. Bib. Lat. 47 Bodl. Lat. bib. f. 3 Bodl. Lyell 7 Bodl. Kennicott 15

mare *sup. ras.* Bodl. Laud Lat. 13 mare et meridie *Hug.* hebr., mare *Iac.*

EV corrected in LV.

33:26 þe most riȝt God EV þe God of þe most riȝtful LV

non est alius ut deus rectissimi *BS* rectissimus *Cavensis* [et al.] Ω^{S} BL Royal 1. A. XI Lambeth Palace 1364 Bodl. Canon. Bib. Lat. 47 Bodl. Canon. Bibl. Lat. 52 Bodl. Lat. bib. f. 3 Wadham Coll. Oxf. A 12. 8

corr. Hug. ut deus rectissimi, id est ut deus populi israel rectissima lege gubernati, Lyra

EV corrected in LV.

I KINGS

21:7 þis [Doech] fedde þe mulys of Saul EV + EIL *om.* LV

þis þat sueþ in summe bokis, and he kepte þe mulis of Saul, is not in Ebreu neþer is of þe text, Lire here (C) (hic pascebat, etc. non est in hebreo nec in libris correctis, Lyra)

pastorum Saul *BS* + hic [Doec] pascebat mulas Saul *Toletanus*[2] *Burgensis* [*et al.*] Ω^{J} BL Add. 15253 BL Royal 1. A. XI BL Royal 1. E. IX Bodl. Canon. Bib. Lat. 47 Bodl. Kennicott 15 Bodl. Laud Lat. 11 Wadham Coll. Oxf. A 12. 8 interlinear gloss 'hic pascebat mulas Saul' *Glossa* 1480/1

BL Harley 616 (BXIII French) BL Add. 40619 (BXIII French)

add. marg. Lambeth Palace 1364 *add.* marg. Bodl. Laud Lat. 13

sumptum est de Iosepho [Josephus] qui dicit, Doech syrus pastor mularum Saul *Hug. corr. Guill.*

Interpolation in EV deleted in LV and restored in three late LV MSS.

24:7–8 þe lord lyueþ for but þe lord smijte hym ouþer þe dai of hym come þat he die ouþer comyng doun in to bataile perische: merciful be to me þe lord þat I putte not my hond in to þe crist of þe lord / [v.8] and Dauid brak to gidre his men wiþ þes woordis and suffride hem not þat þei risen in to Saul EV [+ interpolation] and Dauid . . . Saul *om.* LV

Crist of þe lord, in summe bokis it sueþ, and Dauyþ brak hise men bi siche wordis and suffride not hem þat þey risiden aȝenus Saul [= 24:8], but þis lettre is not in Ebreu neþer in bokis amendid, Lire here (C) (vivit deus, etc. usque ibi exclusiue, Et confregit Dauid, etc., non est in hebreo nec in libris correctis; fuit enim quid appositum per modum glose, Lyra)

propitius mihi . . . meo christo domini *BS* + vivit dominus quia nisi dominus percusserit eum aut dies eius venerit ut moriatur aut descendens in proelium perierit propitius mihi sit dominus ut ne mittam manum meam in christum domini Alcuinian Bibles *Historialis*[2] [*et al.*] Ω^{SJM} all selected Latin Bibles *Glossa* 1480/1

BL Royal 1. C. III (Anglo-Norman) BL Harley 616 (BXIII French)

underlined in red and *corr.* marg. Bodl. Laud Lat. 13

this text belongs at 1 Kings 26[:10–11] *Hug.*, *Iac. corr. Guill.*

EV includes interpolation, but LV omits biblical text and preserves interpolation.

2 KINGS

1:18 and [Dauid] seiþ: Bihold, Israel, for þese þat ben deade vp on þi heeȝe þyngis woundid EV and Dauid seyde: Israel, biholde þou, for þese men þat ben deed, woundid on þin hiȝe placis LV

sicut scriptum est in libro Iustorum *BS* + et ait considera Israhel pro his qui mortui sint super excelsa tua uulnerati *Hubertianus* (and other Theodulfian Bibles) [*et al.*] Ω all selected Latin Bibles *Glossa* 1480/1

underlined in red *corr. supra* in red Bodl. Laud Lat. 13

hebr. et ant[iqui] non habent sed glossa [*Glossa Ordinaria*] exponit *Hug.*

included in the text as glossed by Rabanus Maurus [PL CIX.72], but is without textual authority *Guill.*

Lyra comments on these words, but there is no textual comment

All WB MSS include this interpolation.

1:26 as a moder looueþ hyre oneli sone EV I as a modir loueþ oon aloone sone LV

super amorem mulierum *BS* + sicut mater unicum amat filium ita ego te diligebam [almost all early MSS] all selected Latin Bibles include this interpolation *Glossa* 1480/1

Si come la mere ayme son filz BL Royal 1. C. III (Anglo-Norman)

he[br.] non habet hunc versum Bodl. Laud Lat. 13

[not in Hebrew or Greek, but a gloss] est tamen de textu absque calumpnia *Guill.*

Lyra comments on these words, but there is no textual comment

All WB MSS include this interpolation.

2 CHRONICLES

[**37**] Prayer of Manasseh, inc. 'Lord god almyȝti of our fadris'

lord God, þis preyere of Manasses is not in Ebreu (marg. *al. m. E H* text *A*L_o)

þis is þe preyere of Manasses but it is not in Ebreu neþer it is of þe text, Lire here (C) (ista oratio regis Manasses non est in hebreo nec est de textu, et ideo non intendo eam exquisite exponere sed tamen breuiter pertransire, Lyra)

Incl. Ω^{SJ2} (marg.)^{M} BL Add. 15253 BL Royal 1. E. IX Lambeth Palace 1364 Bodl. Canon. Bib. Lat. 47 Bodl. Canon. Bibl. Lat. 52 Bodl. Kennicott 15 Bodl. Laud Lat. 11 Bodl. Laud Lat. 13 *Glossa* 1480/1

BL Harley 616 (BXIII French) BL Add. 40619 (BXIII French)

est apocrifa et plures libri non habent eam sed Glosa [*Glossa Ordinaria*] exponit Bodl. Laud Lat. 13

All WB MSS include the Prayer of Manasseh.

3 EZRA

Incl. BL Add. 15253 BL Royal 1. B. XII BL Royal 1. E. IX (books of Ezra numbered 1–5) Lambeth Palace 1364 Bodl. Canon. Bibl. Lat. 47 (running-head 'Apocrifa') Bodl. Canon. Bibl. Lat. 52 Bodl. Kennicott 15 Bodl. Lat. bib. f. 3, Wadham Coll. Oxf. A 12. 8 *Glossa* 1480/1

BL Add. 40620 (BXIII French, books of Ezra numbered 1–6) BL Harley 616 (BXIII French)

liber iste inter alios non canonicos qui ponuntur in biblia minoris videtur autoritatis, et ideo ad ipsum exponendum ultimo misi manum, tamen de illis que alibi scribuntur et hic repetuntur intendo breviter transire, Lyra

Incl. EV MSS + I.

ESTHER

3:7 lot is leid in to a vessel þat Ebruely is seid phur EV lot was sent in to a vessel which lot is seid in Ebrew phur LV

phur, is no word of Ebrew but of Persis, and þerfor in Ebreu it is seid phur, goral, so þat goral is an Ebreu word, and signefieþ lot, Lire here (C) (hebraice dicitur, non est per hoc intelligendum quod phur sit nomen hebraicum sed est persicum, unde in hebreo habetur, phur [quod est] goral, quod goral est nomen hebraicum et significat sortem, Lyra)

missa est sors in urnam quae hebraice dicitur phur *BS*

phur, he[br.] non habet Bodl. Laud Lat. 13

All selected Latin Bibles and all WB MSS include this error.

PSALMS

41:3 My soule þristide to God þe quyke welle EV Mi soule þirstide to God þat is a quik welle (q. w. *sup. ras.* A) LV (except MSS noted below)

welle of liyf C_J_E_14ikOP_SRX BL_Add. 31004 BL_Harl. 1896 New Coll. Oxf. 320 *sup. ras.* C Rolle's *Psalter* (Bramley, p. 153) strong quyk B_544D_70D_72R_88UV crossed through and 'welle of lijf' written above in hand of corrector H 'not welle' marg. V

oure bookis han, welle, bi errour of writeris eþer of vnwise amenderis, Lire here B_554 (fortem vivum, sic est in hebreo et in translatione Hieron. iuxta hebraicum, sed vitio scriptorum positum est hic, fontem, in libris nostris communiter propter litterarum similitudinem, vel ex imperitia aliquorum correctorum, Lyra)

sitivit anima mea ad deum fortem vivum *BS* (Gallican Psalter) [fortem viventem Hebrew Psalter]

fontem uiuum *LXX Psalterium Romanum* [most early MSS] Gregory *Moralia in Job* Ω BL Add. 15253 BL Royal 1. E. IX Lambeth Palace 1364 Bodl. Canon. Bib. Lat. 47 Bodl. Canon. Bibl. Lat. 52 Bodl. Lyell 7 Bodl. Kennicott 15 Wadham Coll. Oxf. A 12. 8 *Glossa* 1480/1

fontaigne uiue BL Add. 40620 (BXIII French) fontaine uiue BL Harley 616 (BXIII French) BL Royal 17. E. VII (BHC French)

hebr. et ant[iqui libri] et Ieron. habent, fortem, et de, fonte, nichil *Guill*

See Hargreaves, 'The Latin Text of Purvey's Psalter', 87–9, and the discussion in ch. 6.

106:40 held out is strijf vp on þe princys EV strijf was sched out on princes LV

effusa est contemptio super principes *BS* contentio *Psalterium Romanum* Ω all selected Latin Bibles containing Psalms *Glossa* 1480/1

stryfe Rolle's *Psalter* (Bramley, p. 385)

contencion BL Add. 40620 (BXIII French) contreanz BL Harley 616 (BXIII French)

effusa est contentio, ut patet manifeste in ciuitatibus Lombardie et in aliis locis, Lyra

All WB MSS have this error.

PROVERBS

15:27 Bi mercy and feiþ ben purgid synnes: bi þe drede forsoþe of þe lord bowith doun eche man fro euel EV Synnes ben purgid bi merci and feiþ: ech man bowith awei fro yuel bi þe drede of þe lord LV

conturbat domum suam . . . munera vivet *BS* + per misericordiam et fidem purgantur peccata per timorem autem domini declinat omnis a malo LXX *Cavensis* [*et al.*] Ω^{MSJ} BL Add. 15253 BL Royal 1. A. XI Royal I. B. XII BL Royal 1. E. IX Lambeth Palace 1364 Bodl. Canon. Bibl. Lat. 52 Bodl. Kennicott 15 Bodl. Laud Lat. 11 Wadham Coll. Oxf. A 12. 8 *Glossa* 1481

BL Add. 41751 (BXIII French)

underlined in red *corr.* marg. Bodl. Laud Lat. 13 *del. Hug.* this text belongs at Prov. 16:6 *Guill., Iac.*

Lyra comments on these words, but there is no textual comment

All WB MSS include this interpolation.

SONG OF SONGS

1:9 a tur (crossed through 'as of a turtir' subst. marg. *pr. m.*) *E* as of a turtil EV(*C*) as of a turtle LV

sicut turturis *BS* turis / turris *Toletanus corr.* Ω Geneva BPU lat. 1 Munich Bayerische Staatsbibl. Clm 13001, Vatican Pal. lat. 4 Bodl. Canon. Bib. Lat. 47

E pr. m. corrected in *E* and all other MSS.

2:7 ne makeþ þe leef to waken *E* ('þe' crossed through and expunct. 'my' subst. marg. *pr. m.*) ne makeþ my leef to waken EV(*C*) neþer make to awake þe dereworþe spousesse LV

neque evigilare faciatis dilectam *BS* + meam Ω^S BL Add. 15253 Bodl. Canon. Bibl. Lat. 52 Wadham Coll. Oxf. A 12. 8

m'amie BL Add. 40620 (BXIII French) BL Add. 41751 (BXIII French)

E pr. m. and LV have a better reading than EV.

2:13 riis ('go' inserted *pr. m*) my leef *E* ris go þou my leef EV(*C*) my fayre spousesse rise þou, haste þou LV

surge amica mea *BS* + propera [cf. 2:10] Ω^S BL Add. 15253 BL Royal 1. E. IX Lambeth Palace 1364 Bodl. Canon. Bibl. Lat. 52 Bodl. Laud Lat. 11 Wadham Coll. Oxf. A 12. 8

add. in scribal hand BL Royal 1. A. XI

crossed through Bodl. Kennicott 15 *del. Hug.* Gregorius ant[iqui libri] hebr. non habent, propera *Iac.*

Lyra comments on these words, saying they repeat 2:10, but there is no textual comment

E pr. m. has the best reading.

7:13 see Appendix 2

ECCLESIASTICUS

3:28 shal not han welsum chaunces EV schal not haue prosperitees eþer reste LV

non habebit successus *BS* requiem *Amiatinus Maurdramni* Alcuinian Bibles BL Royal 1. A. XI BL Royal 1. E. IX Bodl. Lyell 7 successus, interlin. gloss, requiem *Glossa Ordinaria* successus *corr. supra* requiem Bodl. Kennicott 15 non habebit successus, prosperos, scilicet sed adversos, Lyra

EV is correct; LV fails to select between alternatives (or is not aware that these are variants).

43:15 see Appendix 2

44:5 in þer wisdam sechinge þe musik manneris EV sekynge maneres of musik in her childhod LV

bokis amendid han, in her childhed, þouȝ summe bokis han, in her kunnyng [Lyra] (C) (in pueritia sua, sic habent libri correcti, Lyra)

in pueritia sua requirentes modos musicos *BS* peritia Theodulfian Bibles Ω^{MS} BL Add. 15253 Lambeth Palace 1364 Bodl. Canon. Bibl. Lat. 52 Bodl. Kennicott 15 Bodl. Lat. bib. f. 3 Bodl. Laud Lat. 11 Wadham Coll. Oxf. A 12. 8

sens BL Add. 40620 (BXIII French) BL Add. 41751 (BXIII French)

Ra[banus] an[tiqui libri] habent, in puericia Bodl. Laud Lat. 13 in puericia, sicut David *Hug.* Rab[anus] ant[iqui libri], in puericia *Iac.*

EV corrected in LV.

ISAIAH

26:1 þe huge cite of oure strengþe, Sion EV Sion *om.* LV

Þat is heuenli citee whois excelence mai not be declarid bi mannus wordis. Þis word, Sion, is neþer in Ebrew neþer in bokis amendid, Lire here (text K) (id est civitas celestis cuius excellentia non potest verbis humanis exprimi propter quod non nominatur hic, quod enim in aliquibus libris ponitur hic, Sion, additum fuit ab aliquo expositore secundum imaginationem, quia non est in hebreo nec in libris correctis, Lyra)

urbs fortitudinis nostrae + Sion *Hubertianus* Ω all selected Latin Bibles *Glossa* 1480/1

BL Add. 40620 (BXIII French) BL Royal 17. E. VII (BHC French)

I[eronimus] an[tiqui libri] he[br.] non habent, Syon Bodl. Laud Lat. 13 *sim. Guill.*, *Hug.*, *Iac.*

EV corrected in LV.

BARUCH

6:72 betir is an vniust (iust *K*) man þat haþ not symylacris *AGH*L_oW_o*XYZ pr. m. K* betere is a iust man þat haþ no symylacris LV

melior est homo iustus qui non habet simulacra *BS* iniustus Ω^{SJ} Lambeth Palace 1364 Bodl. Canon. Bibl. Lat. 52 Bodl. Lat. bib. f. 3 Bodl. Laud Lat. 11 Wadham Coll. Oxf. A 12. 8

Lyra reads 'homo iustus', but does not make a textual comment
EV corrected in *K* LV.

AMOS

3:12 plage or wound of þe litil bed *KAGYHWoLo* plage *X* cuntrei of bed LV
plaga lectuli *BS*

la plaie del lit BL Add. 40620 (BXIII French) la plaie du lit BL Add. 41751 (BXIII French)

id est in regione regni Iudae quae dicitur lectulus ratione templi quod erat ibi, de quo dicitur Cant. 1[:15] lectulus noster floridus, Lyra

LV selects correct alternative from EV.

7:1 aftir þe clippere of floc (*X*) + or kyng *A*(of folc)GHYWoLoZ (of þe k.) after þe clippere of þe kyng (flocke *sup. ras.* I) LV

post tonsorem regis [restored reading *BS*] gregis [most early MSS] BL Add. 15253 BL Royal 1. E. IX BL Royal 1. B. XII Lambeth Palace 1364 Bodl. Canon. Bib. Lat. 47 Bodl. Canon. Bibl. Lat. 52 Bodl. Kennicott 15 Bodl. Lat. bib. f. 3 Bodl. Laud Lat. 13 Wadham Coll. Oxf. A 12. 8

empres ce que les oeilles furent tondus BL Add. 40620 (BXIII French) BL Add. 41751 (BXIII French)

regis *corr.* gregis BL Royal 1. A. XI gregis, vel regis Bodl. Laud Lat. 13 hebr. et Ier., regis *Hug.* regis *Guill.* anti[qui libri], gregis, Glosa, regis vel gregis *Iac.* in hebreo habetur, post tonsionem regis, et videtur hec littera falsificata per imperitiam scriptorum propter similitudinem dictionum, Lyra

LV selects correct alternative from EV.

MATTHEW

4:18 sendende net in to þe se EV castynge nettis in to þe see LV

rete þe nett BL Add. 34305 (Latin–English glossary)

mittentes rete in mare WW, *NT* retia *Dublinensis Egertonensis* [etc.] Lambeth Palace 1364 Bodl. Canon. Bibl. Lat. 52 Bodl. Laud Lat. 11 Bodl. Laud Lat. 13 Bodl. Lyell 7 Wadham Coll. Oxf. A 12. 8

lor roiz Rouen Bibl. municipale A. 211 (BXIII French), Sneddon, 'A Critical Edition of the Four Gospels', II.9.

EV has better reading than LV, *pace WB*, I.xxii.

11:13 til Jon Baptist prophecieden EV (Baptist *om.* *NOP_PUV*[2]) til to Joon prophecieden LV

usque ad Iohannem prophetaverunt WW, *NT* Iohannem + babtistam *Lichfeldensis*

EV corrected in LV and 5 EV MSS.

22:4 my bolis and my volatilis ben slayne EV (v. or fatte beestis *OP_PUV* Tokyo, Takamiys 28) LV as EV

mi boolis & my volatilis BL Royal 17. B. I (concordance to NT) 'The holi prophete Dauid seiþ', ed. Deanesly, *LB*, p. 454

tauri mei et altilia occisa WW, *NT* [no variant recorded]

mes toreax et mes voleilles sont ocises Rouen Bibl. municipale A. 211 (BXIII French), Sneddon, 'A Critical Edition of the Four Gospels', II.69, mes toraux et mes uolailles sont occises BL Royal 17. E. VII (BHC French)

as if from 'alati' (winged things) instead of 'altilia' (fattened things), see Lewis, *NT*, p. 5

5 EV MSS correct the error in EV LV, see Lindberg, *EV*, VII.63.

MARK

5:11 hoggis lesewynge in feeldis EV (in feeldis *om.* P_P*UV*) swyn lesewynge LV

grex porcorum magnus pascens WW, *NT* + in agris [no MSS recorded in WW] BL Add. 15253 Lambeth Palace 1364 Bodl. Canon. Bib. Lat. 47 Bodl. Canon. Bibl. Lat. 52 Bodl. Kennicott 15 Bodl. Laud Lat. 11 Bodl. Lyell 7 Wadham Coll. Oxf. A 12. 8 *Glossa* 1480/1

pessant es chans Rouen Bibl. municipale A. 211 (BXIII French), Sneddon, 'A Critical Edition of the Four Gospels', II.116 BL Royal 17. E. VII (BHC French)

corr. Bodl. Laud Lat. 13 *corr. Guill.*

EV revised in 3 MSS and corrected in LV, see *WB*, I.xxii.

LUKE

1:1–4 included in WB in P_P*UV* only, as a second prologue, inc. 'Forsoþe for many men enforsiden to ordeyne'

The translation is borrowed from Glossed Luke in the *Glossed Gospels*, see *WB*, I.xvii

Incl. BL Add. 34305 (Latin-English glossary based on WB in LV)

Incl. all selected Latin Bibles except Bodl. Kennicott 15.

GALATIANS

4:6 God sente þe spirit of his sone EV God sente his spirit LV

misit deus spiritum filii sui WW, *NT*

dieux enuoia le saint esperit BL Add. 41751 (BXIII French)

EV has the better reading here, *pace WB*, I.xxii.

LAODICEANS

Incl. mopqrstuwx Glasgow Hunterian Museum 176 Bodl. Lyell 26.

Incl. BL Royal 1. A. XI Bodl. Lat. bib. f. 3 Bodl. Laud Lat. 13 inserted in marg. at end of Pauline Epp. Bodl. Lyell 7

2 TIMOTHY

4:13 Penulam, þat is cloþ of Rome or boc (*E*, and see Lindberg, *EV*, VIII.171)

aftir Jerom is clepid a boke & aftir Haymound (Haimo of Auxerre) a cloþe of þe Romayns [*Glossa Ordinaria*] (*QT*)

cloþ (LV) þat is cloþ of Romains, Lyra and Gloss (marg. *V*) (vestis consularis que a romanis data fuit patri Pauli in signum amicitie cum ipso, Lyra)

paenulam quam reliqui *BS*

LV selects correct alternative from EV.

APOCALYPSE

22:14 Blessid þei þat waschen her stoolis in blood of þe lomb EV Blessid be þei þat waischen her stoolis *V* LV

Þis þat is addid in summe bookis, in þe blood of þe lomb, is not of þe text, neiþer is had in elde biblis, Lyra (*V*) (quod autem in aliquibus libris subditur, in sanguine agni, non est de textu nec habetur in antiquis bibliis, Lyra)

beati qui lavant stolas suas + in sanguine agni Ambrose Bede *Dublinensis* BL Add. 15253 Lambeth Palace 1364 Bodl. Canon. Bibl. Lat. 52 Bodl. Kennicott 15 Bodl. Laud Lat. 11 Bodl. Laud Lat. 43 Wadham Coll. Oxf. A 12. 8 *Glossa* 1480/1

BL Add. 41751 (BXIII French) BL Royal 17. E. VII (BHC French)

EV corrected in *V* LV.

APPENDIX 4

Descriptions of select Wycliffite Bible manuscripts

This appendix provides descriptions of complete Wycliffite Bibles and other early and textually significant WB MSS. The information is provided in the following order for each MS: contents; bibliography; date and dialect; ownership history; format; decoration; text.

Codicologists date most WB MSS 's.xv in'. Here I suggest more precise dates, followed by Forshall and Madden's and Lindberg's dates, where available. Forshall and Madden's dates seem frequently too late, as is evidenced by their dating of *G* 'about 1420', when it is known to pre-date 1397.

All EV MSS include the OT prols. detailed in Appendix 1, and LV MSS include the OT prols. to Isaiah and Baruch and the NT prols. detailed in Appendix 1, unless otherwise indicated. LV Prologue to WB is indicated where present.

All MSS are in gatherings of eight, unless otherwise indicated; detail of collation is given only where there are implications for the content of the MS.

The word 'initial' is here used for all initials in designated initial-spaces.

All MSS include the rubrics in Esther, Isaiah, Lamentations, Baruch and Daniel detailed in ch. 4, and EV MSS include the aleph–bet rubrics in Ps. 118, Prov. 31 and Lam. 1–4 and the speaker-rubrics in the Song of Songs detailed in ch. 4, unless otherwise indicated.

CAMBRIDGE

Corpus Christi College, Parker Library 147

WB, no. 116 [S] 454 fols. (no modern foliation), ONT in LV.

Prologue to WB, fols. 1r–18r; lectionary (temporal, commemorations, proper and common of saints, with final fol. lacking), fols. 18v–23v; OT, fols. 24r–370r; NT, fols. 371r–454v, ends in Apoc. 21:18 'jaspis and' (1 fol.

lacking). Lacks Judith 7:18–10:2, Judith 13:8–Esth. 2:5 (2 fols.), Esth. 8:8–14:6 and Job 3:3–6:4; these have been replaced with matching leaves.

M. R. James, *A Descriptive Catalogue of the Manuscripts in the Library of Corpus Christi College, Cambridge*, vol. I (Cambridge University Press, 1912), pp. 335–6; De Hamel, *Book*, fig. 123, p. 175.

Date c. 1410–30; 'perhaps before 1430', *WB*, I.lv; c. 1430, dialect mixed EM, Lindberg, *Judges*, p. 70.

Probably owned (confiscated?) by Geoffrey Blyth, Bp of Coventry and Lichfield 1503–30, since a note by Archbishop Parker (or one of his household) says the annotations on the Prologue are in his hand, fol. 15r.

James says this may be Richard Hunne's copy of WB. According to John Foxe, the [thirteen] articles cited against Richard Hunne at St Paul's Cross on 10 December 1514 were produced by Dr Thomas Head (Commissary of Richard Fitzjames, Bp of London) 'out of the prologue of [Hunne's] English Bible', *Acts and Monuments*, IV.186. The articles certainly derive from a copy of the Prologue to WB; the correspondences are conveniently laid out by Cooper in his account of the Hunne case, 'Richard Hunne', 245–6. The annotations on the Prologue in this MS cannot, however, be associated with the articles cited against Hunne. The passages on which articles II–IV, VII–IX and XI are based are not marked in the margins or annotated, and four of the passages annotated (*WB*, I.43/7, I.43/17–18, I.48/29–30 and I.51/32) are not mentioned in the articles.

There is a note on Wyclif's ignorance of Latin, in the same hand, at Ps. 103:17, fol. 227v (cf. V).

12s; 300 by 195mm; 215 by 130mm; 2 cols., 59/60 lines; a rather uneven and angular bookhand.

Lower margin of fols. 1–17 damp-stained and damaged.

Decoration: three-line (some five-line) initials, gold on rose-mauve and deep-blue background, reproducing the shape of the letter, with green flourishes; initials extended into grotesques in Prophets (some torn out); two-line initials, deep-blue flourished in red, at opening of chapters; one-line initials, alternating blue and red, in Deut. 32 and Ps.-verses; red incipits and explicits; red roman lower-case chapter-numbers; red running-heads (incl. 'Sauter'), complete on verso and recto, with blue paraph on verso and red on recto; red titles in Psalms (but title-glosses in margin outlined in red, and headed 'A glos'); Latin incipits of Psalms underlined in red; lections indexed in the margin, often in red.

Text differs from most LV MSS, Lindberg, *Judges*, p. 70. There are many revised readings, and textual and marginal glosses from Genesis to Joshua and from 1 Chron. to Job, shared with IN, see Lindberg, *KHB*, II.49, and ch. 6, n. 49. Textual glosses are usually underlined in red, sometimes in brown ink. Marginal glosses are enclosed in a red scroll. Frequent marginal 'moral' glosses begin at Num. 11 and continue throughout Numbers and Deuteronomy (Deut. 32–3 are especially heavily glossed in both text and margin). Includes the series of glosses in Chronicles, attributed to 'Li[r]a', and several other (moral) glosses in Chronicles; from Job 1:1–24:12 there are several textual glosses unique to this MS or shared with I (never underlined). There are no glosses in Maccabees.

Emmanuel College 21

WB, no. 118 [P]; i + 350 + ii fols. (not numbered), ONT in LV.

Lectionary (temporal, commemorations, proper and common of saints 'alle vnder oon as þei fallin in þe ȝeer bi ordre', fol. 4r) in LV, fols. 1r–6v; ONT in LV, fols. 7r–350v.

M. R. James, *The Western Manuscripts in the Library of Emmanuel College* (Cambridge University Press, 1904), pp. 17–18.

Date c. 1420, as *WB*, I.lvi; s.xiv ex, James, p. 17; c. 1430, dialect mixed SM, Lindberg, *Judges*, p. 70.

'Iohn Wickleff's translation, performed by him Anno Domini 1383 This copy will give forty pounds', s.xvii, fol. i^{r}.

360 (cropped) by 260 mm; 270 by 180 mm; 2 cols., 60/63 lines; letter 1.5 mm (marginal gloss. 5 mm); an extremely neat and upright bookhand with short ascenders and descenders. Orthography similar to E, *WB*, I.lvi

Opening page of Genesis has an elaborate bar-border in gold, dark-blue and mauve, fol. 7r; six-line initials, gold on a geometrically patterned ground of mauve and deep blue with white tracery, extended into deep-blue borders flourished in red; three-line initials, deep blue flourished in red, at opening of chapters; one-line initials, alternating blue and red, in Ps.-verses; chapter-numbers alternating blue and red upper-case roman; red incipits and explicits; running-heads gold within scroll, complete on verso and recto (incl. 'Sauter'); red Ps.-titles; red Latin incipits of Psalms with blue paraph; margins indexed for lections. Decoration and hand consistent throughout; fine-quality parchment; excellent condition, but cropping of margins has resulted in slight loss of marginal gloss text.

Text 'resembles E and L', though less 'extreme' than E, Lindberg, *Judges*, p. 70.

Textual glosses underlined in ink, never in red; marginal glosses underlined in ink, linked with siglum to biblical text; translational glosses usually 'eþir' but sometimes 'or' (cf. EL). Shares many glosses and readings with EY, and to a lesser extent L. Many marginal glosses throughout OT.

Cambridge University Library Additional 6680 [formerly Ashburnham app. 254]

Lindberg no.191 [C_U_6680]; 404 fols., ONT in LV.

Prefatory Epistles, fols. 1r–3v in LV (not used for Lindberg, *PE*); prol. to Joshua in LV, fols. 3v–4r; prol. to 1 Kings in LV, fols. 4r–5r; prol. to 1 Chronicles in LV, fol. 5r (fol. 6 blank) [for these prols., cf. X]; OT in LV, fols. 7r–324v (no break between Maccabees and Matthew); NT in LV, fols. 324v–404v.

Date c. 1410; c. 1420, dialect SEM or mixed SM, Lindberg, *Judges*, p. 69.

Owned by Henry Sayer, priest, who read through it in twenty-six days in 1576, fol. 404v; William Davenport of Bramhall (1584–1655), who left it to his heirs in 1620, fol. 6v.

378 by 279 mm; 285 by 180 mm; catchwords below right edge of written space, in ink scroll; 2 cols., 85 mm each; 59/60 lines, 5 mm apart; regular bookhand; not ruled for glosses. Not a deluxe MS, but in very good condition except for damp-staining in Jeremiah.

Six-line initials, deep blue and red flourished in both colours; three-line initials, deep blue flourished in red, at opening of chapters; blue paraphs (incl. Ps.-verses); incipits and explicits normally ink but occasionally red; chapter-numbers ink, lower-case roman; chapter-breaks often written in traditional style, with blue paraph; ink running-heads, complete on verso and recto (incl. 'Sauter'); red Ps.-titles.

Text good (but 'average', Lindberg, *Judges*, p. 69). Textual glosses are often underlined in ink, but never in red. There are no marginal glosses. Includes the gloss at Ecclus 28:26, 'in going doun to euerlastinge turment', written within the text with 'Lire here' in the margin, fol. 221r (*WB*, III.178); includes the gloss at Jer. 50:39, 'eþer fendis in licnesse of wodewodis', written within the text, fol. 262r (*WB*, III.461).

Cambridge University Library Dd. 1. 27

WB, no.106 [R]; 533 fols., ONT in LV (bound as 2 vols. in 1976).

(vol. 1) OT, with EV prols. to Job (2), Psalms (2), Proverbs, Ecclesiastes; LV prols. to Wisdom (unique) and Ecclus (unique), Isaiah, Baruch, Ezekiel and Daniel (Ezek. and Dan. otherwise only in M), fols. 1r–418r (lacks fol. 419).

(vol. 2) Lectionary (temporal, proper and common of saints together, commemorations), with months in French, in LV, fols. 420r–426r; NT, fols. 427r–533v; 'Here eendeþ þe Apocalips þe last book of Goddis lawe', fol. 533v.

Date c. 1430; c. 1430–1440, *WB*, I.liv; c. 1435, dialect SEM, Lindberg, *Judges*, p. 70.

Owned by John Moore, Bp of Norwich 1691–1707, fol. 1r.

420 by 270 mm; 280 by 170 mm; some quire and sheet signatures visible; 2 cols., 80 mm each; 64 lines, 5mm apart; square and rather ungainly bookhand with very coarse strokes. In good condition, but fols. 150–156 (end of 4 Kings, beginning of 1 Chron.) badly stained.

Seven miniatures of the Creation in roundels, very badly rubbed, with decorative border, fol. 1r, see Scott, *Later Gothic Manuscripts*, p. 70. Five to ten-line initials, exceptionally fine, green, blue, mauve and orange foliage and fruit on a gold background, extended into elaborate border in the same colours; four-line initials, deep blue flourished in red, at opening of chapters; one-line initials, alternating blue and red, in Ps.-verses and Lam. 1–4 verses; alternating blue and red paraphs; red incipits and explicits; red lower-case roman chapter-numbers, often in the form 'þe x. chapitre'; chapter-breaks sometimes written in traditional style; arabic number in ink adjacent to the column; ink running-heads (incl. Sauter) written across verso and recto; ink lower-case roman chapter-numbers at outer and inner edge of verso and inner and outer edge of recto; Esther rubrics, etc., brown ink underlined in red; Ps.-titles and Latin Psalm incipits underlined in red; beginnings and endings of lections marked in margins.

Text 'later and less uniform' than most LV MSS, Lindberg, *Judges*, p. 70. Has correct reading at Amos 5:17 (*WB*, III.699), and includes missing LV text at Apoc. 20:12.

Textual glosses underlined fairly consistently in ink; sparse marginal glosses written in lozenge shape, very occasionally with a siglum and an attribution. Includes only one or two of the Pentateuch glosses, written within the text; shares glosses on Ps. 145–150 with KOS; lacks almost all glosses in Prophets and Maccabees, and several LV textual glosses in Maccabees.

Cambridge University Library Ee. 1. 10

WB, no.107 [Z]; 193 fols.; originally abridgment of ONT, but surviving text only 2 Chron.–2 Macc.15:1, including the usual prols., in EV.

(part 1) 2 Chron.–Psalms (followed by Canticles and Quicunque vult), fols. 169r–244v (fols. 1–168, Gen.–1 Chron., are now lacking, as quire-signatures demonstrate, see Hargreaves, 'An Intermediate Version of the Wycliffite Old Testament', 130); fol. 224 lacking.

(part 2) Prov.–2 Macc. 15, fols. 1–119 (fol. 94 lacking). Most texts are abridged, but Tobit is nearly complete and the first prol. to 1 Ezra, the commendation of Ezra, the first prol. to Judith and the prols. to Esther, Wisdom and Baruch are complete.

Hargreaves, 'An Intermediate Version of the Wycliffite Old Testament', 129–47.

Date c. 1430, dialect SEM, Lindberg, *Judges*, p. 69. Between Bar. 3:19 and 20 is inserted the note 'Here endiþ the translacioun of N and now bigynneþ þe translacioun of J and of oþere men', fol. 61v; see Hargreaves, 'The Vernacular Scriptures: the Wycliffite Versions', *CHB*, II.400, and De Hamel, *Book*, fig. 121, p. 173.

(part 1) quires 22–31 survive, signed (part 2) quires 1–15 of about 30 survive, signed; catchwords beneath right edge of written space, between stylized scrolls; 215 by 145 mm; 155 by 100 mm; two cols., 44 mm each; thirty-four lines, ruled in red in part 2; 5 mm apart; bounding lines very carefully drawn; regular bookhand.

Four-line initial, deep blue, green and orangey-red on gold background, extended into borders in all colours, at the opening of 2 Chron.; four-line initials (three-line in Psalms), gold on divided mauve and blue background, extended into gold and green borders (some excised); two-line initials, deep blue flourished in red, at opening of chapters; one-line initials, alternating deep blue and red, in Ps.-verses; alternating blue and red paraphs; incipits and (less frequently) explicits underlined in red in part 1, red in part 2; red lower-case roman chapter-numbers, sometimes ink underlined in red, sometimes with blue paraph; ink arabic chapter-numbers adjacent to column, sometimes underlined in red; ink running-heads (not in Psalms) complete on verso and recto with red paraph on verso and blue on recto; Ps.-titles and speaker-rubrics in the Song of Songs underlined in red; Esther and other rubrics in brown ink underlined in red; aleph–bet rubrics in brown ink in Lamentations; textual glosses underlined in red throughout.

Text: intermediate between EV and LV (see Hargreaves), or perhaps rather a blend of the two. Language 'revised', in 'the standard dialect', Lindberg, *Judges*, p. 69. Some textual glosses blend EV and LV readings, e.g. admittid (EV), or receyued (LV) (Tob. 6:20, *WB*, II.588), also Ps. 134:18 and Prov. 26:11; at Job 33:14 includes the LV gloss, but at Jer. 48:1 the gloss, 'þe stronge, man', is at odds with (and less correct than) LV 'þe stronge, citee'.

Cambridge University Library Mm. 2. 15

WB, no. 112 [Q] 362 fols., ONT in LV.

Fols. 1–3 blank (donation poem in English, dated 1 Jan. 1571, sewn on to fol. 3v); title (probably in the same hand as this poem), s.xvi mid, fol. 4r; metrical version of Ps. 82, in the same hand, fol. 4v; OT, fols. 5r–271v; fols. 272–3 blank, ornamented page with text 'Edoverdus Sextus', fol. 274r, and in the same hand 'The true copie of a Prologe whiche John Wicklife wrote to this Bible which he translatid into Englishe about two hundrid yere past, that was in the tyme of kynge Edwarde the thryd, as may iustly be gatherid of the mention that is had of him in diuers auncient Cronicles. Anno domini 1550'; Prologue to WB, fols. 275r–290v; NT, fols. 291r–362r.

Date c. 1410–20; 'about 1430', *WB*, I.liv; c. 1425, dialect SEM (dialect of Prologue Beds., *LALME*, I.68), Lindberg, *Judges*, p. 70; produced in London (?).

Owned by 'Stephanus Tomson, sacri palacii notarii, in anno 1519', fol. 307r, i.e., the Palace of Westminster; also 'anno domini 1522 Stephanus', fol. 329r, see Hudson, *PR*, p. 234; 'An ende of the hoole bible translatid into englische the year of our lorde god [ ]', s.xv, fol. 362r.

OT, Prologue and NT all begin with a new quire, and it is impossible to tell the original order from collation, although some aspects of the decoration imply the Prologue was in its current position.

375 by 260 mm; 285/90 by 190 mm; 2 cols., 87 mm each; 67 lines, 5 mm apart; margins ruled for glosses, outer 37/40 mm and inner 13 mm; regular bookhand; marginal gloss 1 mm. In very good condition.

Six/nine-line initials (i) gold on quartered deep-blue and mauve background reproducing the shape of the letter, with short demi-vinet border in same colours, or (ii) mauve, blue and orange on gold background, with an elaborate border in all colours around all cols.; three-line initials, deep blue flourished in red, at opening of chapters (incl. Prologue); alternating blue and red paraphs (incl. Prologue); red lower-case roman chapter-numbers, often with blue paraph; chapter-breaks often written in traditional style, with a red paraph; red running-heads complete on verso and recto, incl. 'Sauter', with blue paraph and outlined in blue (from fol. 60r onwards, and incl. Prologue); red incipits and explicits. Binding, front 'verbum domini' back 'manet in aeternum' (Is. 40:8) (*pace WB*, I.liv).

Text very good (like G, but not as late, Lindberg, *Judges*, p. 70). Textual glosses underlined in ink until fol. 59v, thereafter usually in red (incl. Prologue). Marginal glosses written right across gloss column; longer glosses sometimes in lower margin; in Daniel, glosses written in all the margins of fols. 242v–243r; sigla (and sometimes lemmata) link text and gloss. Many marginal glosses in OT, incl. nearly all the Pentateuch glosses.

DUBLIN

Trinity College 75

WB, no.151 [*T*]; 281 + ii fols.

Summary harmony of the Gospels, fols. 1r–2v; 'Sermo Doctor Curteyse' (sermon-heads), fols. 2v–3r (fol. 3v blank); lectionary in EV, fols. 4r–11r; prols. to Mark, Luke, John and Apoc.in LV, fols. 11v–13v; NT in EV, with prol. to Matt. in EV, no prols. to other Gospels, prols. to Acts, Cath. Epistles in LV, no prol. to Romans, prol. to Gal. in EV, prols. to 1 and 2 Cor., Eph., Phil., Col., 1 and 2 Thess., 1 and 2 Tim., Titus, Philemon, Hebr. in LV, no prol. to Apoc., fols. 14r–217v; Prologue to WB, fols. 218r–251r; Jerome's prol. to Psalms, fols. 251r–252r, Prologue on Psalms, fol. 252r, and Rolle's prol. on Psalms, fols. 252r–253r (see *WB*, I.37–40); prol. on Psalms written again after Rolle's prol, fol. 253r; opening of Prologue ch. 12, 'But it is to wite . . . haue in heuene', fols. 253r–v; prayer, etc., fols. 253v–254v; copy of letter in Latin to Cardinal Henry Beaufort, Bp of Winchester, from John Witton, curate of Chedynfolde, Surrey, rejecting accusations of heresy (after 1427, when Beaufort became cardinal), fols. 255r–257r; OT lections, in same hand as preceding letter, in LV, fols. 257r–281r.

Marvin L. Colker, *Trinity College Library: Descriptive Catalogue of The Mediaeval and Renaissance Latin Manuscripts*, vol.1 (Aldershot: Scolar Press, 1991), p. 119. Scattergood and Latré, 'Trinity College Dublin MS 75', in Scattergood and Boffey, eds., *Texts and their Contexts*, pp. 223–40. Scattergood and Latré suggest Witton owned the MS. Maureen Jurkowski, 'Lollard Book Producers in London in 1414', pp. 209–10.

Date c. 1425 (but s.xiv ex, *WB*, I.lx).

Note: 'The author of this translation seemeth to have beene John Purvay as Mr Fox calleth him both by the verse in the beginning and the character [i.e., the monogram] in the end of the Apocalipse' (s.xvii, fol. i^r); 'Christus homo factus J. P. prosperet actus', fol. 1r; monogram, fol. 217v (see *WB*, I.lxi). Owned by Sir Henry Gate, who records births and baptisms of his children 1544–55 (fol. i^v, fol. 281v); Francis Burgh, who gave it to Michael Seroien, Lambeth Marsh, 1593 (fol. ii^r and fol. 1r).

295 by 220 mm; 205 by 135 mm (in NT); 235 by 155 mm (in Prol. to WB); 2 cols. (in NT and Prol.); 41 lines (in NT), 44 lines (in Prol.). Five hands: A-D Northants, E Hunts., *LALME*, 1.76–7. Script of Prol. to WB a bastard anglicana, very similar to script of β.

Initials deep blue flourished in red (in NT); red chapter-numbers (in NT); rubrics and red chapter-numbers (OT lections); ink running-heads (NT); red Lombardic initials (Prol. to WB); capitals touched with red (Prol. to WB); titles (of biblical books) in red (Prol. to WB); textual glosses underlined in ink (in NT).

EV text shows a considerable degree of revision, Lindberg, *EV*, VII.24.

HEREFORD

Hereford Cathedral Library O. VII.1

WB, no. 137 [X] 361 fols., lectionary and ONT in LV (originally a two-vol. Bible, Gen.–Ps. and Prov.–Apoc.).

Lectionary, fols. 6r–9v (for final rubric, see pp. 61–2); Prefatory Epistles, fols. 10r–12v, prol. to Joshua, fols. 12v–13r, prol. to Kings, fols. 13r–v, prol. to 1 Chron., fols. 13v–14r (cf. C_U_6680), fols. 6r–14r.

R. A. B. Mynors and R. M. Thomson, *Catalogue of the Manuscripts of Hereford Cathedral Library* (Cambridge: Brewer, 1993), p. 46.

Date c. 1410–20; 'about 1420', *WB*, I.lviii; c. 1420, dialect SEM, Lindberg, *Judges*, p. 71.

'Liber ecclesie cath[edralis Herefordensis ex dono reuerendi] in Christo patris Roberti B[ennet]', Bp of Hereford 1602–1617, fol. 1r (mutilated).

Collation and format: see Mynors and Thomson, *Catalogue . . . Hereford* (pls. 54a–b). Margin not ruled for glosses.

Decoration: see ibid., (pls. 18a–b); aleph–bet rubrics in brown ink underlined in red in margin in Ps. 118 (fols. 181v–182v), within text in Prov. 31 (fols. 191r–v) and in margin in Lam. 1–4 (fols. 245v–246v); speaker-rubrics in margin in Song of Songs (uniquely for an LV MS).

Text 'typical', 'standard', like W, Lindberg, *Judges*, p. 71. Carefully corrected by scribe. Textual glosses carefully underlined in red throughout, incl. lectionary. LV textual glosses lacking in Joshua, in the early part of Judges and sometimes in 1 and 2 Kings. At Ecclus 40:14, a gloss in the lower margin says 'þise twey wordis, *sicut iustus*, is not in sum Latyn book but in sum Latyn book it is sett forþ wiþ þe text and þerfore me þinkiþ þe Englis shude not be drawen wiþ reed'. More extensive glosses are carefully written in the lower margin. Includes the series of glosses in the Pentateuch, but none from 1 Chron. to 2 Macc.

LONDON

British Library Arundel 104

WB, no. 29 [E] ONT in LV. 2-vol. Bible, but originally conceived as a pandect. Late medieval foliation, when the MS was already in two vols.; no modern foliation in vol. 2.

(vol. 1) 375 fols.; lectionary (temporal, commemorations, proper and common of saints together), in LV, fols. 1r–10v; Genesis to Psalms, with the opening verses of Proverbs, fols. 11r–375v; lacks Gen. 42:11–44:25 (1 fol.), 1 Chron. 16:39–18:10 (1 fol.).

(vol. 2) 425 fols.; Proverbs, with the opening verses written again in the upper margin in the scribal hand, to Apocalypse, fols. 1r–425r; 'a table wiþ a riwle þat teechiþ in what book and leef hou me shal finde alle þe firste chapeteris of þe newe testament in þe Bible', fol. 425r. There is no prol. to Jeremiah, *pace WB*, I.xlii.

Stella Panayotova, 'Cuttings from an Unknown Copy of the *Magna Glossatura* in a Wycliffite Bible', *The British Library Journal* 25 (1999), 85–100; De Hamel, *Book*, pp. 182–3 and fig. 129.

Date c. 1430; c. 1450, *WB*, I.xlii; c. 1440, dialect very mixed SM, Lindberg, *Judges*, p. 69.

Owned by Henry Howard, Duke of Norfolk, in late s.xvi (vols. 1 and 2, fol. 1r); note recording the birth and baptism of Henricus Saville, son of Henry Saville de Blatherorde, in 1568, vol. 2, fol. 425r.

405^{+} by 260 mm; 295 by 180 mm; catchwords 50/60 mm below right edge of written space, often within a scroll, sometimes elaborated into a grotesque; 2 cols., 80 mm each; 43/44 lines, 7 mm apart; letter 3.5 mm, marginal gloss 2 mm; margin not ruled for glosses. Very thick vellum, in very good condition, but not a beautiful volume.

Eight-line initial with symbols of four Evangelists at opening of Matt., vol. 2, fol. 251r (see fig. 7); fine three/seven-line initials, orange, pinky-beige and blue on a gold background and foliate borders in the same colours; some fine illuminated initials in Psalms taken from an MS of Peter Lombard's Gloss on Psalms and pasted in (some since excised), see Panayatova; two-line initials, deep blue flourished in red, at opening of chapters; one-line initials, alternating blue and red, in Ps.-verses; most incipits left blank in vol. 1, but red incipits (no explicits) throughout vol. 2; chapter-numbers alternating deep-blue and red upper-case roman; running-heads in ink only and often cropped from Gen. 7 to 4 Kings, elsewhere alternating deep blue and red upper-case letters, complete on verso and recto (incl. 'Sauter'), in the first chapters of Genesis flourished in red and throughout vol. 2 flourished in both colours; red Ps.-titles; red Latin Psalm incipits.

Text 'bad' (Lindberg, *Baruch*, p. 48), with 'many late and dubious forms and readings', *Judges*, p. 69. Includes coda to Acts (28:31), only otherwise in BL Harl. 4890 and BL_Lansdowne 455, and with IL restores interpolated text at 1 Kings 21:7 (see Appendix 3).

Textual glosses are very occasionally underlined in ink. In Genesis and Exodus, and in Isaiah and Jeremiah, several textual glosses are disordered, the scribe writing the gloss before the word(s) being glossed, e.g., at Gen. 49:17 'þat is an horned eddre, cerastes', fol. 39r; translational glosses have 'or' not 'eþer'; shares many readings with LPY, and in Maccabees follows Y's practice of writing glosses within the text in a smaller gloss hand, with attribution to Lyra. Many marginal glosses in OT; at Num. 11:17 the lengthy gloss is written within the text, not underlined but attributed 'Lire here' (marg. BCdEKLPQX, *WB*, I.397), fol. 94r.

British Library Cotton Claudius E. II

WB, no. 9 [C]; 352 fols., ONT in LV (except for a small part of NT in EV, see below).

Half-page miniature of Creation and Fall and eight-line initial 'O', s.xvi, fol. 1r; part of French paraphrase of Genesis, s.xvi, fol. 1v; fol. 2 blank except for Cotton's title; OT, inc. Gen. 9:23, fols. 3r–278v; NT in LV, fols. 279r–351v, but in EV (in same hand) from Luke 19:12 to 20:10, and throughout Philemon (but the prol. to Philemon is in LV); names of books 'in ordre in þis Bible' (excluding 3 Ezra and Laodiceans) with number of chapters in each, fols. 351v–352r, concluding that 'þe sume of bookis wiþ þe prolog conteyneþ [l]xxiii & xi'. The collation shows that this MS did not contain the Prologue at the time it was bound (only two leaves are missing at the opening, and these must have contained Gen. 1–9:23).

Date c. 1410; 'before 1420', *WB*, I.xl; c. 1420, dialect SM, Lindberg, *Judges*, p. 69.

380 by 260 mm; 263 by 170 mm; first quire (confirmed by quire and sheet signatures) lacks 1–2; catchwords centred 53 mm below inner col., sometimes outlined in red; 2 cols., 80 mm each; 62/63 lines, 4 mm apart;

bounding-lines carefully drawn; letter 1.5 mm (marginal gloss 1mm); column ruled for marginal glosses throughout OT but not NT, width 35 mm (outer), 23/24 mm (inner); carefully written and corrected in one even but not elegant bookhand; Dan. 6 was omitted and then added in the lower margin, fol. 250r.

Eight/ten-line initials, deep blue and red flourished in both colours; three-line initials, deep-blue flourished in red, at opening of chapters; one-line initials, alternating deep blue and red, in Ps.-verses; alternating blue and red paraphs; red incipits and explicits; red lower-case roman chapter-numbers, 'capitulum i', or c^m^ i, etc.; ink lower-case roman chapter-numbers with alternating blue and red paraph centrally above each column (red without paraph in NT); ink running-heads, with alternating blue and red paraph, complete on verso and recto (incl. Psalms), red with blue paraph in NT; red Ps.-titles. A workmanlike rather than beautiful MS.

Text good (but 'average', Lindberg, *Judges*, p. 69). EV text revised, Lindberg, *EV*, VII.22. Textual glosses are written in the margin in Genesis and the first part of Exodus; thereafter, textual glosses are usually underlined in ink but sometimes in red.

This is by far the most heavily glossed MS of the OT, containing nearly all the series of glosses (except those in 1–2 Macc.) and many unique glosses, especially in Prov.–Is. 8:4. Marginal glosses are written across the full width of the margin and also in the upper and lower margins from Proverbs to Is. 8:4; cropping has caused slight loss of gloss text on fol. 178; from 2 Chron. 21 to 1 Ezra 9 (fols. 121v–129r) marginal glosses are headed 'glos(e)', as are the Psalm title-glosses; in Psalms the word is outlined in red. Lemmata, underlined in ink or in red, always link biblical text and marginal gloss; sigla link biblical text and marginal gloss in the upper or lower margin, or where the gloss is at some distance from the biblical text; glosses are always completed on the same page as the biblical text, with the exception of the gloss on Dan. 11, fols. 252r–v, where a rubric instructs 'turne ouer þe leef'.

British Library Egerton 617–618

WB, no. 32 [*G*], **617**: 224 fols., Proverbs–Maccabees in EV **618**. 177 fols., NT in EV. Originally a three-vol. Bible.

NT order: Gospels, Acts, Catholic Epistles, Pauline Epistles, Apocalypse; lacks 1 fol. after 102 (1 John 5:9–end, 2 John and 3 John, Jude 1:1–3), incipit 'The prologe of Poulis pistle to Romayns', but no prol., fol. 104v; fol. 105r blank (production break between Catholic Epistles and Pauline Epistles);

lacks one fol. after 113 (1 Cor. 1:1–3:9); lacks one fol. after 142 (Titus); lacks prols. to Matt., Mark, Acts, Catholic Epistles, all Pauline Epistles except Philemon (but leaves space for prols. to other Pauline Epp.), Apoc. (leaves space to add prol.). Lectionary in EV, with incipits in Latin in red, trans. 'þat is to saye [etc.]', temporal, proper of saints, common of saints, commemorations, fols. 160r–177r.

Song of Songs printed from this MS by its then owner Adam Clarke, *The Holy Bible . . . with a Commentary*, vol. IV (Lutterworth, 1825), 15P3–Q1; Clarke names John Hunter as former owner, fol. 55v.

Doyle, 'English Books In and Out of Court', p. 168; Krochalis, 'The Books and Reading of Henry V and his Circle', 51; Scott, *Later Gothic Manuscripts*, p. 70.

Before 1397, but 'about 1420', *WB*, I.xliii; c. 1425, dialect SEM (slightly more N. before Bar. 3:20), Lindberg, *Judges*, p. 68.

Owned by Thomas Duke of Gloucester (whose arms appear on fol. 2r), *pace WB*, I.xliii and Sven L. Fristedt, 'A Weird Manuscript Enigma in the British Museum', *Stockholm Studies in Modern Philology*, n.s. 2 (1964), 116–21. This MS was included among Gloucester's forfeited possessions in 1397, and valued at 40 shillings; it is the 'earliest datable manuscript of EV', Hudson, *PR*, p. 247 (for 'Harley' read 'Egerton').

435 by 290 mm; 315 by 190 mm; 2 cols., 46 lines; letter 3 mm, a large and sometimes slightly tremulous bookhand.

On the decoration in this Bible (masks and dragons) see Scott, *Later Gothic Manuscripts*, p. 70, and cf. Trinity Hall Camb. 17 (Roger Dymmock, *Liber Contra Duodecim Errores*, 1395–99). Elaborately decorated bar-border in gold, mauve, pink and blue, with touches of olive green, at the opening of each book; seven-line initial with coiled mauve and blue foliage on gold background, 618, fol. 1r; two-line initials, gold on mauve and blue background with white tracery, at opening of chapters; one-line initials, alternating gold on deep blue and deep blue flourished in red, in some parts of the NT and throughout the lectionary (cf. Bodl. Fairfax 11); red incipits; red roman lower-case chapter-numbers; red running-heads, complete on verso and recto, undecorated; the beginnings and endings of lections are written in red within the text throughout NT; many omissions in text carefully corrected, often within lozenges, in margin; lower corners of first 24 fols. affected by damp, affecting text of Prov. 1–12.

Text 'average', Lindberg, *Judges*, p. 68; text of NT 'ordinary', Lindberg, *EV*, VII.22. Textual glosses usually underlined in ink (very occasionally in red in Isaiah and Ezekiel); in Isaiah and Jeremiah the glosses are frequently added later.

British Library Harley 5017

WB, no. 22 [e]; 117 fols., 1 Macc.–Apoc. in LV.

1–2 Maccabees in LV, fols. 1r–25r, NT in LV, fols. 25r–117r (fol. 117 now a stub); part of same set as BL Royal I. C. IX; presumably originally a three-vol. Bible, now missing the second vol., Ps.–Malachi.

Hargreaves, 'The Marginal Glosses to the Wycliffite New Testament', 285–300.

Date c. 1400–10; 'not later than 1410', *WB*, I.xl; c. 1420, for Royal I. C. IX, Lindberg, *Judges*, p. 69.

Base text of John Russell's projected edition of WB.

Owned by Rob. Keck in s.xvii, fol. 1*r.

385 by 275 mm; 310 by 175 mm; quire and sheet signatures ('a' onwards) written within bounding-lines 30 mm below outer col. of recto, quire letter above arabic leaf number; catchwords written 30 mm below right edge of written space, outlined in red; 2 cols., 83 mm each; 50 lines, 5 mm apart; margin ruled for marginal glosses, inner and outer, 17 mm; regular bookhand. In rather poor condition, but a carefully written MS.

Blue initial on gold background and decorative border in gold, pink, light blue and deep blue, somewhat clumsily executed, at the opening of Matt., fol. 25r; five/six-line initials, deep blue and red flourished in both colours; two-line initials, deep blue flourished in red, at opening of chapters; blue and red paraphs; red incipits and explicits; red running-heads, complete on verso and recto, with blue paraphs; red lower-case roman chapter-numbers above outer and inner edges of verso cols. and inner and outer edges of recto cols.; red chapter-numbers in English, 'þe firste c^{o}', etc., but sometimes red lower-case roman; chapter-breaks sometimes written in traditional style; margins damp-stained throughout, and opening and closing fols. badly rubbed. Original Harleian Library spine, pasted onto flyleaf of the 1964 binding, attributes translation to Wyclif.

Textual glosses in Maccabees are in the margin, as in Royal I. C. IX. Textual glosses in the NT are not underlined. Includes many marginal glosses in the NT, but in Apoc. only in ch. 1; most of these glosses are shared with *V*, see Hargreaves, and Appendix 2.

British Library Royal 1. C.VIII

WB, no. 6 [A]; 372 + i fols., ONT in LV.

Prologue to WB, ch. 1 only, bookhand c. 1475–1500, fols. 1r–v, originally wrapper, with arms of Henry VII incorporated in the lower decorated border of fol. 1r; OT in LV, fols. 2r–299r; prol. to Matthew, fol. 299v; NT, fols. 300r–372v.

Forms base text of ONT in LV in *WB*.

Date c. 1400–10; 'probably before 1420', *WB*, I.xxxvii; c. 1420, Lindberg, *Judges*, p. 69; dialect Bucks, *LALME*, I.114; decoration c. 1400–1410; almost certainly a London production.

375 by 255 mm; 280 by 180 mm; quire and sheet signatures often cropped (MS is complete at beginning); catchwords 65 mm below right edge of written space; 2 cols., 86 mm each; 57 lines, 5 mm apart; an even, slightly angular bookhand.

Miniature of John the Evangelist with his eagle at the opening of John, fol. 325v (see fig. 6); seven/eight-line initials, pinky-red and deep blue on gold background, with decorated bar-border in the same colours at the opening of each book; four-line initials, gold on quartered pinky-red and deep-blue background, sometimes reproducing the shape of the letter; three-line initials, deep blue flourished in red, at opening of chapters; one-line initials, alternating deep blue and red, in Ps.-verses; blue paraphs; red incipits and explicits; red lower-case roman chapter-numbers; ink running-heads with blue paraph, complete on verso and recto (not in Psalms); red Ps.-titles and glosses; aleph–bet rubrics in Lamentations, fols. 369r–372r; badly stained but with no loss of text. A very fine MS.

Text very good ('average', *Judges*, p. 69), but revised. The missing portion of Wisd. 12:9 is added in the margin in the scribal hand, fol. 199r, and of Apoc. 20:12 in the lower margin in the scribal hand, fol. 372r. On other textual corrections in this MS, see *WB*, I.xxxix–xl and Appendix 2. There is also considerable correction *sup. ras.* in Song of Songs.

Translational variants sometimes cut to one of the alternatives from Gen. 1 to Numbers 20 (four in Genesis, five in Exodus, five in Leviticus, seven from Num. 1–20), present from there to Job, and then omitted to the end of the OT. Textual glosses are underlined in red or in brown ink.

There are only a few marginal glosses; in Psalms, the title-glosses are incorporated into the title rubrics (but signalled 'a glos') and rubricated throughout; from Ps. 54 to Ps. 68 (fols. 174r–176r) the titles incorporate references to the Hebrew title and to Jerome. Includes a unique marginal gloss at Ecclus 28:15 inc. 'a dowble tungid man is he' (*WB*, III.77), fol. 208v.

British Library Royal 1. C. IX

WB, no. 7 [B]; ii + 233 fols., Genesis to Job in LV.

Companion vol. to Harley 5017, presumably originally a three-vol. Bible, now lacking the second vol., Psalms to Malachi.

Initial rubric: ‘here biginneþ þe Bible playnly þe text & where þat ony maner clause is set in þe text and is not þerof Lire certifieþ it plainly’, fol. 1r (see also d), *WB*, I.79.

Date c. 1400–10; ‘not later than 1410’ (for Harley 5017), *WB*, I.xl; c. 1420 (for this MS), dialect CM, Lindberg, *Judges*, p. 69.

395 by 285 mm; 315 by 180 mm; quire and sheet signatures 30 mm below right edge of written space, letter above number; catchwords 30 mm below right edge of written space, outlined in red; 2 cols., 88 mm each; 50 lines, 5 mm apart; margins ruled for glosses, inner and outer, 17 mm; two main hands, with hand 2 beginning at fol. 169r (4 Kings 19).

Five/six-line initials, deep blue and red flourished in both colours; two-line initials, deep blue flourished in red, at opening of chapters; blue paraphs; red incipits and explicits; red running-heads, complete on verso and recto, with blue paraphs; red lower-case roman chapter-numbers above outer and inner edges of verso cols. and inner and outer edges of recto cols.; red chapter-numbers in English, ‘þe firste chapiter’ or ‘chapitil’, etc., but sometimes red lower-case roman; chapter-breaks are sometimes written in traditional style. Not elaborately decorated but a handsome, carefully written MS.

Text ‘like A’, an ‘ordinary copy’ of LV, Lindberg, *Judges*, p. 69. Textual glosses are underlined sometimes in red and sometimes in ink; usually, however, they are written in the margin, underlined in red, with red sigla linking the gloss and the text. The biblical text was apparently corrected before the marginal glosses were written, since in several places the marginal gloss is written around the added text. The textual glosses were apparently written before the marginal glosses, since at e.g. Judith 15:4 the marginal gloss is written around the textual gloss in the margin, ‘propir, eþer synguler’, fol. 215r.

In the marginal glosses, lemmata (which occur sporadically) are underlined in red; where they are extensive, the lower margin is also used; where they are very extensive, the glosses also intrude into the biblical text cols., showing that the biblical text must have been written with knowledge of the glosses to be added: fols. 209v–210r (Tob. 12), fol. 213r (Judith 9), fol. 216v (Esther 3), fol. 217v (Esther 7) and throughout Job (fols. 220v–233r), cf. *Glossa Ordinaria* format. In Job, the marginal gloss becomes continuous, and the separate lemmata, underlined in red, are not indicated by the usual alphabetical and other sigla in the biblical text, so that only the first lemma is signalled; at Job 31:38, the gloss on ‘if my hond crieþ’ begins on fol. 229v and ends on fol. 230r; the glosses on Job 39:35 and Job 40:3 are written twice, on fol. 232 verso and recto; there are many marginal glosses ascribed to Lyra throughout, but none is ascribed to the Gloss (contrast Harley 5017); *WB* does not record these glosses after the end of Deuteronomy (see Appendix 2). There are a number of unique glosses in 4 Kings 22–5, fols. 170r–172r, in 2 Chron. 20–5, fols. 189v–192r, and also sporadically throughout: these are not recorded in *WB*, but see Appendix 2.

Lambeth Palace 25

WB, no. 46 [U]; iv + 369 fols., Pentateuch in EV, Joshua–Apocalypse in LV.

Prefatory Epistles in EV, fols. 1r–4r; Pentateuch in EV, fols. 4r–76v (LV catchwords for Josh. 1:1, fol. 76v), Joshua to end of OT in LV, fols. 77r–301v; NT in LV, fols. 302r–368v (fol. 369 blank). Perhaps originally a two-vol. Bible, since the opening of Matt., fol. 302r, is badly soiled.

M. R. James, *A Descriptive Catalogue of the Manuscripts of the Library of Lambeth Palace*, part I (Cambridge University Press, 1930), pp. 40–1; Pickering and O'Mara, *Manuscripts in Lambeth Palace Library*, pp. 1–2.

Date c. 1390–1400; c. 1400, *WB*, I.xlv; 'after 1400', dialect SEM throughout, Lindberg, *Judges*, pp. 68, 70.

Owned by Edmund Bonner, Bp of London from 1540 (see *WB*, I.xlv, and Bodl MS Engl. hist. c. 147, fol. 139v); an Essex provenance is suggested by the names of Tey sponsors (1543–47) pasted on fol. iv[r].

395 by 250 mm; 280 by 185 mm; catchwords 15/35 mm below right edge of written space; 2 cols., 57/69 lines (69 on last fol. of 2 Macc.); 4/5 mm apart; three regular bookhands.

Five-line gold initial extended into decorative border in gold, blue, mauve and orange (all very faded) at the opening of Matt., fol. 302r; five/six-line initials, deep blue with saw-tooth pattern flourished in red with touches of violet; two-line initials, deep blue flourished in red, at opening of chapters; one-line initials, alternating deep blue and red, in Ps.-verses; verses touched in red to end of Genesis; red roman lower-case chapter-numbers within col., sometimes with decorative red line-fillers; chapter-breaks sometimes written in traditional style, with blue paraph; red running-heads with blue paraph, complete on verso and recto; red incipits and explicits ('here endiþ . . . here bigynneþ'); red Ps.-titles incorporate title-glosses, cf. A (rubric 'a glos', with blue paraph, in margin).

Text of EV portion 'less uniform' than most EV MSS, Lindberg, *Judges*, p. 68; very good (but 'good', Lindberg, *Baruch*, p. 49) in LV. Corrects LV at Amos 5:17 (*WB*, III.699). Textual glosses sometimes underlined in ink (very occasionally in red); textual glosses in Psalms sometimes attributed to

Lyra within text, in glosses shared with B_554KV, e.g., 'dresside my werkis, li. he.' (Ps. 58:5), fol. 185r; see Appendix 2. Marginal glosses are sometimes linked to the biblical text with sigla, sometimes have a red lemma and blue or red paraph, and are sometimes red throughout. There are glosses on Dan. 11:36–45 and 12:11 (shared with CQ) in all the margins of fols. 275r–v. In the EV portion, a few LV glosses are written in the lower margin; the gloss lemmata are in EV at Gen. 6:6 (*WB*, I.89–90), fol. 5v, and at Exd. 4:21 (*WB*, I.201), fol. 24r. There are unique glosses on 'locuste' and 'bruke' (Joel 1:4, *WB*, III.686–687), fol. 278v.

LONGLEAT HOUSE, WARMINSTER

Longleat 3

Lindberg no.178 [L_o]; 398 fols., ONT in EV.

OT, with space left for prols. to Ezekiel, Daniel and all the Minor Prophets, fols. 1r–326v; NT, lacking all prols., fols. 327r–398r. Four fols. are torn, involving loss of text: fol. 37 (Exd. 40 and Lev. 1–3), fol. 134 (part of 4 Kings 25 and opening of 1 Chron.), fol. 310 (a few verses of Mal. 3 and 1 Macc.1) and fol. 398 (Apoc. 22:20–1).

Date c. 1390–1400; c. 1400–1410, Madden; c. 1400, dialect NM, Lindberg, *Judges*, p. 68.

John Spelman (c. 1480–1546) 'de Narburgh' (Narborough, Norfolk) gave this MS to his son Henry Spelman (d. 1581) of Congham (Norfolk), who gave it to his son Henry (legal historian and antiquary, 1563/4–1641); inscription dated 1582, flyleaf iii^{r} (transcribed from previous inside cover). Thomas Thynne, Lord Bath, bought this MS at one of the sales of Spelman's books in 1709–10; see Kate Harris, 'An Augustan Episode in the History of the Collection of Medieval Manuscripts at Longleat House', in Edwards *et al.* eds., *The English Medieval Book*, pp. 237–8.

395 × 285 mm; 255 x 180 mm; catchwords 65 mm below right edge of written space, enclosed in rectangle; 2 cols., 85 mm each; 56 lines, 4 mm apart; one clear bookhand.

Eight-line initial, blue flourished in red, at the opening of the Prefatory Epistles, fol. 1r, and Matthew, fol. 327r; eight-line initial, deep blue with foliate pattern in pink and brown, and very elaborate red and violet penwork, at opening of Luke, fol. 344r; bar-border in blue and red, flourished in red, at opening of Genesis, fol. 3v; six-line initials, deep blue and red, flourished in both colours, at opening of each book; four-line initials, deep blue (faded) flourished in red, at opening of chapters in OT; two-line initials, deep blue flourished in red, outset, at opening of chapters in NT (cf. *E*); capitals in Ps.-verses touched with red. Opening of chapters sometimes written in large letters, and top-line ascenders sometimes extended and decorated, to the end of Judges only. Occasional incipits and explicits in ink, in Latin, in the early books of the OT; occasional red incipits and explicits, sometimes in Latin and sometimes in English, from 2 Chron. to Baruch; from Romans onwards, there are red incipits and explicits in English; ink chapter-numbers, lower-case roman, from Genesis to Romans, red chapter-numbers from Romans onwards; ink running-heads, Latin, from Genesis to Romans (not in Psalms), red running-heads from Romans onwards, English, complete on verso and recto. Includes rubric at 2 Chron. 37 (Prayer of Manasseh), Esther rubrics, etc., in brown ink, not underlined; red Ps.-titles and numbers. Lections indicated in ink in lower margin, in OT, and in margin beside opening of lection in Latin, in NT; red abc marking lections in NT. Parchment of medium quality. Opening fols. badly stained and worn. A workmanlike MS.

Text: 'one of the best MSS of EV', Lindberg, *Baruch*, p. 48; often agrees with *CE*, Judges, p. 68. It is uniquely correct among EV MSS at Judges 9:15, 'deuowre þe see\d/ris of Liban' (*cedros*), see Lindberg, *Judges*, pp. 72, 242. With *XY* has correct reading at Bar. 4:20, 'I shal crie to þe heȝest' [bihest *AGK*]. At Ecclus 32:15, 'tiffe þou þee not' is *corr.* in margin 'haue þou not a sloow wil' (cf. *C pr. m. E*, Lindberg, *EV*, IV.346). Has a slightly revised text of EV in NT, Lindberg, *EV*, VII.22. Textual glosses are sporadically underlined in ink, never in red. Translational variants are often added in the margin in the prophetical books. Includes the LV gloss on Priapus, 'þat is an idol liyk a man wiþ outragiouse membre of man' (3 Kings 15:3, *WB*, II.209), in the scribal hand, headed 'þe glos'. There are lengthy Middle English glosses on some Psalms.

OXFORD

Bodley 277

WB, no. 60 [I] 377 fols., ONT in LV.

Ch. 1 of Prologue to WB, fol. 1r; OT, incl. 3 Ezra (lightly revised), fols. 1v–301v (lacks 3 Kings 22:11–4 Kings 2:16); NT, incl. the EV long prol. to Romans, 'First us bihoueþ vndirstonde' (Stegmüller, *RBMA*, no. 669), fols. 301v–376r (fol. 377 blank). In several places the scribe seems to have misjudged the space necessary for prols., most notably the EV long prol. to Romans, where an extra portion of leaf, one column wide, has been inserted (fol. 334, ii).

Ed. Lindberg, *KHB*.

De Hamel, *Book*, figs. 130–1, pp. 184–5; Scott, *Later Gothic Manuscripts*, p. 70. Fol. 1r frontispiece in Lindberg, *KHB*, I.

Date c. 1425–35 (?), 'perhaps 1440', *WB*, I.xlvii; c. 1450, Lindberg, 'The Alpha and Omega of the Middle English Bible', p. 192; c. 1430, dialect mixed EM, *Judges*, p. 70.

'Hic liber erat quondam Henrici Sexti', who gave it to the London Charterhouse, fol. 375r; see Hudson, *PR*, p. 23.

140 mm thick incl. boards; 405 by 250 mm; 290 by 180 mm; catchwords not visible; 2 cols., 85 mm each; 64 lines, 5 mm apart; bounding lines very carefully drawn; outer margin ruled for glosses 35 mm, inner margin 15 mm; letter 2 mm (marginal gloss 1.5 mm); an even bookhand. In excellent condition throughout; an exceptionally sumptuous volume.

Bar-borders at the opening of each book, in gold, blue, pink, orangey-red and green (especially sumptuous for the opening of Genesis, fol. 1v, Psalms, fol. 167r, Matthew, fol. 300r, Romans, fol. 335r and the Apocalypse, fol. 370r); six-line initials in the same colours; three-line initials, deep blue flourished in red, at opening of chapters; one-line initials, alternating deep blue and red, in Ps.-verses; red incipits and explicits; red chapter-numbers, upper-case roman with blue paraph, within the col., in OT (incl. Psalm-numbers), alternating blue and red upper-case roman chapter-numbers without paraph in NT; chapter-breaks sometimes written in traditional style (e.g. at the conclusion of 2 Kings 11, fol. 91r); red running-heads with blue paraphs, English, complete on verso and recto in OT (incl. 'Sauter'), but in alternating blue and red letters written across verso and recto in NT; omissions to text in the margin often in a lozenge bounded by elaborate red penwork. Lections are marked in red in the margin and the opening of each lection is marked in red in the text.

The text is carefully corrected throughout. Textual glosses are underlined in ink, never in red; marginal glosses are underlined in ink and linked by rubricated sigla to the biblical text; longer glosses are written in the lower margin, e.g., at Exd. 25:16, fol. 25r. The text is revised stylistically throughout; see Lindberg, *KHB* (text 'remarkable', *Judges*, p. 74). There are corrections to LV text at Song 7:13 and Hab. 1:12. Many textual glosses present in other LV MSS are missing here from Genesis to Psalms, with the text often following the EV translation. There are many readings and glosses shared with S in Gen.–Joshua and 1 Chron.–Job, and with N in 1 Chron.–2 Ezra (see Lindberg, *KHB*, II.49). Translational textual glosses up to and incl. Psalms always follow the formula '[x] *or* [y]', but in Wisdom and Ecclus commonly '[x] *eþer* [y]', and in the prophetic books almost always '[x] *eþer* [y]'. Some glosses in Psalms are shared with B_554KUV; Psalm title-glosses begin at Ps. 92; from Proverbs to the end of the OT textual glosses are shared with most LV MSS. There are unique glosses from Gregory and Ambrose in 3 Kings, not recorded in *WB* (see Appendix 2).

Bodley 959

WB, no. 65 [*E*]; 333 fols., Gen. to Bar. 3:20 in EV, expl. 'of hem risen / þe ʒunge' (end of fol. 332r, fol. 333v blank)

Lacks prol. to Judith and 1:1–4:16 (1 fol.); fols. 232v–233r blank (booklet boundary between second prol. to Ps. and Ps. 1); a few French words with English equivalents scribbled in a s.xiv hand (transcribed Fristedt, *WB*, *I*.70–1), fol. 333r; 'þat þing þat ʒe spac of touchynge Sauages douʒter wole not ʒet be', in a s.xv hand, lower marg. fol. 333v.

Forms text of Lindberg's edition of this part of OT in EV (*EV*, I–V).

Lindberg, *EV*, I.7–25; De Hamel, *Book*, pp. 170–1, fig. 119; Hudson, *PR*, p. 279.

Date: c. 1380–90; 'certainly before 1390', *WB*, I.xlvii; c. 1400, Lindberg, *Judges*, p. 68; dialects (see below).

Donated to Bodleian Library by Springham via Sir Thomas Bodley, 1602.

12s, 330+ by 230+ mm; 210/230 by 150/160 mm; catchwords in various positions, but most 10 mm below right edge of written space; 2 cols., 53–66 lines, 3–4 mm apart; letter 1–2 mm; at least four hands:

hand A, fols. 1r–44v (Pref. Epp. to end of Exodus), dialect WM plus EM, Lindberg, *EV*, I.15 (hands 1/2, fols. 44v–45r, Lindberg, *EV*, I, pl. opp. p. 156)

hand B, fols. 45r–93v (Leviticus to Judges 7:13), dialect WM with S features, Lindberg, *EV*, II.18 (hands 2/3, fol. 93v, Lindberg, *EV*, II, pl. opp. p. 216)

hand C, fols. 93v–288r? (Judges 7:13 to Ecclus 48:6?), dialect NEM, Lindberg, *EV*, III.18, Soke, *LALME*, I.146

hand D [or E], fols. 288r–332r (Ecclus 48:6 to end), dialect EM, Lindberg, *EV*, IV.16, Northants, *LALME*, I.146 (fol. 288r, Lindberg, *EV*, IV, pl. opp. p. 362). *WB* and Lindberg both think a separate hand probably wrote some part of Judges 7:13 to Ecclus 48:6, but cannot determine where this fourth hand begins (*WB*, I.xlvii; Lindberg, following Fristedt, *WB*, *I*.63, begins *EV*, IV with 1Ezra [fols. 190v–191r, end of 2 Chron. and opening of 1Ezra, Lindberg, *EV*, III, pl. opp. p. 310, also fol. 254v, Lindberg, *EV*, VI, pl. opp. p. 300]).

Four/twelve-line (most four) initials, red flourished in deep blue, crudely executed; two/three-line (most three-line) red Lombardic initials, outset (cf. L_o), at opening of chapters; red (but from fol. 95v onwards usually ink); running-heads at first on verso only, but from Judges 19 onwards usually complete on verso and recto (verso only in 'Sauter'); red incipits and explicits; no paraphs; ink chapter-numbers, arabic; textual rubrics in Esther in ink; red title-rubrics in Psalms; one-line red initials in Ps.-verses; first two speaker-rubrics in Song of Songs *om.* and supplied in the margin *pr. m.*

On the text of *E*, see intros. to Lindberg, *EV*, I–V; 'the best' text of this part of OT in EV, Lindberg, *Baruch*, p. 47. *E pr. m.* shares readings with LV, see Lindberg, *EV*, I.20–1 (etc.), and has many unique readings, see Lindberg, *EV*, I.17–18 (etc.). There are corrections/revisions throughout (typically three or four per page), some in scribal hand(s) but many more in another hand, in the text *sup. ras.*, or with the text erased and/or crossed through, or expuncted, and an interlinear and/or marginal correction. Dialectal corrections include addition of final –e, addition of *–n* or *-en* to infinitive or plural present and erasure of prefix *I-*, *y-* in Prefatory Epistles and Genesis, see Lindberg, *EV*, I.18–19.

Bodleian Douce 369, part 1

WB, no. 87 [*C*]; 250 fols.

Num. 20:2–Bar. 3:20, fols. 1r–250r, lacks Jud. 1:21–Jud. 4:4 (1 fol.); 'Explicit translacioun Nicholay de herford', fol. 250r. De Hamel says Hereford may have added the colophon naming himself, in the same hand as the corrections and chapter-numbers (*Book*, pp. 171–3, fig. 120 at p. 171).

Forms the text in EV in *WB* from 1 Ezra to Bar. 3:20.

Date: 'before 1390', *WB*, I.l; 1382–5, De Hamel, *Book*, p. 172; before 1400, dialect NM, Lindberg, *Judges*, p. 68.

365 by 250 m; 250 by 150 mm; catchwords 10 mm below right edge of written space; 2 cols., 56 lines, 4 mm apart, letter 2 mm; three hands, of which the third (Esth. 2:5 to the end) is that of the final scribe of Bodl. 959, according to *WB*, I.l; De Hamel, however, thinks it is 'probably not', *Book*, p. 172.

Three-line initials (a few six-line initials), alternating deep blue and red flourished in the other colour, sometimes with a human face (e.g., fols. 63v, 87v), roughly executed, at opening of books and chapters; no paraphs; occasional red incipits and explicits, Latin; ink chapter-numbers, arabic, adjacent to col.; ink running-heads in upper left-hand margin of verso (incl. 'Salterium'); textual rubrics in Esther in brown ink; one-line initials, alternating deep blue and red, in Ps.-verses; red Ps.-titles; lections occasionally outlined in red, e.g. at Deut. 31:24–30, fols. 21r–v.

Text 'less uniform [than most EV MSS] but more correct', Lindberg, *Judges*, p. 68.

Textual glosses usually written in the margin and linked by sigla to the biblical text, in the same hand as the corrections, chapter-numbers and colophon, but occasionally within text and underlined in ink, e.g., 'þe swalewe and, þe somer foule þat is clepid, cyconye' (Jer. 8:7), fol. 230r.

Bodleian Fairfax 2

WB, no.71 [K]; ii + 388 fols.; ONT in LV.

Prefatory Epistles in EV, fols. 1r–3r; Gen.–Ps., fols. 3r–187r, with prols. in EV; summary of Canticles with book and chapter nos., fols. 187r–v; Quicunque vult, fol. 187v; lectionary (temporal, proper of saints for each month, beginning January, with dominicals and ferials listed at the end of each month and commemorations listed in the lower part of fols. 192v–193r), book and chapter-numbers and indexing letters of each lection are provided, but not the opening and closing words, fols. 188r–193v (perhaps lectionary misplaced, but possibly this was originally a two-vol. Bible, with lectionary concluding vol. 1); Prov.–2 Macc., fols. 194r–312r; with prols. in EV (but lacks prols. to Wisdom and Jeremiah); sometimes the room needed for the prol. is misjudged (e.g. to Proverbs, fol. 194r); prol. to Isaiah inc. 'anoþer prolog on Isayee and oþere profetis', but there is only the LV prol., fol. 223r (*pace WB*, it is not misplaced); NT, fols. 312r–385v; a 'table', that is, a *capitula*-list of books of the NT, inc.'i. Of þe generacion of Crist. Hou Josep spousid Marie ii. Of Cristis birþe', expl. '[Apocalypse] xxiiii. To ʒelde to ech man vp hise werkis' (cf. Lambeth Palace 547), fols. 385v–388v.

'Þe ʒeer of þe lord m.cccc & viiij þis book was endid', with fourth 'c' erased, fol. 385r, *WB*, I.xlviii; Andrew G. Watson, *Catalogue of Dated and Datable Manuscripts c. 435–1600 in Oxford Libraries*, vol. I (Oxford: Clarendon Press, 1984), no. 485, p. 78; Kathleen L. Scott, *Dated and Datable English Manuscript Borders c. 1395–1499* (London: British Library, 2002), pp. 40–1; De Hamel, *Book*, p. 182 and fig. 128. Note dating MS 1318, and later corrected, in a s.xvii hand, 1308, or perhaps 1408 'which is 25 years after Wickleff finished ye translation' [i.e. 1383]; in the same hand, this MS is 'more legible but not so antient or correct as [Bodley 277]. That it is not so antient I suppose from ye figure of ye letter, & because some notes that are in that copy added in y[e] margent in this are crept into y[e] text', fol. i[r]. Dialect mixed CM, Lindberg, *Judges*, p. 70.

425 by 275 mm; 300 by 195 mm; 95 mm thick excluding boards; original red roman sheet signatures sometimes visible, s.xv quire and arabic sheet signatures (side by side) clearly visible; catchwords close to inner gutter 40 mm below written space; 2 cols., 90 mm each; 60/61 lines; letter 2 mm (also marginal gloss); a regular bookhand with rather thick strokes. In very good condition.

Three-sided border in blue, mauve and gold, with a curve in the middle of the vertical, fols. 1r, 3r; six-line initial, gold on mauve and blue quartered background with white filigree work, at opening of Prefatory Epistles, fol. 1r; fifteen-line Lombardic initial, deep blue flourished in red, at the opening of Matt., fol. 312r; two/eight line (most two-line) Lombardic initials, deep blue flourished in red, at opening of books and chapters; very occasional red paraphs within the text; chapter-numbers (and Ps.-numbers) ink, arabic, adjacent to text; chapter-breaks frequently written in traditional style, with red paraph; explicits and incipits (beginning 'Se now') usually underlined in red; red running-heads, with blue paraph, complete on verso and recto (Joshua titled 'þe book of domes', Psalms titled 'Dauid', 2 Ezra 'Esdre or Neemye'); one-line initials, alternating deep blue and red, in Ps.-verses; Ps.-titles and Latin Psalm incipits underlined in red; rubrics in Esther etc. underlined in red; margins indexed for lections.

Text very good ('good', Lindberg, *Baruch*, p. 49); carefully corrected throughout. Summary of contents often indicated in ink in the upper margin, especially in the historical books, but also e.g. at Jer. 36 'Joachym king of Juda brent þe book þat Jeremye made', fol. 250r. At Wisdom 15:14 has the unique corrected reading 'comaunden' where other LV MSS have 'vpbreyden' (*imperantes BS* var. *improperantes*), see Lindberg, *KHB*, III.46, fol. 208v. From Num. 30 onwards, glosses are usually underlined in red within the text.

Includes most of the series of glosses in the Pentateuch, and a few unique glosses; shares a few marginal glosses in Kings with BC (see Appendix 2); shares many title-glosses and textual glosses (written within the text) in Psalms with B_554V, and has some unique glosses in Ps.; the title glosses are added later, and sometimes related to the wrong psalm, e.g. the title-gloss to Ps. 75 is adjacent to Ps. 76, fol. 177r (see Appendix 2); in Proverbs, ink sigla link the biblical text and numerous unattributed marginal glosses, often shared with CNa but sometimes unique (see Appendix 2); Is. 5:1–4 is heavily glossed within the text and the whole text is underlined in red, concluding 'Li[re] he[re]' (*WB*, III.234), cf. BL Lansdowne 455, fol. 224r; Is.

26 is glossed within the text, with the glosses (unique to this MS) underlined in red and attributed 'Li[re] he[re]' (*WB*, III.268–9), fols. 228v–229r (for the gloss on Is. 26:1, see Appendix 3). There are other unique glosses *passim*.

A note at the beginning of Matthew says 'mark wel þis booc and alle þe bookis swynge', fol. 312r.

Christ Church 145 (formerly E. 4)

WB, no. 91 [*X*]; iv + 386 fols., ONT in EV.

Lectionary in LV (temporal, sanctoral 'boþe of þe propre and of þe comoun to gidere', fol. 5v, commemorations), in a slightly later hand than the text of the Bible, fols. 1r–9r (this is an added quire, fol. 9 being the original wrapper of the MS; fol. 9v blank); OT, fols. 10r–307r; NT, with Ephesians following 2 Thessalonians, incl. prols. to the Gospels but lacking all other NT prols., fols. 307r–385r; list of number of chapters in biblical books (incl. 3 Ezra, and with the number of chapters in 2 Chron. listed as 36 not 37), and number of 'bokis of þe owlde lawe' (47), and numbers of chapters in NT, only as far as Galatians, in a different hand, s.xv ex, fol. 385v (fol. 386 blank).

Forms the base of Lindberg's text of Baruch 3:20 to end of NT, *EV*, VI–VIII.

Gibson, *The Bible in the Latin West*, pp. 74–5.

Date c. 1390–1400; 'not much after 1400', *WB*, I.li; 'a very fine and Early MS' (Forshall, letter, fol. i[v]); 1400–10, dialect SEM, Lindberg, *EV*, VI.31, but NM, Lindberg, *Judges*, p. 68.

Owned by Robert Claye, Vicar of Flower, Northants, who gave it to Edward Saunders of Flower in 1575. Donated to Christ Church by Edward Saunders's son, of the same name (front pastedown; ex dono inscription, fol. 1r); a letter from Josiah Forshall (dated 14 July c. 1842) thanking the Dean [Gaisford] for lending the MS to himself and to Frederic Madden, pasted in, fols. i[r]–ii[r].

385 by 265 mm; 262 by 182 mm; catchwords immediately below right edge of written space; 2 cols., 85 mm each; single boundary-lines very carefully ruled; 58 lines, 4 mm apart; hand 'a good plain *textualis*', Gibson, p. 74. In very good condition.

Thirteen-line initial, pinky-mauve and blue foliated on gold background with bar-border in gold, mauve and blue, at the opening of the Prefatory Epistles, fol. 10r; seventeen-line initial, deep blue and red flourished in red and violet, at the opening of Genesis, fol. 12r; eight-line initial, deep blue and red flourished in red and violet, at the opening of Psalms, fol. 174v;

three-line initials, deep blue flourished in red, at opening of books (incl. Matt., fol. 307r) and chapters; one-line initials, alternating blue and red, in Ps.-verses; capitals touched with red (Gen.–Job only); alternating blue and red upper-case roman chapter-numbers; chapter-breaks sometimes written in traditional style, e.g., at Joshua 6 and 7, fol. 71r (see fig. 5); alternating blue and red Lombardic capitals in running-heads, across verso and recto (incl. 'Salterium') [see '(JO)SUE', fig. 5], also ink in left-hand margin one line above upper line of text; no incipits or explicits within text except incipit to Psalms, Song of Songs, Wisdom and Lamentations; red Ps.-titles; red Latin Psalm incipits.

One of the best texts of EV, Lindberg, *Baruch*, p. 47; overall the most literal text of EV, Lindberg, *EV*, VI.43. Text of Gospels 'the most conservative' of surviving MSS, but there are nevertheless revisions and errors, Lindberg, *EV*, VII.24. Uniquely, it has an accurate translation at Matt. 11:5 (see ch. 6).

Includes one marginal gloss (LV textual gloss) in Genesis, in scribal hand, 'bdellyum, þat is a tre of spicery' (2:12, *WB*, I.82), fol. 12v, and two marginal glosses (LV) in Exodus, in scribal hand, 'Adonay, þat is tegramaton þat signyfieþ goddis beinge nakydli wiþoute consideration to creature' (6:3, *WB*, I.204), fol. 27v, and 'gomor, conteyneþ a quart and half' (16:18, *WB*, I.230), fol. 30v. Psalm title-glosses (LV) are added, in the margin, in another hand; includes LV marginal gloss at Ps. 101:4, 'critons, [a gloos *X*] þat is þat þat dwelliþ in þe panne of þe friyng' (*WB*, III.840), in the same hand as the Psalm title-glosses. Includes the EV glosses 'bouȝte þe corn floor, for vi. hundrid siclis of gold' (2 Kings 24:24, *WB*, II.157), underlined in ink, and 'epynychion, þat is to þe god ouercomere victorie & preysyng' (1 Chron 15:21, *WB*, II.351), not underlined. Omits many of the later OT EV textual glosses (beginning at Wisd. 4:17), see Lindberg, *EV*.

Corpus Christi College 4

WB, no. 94 [*A*]; ii + 388 fols., ONT in EV.

Lower margin of fol. 1 cut away (probably to remove ownership inscription); lectionary in EV, in scribal hand (temporal, proper of saints, common of saints, commemorations), fols. 1r–6r; names of biblical books in English (*om.* 3 Ezra), with separate heading for books 'of þe newe lawe', and Paul's letters listed as twelve (1 and 2 Tim. separately), fol. 6v; 'the interpretation of certaine [48] harde wordes in this booke', in outer marg., s.xvi, fol. 6v; OT (with prol. to 1 Ezra titled 'þe proloog of þe þree bookis of Esdre', fol. 145r), fols. 7r–310v. NT, lacking all prols., fols. 311r–386v.

At the end of Apocalypse, in hand of Thomas Moulder, 'Anime eorum et omnium fidelium defunctorum per uniuersam dei misericordiam in pace requiescant. Amen. So be it', fol. 386v (fols. 387–388 blank).

Forms the text of *WB* in EV from Genesis to 3 Kings and Ezek. 1:26 to 32:23.

Date c. 1400–10; 'before 1420', *WB*, I.li; c. 1425, dialect mixed CM, Lindberg, *Judges*, pp. 67–8.

Owned by Thomas Moulder, gentleman, s.xvi, fol. 387r; Thomas Reuely, s.xvi, fol. i^r, donated Anthony Langford, 1615, fol. 1r (donor inscription, *WB*, I.li). Frederic Madden's diary entry for Saturday 5 June 1830, describes this MS as 'magnificent', Bodl. MS Engl. hist. c. 147, fol. 174r.

130 mm thick (incl. boards); 440 by 300 mm; 315 by 205 mm; some quire and sheet signatures visible; catchwords usually close to gutter 75 mm below written space; 2 cols., 95 mm each; 59 lines, 5 mm apart; letter 3 mm.

Eight-line Lombardic initials, deep blue flourished in red touched with blue, at opening of each book and for Psalm nocturns; decorative border for each book, deep blue flourished in red; three-line initials, deep blue flourished in red, at opening of chapters and in lectionary; two-line initials, deep blue, in lectionary; one-line initials, alternating deep blue and red, in Ps.-verses, and deep blue and red decorative line-fillers (each verse begins on a new line); alternating deep blue and red paraphs within text, fols. 7r–30r only; red chapter-numbers, lower-case roman within col., but sometimes adjacent to col. in early Genesis (also ink lower-case roman or arabic adjacent to col.); red running-heads, English (not in Psalms), complete on verso and recto; red incipits and explicits ('here endiþ . . . and now bigynneþ'); red Ps.-titles; Latin incipits of Psalms underlined in red, with three-line initial; rubric 'þis preyer of Manasses not in Ebrew' (2 Chron. 37) within text and not underlined, fol. 145r (see Appendix 2). A very well-written if scarcely 'magnificent' MS.

Text 'ordinary', relatively unrevised, though occasionally corrected *al. m.*, Lindberg, *EV*, VII.21. First underlining of textual gloss in red is at 2 Kings 24:25, fol. 104r; textual glosses underlined regularly from Bar. 3:23, fol. 263v, onwards.

Corpus Christi College 20

WB, no. 93 [H]; i + 230 fols., 1 Ezra–2 Macc.in LV.

Expl. 'here endeþ þe secounde book of Machabeis. Blessid be þe holi trinyte. Amen' (scribal hand, fol. 229v); no indication of NT, so perhaps originally a two-vol OT.

Date c. 1410; c. 1425, dialect SEM, Lindberg, *Judges*, p. 70.

Owned 'per me Nicholaii Hille' (fol. 1v), Frauncis Vaughan (both s.xvi/xvii).

350 by 205 mm; 255 by 145 mm; catchwords 50 mm below right edge of written space, enclosed in rectangle; 2 cols., 70 mm each; 46/51 lines, bounding-lines very carefully drawn; letter 2 mm (also marginal gloss), two hands, (1) 1 Ezra to end of Job ('blessid be þe hooly Trynyte Amen' at end of Job, fol. 50v) (2) Psalms to 2 Maccabees, a very elegant upright bookhand. In excellent condition.

Five/seven-line initials, orangey-red and deep-blue penwork with saw-tooth pattern flourished in both colours; three-line initials, deep blue flourished in red, at opening of chapters; one-line initials, alternating deep blue and red, in Ps.-verses; red paraphs within text; chapter-numbers red roman lower-case, adjacent to col.; red incipits and explicits, English; red running-heads with blue paraph, complete on verso and recto, English (incl. 'Sauter'); alternating deep blue and red paraphs in Psalms; red Ps.-titles; Latin Psalm incipits in ink in later hand.

Text excellent (but 'good', Lindberg, *Baruch*, p. 48, and 'very ordinary', *Judges*, p. 70). At Ps. 41:3, shares reading 'strong quyk' with B_544 and other good MSS (see Appendix 3), but this has been crossed through and 'welle of lijf' written above in the hand of a corrector.

Textual glosses are very carefully underlined in red, marginal glosses are underlined in red and outlined in red.

Lincoln College Latin 119

WB, no. 96 [G]; iii + 351 fols., ONT in LV.

OT books from Exodus onwards prefaced by their descriptions in the Prologue to WB, with the exception of the usual LV prols. to Isaiah and Baruch (the openings of the sections on Tobit, Judith and Ecclus have been adjusted to remove doubts about canonicity, see ch. 4), fols. 1r–279r; lacks Job 9:18 (end of quire) to Ps. 17:38. Chs. 1–3 of Prologue to WB, as far as 'in alle þingis do his wille' (end of description of Genesis) follow 2 Maccabees, inc. 'Here bigynneþ a reule þat telliþ of þe bookis of þe oolde testament whiche ben of very feiþ & whiche ben not of feiþ. But alle þe bookis of þe newe testament ben of feiþ & of bileeue, & also here bigyneþ þe prolog of Genesis in [to] þe ende', expl. 'here endiþ þe prolog of Genesis', fols. 279r–v. A rubric below the first col. of fol. 1r explains 'Seke þou þe prolog of Genesis at þe ende of Machabeis þat is bitwixe þe olde lawe and þe newe'.

NT, fols. 280r–351r.

Date c. 1410; 'about 1420', *WB*, I.lii; c. 1430, standard EM dialect (dialect of Prologue Hunts, *LALME*, I.153), Lindberg, *Judges*, pp. 69–70.

'Proposals for Printing by Subscription, the Holy Bible . . . Translated into English . . . by John Wickleffe', by John Russell, 1719, pasted onto fols. ii^r^–iii^v^. Many notes in s.xvi/xvii hand in margins.

410 by 270 mm; 300 by 190 mm; catchwords usually 15 mm below right edge of written space and enclosed within scroll; 2 cols., 82 mm each; 65 lines; outer margin ruled 40 mm, inner margin 20 mm; letter 2 mm (marginal gloss 1 mm); an even bookhand, probably the same scribe as CUL Kk. 1. 8.

Deep-blue and red saw-tooth borders at the opening of each book; seven-line initials, deep blue and red flourished in both colours; three-line initials, deep blue flourished in red, at opening of chapters; one-line initials, alternating deep blue and red, in Ps.-verses; alternating deep blue and red paraphs; red running-heads, with blue paraph and outlining, complete on verso and recto (incl. 'Sauter'); red lower-case roman chapter-numbers, usually with blue paraph, within col.; red incipits and explicits, English; Psalm title-rubrics with blue paraph (but title-glosses in ink in the margin); lections indexed in ink in margin; average quality parchment; not a luxury MS.

Text good (but 'average', Lindberg, *Judges*, p. 70). Textual glosses sometimes underlined in ink (very occasionally in red) from Genesis to 1 Kings 8 (not the end of a quire), and often, but not consistently, underlined in red from 1 Kings 8:12 to end of NT. Nearly all the series of glosses in the Pentateuch are written in the margin and linked to the biblical text with sigla and/or lemmata; marginal glosses are written very neatly across the ruled margin or sometimes, where they are more extensive, in the lower margin, e.g., glosses on Lev. 11:29–30 (*WB*, I.316), fol. 30r. Exceptionally, the scholia gloss on Dan. 2:1 (*WB*, III.623–4) is written across the whole width of the lower margin, fol. 245r.

Includes most of the series of glosses on the Pentateuch, Chronicles and Maccabees. The glosses at Rom. 6:16 and 1 Cor. 14:34 marked 'G' in *WB* are not from this MS.

Queen's College 388

WB, no. 101 [M] i + 443 + i fols., ONT in LV.

Lectionary in LV (temporal, commemorations, proper and common of saints together), fols. 1r–7v (fol. 8 blank); OT, inc. Gen. 1:20 'þe erþe vndur þe firmament' (1 fol. lacking, there must therefore have been a prologue), fols. 9r–354v; lacks 1 Chron. 29:7–2 Chron. 3:1 (1 fol.). Unique prols. to all books from Exodus to Ecclesiastes (except 2 Chron.) and to Wisdom, Jeremiah and 1 Maccabees. Shares prols. to Ezekiel and Daniel with R; has usual prols to Isaiah and Baruch; NT, fols. 355r–443v.

Date c. 1410–20; 'about 1420', *WB*, I.liii; c. 1420, dialect SEM, Lindberg, *Judges*, p. 70.

Owner inscription 'Ego Willm. Smyth seruiens scutellie dominae Reginae Elizabethae incepi legere 2° die Octob. 1561 et finem feci 10 die Junii a° 1563 iterum relegere incepi 12° Junii an° praedicto', fol. 8v. Loaned to Forshall 9 July 1831, returned 2 Aug. 1844 (fol. i^v).

432 by 300 mm; 325 by 210 mm, some quire and sheet signatures visible, quire 1 lacks 1; 2 cols., 97 mm each; 60/61 lines, 5 mm apart; bounding-lines carefully drawn; letter 2.5 mm, one regular bookhand with rather thick strokes.

Decorated foliate border with gold and green at opening of Matt. (initial torn out); seven/eight-line initials, gold on patterned mauve and deep blue background reproducing the shape of the letter, with extenders in all colours and green (most torn out), six/seven-line initials, deep blue and red with saw-tooth pattern flourished in red with touches of violet; three-line initials, deep blue flourished in red extended into borders, at opening of chapters; alternating blue and red paraphs; red roman lower-case chapter-numbers; red titles; red incipits and explicits, 'here endiþ . . . and here bigynneþ'; red running-heads with blue paraph, English, above each col. on verso and recto (incl. 'Sauter'); one-line initials, alternating deep blue and red, in Ps.-verses (Latin Psalm incipits in ink in a later hand); one-line blue initials and blue paraphs in lectionary; margins indexed for lections. Much discoloration and rubbing, but a handsome volume.

Text good (but 'ordinary', Lindberg, *Judges*, p. 70). Textual glosses are often but not always underlined in ink (never in red). There are no marginal glosses. Includes a few of the series of glosses in the Pentateuch, written within the text, and the gloss 'in goinge doun to euerlastinge turment, li[re] here' (Ecclus 28:26, *WB*, III.178), written within the text (this is the only attribution to Lyra in this MS), fol. 247r.

PRINCETON

William H. Scheide 12 (conserved in Princeton University Library)

WB, no. 154 [P_S]; ii + 405 + ii fols., ONT in LV.

'The Bybyll complett yn Englyshe' (s.xvi, fol. ii^v). Prologue to WB (complete), fols. 1r–17r; lectionary (temporal, commemorations, proper of saints, common of saints), fols. 17v–22v; OT, fols. 24r–325r; NT, fols. 325v–403r, expl. 'here endiþ þe Apocalips & blessid be þe hooly trinite amen amen amen', 'here endyth the Bybyll ffull and complete' (latter in same hand as fol. ii[v]). There are four prols. to Galatians (see *WB*, I.xxx and Appendix 1), fols. 271r–v. Above the prol. to Apocalypse is a note in John Bale's handwriting 'Hunc prologum Gilberti Porretani in Apocalipsim transtulit Joannes Wiclevus in Anglicum sermonem', fol. 397r.

Date c. 1400–10, as *WB*, I.lxi; dialect SM (Prologue, Bucks., *LALME*, I.154), 'very like A in most respects, though earlier', Lindberg, *Judges*, p. 69.

According to ownership notes on fols. 403v–404r, it passed from Robert [or Richard] Mery of Hatfield, Herts, fl. 1461–1483, to his son Thomas, and thence to Joane Mery, who 'was brought up by her Uncle Willyam Mery grocer of London in whose house the true relygion of the Ghospell of our Saviour Jesus Christ was zealously professed and the sayd Joane therein instructed and trayned in her youthe . . . by whome the sayd Thomas Bowyer [Joane m. Thos Bowyer, grocer, of London, in 1531] had this Boke a singuler jewell of antiquite & carefully preserved . . .' (signature of Richard Bowyer, son of Thomas and Joane, fol. 403v), now in the time of Elizabeth I its owner, Thomas Bowyer, 'doth veryly by Gods grace purpose to kepe this boke which in those superstitious tymes was kept in huggremuggre' (signature of T. Bowyer, fol. 404r); thence passed down through Morley and Palmer families to Acland family, and sold by Alexander Peregrine Fuller-Acland-Hood to Quaritch in 1931, who sold it to John H. Scheide for £2375; see Percy A. Bowyer, 'Notes Concerning the Bowyer Family', *Sussex Archaeological Collections* 64 (1923), 105–8.

'This is my wiues booke, T[homas] Palmer' (of Fairfield, Somerset, antiquarian) (s.xviii in, fol. i[r]), and this same T. Palmer is the author of other ownership notes (dated 1723, fols. 404v–405r).

12s; 290 by 190 mm; 210 by 130 mm; 2 cols., 60 lines; 3 mm apart; letter 1.5 mm (marginal gloss 1 mm); two main bookhands, the first more upright and less even than the second. In very good condition (slight loss of text in Is. 24–5, fol. 241), although some books, especially Psalms, somewhat rubbed and discoloured through use.

Four/seven-line initials, deep blue and red flourished in both colours, decorating the whole length of the bounding line in blue and red; two-line initials, deep blue flourished in red, often extended in margins, at opening of chapters; alternating blue and red paraphs in Ps.-verses and Lam. 1–4 verses; rubrics and blue paraphs in lectionary; chapter-numbers red roman, followed by red pen flourish; alternating blue and red Lombards in running-heads, written across verso and recto, to fol. 91v (end of quire), thereafter blue paraph and red letters usually on recto only but sometimes verso and recto; incipits and explicits lacking from Genesis to 2 Chronicles, then usually present, red Ps.-titles; Latin Psalm incipits in ink, in a later hand. Early s.xviii binding.

Revised text from Psalms to end of OT. Shares some readings with A alone, and has unique LV readings at Ps. 105:29, Ps. 106:29, Lam. 5:16, Ezek. 1:10, Ezek. 7:13, Ezek. 33:6, and one reading shared with C_J_E.14 at Ps. 119:7 (see Appendix 2).

Textual glosses are usually underlined in ink, but sporadically in red in the Prophets. Marginal glosses, in hand of biblical text, are linked to the biblical text with ink sigla; longer glosses are neatly written in the lower margin. Includes the series of glosses in the Pentateuch as far as Gen. 35, written in the margin (and is uniquely correct in the gloss on Gen. 6:6, see p. 169). Other OT marginal glosses include those at Bar. 6:42 (*WB*, III.498), Ezek.45:10–12 (*WB*, III.610) and Dan. 4:31 (*WB*, III.639).

Select bibliography

Manuscripts (see also Appendix 3 for Latin and French Bibles, and Appendix 4 and Index of MSS for WB MSS):

Cambridge, University Library Ff. 6. 31 (John Colop's common-profit book)
University Library Ii. 6. 26 (tracts in favour of scriptural translation)
London, British Library Burney 3 (Latin Bible, Canterbury, 1230–40)
Bodl. Engl. hist. 147, 148, 155, 163 (volumes of Frederic Madden's diary)
Magdalen College lat. 55 (Wyclif, part of *Postilla in totam Bibliam*)
Magdalen College lat. 98 (Wyclif, *De Mandatis Divinis*)
Magdalen College lat. 117 (Wyclif, part of *Postilla in totam Bibliam*)
St John's College 171 (Wyclif, part of *Postilla in totam Bibliam*)
Paris, Bibliothèque Nationale fr. 1 (Gen.-Hebrews in Anglo–Norman, s.xiv in)
Rouen, Bibliothèque Municipale A. 211 (BXIII, France, s.xiii)
Vienna, Österreichische Nationalbibliothek 1342 (Wyclif, part of *Postilla in totam Bibliam*)
Österreichische Nationalbibliothek 4133 (Richard Ullerston on biblical translation)

PRIMARY SOURCES AND REFERENCE WORKS

Augustine, *De Doctrina Christiana*, ed. J. Martin, CCSL XXXII (Turnhout: Brepols, 1962)
Enarrationes in Psalmos, ed. E. Dekkers and J. Fraipont, CCSL XXXVIII–XL, 3 vols. (Turnhout: Brepols, 1956)
Epistola XCIII, ad Vincentium Donatistam, ed. A. Goldbacher, CSEL XXXIV (Vienna: Tempsky, 1895), pp. 445–96
Bacon, Roger, *Opus Minus, Opus Tertium and Compendium Studii*, ed. J. S. Brewer, *Rogeri Bacon Opera Quedam Hactenus Inedita*, Rolls Series (London, 1859)
Bale, John, *Illustrium Maioris Britanniae Scriptorum . . . Summarium* (Wesel, 1548)
Scriptorum Illustrium Maioris Brytanniae . . . Catalogus, 2 vols. (Basle, 1557–9)
Index Britanniae Scriptorum: John Bale's Index of British and Other Writers, ed. Reginald Lane Poole and Mary Bateson (Woodbridge: Brewer, 1990)
Barton, John, and John Muddiman, eds., *The Oxford Bible Commentary* (Oxford University Press, 2001)

Bede, *Historia Ecclesiastica*: Bertram Colgrave and R. A. B. Mynors, eds., *Bede's Ecclesiastical History of the English People* (Oxford: Clarendon Press, 1969)

Bernard, Edward *et al.*, eds., *Catalogi Librorum Manuscriptorum Angliae et Hiberniae* (Oxford, 1697)

Bible [English]: Anna C. Paues, ed., *A Fourteenth Century English Biblical Version Consisting of a Prologue and Parts of the New Testament* (Cambridge University Press, 1902)

Bible [English]: M. J. Powell, ed., *The Northern Pauline Epistles*, EETS e.s. 116 (London, 1916)

Bible [Latin]: *Biblia Sacra Iuxta Latinam Vulgatam Versionem*, 18 vols. (Rome: Vatican, 1926–1995) (OT only)

Bible [Latin]: Robert Weber, ed., *Biblia Sacra Iuxta Vulgatam Versionem* (Stuttgart: Deutsche Bibelgesellschaft, 1969)

Bible [Latin]: John Wordsworth and Henry Julian White, eds., *Nouum Testamentum Domini Nostri Iesu Christi Latine Secundum Editionem Sancti Hieronymi*, 3 parts (Oxford: Clarendon Press, 1888–1954)

Bible [Latin] with *Glossa Ordinaria*: Margaret Gibson and Karlfried Froehlich, eds., *Biblia Latina cum Glossa Ordinaria, Facsimile Reprint of the Editio Princeps, Adolph Rusch of Strassburg, 1480/1*, 4 vols. (Turnhout: Brepols, 1992)

Bible [Wycliffite], Prologue: John Gough, ed., *The Dore of Holy Scripture* (London, 1536)

Bible [Wycliffite], Prologue: Robert Crowley, ed., *The Pathwaye to Perfect Knowledge* (London, 1550)

Bible [Wycliffite]: Prologue, ch. 15, ed. Anne Hudson, *Selections from English Wycliffite Writings* (Cambridge University Press, 1978), pp. 67–72, 173–7

Bible [Wycliffite]: John Lewis, ed., *The New Testament of Our Lord and Saviour Jesus Christ Translated out of the Latin Vulgat* (London: Page, 1731)

Bible [Wycliffite]: Henry Hervey Baber, ed., *The New Testament Translated from the Latin in the Year 1380 by John Wiclif, to which are Prefixed Memoirs of the Life, Opinions, and Writings of Dr. Wiclif* (London: Hamilton, 1810) [1824 printing includes the prologues 'Seynt Austyn seiþ in þe secunde book', and 'Oure Lord Jesu Crist verri god and verri man']

Bible [Wycliffite]: Song of Songs in EV: Adam Clarke, ed., *The Holy Bible . . . with a Commentary*, vol. IV (Lutterworth, 1825), 15P3–Q1

Bible [Wycliffite]: Samuel Bagster, ed., *The English Hexapla: Exhibiting the Six Most Important English Translations of the New Testament Scriptures* (London: Bagster, 1841)

Bible [Wycliffite]: Lea Wilson, ed., *The New Testament in English* (London, 1848)

Bible [Wycliffite]: Josiah Forshall and Frederic Madden, eds., *The Holy Bible, Containing the Old and New Testaments, with the Apocryphal Books, in the Earliest English Versions Made from the Latin Vulgate by John Wycliffe and his Followers*, 4 vols. (Oxford: Clarendon Press, 1850) [reprinted New York: AMS, 1978]

Bible [Wycliffite]: Walter W. Skeat, ed., *The New Testament in English* (Oxford: Clarendon Press, 1879) [*WB* text in LV]

Bible [Wycliffite]: Walter W. Skeat, ed., *The Books of Job, Psalms, Proverbs, Ecclesiastes and the Song of Solomon* (Oxford, 1881) [*WB* text in LV]

Bible [Wycliffite]: Conrad Lindberg, ed., *The Earlier Version of the Wycliffite Bible*, vol. I *SSE* 6 (Stockholm: Almqvist and Wiksell, 1959), vol. II *SSE* 8 (1961), vol. III *SSE* 10 (1963), vol. IV *SSE* 13 (1965), vol. V *SSE* 20 (1969), vol. VI *SSE* 29 (1973), vol. VII *SSE* 81 (1994), vol. VIII *SSE* 87 (1997)

Bible [Wycliffite]: Conrad Lindberg, ed., *The Middle English Bible 1: Prefatory Epistles of St. Jerome* (Oslo: Norwegian University Press, 1978)

Bible [Wycliffite]: Conrad Lindberg, ed., *The Middle English Bible 2: The Book of Baruch* (Oslo: Norwegian University Press, 1985)

Bible [Wycliffite]: Conrad Lindberg, ed., *The Middle English Bible 3: The Book of Judges* (Oslo: Norwegian University Press, 1989)

Bible [Wycliffite]: *The New Testament in English* (Portland, Oregon: International Bible Publications, 1986) (facsimile of Bodl. Rawlinson C. 259)

Bible [Wycliffite]: Conrad Lindberg, ed., *King Henry's Bible, MS Bodl 277: The Revised Version of the Wyclif Bible*, vol.I *SSE* 89 (Stockholm: Almqvist and Wiksell, 1999), vol. II *SSE* 94 (2001), vol. III *SSE* 98 (2002), vol. IV *SSE* 100 (2004)

Bible [Wycliffite]: *Wycliffite Manuscript: The New Testament*, CD-ROM, Oakland, 1999 (facsimile of Southern Methodist University, Bridwell Library Prothro B-01)

Bible [Wycliffite]: William Cooper, ed., *The Wycliffe New Testament, 1388, an Edition in Modern Spelling* (London: British Library, 2002) [based on *WB* text in LV]

Chichele, Henry: E. F. Jacob, ed., *The Register of Henry Chichele, Archbishop of Canterbury, 1414–1443*, 4 vols. (Oxford: Clarendon Press, 1943–7)

De Oblacione Iugis Sacrificii: Anne Hudson, ed., *The Works of a Lollard Preacher: The Sermon 'Omnis plantacio', the Tract 'Fundamentum aliud nemo potest ponere', and the Tract 'De oblacione iugis sacrificii'*, EETS 317 (Oxford University Press, 2001)

De Officio Pastorali: Conrad Lindberg, ed., *English Wyclif Tracts* (Oslo: Norwegian University Press, 1991), no. 1

Dymmo(c)k, Roger, *Liber Contra Duodecim Errores et Hereses Lollardorum*: ed. H. S. Cronin (London: Wyclif Society, 1922)

Emden, A. B., *A Biographical Register of the University of Oxford to AD 1500*, 3 vols. (Oxford: Clarendon Press, 1957–9)

English Wycliffite Sermons: Pamela Gradon and Anne Hudson, eds., *English Wycliffite Sermons*, 5 vols. (Oxford: Clarendon Press, 1983–96)

Fasciculi Zizaniorum: W. W. Shirley, ed., *Fasciculi Zizaniorum Magistri Johannis Wyclif cum Tritico*, Rolls Series (London, 1885)

'First seiþ Bois': C. F. Bühler, ed., 'A Lollard Tract: On Translating the Bible into English', *Medium Ævum* 7 (1938), 167–83

Foxe, John: S. R. Cattley and J. Pratt, eds., *The Acts and Monuments of John Foxe*, 8 vols. (London: Religious Tract Society, 1877)

Gregory the Great, *Homiliae in Hiezechielem*, ed. M. Adriaen, CCSL CXLII (Turnhout: Brepols, 1971)

Grosseteste, Robert: S. Harrison Thomson, *The Writings of Robert Grosseteste, Bishop of Lincoln* (Cambridge University Press, 1940)

Guido de Baysio, *Rosarium super Decreto* (Venice, 1495)

Hanna, Ralph, *The Index of Middle English Prose: Handlist I* (Huntington Library) (Cambridge: Brewer, 1984), pp. 14–15 [MSS of WB]

A Descriptive Catalogue of the Western Medieval Manuscripts of St John's College Oxford (Oxford University Press, 2002)

Herbert, Arthur Sumner, rev. T. H. Darlow and H. Moule, *Historical Catalogue of Printed Editions of the English Bible 1525–1961* (London: British and Foreign Bible Society, 1968)

Higden, Ranulph, *Polychronicon*: Joseph Rawson Lumby and Churchill Babington, eds., *Polychronicon Ranulphi Higden*, 9 vols., Rolls Series (London, 1865–86)

Historia Vitae et Regni Ricardi Secundi, ed. George B. Stow (Philadelphia: University of Pennsylvania Press, 1977)

'The holi prophete Dauid seiþ', ed. Deanesly, *LB*, pp. 445–56. Selections ed. Stephen Shepherd, in Jocelyn Wogan-Browne *et al.*, eds., *The Idea of the Vernacular* (1999), pp. 149–56

Hus, John: Jaroslav Eršil, ed., *Magistri Iohannis Hus: Opera Omnia*, vol. 22, *Polemica* (Prague, 1966)

James, Thomas, A *Treatise of the Corruption of Scripture, Councels and Fathers by the Prelats, Pastors and Pillars of the Church of Rome, for Maintenance of Popery and Irreligion* (London: Lownes, 1612)

Jerome, *Commentarii in Prophetas Minores*, ed. M. Adriaen, CCSL LXXVI pars 1, vol. 6 (Turnhout: Brepols, 1969)

Liber de Optimo Genere Interpretandi (Epistola LVII ad Pammachium), ed. G. J. M. Bartelink, *Mnemosyne*, supplement 61 (Leiden: Brill, 1980)

Ker, Neil R., *Medieval Manuscripts in British Libraries*, vol. I (Oxford: Clarendon Press, 1969), vol. II (1977), vol. III (1983), vol. IV (1992), vol. V (2000)

Ker, Neil R., and Andrew G. Watson, *Medieval Libraries of Great Britain: A List of Surviving Manuscripts*, 2nd edn (London: Royal Historical Society, 1964)

Knighton, Henry: Geoffrey H. Martin, ed., *Knighton's Chronicle, 1337–1396* (Oxford: Clarendon Press, 1995)

Kurath, H., S. M. Kuhn *et al.*, eds., *Middle English Dictionary* (Ann Arbor: University of Michigan, 1952–2001)

Leland, John, *Commentarii de Scriptoribus*, ed. Anthony Hall, 2 vols. (Oxford, 1709)

Lewis, R. E., N. F. Blake and A. S. G. Edwards, *Index of Printed Middle English Prose* (New York: Garland, 1985), pp. 41–3 [MSS of WB]

Lewis, John, *The History of the Life and Sufferings of the Reverend and Learned John Wicliffe* (London: Knaplock, 1720)

Lindberg, Conrad, 'The Manuscripts and Versions of the Wycliffite Bible: A Preliminary Survey', *Studia Neophilologica* 42 (1970), 333–47

Love, Nicholas, *Mirror of the Blessed Life of Jesus Christ*, ed. Michael M. Sargent (New York: Garland, 1992)

Lyndwood, William, *Provinciale seu Constitutiones Anglie* (Antwerp: Francis Bryckman, 1525)

Lyra, Nicholas of: *Biblia Latina cum Postillis Nicolai de Lyra*, 4 vols. (Venice, 1481)

Matthew, H. G. C, and Brian Harrison, eds., *The Oxford Dictionary of National Biography*, 61 vols. (Oxford University Press, 2004)

McIntosh, Angus, M. L. Samuels and Michael Benskin, *A Linguistic Atlas of Late Mediaeval English*, 4 vols. (Aberdeen University Press, 1986)

The Mirror of Our Lady: John H. Blunt, ed., *The Myroure of Oure Ladye*, EETS e.s. 19 (London, 1873)

More, Sir Thomas, *A Dialogue Concerning Heresies*: Thomas C. M. Lawler, Germain Marc'hadour and Richard C. Marius, eds., *The Complete Works of St. Thomas More*, vol. VI (New Haven: Yale University Press, 1981)

Netter, Thomas, *Doctrinale Antiquitatum Fidei Cathholicae Ecclesiae*, ed. B. Blanciotti, 3 vols. (Venice, 1757–9)

Pecock, Reginald, *Repressor of Over Much Blaming of the Clergy*, ed. Churchill Babington, 2 vols. Rolls Series (London, 1860)

Petrus Aureoli, *Compendium Litteralis Sensus Totius Divinae Scripturae*, ed. P. Seeboeck (Quaracchi, 1896)

Pickering, Oliver S., and V. M. O'Mara, *The Index of Middle English Prose, Handlist XIII: Manuscripts in Lambeth Palace Library, Including Those Formerly in Sion College Library* (Cambridge: Brewer, 1999), pp. 1–2 [WB MSS]

Richter, E. and E. L. Friedberg, eds., *Corpus Iuris Canonici*, 2 vols. (Leipzig: Tauchnitz, 1879–81)

Rolle, Richard: H. R. Bramley, ed., *The Psalter or Psalms of David and Certain Canticles . . . by Richard Rolle of Hampole* (Oxford: Clarendon Press, 1884)

Ross, Woodburn O., ed., *Middle English Sermons, Edited from BM MS Royal 18 B XXIII,* EETS o.s. 209 (London, 1940)

Severs, J. Burke, *A Manual of the Writings in Middle English, 1050–1400* (New Haven: Connecticut Academy of Arts and Sciences, 1970)

Sharpe, Richard, *A Handlist of the Latin Writers of Great Britain and Ireland before 1540* (Turnhout: Brepols, 2001)

Stegmüller, F., and N. Reinhardt, *Repertorium Biblicum Medii Aevi*, 11 vols. (Madrid: Consejo Superior de Investigaciones Científicas, 1950–80)

The Thirty-Seven Conclusions: Josiah Forshall, ed., *Remonstrances against Romish Corruptions of the Church: Addressed to the People and Parliament of England in 1395, 18 Ric. II* (London: Longman, 1851)

Trevisa, John, 'Dialogus inter Dominum et Clericum': Ronald Waldron, ed., 'Trevisa's Original Prefaces on Translation: A Critical Edition', in E. D. Kennedy, R. Waldron and J. S. Wittig, eds., *Medieval English Studies Presented to George Kane* (Cambridge: Brewer, 1988), pp. 285–99; J. A. Burrow and

Thorlac Turville-Petre, eds., *A Book of Middle English* (Oxford: Blackwell, 1992), pp. 213–20

Two Wycliffite Texts: The Sermon of William Taylor 1406, The Testimony of William Thorpe 1407, ed. Anne Hudson, EETS o.s. 301 (Oxford University Press, 1993)

Tyndale, William, *Obedience of a Christian Man*, ed. David Daniell (London: Penguin Books, 2000)

Ussher, Archbishop James: Henry Wharton, ed., *Jacobi Usserii, Armachani Archiepiscopi, Historia Dogmatica Controversiae inter Orthodoxos et Pontificios de Scripturis et Sacris Vernaculis* (London, 1690)

Walsingham, Thomas, *Chronicon Angliae*, ed. E. M. Thompson, Rolls Series (London, 1869)

Waterland, Daniel: *The Works of Daniel Waterland*, 10 vols. (Oxford, 1823)

Wharton, Henry, *Auctarium Historiae Dogmaticae Jacobi Usserii* (London, 1689)

Wilkins, David, ed., *Concilia Magnae Britanniae et Hiberniae*, 4 vols. (London, 1737)

Wyclif, John, *De Simonia*, ed. Sigmund Herzburg-Fränkel and M. H. Dziewicki (London: Wyclif Society, 1898)

De Triplico Vinculo Amoris, ed. Rudolf Buddensieg, *John Wiclif's Polemical Works in Latin*, vol. II (London: Wyclif Society, 1883), pp. 153–98

De Veritate Sacrae Scripturae, ed. Rudolf Buddensieg, 2 vols. (London: Wyclif Society, 1905); partially trans. by Ian Christopher Levy, *John Wyclif: On the Truth of Holy Scripture* (Kalamazoo, Michigan, 2001; published for TEAMS by Medieval Institute Publications)

Opus Evangelicum, ed. Johann Loserth, 2 vols. (London: Wyclif Society, 1895)

Postilla in Totam Bibliam, selections ed. Gustav A. Benrath, *Wyclifs Bibelkommentar* (Berlin: De Gruyter, 1966)

Trialogus, ed. Gotthard Lechler (Oxford: Clarendon Press, 1869)

Thomas Arnold, ed., *Select English Works of John Wyclif*, 3 vols. (Oxford: Clarendon Press, 1871)

F. D. Matthew, rev. edn, *The English Works of Wyclif*, EETS o.s. 74 (London, 1902)

SECONDARY SOURCES

Ackroyd, P. R., and C. F. Evans, eds., *The Cambridge History of the Bible, Volume 1: From the Beginnings to Jerome* (Cambridge University Press, 1970)

Aers, David, *Faith, Ethics and Church Writing in England, 1360–1409* (Cambridge University Press, 2000)

Aston, Margaret, 'Lollardy and Sedition, 1381–1431', *Past and Present* 17 (1960), 1–44

Aston, Margaret, *Lollards and Reformers: Images and Literacy in Late Medieval Religion* (London: Hambledon Press, 1984)

Aston, Margaret, and Colin Richmond, eds., *Lollardy and the Gentry in the Later Middle Ages* (Stroud: Sutton, 1997)

Barr, Helen, and Ann M. Hutchison, eds., *Text and Controversy from Wyclif to Bale: Essays in Honour of Anne Hudson* (Turnhout: Brepols, 2005)

Berger, Samuel, *La Bible française au Moyen Age* (Paris, 1884)

Histoire de la Vulgate pendant les premiers siècles du moyen âge (Paris, 1893)

Bose, Mishtooni, 'Reginald Pecock's Vernacular Voice', in Somerset *et al.*, eds., *Lollards and their Influence in Late Medieval England* (Woodbridge: Boydell Press, 2003), pp. 217–36

Boyle, Leonard E., 'Innocent III and Vernacular Versions of Scripture', in Walsh and Wood, eds., *The Bible in the Medieval World* (1985), pp. 97–107

Breeze, Andrew, 'The Wycliffite Bible Prologue on the Scriptures in Welsh', *Notes and Queries* n.s. 46 (1999), 16–17

Burnley, J. D., 'Late Medieval English Translation: Types and Reflections', in Ellis, ed., *The Medieval Translator I* (1989), pp. 37–53

Cahn, Walter, *Romanesque Bible Illumination* (Ithaca: Cornell University Press, 1982)

Cameron, Euan, *Waldenses: Rejections of Holy Church in Medieval Europe* (Oxford: Blackwell, 2000)

Carr, Joseph, *Über das Verhältnis der Wiclifitischen und der Purvey'schen Bibelübersetzung zur Vulgata und zu einander* (Leipzig, 1902)

Christianson, C. Paul, *Memorials of the Book Trade in Medieval London: The Archives of Old London Bridge* (Cambridge University Press, 1987)

Cigman, Gloria, '*Luceat Lux Vestra*: The Lollard Preacher as Truth and Light', *Review of English Studies* 40 (1989), 479–96

Cole, Andrew, 'Chaucer's English Lesson', *Speculum* 77 (2002), 1128–67

Coleman, Janet, *English Literature in History 1350–1400: Medieval Readers and Writers* (London: Hutchinson, 1981)

Cooper, W. R., 'Richard Hunne', *Reformation* 1 (1996), 221–51

Copeland, Rita, 'The Fortunes of "Non Verbum pro Verbo": or, why Jerome is not a Ciceronian', in Ellis, ed., *The Medieval Translator* I (1989), pp. 15–35

Copeland, Rita, 'Rhetoric and the Politics of the Literal Sense in Medieval Literary Theory: Aquinas, Wyclif, and the Lollards', in Piero Boitani and Anna Torti, eds., *Interpretation: Medieval and Modern* (Cambridge University Press, 1993), pp. 1–23

'Childhood, Pedagogy and the Literal Sense', in Wendy Scase, Rita Copeland and David Lawton, eds., *New Medieval Literatures* I (Oxford University Press, 1997), pp. 125–56

Pedagogy, Intellectuals, and Dissent in the Later Middle Ages: Lollardy and Ideas of Learning (Cambridge University Press, 2001)

Crompton, James, 'John Wyclif: A Study in Mythology', *Transactions of the Leicestershire Archaeological and Historical Society* 42 (1966–7), 6–34

Crystal, David, *The Stories of English* (London: Penguin Books, 2005)

Cummings, Brian, *The Literary Culture of the Reformation: Grammar and Grace* (Oxford University Press, 2002)

Dahan, Gilbert, *L'exégèse chrétienne de la Bible en Occident médiéval: XIIe –XIVe siècle* (Paris: Cerf, 1999)

Dahmus, Joseph, *William Courtenay, Archbishop of Canterbury, 1381–1396* (Philadelphia: Pennsylvania State University Press, 1966)

Daniell, David, *The Bible in English: Its History and Influence* (New Haven: Yale University Press, 2003)

Deanesly, Margaret, *The Lollard Bible and Other Medieval Biblical Versions* (Cambridge University Press, 1920, reprinted 1966)

The Significance of the Lollard Bible (London: Athlone, 1951)

De Hamel, Christopher, *The Book: A History of the Bible* (London: Phaidon, 2001)

De Libera, Alain *et al.*, eds., *Etudes de philosophie médiévale, langages et philosophie: Hommage à Jean Jolivet* (Paris: Vrin, 1997)

Dinshaw, Carolyn, *Getting Medieval: Sexualities and Communities, Pre-Modern and Postmodern* (Durham, N.C.: Duke University Press, 1999)

Dove, Mary, 'Love *ad litteram*: the Lollard Translations of the Song of Songs', *Reformation* 9 (2004), 1–23

Doyle, A. I., 'English Books In and Out of Court from Edward III to Henry VII', in V. J. Scattergood and J. W. Sherborne, eds., *English Court Culture in the Later Middle Ages* (London: Duckworth, 1983), pp. 168–9

Doyle, A. I., 'Reflections on Some Manuscripts of Nicholas Love's *Myrour of the Blessed Lyf of Jesu Christ*', *Leeds Studies in English* n.s. 14 (1983), 82–93

Edwards, A. S. G., Vincent Gillespie and Ralph Hanna, eds., *The English Medieval Book: Studies in Memory of Jeremy Griffiths* (London: British Library, 2000)

Ellis, Roger, ed., *The Medieval Translator: The Theory and Practice of Translation in the Middle Ages*, vol. I (Cambridge University Press, 1989)

Evans, G. R., *John Wyclif: Myth and Reality* (Oxford: Lion, 2005)

Fowler, David C., 'John Trevisa and the English Bible', *Modern Philology* 58 (1960), 81–98

The Bible in Early English Literature (London: Sheldon Press, 1977)

The Bible in Middle English Literature (Seattle: University of Washington Press, 1984)

Review of Anne Hudson, *The Premature Reformation*, *Studies in the Age of Chaucer* 12 (1990), 296–305

The Life and Times of John Trevisa, Medieval Scholar (Seattle: University of Washington Press, 1995)

Fristedt, Sven L., *The Wycliffe Bible, Part I. The Principal Problems Connected with Forshall and Madden's Edition*, *SSE* 4 (Stockholm: Almqvist and Wiksell, 1953)

The Wycliffe Bible, Part II: The Origin of the First Revision as Presented in De Salutaribus Documentis, *SSE* 21 (Stockholm: Almqvist and Wiksell, 1969)

The Wycliffe Bible, Part III: Relationships of Trevisa and the Spanish Medieval Bibles, *SSE* 28 (Stockholm: Almqvist and Wiksell, 1973)

'The Authorship of the Lollard Bible: Summary and Amplification of *the Wycliffite Bible. Part I*', *Stockholm Studies in Modern Philology* 19 (1956), 28–41

'The Dating of the Earliest Manuscript of the Wycliffite Bible', *Stockholm Studies in Modern Philology* n.s. 1 (1960), 79–85

'A Weird Manuscript Enigma in the British Museum', *Stockholm Studies in Modern Philology* n.s. 2 (1964), 116–21 [BL MSS Egerton 617/618]

'New Light on John Wycliffe and the First Full English Bible', *Stockholm Studies in Modern Philology* n.s. 2 (1968), 61–86

'A Note on Some Obscurities in the History of the Lollard Bible', *Stockholm Studies in Modern Philology* n.s. 4 (1972), 38–45

'Spanish Influence on Lollard Translation. *Amplification of The Wycliffe Bible. Part III*', *Stockholm Studies in Modern Philology* n.s. 5 (1975), 5–10

Gameson, Richard, ed., *The Early Medieval Bible: Its Production, Decoration and Use* (Cambridge University Press, 1994)

Gasquet, Francis A., 'The Pre-Reformation English Bible', in *The Old English Bible and Other Essays* (London: Nimmo, 1897), pp. 102–55

Ghosh, Kantik, *The Wycliffite Heresy: Authority and the Interpretation of Texts* (Cambridge: Cambridge University Press, 2001)

Gibson, Margaret T., *The Bible in the Latin West* (Indiana: University of Notre Dame Press, 1993)

Gillespie, Vincent, 'The Book and the Brotherhood: Reflections on the Lost Library of Syon Abbey', in Edwards, etc., eds., *The English Medieval Book*, pp. 185–208

Gillespie, Vincent, 'The Mole in the Vineyard', in Barr and Hutchison, eds., *Text and Controversy*, pp. 131–61

Gradon, Pamela, and Anne Hudson, 'Aspects of Biblical Translation', in *English Wycliffite Sermons*, vol. III (Oxford: Clarendon Press, 1990), pp. lxviii–xcviii

Gradon, Pamela, 'Wyclif's *Postilla* and his Sermons', in Barr and Hutchison, eds., *Text and Controversy*, pp. 67–77

Hanna, Ralph, 'The Difficulty of Ricardian Prose Translation: The Case of the Lollards', *Modern Language Quarterly* 51 (1991), 319–40

'English Biblical Texts before Lollardy', in Somerset *et al.*, eds., *Lollards and Their Influence in Late Medieval England*, pp. 141–53

Hargreaves, Henry, 'The Latin Text of Purvey's Psalter', *Medium Ævum* 24 (1955), 73–90

'An Intermediate Version of the Wycliffite Old Testament', *Studia Neophilologica* 28 (1956), 129–47

'The Marginal Glosses to the Wycliffite New Testament', *Studia Neophilologica* 33 (1961), 285–300

'*The Mirror of Our Lady*', *Aberdeen University Review* 42 (1968), 267–80

'The Vernacular Scriptures: the Wycliffite Versions', in *CHB*, II, pp. 387–415

'Popularising Biblical Scholarship: The Role of the Wycliffite *Glossed Gospels*', in Lourdaux and Verhelst, eds., *The Bible and Medieval Culture*, pp. 171–89

Harriss, Gerald, *Shaping the Nation: England 1360–1461* (Oxford: Clarendon Press, 2005)

Hudson, Anne, *Lollards and their Books* (London: Hambledon Press, 1985)

'Wyclif and the English Language', in Anthony Kenny, ed., *Wyclif in his Times* (Oxford: Clarendon Press, 1986), pp. 85–103

'Biblical Exegesis in Wycliffite Writings', in *John Wyclif e la traduzione degli studi biblici in Inghilterra* (Genoa: Melangolo, 1987), pp. 61–79

'Two Notes on the Wycliffite *Glossed Gospels*', in Oshitari *et al.*, eds., *Philologia Anglica*, pp. 379–84

The Premature Reformation: Wycliffite Texts and Lollard History (Oxford: Clarendon Press, 1988)

'Lollard Book Production', in Jeremy Griffiths and Derek Pearsall, eds., *Book Production and Publishing in Britain 1375–1475* (Cambridge University Press, 1989), pp. 125–42

'The Variable Text', in A. J. Minnis and Charlotte Brewer, eds., *Crux and Controversy in Middle English Textual Criticism* (Cambridge University Press, 1992), pp. 49–60

Hudson, Anne, ed., *Wyclif: Political Ideas and Practice: Papers by Michael Wilks* (Oxford: Oxbow, 2000)

Hurley, Michael, '"Scriptura sola": Wyclif and his Critics', *Traditio* 16 (1960), 275–352

Hunt, Simon, 'An Edition of Tracts in Favour of Scriptural Translation and of Some Texts connected with Lollard Vernacular Biblical Scholarship', D.Phil. Dissertation, 2 vols., University of Oxford (1994)

Johnson, Dudley R., 'The Biblical Characters of Chaucer's Monk', *PMLA* 66 (1951), 827–43

Jurkowski, Maureen, 'New Light on John Purvey', *English Historical Review* 110 (1995), 1180–90

'Heresy and Factionalism at Merton College in the Early Fifteenth Century', *Journal of Ecclesiastical History* 48 (1997), 658–81

'Lollard Book Producers in London in 1414', in Barr and Hutchison, eds., *Text and Controversy*, pp. 201–26

Justice, Steven, *Writing and Rebellion: England in 1381* (Berkeley: University of California Press, 1994)

Kenyon, F. G., *Our Bible and the Ancient Manuscripts*, 2nd edn (London: Eyre and Spottiswode, 1896)

Krey, Philip D. W., and Lesley Smith, eds., *Nicholas of Lyra: The Senses of Scripture* (Leiden: Brill, 2000)

Krochalis, Jeanne E., 'The Books and Reading of Henry V and his Circle', *The Chaucer Review* 23 (1988), 50–77

Kuhn, Sherman M., 'The Preface to a Fifteenth-Century Concordance', *Speculum* 43 (1968), 258–73

Lambert, Malcolm, *Medieval Heresy: Popular Movements from the Gregorian Reform to the Reformation*, 3rd (Oxford: Blackwell, 2002)

Lampe, G. W. H., ed., *The Cambridge History of the Bible, Volume 2: The West From The Fathers To The Reformation* (Cambridge University Press, 1969)

Lawton, David, 'Englishing the Bible: 1370–1549', in Wallace, ed., *The Cambridge History of Medieval Literature*, pp. 454–82

Levy, Ian C., 'Defining the Responsibility of the Late Medieval Theologian: The Debate between John Kynyngham and John Wyclif', *Carmelus* 49 (2002), 5–29

John Wyclif: Scriptural Logic, Real Presence, and the Parameters of Orthodoxy (Milwaukee: Marquette University Press, 2003)

Levy, Ian C., ed., *A Companion to John Wyclif: Late Medieval Theologian* (Leiden: Brill, 2006)

Light, Laura, 'Versions et revisions du texte biblique', in Riché and Lobrichon, eds., *Le Moyen Age et la Bible*, pp. 55–93

'French Bibles c. 1200–30: A New Look at the Origin of the Paris Bible', in Gameson, ed., *The Early Medieval Bible*, pp. 155–76

Lindberg, Conrad, 'The Break at Baruch 3:20 in the Middle English Bible', *English Studies* 60 (1979), 106–10

'The Language of the Wyclif Bible', in W. D. Bald and H. Weinstock, eds., *Medieval Studies Conference Aachen 1983: Language and Literature* (Frankfurt: Lang, 1984), pp. 103–110

'Who Wrote Wiclif's Bible?', *Stockholm Studies in Modern Philology* n.s. 7 (1984), 127–35

'A Note on the Vocabulary of the Middle English Bible', *Studia Neophilologica* 57 (1985), 129–31

'A Note on Wyclif's English', in Oshitari *et al.*, eds., *Philologia Anglica*, pp. 385–8

'Reconstructing the Lollard Versions of the Bible', *Neuphilologische Mitteilungen* 90 (1989), 117–23

'Towards an English Wyclif Canon', in L. E. Breivik *et al.*, eds., *Essays on English Language in Honour of Bertil Sundby* (Oslo: Norwegian University Press, 1989), pp. 179–84

'From Jerome to Wyclif, an Experiment in Translation: The First Prologue', *Studia Neophilologica* 63 (1991), 143–5

'Literary Aspects of the Wyclif Bible', *Bulletin of the John Rylands Library* 77:3 (1995), 79–85

'The Alpha and Omega of the Middle English Bible', in Barr and Hutchison, eds., *Text and Controversy*, pp. 191–200

Lobrichon, Guy, 'Les éditions de la bible latine dans les universités du XIIIe siècle', in Giuseppe Cremascoli and Francesco Santi, eds., *La bibbia del XIII secolo: storia del testo, storia dell'esegesi* (Florence: SISMEL, 2004), pp. 15–34

Lourdaux, Willem, and D. Verhelst, eds., *The Bible and Medieval Culture* (Louvain: Louvain University Press, 1979)

McHardy, Alison, '*De Heretico Comburendo*, 1401', in Aston and Richmond, eds., *Lollardy and the Gentry*, pp. 112–26

McNiven, Peter, *Heresy and Politics in the Reign of Henry IV: The Burning of John Badby* (Woodbridge: Boydell Press, 1987)

McSheffrey, Shannon, 'Heresy, Orthodoxy and English Vernacular Religion', *Past and Present* 186 (2005), 47–80

McSheffrey, Shannon, and Norman Tanner, eds., *Lollards of Coventry 1486–1522* (Cambridge University Press, 2003; Camden Society)

Martin, Geoffrey H., 'Knighton's Lollards', in Aston and Richmond, eds., *Lollardy and the Gentry*, pp. 28–40

Matthew, F. D., 'The Authorship of the Wycliffite Bible', *English Historical Review* 10 (1895), 91–9

Minnis, Alastair J., '"Authorial Intention" and "Literal Sense" in the Exegetical Theories of Richard FitzRalph and John Wyclif: An Essay in the Medieval History of Biblical Hermeneutics', *Proceedings of the Royal Irish Academy* 75, Section C, no. 1 (Dublin, 1975)

Minnis, Alastair J., *Medieval Theory of Authorship: Scholastic Literary Attitudes in the Later Middle Ages*, 2nd edn (Aldershot: Scolar Press, 1988)

Minnis, Alastair J., ed., *Latin and Vernacular: Studies in Late-Medieval Texts and Manuscripts* (Cambridge: Brewer, 1989)

Minnis, Alastair J., and A. B. Scott with David Wallace, eds., *Medieval Literary Theory and Criticism c. 1100–c. 1375: The Commentary-Tradition* (Oxford: Clarendon Press, 1988)

Moessner, Lilo, 'Translation Strategies in Middle English: The Case of the Wycliffite Bible', *Poetica: An International Journal of Linguistic–Literary Studies* 55 (2001), 123–54

Ng, Su Fang, 'Translation, Interpretation and Heresy: The Wycliffite Bible, Tyndale's Bible and the Contested Origin', *Studies in Philology* 98 (2001), 315–38

Oberman, Heiko A., *The Harvest of Medieval Theology: Gabriel Biel and Late Medieval Nominalism*, rev. edn (Grand Rapids: Eerdmans, 1967)

Ocker, Christopher, *Biblical Poetics before Humanism and Reformation* (Cambridge University Press, 2002)

Oshitari, Kinshiro, *et al.*, eds., *Philologia Anglica: Essays Presented to Professor Yoshio Terasawa on the Occasion of his Sixtieth Birthday* (Tokyo: Kenkyusha, 1988)

Peikola, Matti, *Congregation of the Elect: Patterns of Self-Fashioning in English Lollard Writings*, Anglicana Turkuensia 21 (Turku: University of Turku Press, 2000)

Riché, Pierre, and Guy Lobrichon, eds., *Le Moyen Age et la Bible* (Paris: Beauchesne, 1984)

Ro, Anne Karin, '"Symple men" and "worldli clerkis": Lollard sentiments in the General Prologue to the Wycliffite Bible', in Leiv E. Breivik *et al.*, eds., '*These Things Write I vnto thee . . .*': *Essays in Honour of Bjørg Bækken* (Oslo: Novus Press, 2006), pp. 227–39

Robinson, P. R., *Catalogue of Dated and Datable Manuscripts c.737–1600 in Cambridge Libraries*, vol. I (Cambridge: Brewer, 1988)

Robson, J. A., *Wyclif and the Oxford Schools* (Cambridge University Press, 1961)

Scase, Wendy, 'Reginald Pecock, John Carpenter and John Colop's "Common-Profit" Books: Aspects of Book Ownership and Circulation in Fifteenth-Century London', *Medium Ævum* 61 (1992), 261–74

'The Audience and Framers of the *Twelve Conclusions*', in Barr and Hutchison, eds., *Text and Controversy*, pp. 283–301

Scott, Kathleen L., *Later Gothic Manuscripts, 1390–1490*, 2 vols. (*A Survey of Manuscripts Illuminated in the British Isles*, ed. J. J. G. Alexander, vol. VI) (London: Harvey Miller, 1996)

Dated and Datable English Manuscript Borders c. 1395–1499 (London: British Library, 2002)

Simpson, James, *The Oxford English Literary History*, Volume 2, *1350–1547: Reform and Cultural Revolution* (Oxford University Press, 2002)

Smalley, Beryl, review of Margaret Deanesly, *The Significance of the Lollard Bible, Medium Ævum* 22 (1953), 49–52

'John Wyclif's *Postilla super Totam Bibliam*', *Bodleian Library Record* 4 (1953), 186–205

'The Bible and Eternity: John Wyclif's Dilemma', *Journal of the Warburg and Courtauld Institutes* 27 (1964), 73–89

'Wyclif's *Postilla* on the Old Testament and his *Principium*', in *Oxford Studies Presented to Daniel Callus, O. P.* (Oxford: Clarendon Press, 1964), pp. 253–96

The Study of the Bible in the Middle Ages, 3rd edn (Oxford: Blackwell, 1983)

Sneddon, Clive R., 'A Critical Edition of the Four Gospels in the Thirteenth-Century Old French Translation of the Bible', D.Phil. Dissertation, 2 vols., Oxford, 1978

'The "Bible du XIIIe siècle": Its Medieval Public in the Light of its Manuscript Tradition', in Lourdaux and Verhelst, eds., *The Bible and Medieval Culture*, pp. 127–40

'Translation Technique and the *Old French Bible*', *Forum for Modern Language Studies* 35 (1999), 339–49

'On the Creation of the Old French Bible', *Nottingham Medieval Studies* 46 (2002), 25–44

'Rewriting the Old French Bible: The New Testament and Evolving Reader Expectations in the Thirteenth and Early Fourteenth Centuries', in Rodney Sampson and Wendy Ayres-Bennett, eds., *Interpreting the History of French. A Festschrift for Peter Rickard* (Amsterdam: Rodopi, 2002), pp. 35–59

Somerset, Fiona, *Clerical Discourse and Lay Audience in Late Medieval England* (Cambridge University Press, 1998)

Somerset, Fiona, Jill C. Havens and Derrick G. Pitard, eds., *Lollards and Their Influence in Late Medieval England* (Woodbridge: Boydell Press, 2003)

Southern, R. W., *Robert Grosseteste: The Growth of an English Mind in Medieval Europe*, 2nd edn (Oxford: Clarendon Press, 1992)

Spencer, H. Leith, *English Preaching in the Late Middle Ages* (Oxford: Oxford University Press, 1993)

Strohm, Paul, *England's Empty Throne: Usurpation and the Language of Legitimation, 1399–1422* (New Haven: Yale University Press, 1998)

Summerson, Henry, 'An English Bible and Other Books Belonging to Henry IV', *Bulletin of the John Rylands Library* 79 (1997), 109–15

Talbert, Ernest W., 'A Note on the Wyclyfite Bible Translation', *Texas Studies in English* 20 (1940), 29–38

Tanabe, Harumi, 'On Some English Readings in the Vocabulary of the Wycliffite Bible', in Oshitari *et al.*, eds., *Philologia Anglica*, pp. 389–401

Thomson, Williell R., *The Latin Writings of John Wyclif* (Toronto: University of Toronto Press, 1983)

Tov, Emmanuel, *Textual Criticism of the Hebrew Bible*, 2nd edn (Minneapolis: Fortress Press, 1992)

Von Nolcken, Christina, 'Lay Literacy, the Democratization of God's Law and the Lollards', in John L. Sharpe III and Kimberly Van Kampen, eds., *The Bible As Book: The Manuscript Tradition* (London: British Library, 1998), pp. 177–95

Wallace, David, ed., *The Cambridge History of Medieval Literature* (Cambridge University Press, 1999)

Walsh, Katherine, and D. Wood, eds., *The Bible in the Medieval World: Essays in Memory of Beryl Smalley*, Studies in Church History, Subsidia 4 (Oxford: Blackwell, 1985)

Watson, Nicholas, 'Censorship and Cultural Change in Late-Medieval England: Vernacular Theology, the Oxford Translations Debate and Arundel's *Constitutions* of 1409', *Speculum* 70 (1995), 822–64

White, H. J., 'Vulgate', in James Hastings, ed., *A Dictionary of the Bible*, vol. IV (Edinburgh: Clark, 1902), pp. 873–90

Wilks, Michael, 'Misleading Manuscripts: Wyclif and the Non-Wycliffite Bible', *Studies in Church History* 11 (1975), 147–161

'John Wyclif: Reformer', in Hudson, ed., *Wyclif: Political Ideas and Practice*, pp. 1–15

Wogan-Browne, Jocelyn, Nicholas Watson, Andrew Taylor and Ruth Evans, *The Idea of the Vernacular: An Anthology of Middle English Literary Theory, 1280–1520* (Exeter University Press, 1999)

Workman, Herbert B., 'The First English Bible', *London Quarterly Review* 135 (1921), 187–99

John Wyclif: A Study of the English Medieval Church, 2 vols. (Oxford: Clarendon Press, 1926)

Wright, Laura, 'About the Evolution of Standard English', in M. J. Toswell and E. M. Tyler, eds., *Studies in English Language and Literature: 'Doubt wisely'. Papers in Honour of E. G. Stanley* (London: Routledge, 1996), pp. 99–115

Yonekura, Hiroshi, *The Language of the Wycliffite Bible: The Syntactic Differences Between the Two Versions* (Tokyo: Aratake Shuppan, 1985)

Yonekura, Hiroshi, 'John Purvey's Version of the Wycliffite Bible: A Reconsideration of His Translation Method', *Studies in Medieval Language and Literature* 1 (1986), 67–91

Index of manuscripts of the Wycliffite Bible

This index is arranged alphabetically by place and by institution or private owner within that place. All MSS known to me are included here, but since I do not cite every MS individually not all entries have references to pages in this book. The MSS are listed numerically in *WB*, and in Lindberg, *MSS*.

MSS in italics are described in full in Appendix 4.

Numbers in bold roman font are the numbers given in *WB*; numbers in bold italics are numbers given by Lindberg.

Where no date is given, the date is s.xv in.

+L = Epistle to the Laodiceans included

ABERYSTWYTH

National Library of Wales 7855A — Matt. 6:14–13:4 in LV
Ker, *MMBL*, II.22.

ALNWICK

Duke of Northumberland 788 ***225*** Gospels in LV

BEL AIR, CALIFORNIA

Dr Steve Sohmer — NT in LV
Olim Endowment for Biblical Research, Boston. Judith Oliver, ed., *Manuscripts Sacred and Secular* (Boston: Endowment for Biblical Research, 1985), pp. 13–15; De Hamel, *Book*, p. 186 and fig. 132, p. 336. Ownership inscription on the back flyleaf: 'Iste liber constat Thome Downe de haloghton', c. 1500.
pp. 61, 126

BERKELEY, CALIFORNIA

Bancroft Library 13 — Matt.9–Apoc. in LV
Bancroft Library 128 ***226*** Lectionary, NT, OT lections in LV
Date: s.xiv ex according to Digital Scriptorium database. The script and decoration are, however, very similar to those of Bodl. Fairfax 11.
p. 59

CAMBRIDGE, ENGLAND

Christ's College 10 **115** NT in LV

Corpus Christi College Parker 147 (S) **116** Prologue, Lectionary, ONT in LV
pp. 17, 59, 65, 88, 96, 106, 120, 127, 146, 156–7, 170, 171, 174–5, 186, 215, 235–7, 239, 254

Corpus Christi College 440 **117** Lectionary (gospels only), Gospels in LV
p. 60

Emmanuel College 21 (P) **118** Lectionary, ONT in LV
pp. 17, 59, 65, 88, 96, 106, 156, 166, 237–8, 245

Emmanuel College 34 **119** Lectionary, NT in LV
Date: post-1937. Robinson, *Catalogue of Dated and Datable Manuscripts c. 737–1600 in Cambridge Libraries*, I.64.

Emmanuel College 108 (p) **120** Lectionary, NT (+L) in LV
pp. 15, 59, 205, 206, 207, 208, 209, 234

[Fizwilliam Museum McClean 133 Matthew in EV, from the *Glossed Gospels*]

Gonville and Caius College 179/212 **113** Matthew–Mark in LV

Gonville and Caius College 343/539 (c) **114** Gospels, Lect. / Rom.-Apoc. in LV
Date: post-1397 (cf. Emmanuel Coll. Camb. 34).
p. 59

Jesus College 30 (J) **122** Matt.–Luke in LV

Jesus College 47 (s) **121** Lectionary, NT (+L) in LV
pp. 234, 245

Magdalene College F. 4. 6 (*O*) **126** NT in ELV (and EV rev.)
Matt. prol., Matt., Mark and Luke in EV, rev. ('clearly influenced by LV'), Lindberg, *EV*, VII.23; the rest (including prologues) in LV.
pp. 105, 179–80, 232, 233

Magdalene College Pepys 15, 16 **124** Gospels, Lectionary / Rom.–Apoc. in LV
Date: 1416(?), 1437 *sup.ras.*, vol. 1, fol. 194v; a '6' is visible, and evidence from the Calendar suggests 1416 is more likely than 1406; see Rosamond McKitterick and Richard Beadle, *Catalogue of the Pepys Library at Magdalen College Cambridge*, vol. V, i (Cambridge: Brewer, 1992), pp. 2–3.

Magdalene College Pepys 1603 (d) **123** Genesis–Ruth in LV
Date: c. 1430, McKitterick and Beadle, *Catalogue of the Pepys Library*, vol. V, i, pp. 24–25. Dialect SEM, Lindberg, *Judges*, p. 70.
pp. 141, 156, 184, 200, 225, 250

Magdalene College Pepys 2073 (w) **125** OT lections, Lectionary, NT (+L) in LV
Owner inscription of William Weston, last Lord Prior of St John's of Jerusalem in England (1530–33), 1540, fol. 351v. McKitterick and Beadle, *Catalogue of the Pepys Library*, vol. V, i, pp. 48–50.
pp. 53, 234

Sidney Sussex College 99 (*N*) **127** Lectionary, NT, OT lections in EV
Prols. to NT in LV; NT in slightly rev. EV, Lindberg, *EV*, VII.22–3.
pp. 142, 179, 232

St John's College E. 13 **128** Lectionary (epistles only), Rom.–Apoc. in LV
p. 60

St John's College E. 14 (C_J_E.14) **129** Psalms, Cant., Quicunque vult, Prov.–Ecclus in LV
Quicunque vult includes Rolle's commentary; prol. to Wisdom in EV, fol. 120v; part of the lections for the Office of the Dead, in a later hand, fol. 182v. Shares a few glosses with CV in Prov.–Ecclus. Owned by Clemens Ridley, servant to Robert Shurton, priest, who bequeathes his soul to god 'et b. marie et omnibus sanctis', and his body to be buried at St Katherine-iuxta-Turrem, London (s.xv, fol. ii[r]).
pp. 54, 96, 141, 203, 219, 288, 266

St John's College E. 18 **132** John in LV
Also Articles of Faith and Psalms of the Passion.
St John's College G. 25 Apocalypse in LV
Dialect Cambs., *LALME*, I.64. Also incl.ME *Elucidarium*; 'how in þe sacrament of þe auter Crist is [to] be resceyued worþil and deuotly', fols. 85r–93r [unpublished], *Vae octuplex*, and 'Of ministers in the church', appended to the Wycliffite Sermon Cycle (ed. Pamela Gradon, *English Wycliffite Sermons*, II.328–78); see Hanna, 'English Biblical Texts before Lollardy', in Somerset *et al.*, eds., *Lollards and their Influence*, pp. 149–50.

St John's College G. 26 (C_J_G.26) **130** Prov.–Ecclus in LV, Tobit in EV
p. 220

St John's College N. 4 **131** Gospels in LV

St John's College Aa. 5. 1, item 72 Fragment of Dan., Joel, Amos in LV
Two strips of inner column, 50 lines, 2–4 words per line; (1) inc. 'in tyme ordeyn[ed]' (Dan. 11:29), expl. Dan. 13:22; 2) inc. 'in to speris' (Joel 3:10), expl. Amos 3:11. Date: c. 1390–1400. Six-line initial Þ, deep blue (Amos 1:1). Probably from a complete WB or OT.
p. 221

[Trinity College B. 1. 38 Matt., John in EV, from the *Glossed Gospels*]

Trinity College B. 2. 8 (T) **133** Pentateuch in LV
pp. 75, 156

Trinity College B. 10. 7 **134** Matt. 5:38–Apoc. 16:15 in LV
Trinity College B. 10. 20 **135** NT, Lectionary, OT lections in LV
p. 58

Trinity College O. 7. 26 Gospels in LV
University Library Add. 6680 (C_U_6680) ***191*** ONT in LV
pp. 17, 65, 88, 94, 96, 105, 106, 138, 141, 156, 162, 193, 199, 200, 201, 238

University Library Add. 6681 (*H*) **155** OT in EV
Date: c. 1400. Text 'uniform', dialect EM, Lindberg, *Judges*, p. 68. Has title (but no text) for 'þe prologe in Amos', fol. 329r.
pp. 18, 99, 104, 214

University Library Add. 6682 ***213*** NT in EV
Date: s.xiv ex. Matt. 1 headed 'þe gospel of þe natyuyte of oure lady & of concepcioun', fol. 1v. Text 'insignificant', Lindberg, *EV*, VII.21.
pp. 60, 142

University Library Add. 6683 (C_U_6683) ***176*** Lectionary, NT, OT lections in LV
Three-line initials, gold on a mauve and blue background (several excised), and bar borders in gold, mauve and blue at opening of each book; three-line initials, deep blue flourished in red.
pp. 59, 62, 64

University Library Add. 6684 ***229*** Lectionary (gospels only), Gospels in LV
Fine seven-line gold initial at opening of Matt., fol.10r.

University Library Dd. 1.27 (R) **106** OT, Lectionary, NT in LV
pp. 17, 59, 74, 88, 90, 94, 96, 97, 100, 106, 107, 156, 186, 187, 202, 203, 204, 228, 238–9; fig.3
University Library Ee. 1. 10 (Z) **107** 2 Chron.–2 Macc. + Canticles, abridged in EV (rev.)
pp. 52, 78, 88, 103, 239–41

DRESDEN

Sächsische Landesbibliothek Od 83 ***182/227*** Lectionary, NT, OT lections in LV

Hunt, *TFST*, I.153–5.
pp. 16, 52, 130, 205, 206

DUBLIN

Trinity College 66 (*F*) **150** Genesis–Psalms prol. in EV

The first vol. of a two-vol. Bible, the second vol. of which is *Y*; see Lindberg, *EV*, VI.36.

Date: c. 1400; text 'uniform', dialect, mixed NM, Lindberg, *Judges*, p. 68.

p. 17

Trinity College 67 (Y) **149** Prov.–Apoc., Lectionary in LV

Date: c. 1410–20. Dialect SE or SEM, text 'average', Lindberg, *Judges*, p. 71. On animal-head decoration, see Scott, *Later Gothic Manuscripts*, p. 70. Shares some readings with ELP. Marginal glosses are written in a careful miniature version of the main hand; at Is.17:6, 28:15 and 29:1 the glosses are disarranged, with the gloss in the text and the word(s) being glossed supplied in the margin; at Is.35:4 the gloss is written first; at Jer. 20:14 the whole gloss is written in the text before the text glossed. Sometimes in Prophets and typically in Maccabees the miniature marginal gloss writes glosses within the text; these glosses are sometimes written before the words being glossed (as in Macc. in E).

pp. 18, 88, 90, 96, 106, 162–3, 166, 245

Trinity College 70 (D_70) Ps. 2:8–150, Canticles, Quicunque vult in LV

Also the Primer and the Ten Commandments in English, and many short works of spiritual instruction. Dialect Beds., *LALME*, I.76.

pp. 218, 219, 229

Trinity College 72 (D_72) Lect., Prol. to Psalms, Psalms, Canticles in LV

pp. 63, 120, 129, 229

Trinity College 73 **152** Lectionary, NT in LV

Trinity College 74 (D_74) NT in EV

Text 'unimportant', Lindberg, *EV*, VII.23.

p. 142

Trinity College 75 (*T*) **151** Lect. in EV, Prologue, NT, OT lections in ELV

pp. 77–8, 105, 120, 123, 142, 202, 234, 242–3

Trinity College 76 (D_76) Gospels in EV
Hunt, *TFST*, I.145. Text 'unimportant', Lindberg, *EV*, VII.23. Dialect EM, *LALME*, I.77.
pp. 16, 130, 142, 205

DUNEDIN, NEW ZEALAND

Public Library Reed 6 ***224*** Gospels in LV
Margaret M. Manion, Vera F. Vines and Christopher de Hamel, *Medieval and Renaissance Manuscripts in New Zealand Collections* (Melbourne: Thames and Hudson, 1989), p. 86.
Public Library Reed fragment 20 1 fol. from a Lectionary in LV
Epistle lections for part of Whitsun xvii; probably from the same MS as Sotheby's, 3.7.84, lot 6, now Tokyo, Takamiya. Manion, Vines and De Hamel, *Medieval and Renaissance Manuscripts in New Zealand Collections*, pp. 98–9.
p. 61

DURHAM

Durham University Cosin V. v. 1 **136** NT in EV (– Gospel prologues)
Text 'standard', Lindberg, *EV*, VII.22.
p. 142

EDINBURGH

National Library of Scotland Adv. 18. 6. 7 (*Q*) **145** Lectionary, NT in EV (– prologues Rom.–Apoc.)
Text has some revised readings, Lindberg, *EV*, VII.23.
pp. 106, 142, 234

[National Library of Scotland 6124 Matt. 3:16–4:4, 5:10–12 in EV, from the *Glossed Gospels*]
National Library of Scotland 6127 ***200*** Pauline Epistles in EV

ETON

Eton College 24 Apocalypse in LV
Each verse in Latin and in WB; includes commentary of Berengaudus. Date: 1455, Ker, *MMBL*, II.650–1.
p. 50

GLASGOW

Hunterian Museum 176 **146** NT (+L) in LV
p. 234

British Library Add. 10046 (i) **36** Prologue (part of ch. 12), Psalms, Cant., Quicunque vult (with Rolle's commentary) in LV. On Prologue extract, see ch. 5, n. 83.

130 × 90 mm. Initials rose, deep blue and gold (highly professional work in N. French style).

pp. 120, 129, 202, 228

British Library Add. 10047 (k) **37** Psalms 1–73 in LV

Date: s.xv ex, *WB*, I.xliv.

pp. 59, 217, 228

British Library Add. 10596 (g) **38** Tobit, Dan.13 (Susanna) in LV

Date c. 1430.

pp. 53–4,

British Library Add. 11858 (*U*) **39** NT in ELV (and rev. EV)

Matt.–Luke 19:13, and prols. to Matt. and Luke, in EV, with Mark, Luke and part of Matt. in rev. EV, 'clearly influenced by LV', Lindberg, *EV*, VII.24; the rest (including prols.) in LV.

In the same hand as b; perhaps the fourth vol. of a four-vol. Bible. Date c. 1410–20.

pp. 18, 105, 142, 179–80, 205, 206, 232, 233

British Library Add. 15517 **40** Gospels in LV

[British Library Add. 15521 (y) Additional prologues

Transcribed by Joseph Ames from 'Thomas Granger's MS' and corrected by Madden; said to be dated 1424 (fol. 2r), location now unknown, *WB*, IV.699. Includes OT lections in LV transcribed by Ames from 'Jennings' MS'.]

pp. 205, 206, 207, 208, 209

British Library Add. 15580 (*Y*) **41** Lectionary, Prov.–Apoc. in EV

The second vol. of a two-vol. Bible, the first vol. of which is *F*; Lindberg, *EV*, VI.36.

Date: c. 1400–10; text 'uniform' EV, dialect EM, Lindberg, *Judges*, p. 69; text 'less corrupt than all the other MSS [containing Bar. 3:20 onwards] (*X* excepted)', Lindberg, *EV*, VI.36. Text of Gospels 'standard', Lindberg, *EV*, VII.24. Rough red Lombardic penwork initials.

pp. 17, 59, 61, 91, 104, 106, 142

[British Library Add. 28026 Matt. in EV, from the *Glossed Gospels*]

British Library Add. 28256 ***183*** Apocalypse in LV

Lindberg gives the number as 28856.

British Library Add. 31044 ***184*** Prol. (Ps.–Ecclus.), Ps.–Ecclus in LV

Also prologue to Rolle's *Psalter*. Date: c. 1400. On Prologue extract, see ch.5, n. 82.

pp. 120, 124, 129, 202, 218, 228, 232

[British Library Add. 34305 Latin–English glossary based on WB in LV]

179 fols. Inc. Creauit made of now3t. Inanis ydyll. OT in Hebrew order, not WB order. Old chapter-numbers in Ezra (includes 3 Ezra). Lacks Psalms. Includes Luke 1:1–4.

pp. 85, 86, 137, 179, 180, 233

British Library Add. 35284 Psalms 45–150, Canticles, Litany in LV

Date: c. 1400. 115 × 85 mm; single column.

[British Library Add. 41175 Matt., Mark in EV, from the *Glossed Gospels*]

British Library Arundel 104 (E) **29** Lectionary, ONT in LV

pp. 17, 59, 63, 65, 88, 90–1, 96, 106, 156, 162–3, 166, 226, 237, 238, 244–5; *fig. 7*

British Library Arundel 254 **30** Cath. Epistles, part of OT lections in EV

Also *Oon of Foure.*

British Library Burney 30 **31** John, Hebrews, OT lections in LV

British Library Cotton Claudius E. II (C) **9** ONT in LV

pp. 17, 96, 99–100, 105, 106, 119, 127, 151, 155, 163–4, 165–6, 167–72, 181–2, 184, 185, 186, 187, 210, 213, 216, 220, 225, 226, 228, 231, 245–6, 252; *fig. 11*

British Library Egerton 617/618(G) **32** Prov.–2 Macc. / NT, Lectionary in EV

pp. 14, 18, 44, 58, 61, 64–5, 90, 93, 105, 106, 141–2, 158, 246–7; *fig. 8*

British Library Egerton 1165 **33** Lectionary, NT in LV

[BL Egerton 2880 Scots translation of WB NT in LV, c. 1520–26]

British Library Egerton 1171 **34** Lectionary, NT in LV

British Library Harley 272 **10** NT in LV
p. 74

British Library Harley 327 **11** Rom.–Apoc. in LV
p. 74

British Library Harley 940 **12** Rom.–Apoc. in LV
p. 74

British Library Harley 984 **13** Matthew in LV
p. 74

British Library Harley 1029 OT and NT lections in EV
Temporal, proper of saints, common of saints and commemorations. Rough red Lombardic initials. Clearly written, but a working volume.
pp. 64, 65–6

British Library Harley 1212 (u) **14** Lectionary, NT (+L) in LV
pp. 74, 234

British Library Harley 1666 (α) **15** Prologue to WB
125 × 95 mm; single column.
pp. 67, 74, 111, 120, 123, 134, 200

British Library Harley 1710 OT and NT lections in EV
Date: c. 1390–1400. Dialect EM. Clearly written, but a working volume.
pp. 64, 65–7; *fig. 4*

British Library Harley 1896 **16** Psalms, Canticles in LV
Each verse in Latin and English, as in Worcs. Cathedral F. 172.
pp. 63, 228

British Library Harley 2249 (b) **17** Joshua 19:19-Ps. 144:13 in LV
In the same hand as *U*; perhaps the second vol. of a 4-vol. Bible. Date: c. 1410–20. Dialect SEM, Lindberg, *Judges*, p. 70.
pp. 18, 217, 218

British Library Harley 2309 **18** Gospels in LV
British Library Harley 3903 (f) **19** Job, Tobit in LV
pp. 52, 97

British Library Harley 4027 **20** Lectionary, NT in LV
British Library Harley 4890 **21** Lectionary, NT in LV
pp. 59, 187, 245

British Library Harley 5017 (e) **22** 1 Macc.–Apoc. in LV
The third vol. of a three-vol. Bible, the first vol. of which is B. The NT from this MS is transcribed in BL Add. 5890–1. Date: c. 1400–10.
pp. 18, 74, 88, 142, 156, 165, 169–70, 221, 248

British Library Harley 5767 **23** Luke, John in LV
British Library Harley 5768 **24** James–Apoc. in LV (– prologues)
British Library Harley 6333 (o) **25** Gospel prols., Rom.–Apoc. (+L), Lect. in LV
Hunt, *TFST*, I.172.
pp. 52, 187, 206, 234

British Library Lansdowne 407 **26** Lectionary, NT in LV
British Library Lansdowne 454 (D) **27** Genesis–Psalms in LV
Date c. 1420. Dialect mixed SM, Lindberg, *Judges*, p. 69. Decorative border in blue, reddish brown, green and traces of gold at opening of Genesis; seven-line initial blue, pink and reddish-brown coiled foliage on gold background at opening of Psalms, fol. 253r; five to six-line gold initials on quartered blue and reddish brown (perhaps originally mauve) background.
pp. 18, 19, 156

British Library Lansdowne 455 **28** Part of OT, OT Lect., NT in LV, Lect. in ELV
Shares glosses on Is. 5:1–4 with K (only).
pp. 206, 245, 258

British Library Royal 1. A. IV **1** Lectionary, NT in LV
British Library Royal 1. A. X **2** Lectionary, NT in LV
Lection incipits in Latin within the text, from Matt. to 1 Cor.
p. 61

British Library Royal 1. A. XII **3** NT in LV
Presented to Queen Elizabeth I by her chaplain John Bridges.
p. 193

British Library Royal 1. B. VI (*M*) **4** Lect. in LV, NT in EV (– prols., *pace WB*, I.xxxix)
Text 'standard', with some revised readings, Lindberg, *EV*, VII.[illegible]. Date: c. 1400.
pp. 59, 105, 142, 193, 199

British Library Royal 1. B. IX **5** John in LV
Also the interlinear English text of John from the Lindisfarne Gospels.
British Library Royal 1. C. VIII (A) **6** Prologue (ch. 1), ONT in LV (rev.)
pp. 17, 44, 88, 91, 96, 106, 120, 127, 141, 149, 150, 155, 156, 165, 183, 186, 187, 199, 210, 217, 218, 219, 220, 221, 248–9, 250, 265, 266; *fig. 6*

British Library Royal 1. C. IX (B) **7** Genesis–Job in LV
pp. 18, 88, 90, 96, 99, 100, 156, 157, 163–4, 166, 167–70, 184, 210–16, 249–51

British Library Royal 17. A. XXVI **8** John in EV
Also Apoc. in English (not WB) with commentary, and several works of spiritual instruction.
p. 142
[British Library 17. B. I Concordance to NT of WB]
170 fols. Sherman M. Kuhn, 'The Preface to a Fifteenth-Century Concordance', *Speculum* 43 (1968), 258–73; Hudson, *PR*, pp. 234–5. At each letter of the alphabet, a two-line initial, deep blue flourished in red.
pp. 18, 180, 233

Lambeth Palace Library 25 (U) **46** Gen.–Deut. in EV, Joshua–Apoc. in LV
pp. 17, 54, 88, 96, 106, 140, 156, 166, 187, 217, 218, 219, 229, 251–2

Lambeth Palace Library 369 (x) **47** NT (+L), OT lections (frag.) in LV
Dialect: Hunts., *LALME*, I.118. There are some EV textual glosses in Acts. Pickering and O'Mara, *Manuscripts in Lambeth Palace Library*, pp. 25–26.
p. 234

Lambeth Palace Library 532 **48** Lectionary, NT, OT lections in LV
Pickering and O'Mara, *Manuscripts in Lambeth Palace Library*, pp. 46–7.
Lambeth Palace Library 547 **49** Gospels, Cath. Epistles in LV
Also a *capitula*-list for Matt.1–John 17 (cf. K). Pickering and O'Mara, *Manuscripts in Lambeth Palace Library*, pp. 51–2.
pp. 88, 257

Lambeth Palace Library 1033 (V) **50** 2 Chron. 2:7–Baruch in LV
Date: c. 1410–20. Dialect SEM, text 'average', Lindberg, *Judges*, p. 71. Includes some unique glosses in Job, and shares glosses with B_554K in Psalms (see Appendix 2). Pickering and O'Mara, *Manuscripts in Lambeth Palace Library*, p. 60.
pp. 18, 96, 106, 162, 175, 216, 217, 218, 219, 229, 236

Lambeth Palace Library 1150/1151 **51** Lectionary, Gospels / Rom.–Apoc. in LV
Pickering and O'Mara, *Manuscripts in Lambeth Palace Library*, p. 66.
Lambeth Palace Library 1366 ***185*** Lectionary, Gospels in LV
Date: s.xiv/xv, Ker, *MMBL*, I.98; Pickering and O'Mara, *Manuscripts in Lambeth Palace Library*, p. 67.

Sion College ARC L 40.2 / E.1 (F) **42** Prefatory Epistles, OT in LV
Also notes on the Prophets. Conserved at Lambeth Palace. Date: c. 1420. Dialect mixed CM, Lindberg, *Judges*, p. 69. Ker, *MMBL*, I.287–8; Pickering and O'Mara, *Manuscripts in Lambeth Palace Library*, p. 79. Has one unique marginal gloss: 'ioyned to trowȝis, to be baþid ynne' [Lyra] (Song of Songs 7:5; *WB*, III.81).
pp. 18, 96, 106, 124, 138, 141, 156, 199

Sion College ARC L 40.2 / E.2 **43** NT, OT lections in LV
Conserved at Lambeth Palace. Date: c. 1420–30. Ker, *MMBL*, I.288; Pickering and O'Mara, *Manuscripts in Lambeth Palace Library*, pp. 79–80.
Westminster Abbey 8 **45** Lectionary, NT in LV
Dr Williams's Library Anc. 7 ***187*** NT in LV
Date: s.xiv/xv, Ker, *MMBL*, I.429–30. Perhaps London.

LONGLEAT HOUSE, WARMINSTER
(property of the Marquess of Bath)

Longleat 3 (L_0) ***178*** ONT in EV (- NT prologues)
pp. 17, 87, 88, 99, 104, 105, 142, 143, 214, 252–3

Longleat 5 ***179*** Lectionary, NT in LV
OT lections written in full (lacks saints Sept.–Oct., and commemorations). Includes annotations from the *Glossed Gospels* in Matt. 4 and Luke 1–5, 14:16–35 and 16:19–25: see Hargreaves, 'Marginal Glosses to the Wycliffite New Testament', 294; Hudson, 'Two Notes on the Wycliffite *Glossed Gospels*', in Oshitari *et al.*, eds., *Philologia Anglica*, pp. 381–2.
p. 61

MANCHESTER

Chetham's Library 6723 **143** Lectionary, NT in LV
Ker, *MMBL*, III.355–6.
p. 59
John Rylands Library Eng. 3 ***204*** Luke, John, Matt., Mark in LV
Ker, *MMBL*, III.400–1.
John Rylands Library Eng. 75 **167** Rom.–Apoc. in LV
Date: s.xiv/xv, Ker, *MMBL*, III.403.
John Rylands Library Eng. 76 (R_76) ***205*** Lectionary, Matt. 2–Heb. 2, Acts 8–James 2 in LV
Ker, *MMBL*, III.404.
p. 59

John Rylands Library Eng. 77 (R_77) **158** Lectionary, NT in LV
Date: s.xiv/xv, Ker, *MMBL*, III.404–5; Hunt, *TFST*, I.163. Forms the base text of WB NT in Samuel, Bagster *The English Hexapla* (London: Bagster, 1841) (prologues not included).
pp. 16, 47–53, 58–9, 61, 62–3, 130, 205; *figs. 1, 2*

John Rylands Library Eng. 78 (R_78) **160** Lectionary, Matt.–2 Cor. 7 in LV
Ker, *MMBL*, III.405.
p. 59

John Rylands Library Eng. 79 (R_79) **159** NT in LV
Ker, *MMBL*, III.405.
p. 61

John Rylands Library Eng. 80 (r) **157** Lectionary, NT (+L) in LV
Date: 1444. Ker, *MMBL*, III.406.
pp. 206, 234

John Rylands Library Eng. 81 (R_81) **156** NT in EV (− prologues)
Date: s.xiv/xv, Ker, *MMBL*, III.406–7. Forms the base text of Lea Wilson, ed., *The New Testament in English* (London, 1848). Text 'standard', Lindberg, *EV*, VII.23.
pp. 53, 105, 142

John Rylands Library Eng. 82 (ç) **44** Parts of Kings-Chron. and Sapiential books in LV
1 Kings 28:5 to 4 Kings, 2 Chron., Prov. 1–19:4 ('ricchessis'), Eccl. 2:6 ('wode of trees') to 12:3 ('þe hous schulen'), Song 4:5 ('fed among lilies') to 8:1 ('who'), Wisd. 1:8 ('not passe') to 19:13 ('abhomynable'), Ecclus 1:12 ('and ioie in to') to 16:2 ('of hem'). Ker, *MMBL*, III.407.
p. 52

John Rylands Library Eng. 83 (R_83) ***206*** Extracts from Sapiential books in LV
Date: s.xiv/xv, Ker, *MMBL*, III.407–8. Proverbs; extracts from Eccl. (ch. 12 entire); Song of Songs 8:6–7; Wisdom 1–9; extracts from Ecclus, finishing at Ecclus 37:23
p. 52

John Rylands Library Eng. 84 (R_84) **161** Acts in ELV
Date: s.xiv/xv, Ker, *MMBL*, III.408. Acts 7:31–10:6 in EV, the rest in LV.
p. 60

John Rylands Library Eng. 88 (R_88) ***207*** Psalms, Song of Songs in LV

Ker, *MMBL*, III.412.

p. 229

John Rylands Library Eng. 89 (R_89) ***208*** Parts of Prophets in ELV

Ker, *MMBL*, III.412–13. Ezek., abridged, in EV; Dan. in LV; Minor Prophets abridged (but Jonah and Malachi complete) in EV; 1 Macc. 1–9 abridged in EV; see Lindberg, *EV*, VI.39.

pp. 52, 156, 221

John Rylands Library Eng. 91 (R_91) ***209*** Lect., Prov.–Apoc. in LV

272 fols. Ker, *MMBL*, III.414. Date: 1410–20. Dialect EM, Lindberg, *Judges*, p. 70. Revised: the missing words of Wisd.12:9 are added in the margin, and Song of Songs 7:13 is corrected, cf. A. Shares several glosses in Proverbs with CKNa (some with N only), all written within the text. Opening of each book sumptuously decorated with foliate borders in gold and subtle pinks and blues.

pp. 18, 59, 96, 106, 119, 156, 186, 220

NEW HAVEN, CONNECTICUT

Yale University Beinecke Library 125 (*W*) **168** Matt. 3:4–1 Tim. 1:15 in EV (rev.)

Lacks Gospel prologues. Text 'ordinary', 'some revised readings', Lindberg, *EV*, VII.24. Date: c. 1400, Barbara A. Shailor, *Catalogue of Medieval and Renaissance Manuscripts in the Beinecke Rare Book and Manuscript Library*, vol. I (Binghampton: Medieval and Renaissance Texts and Studies, 1984), pp. 172–3.

p. 142

Yale University Beinecke Library 360 Psalm 2:9–150, Canticles, Quicunque vult in LV

Also the Litany, Hours of the Virgin and Office of the Dead, in English. Shailor, *Medieval and Renaissance Manuscripts in the Beinecke Library*, vol. II (1987), pp. 204–6.

p. 63

NEW YORK

American Bible Society B. 3. 66 NT in LV

Columbia University Plimpton 269 **172** Rom.–Apoc. in LV

Ker, *MLGB*, p. 138. Date: s.xv med., Malcolm Parkes, Digital Scriptorium database.

p. 54

Columbia University Plimpton Add. 03 ***194*** NT in ELV, OT lections in LV

Matt. and Mark (w. prologues) in slightly rev. EV (Lindberg, *EV*, VII.22), the rest in LV.

Date: s.xiv/xv, Malcolm Parkes, Digital Scriptorium database.

p. 142

Pierpont Morgan 362 ***221*** Lectionary, NT in LV

Verlyn Klinkenborg, *British Literary Manuscripts, Series I* (New York, 1981), no. 8, pl.

Pierpont Morgan 400 NT in LV

Public Library 64 ***201*** Lectionary, NT, OT lections in LV

Description and images at Digital Scriptorium database.

Public Library 65 **171** Lectionary, NT in LV

Date: c. 1430, Paul Acker, Digital Scriptorium database.

Public Library 66 ***202*** Lectionary, NT in LV

Date: c. 1420, Paul Acker, Digital Scriptorium database.

Public Library 67 (*S*) **162** Part of Lectionary, NT in EV

Date: c. 1390, Paul Acker, Digital Scriptorium database. Text 'conservative', Lindberg, *EV*, VII.23.

pp. 59, 105, 141, 142, 206, 207, 208, 209

NORWICH

Norfolk Heritage Centre I h 20 (W) **144** Gen.–Prov. 7:10 in LV

208 fols.. 'Liber Jacobi Boolene manentis in Blicklingia', Sir James Boleyn, d. 1561 (fol. i^v)

Date: c. 1420. Dialect mixed SEM, text standard, Lindberg, *Judges*, p. 71. Fine gold and multicoloured borders (including green) at opening of each book; gold initials on mauve and deep-blue geometrically patterned background, also gold initials on deep-blue, orange, pink and cream interlaced background.

pp. 18, 96, 243

ORLANDO, FLORIDA

Van Kampen 637 (q) **163/*215*** Matt. 3:5–Apoc.17:14 (+L) in LV

Olim Cardwell; bought from the Goyder Trust at Sotheby's, 22.6.93, lot 83, pp. 83–5, pl. at 83.

De Hamel, *Book*, p. 181 and fig. 27, p. 336.

pp. 206, 234

Van Kampen 638 ***175*** Matt.19:4-John 9:31 in LV

Olim Kerslake; bought from the Goyder Trust at Sotheby's, 22.6.93, lot 85, p. 88, pl. at 82.

Van Kampen 639 Lectionary, Gospels in LV
Sotheby's, 24.6.86, lot 69. Gospel lections for the temporal only. An inscription on the final flyleaf reads 'Thys booke was founde under a payr of Stayres in the prests hawlle at litchfield, a° 1542.'

Van Kampen 640 NT in LV
Bought from the Goyder Trust at Sotheby's, 22.6.93, lot 84, pp. 86–7, pl.at 87. Previously unrecorded.

Van Kampen 641 Part of OT lections in LV
Christie's, 2.12.87, lot 19. 16 fols., Lent i. to Easter Eve; Whitsun Eve to Sat. after Whitsun; with the OT lections written in full. Perhaps from the same MS as Dunedin Public Library Reed fragment 20 and Tokyo, Takamiya.
p. 61

Van Kampen 642 1 Cor.1:11–Acts in LV

OXFORD

[Bodley 143 Luke in EV, from the *Glossed Gospels*]

Bodley 183 (a) **90** Lectionary, NT, part of OT in ELV
Bodl. Fairfax 11 is written by the same scribe and decorated by the same illuminator, De Hamel, *Book*, p. 179 and figs. 125–6. Includes Tobit, Judith, Esther, Prov., Eccl., Song, Wisd., Ecclus in LV; prologues to these books, except Tobit, in EV (slightly rev.)
pp. 59, 94, 96, 98, 100, 141, 156, 202, 203

[Bodley 243 Luke, John in EV, from the *Glossed Gospels*]

Bodley 277 (I) **60** Prologue (ch.1), ONT in LV (rev.)
pp. 17, 40, 44, 65, 88, 90, 96, 101, 106, 120, 127, 139, 140, 146–7, 149, 150–2, 155, 156–7, 158, 170, 180, 186, 206, 211, 215, 219, 220, 225, 226, 227, 228, 232, 236, 237, 253–5

Bodley 296 (L) **61** Gen.–Psalms in LV
Date: c. 1420–30. Dialect mixed SM, Lindberg, *Judges*, p. 70. Shares many readings with E (and some with PY). Presumably vol. 1 of a two-vol. Bible.
pp. 18, 96, 156, 226, 237, 238, 245

Bodley 531 **62** Lectionary, NT in LV
OT lections written in full in the Lectionary.
pp. 59, 61

Bodley 554 (B_554) **66** Psalms, Canticles in LV

Also an extract from Rolle: see Michael Kuczynski, 'A Fragment of Richard Rolle's *Form of Living* in MS. Bodley 554', *Bodleian Library Record*, Oct. 1994, 20–32. Date: c. 1400. 89 fols.; single col. There are extensive glosses throughout, from Lyra and Augustine.

pp. 156, 161, 170, 183, 210, 216, 217, 218, 219, 229

Bodley 665 **63** Lectionary, NT in LV

p. 59

Bodley 771 **64** Extracts from Epistles, Acts, OT in EV

Ker, *MLGB*, p. 179. Dialect Hunts., *LALME*, I.146.

pp. 52, 54

Bodley 959 (E) **65** Gen.–Bar. 3:20 in EV

pp. 88, 99, 103–4, 141, 143–4, 146, 148, 153, 175–7, 178, 199, 214, 223, 224, 225, 230, 234, 253, 255–6; *fig. 10*

Bodley 978 Lectionary in EV, 1 John–Apoc. in LV

Also *Oon of Foure.*

Bodley 979 **67** NT in LV

Bodl. Ashmole 1517 **89** Matt. 2:5–Jude, part of Lect. and OT lects. in LV

Bodl. Douce 36 **84** Tobit in LV

pp. 52, 79–8; *fig. 9*

Bodl. Douce 240 **85** NT, Lectionary in LV

Bodl. Douce 258 James–3 John:3 in LV

Also gospels for Easter Day (Mark 16), Ascension Eve (John 17), Ascension Day and St Thomas's Day (John 20), in LV, and part of Rolle's *Psalter*.

Bodl. Douce 265 **86** Lectionary (NT lections only), NT in LV

Bodl. Douce 369 (pt 1 C) **87** Pt 1 Num.20-Bar. 3:20 in EV

pp. 18, 71–2, 103–4, 141, 142, 148, 199, 253, 256–7

(pt. 2 *K*) Pt 2 Isaiah–Acts in EV (rev. in Luke–John)

Date: c. 1420. NT text 'conservative' in Matt.–Mark, somewhat revised in Luke–John, Lindberg, *EV*, VII.22. Dialect EM, Lindberg, *Judges*, p. 68; Soke, *LALME*, I.148. Shares correct reading with LV at Bar.6:72, see Appendix 3.

pp. 18, 88, 106, 142, 199, 231

Bodl. Douce 370 (*B*) **88** Genesis–2 Chron. in EV

Base text of EVin *WB*, from 4 Kings to 2 Chron. Date: c. 1400; 'literal version' of EV, dialect mixed NM, Lindberg, *Judges*, p. 68.
pp. 18, 141, 199

Bodl. Dugdale 46 (n) **76** Pauline Epistles in LV
p. 206
Bodl. e. Musaeo. 110 **70** NT in LV
Bodl. Eng. Misc. C. 27 ***188*** Fragments of Isaiah 30–3
Probably from a complete Bible or Old Testament (large format, letter 2.5 mm).
Bodl. Fairfax 2 (K) **71** ONT, Lectionary in LV
pp. 15, 17, 59, 63, 65, 88, 94, 96, 97, 98, 100, 106, 141, 165, 166, 170, 185, 186, 199, 200, 201, 202, 203, 210, 215, 216, 217, 218, 219, 220, 221, 231, 239, 257–9

Bodl. Fairfax 11 **72** Lectionary, NT in LV
Date: c. 1420. MS a written by the same scribe and decorated by the same illuminator, De Hamel, *Book*, p. 179 and figs. 125–6.
pp. 58, 59, 72–3, 247, 281

Bodl. Fairfax 21 **73** Lectionary (NT lections only), Rom.–Apoc. in LV
pp. 59, 61

Bodl. Gough Eccl. Top. 5 **83** NT in LV, Lectionary (NT lections only) in EV
Forms the base text of the Gospels in Lewis, *NT*.
pp. 61, 75

Bodl. Hatton 111 **74** Lect., Gospels, James–Apoc. in EV (−prologues)
Also the office of Compline in English, and a *capitula*-list for Matt.1–Luke 20. Text 'unimportant', 'a few corrected readings', Lindberg, *EV*, VII.22.
pp. 59, 65, 142

Bodl. Holkham misc. 40 Gospels in LV
Hanna, 'English Biblical Texts before Lollardy', in Somerset *et al.*, eds., *Lollards and their Influence*, pp. 148–9.

Bodl. Junius 29 **75** Part of Lectionary, NT in LV
Bodl. Laud Misc. 24 **52** Matt.–Mark in LV
Bodl. Laud Misc. 25 **53** Gospels in LV
Bodl. Laud Misc. 33 **54** Pauline and Cath. Epistles, Apoc. in LV
p. 72

Also a *capitula*-list for the NT (as in K). Dialect: Northants, *LALME*, I.152.

Christ Church 147 **93** Gal.–Hebr. in LV

Corpus Christi College 4 (A) **94** Lectionary, ONT in EV (—prols. in NT)
pp. 17, 59, 65, 87, 88, 95, 99, 105, 142, 193, 199, 214, 260–1

Corpus Christi College 20 (H) **95** 1 Ezra-2 Macc. in LV
pp. 18, 96, 106, 156, 183, 220, 229, 261–2

Lincoln College Latin 119 (G) **96** Prologue, ONT in LV
pp. 17, 74, 88, 96, 97, 98, 102, 106, 107, 120, 123, 124, 127, 152, 156, 242, 262 –3

New College 66 (O) **97** Gen.–Psalms in LV
Extracts from *Glossa Ordinaria* on Genesis and Joshua (s.xiii, fols. 1r–2v); Pref. Epistles in LV, fols. 3r–6r; Genesis-Psalms in LV (incipit of Proverbs), with prols. to 2 Chronicles, Ezra, Tobit, Judith, Esther and Psalms in EV, and to Joshua, 1 Kings (follows the text at fols. 115v–116v) and 1 Chron. in LV, fols. 6v–234v. Date c. 1410–20. Dialect SEM, text 'standard', Lindberg, *Judges*, p. 70.
pp. 18, 94, 96, 97, 98, 100, 138, 141, 156, 199, 200, 201, 202, 217, 228, 239

New College 67 (*V*) **98** NT in EV (rev.)
Text 'very much revised' and strongly influenced by LV, Lindberg, *EV*, VII.24.
pp. 142, 152, 165, 166, 169–70, 179–80, 221, 223, 233, 234, 248

New College 320 **99** Psalms, Canticles in LV
Date: c. 1500, De Hamel, *Book*, p. 179.
p. 228
Oriel College 80 **100** Lectionary, Matt.–Luke 20:32 in LV
Queen's College 369 **102** Matt.–1 Tim.2.12 in EV
Text 'ordinary', Lindberg, *EV*, VII.23.
p. 142
Queen's College 388 (M) **101** Lectionary, ONT in LV
pp. 17, 59, 62, 65, 96, 99, 100, 106, 107, 127, 129, 156, 193, 200, 201, 202, 203, 204, 263–4
St John's College 7 (N) **103** OT (–Psalms) in LV

266 fols. Hanna, *A Descriptive Catalogue of the Western Medieval Manuscripts of St John's College Oxford*, pp. 8–9. Psalms detached. Quires 1–2 (16 fols.) are lacking (perhaps contained Prologue), see Hanna. Date: c. 1420. Dialect SEM, Lindberg, *Judges*, p. 70. Text 'average', Lindberg, *Judges*, p. 70. Includes most of the series of Pentateuch glosses; shares idiosyncratic glosses in text of 2 Chron.–2 Ezra 5:3 with IS (see Lindberg, *KHB*, II.49), and like IS, omits many LV textual glosses. Shares many glosses in Proverbs with aCK, nearly always attributing them to Lyra within the text.

pp. 18, 63, 72, 96, 97, 106, 127, 156–7, 163, 170, 236, 254

St John's College 79 **104** Matt.–John 13:4 in LV

Hanna, *A Descriptive Catalogue of the Western Medieval Manuscripts of St John's College Oxford*, p. 107.

[Trinity College 93 Summary of Genesis to opening of James]

Date: c. 1450, Ker, *MMBL*, III.713. Includes 3–4 Ezra, and glosses from Lyra and the *Glossa Ordinaria*; the compiler makes use of LV, and perhaps EV.

p. 52

University College 96 (β) **105** Prologue, gospel lections in LV

Probably written by the same scribe as Prol. to WB in *T* (script a bastard anglicana). Gospel lections for Holy Week and Easter only.

pp. 120, 123, 243

Worcester College E. 10. 7 (binding) ***190*** 2 fols. of Deuteronomy in LV

Neil R. Ker, *Fragments of Medieval Manuscripts used as Pastedowns in Oxford Bindings* (Oxford: Bibliographical Society, 2004), no. 1527, p. 140.

PHILADELPHIA

Penn University Library 120 (P_P) ***203*** NT in EV (rev.), Lectionary in EV

Text 'interesting' and 'clearly revised', Lindberg, *EV*, VII.23.

pp. 142, 179–80, 205, 232, 233

PRINCETON

William H. Scheide 12 (P_S) **154** Lectionary, Prologue, ONT in LV

pp. 17, 41–3, 65, 88, 96, 106, 120, 127, 150, 155, 156, 169, 206, 210, 219, 220, 221, 228, 264–6

William H. Scheide 13 **169** NT, Lectionary in LV

SAN MARINO, CALIFORNIA

Huntington Library HM 134 ***198*** Lect. (fragment of proper of saints), NT in LV

Matt. 4:20–13:33 in revised EV. C.W. Dutschke, *Guide to Medieval and Renaissance Manuscripts in the Huntington Library* (San Marino: Huntington Library, 1989), pp. 178–9. Images available at Digital Scriptorium database.

p. 142

Huntington Library HM 501 ***199*** Deut 34:4–12, Bar. 1–6:68, Tobit 1:10–14:17, in LV, both EV prols to Ps., part of Prol. (Ps, opening of ch. 12), Psalms, Canticles, Litany, extracts from Ps. in LV, *Oon of Foure* [etc.], see Hanna, *The Index of Middle English Prose Handlist 1*, pp. 25–30.

pp. 52, 120, 129

TAUNTON, SOMERSET

Heneage 3182 ***217*** Epistles in LV

On deposit in Somerset Record Office.

TOKYO

Keio University Library 170 X 9.6 Extracts from OT in LV; Prologue (chs. 11–15)

This MS formed part of the same MS as Huntington Library HM 501.

pp. 52, 120

Takamiya 28 ***193*** Matthew, Acts in EV (rev.)

Olim Bristol Baptist College Z. f. 38. Date: s.xiv/xv, Ker, *MMBL*, II.200–1. Text 'clearly revised', Lindberg, *EV*, VII.21–2.

pp. 142, 180, 233

Takamiya 31 ***219*** NT in LV

Olim Boies Penrose. Includes marginal annotations from the *Glossed Gospels* in Matt. 8, Luke 2, 5, 10–11, 12, 15–16, and John 4, 13; provides evidence of the text of the Long Gloss on John, see Hudson, 'Two Notes on the Wycliffite *Glossed Gospels*', pp. 382–4.

Takamiya 1 fol. from a Lectionary in LV

From the proper of saints, Purification to St Mark, with OT lections for Purification, Valentine, Julian, Tiburtius and Valerian written in full. Sotheby's, 3.7.84, lot 6.

Probably from the same MS as Dunedin Public Lib. Reed fragment 20.

p. 61

WINCHESTER

Winchester College 42 **139** Lectionary, NT in LV
Ker, *MMBL*, IV.630.

WINDSOR

Dean and Canons Library 4 ***177*** Part of Lectionary, NT in LV
Ker, *MMBL*, IV.644–5.

WOLFENBUTTEL

Herzog-August-Bibl., Guelf. Aug. A. 2 (W_o) **153** Lect., ONT in EV (−prols. to Mark, Luke)

Date: c. 1400, De Hamel, *Book*, p. 175. 'Standard' text, cf. *BFH*, mixed Midl. dialect, Lindberg, *Judges*, p. 68. Text of Gospels 'ordinary', Lindberg, *EV*, VII.24.

Belonged to Thomas of Lancaster (c. 1388–1421), brother of Henry V, before he was created Duke of Clarence in 1412: De Hamel, *Book*, pp. 173–4; fig. (with historiated initial) 122, p. 174. The decoration is 'rather later in style than Egerton': Doyle, 'English Books In and Out of Court', in Scattergood and Sherborne, eds., *English Court Culture*, pp. 168–9. Probably made in London, De Hamel, *Book*, p. 174. Plates: Milde, ed., *Mittelalterliche Handschriften der Herzog August Bibliothek*, pp. 182–3.

pp. 17, 44, 65, 90, 142

WORCESTER

Worcester Cathedral F. 172 ***212*** Prologue (Ps.–Ecclus), Psalms 1–83, Acts in LV

Each verse of Psalms in Latin and English, as in BL Harl. 1896. Also the Gospel of Nicodemus in English, Rolle's *Emendatio Vite*, Hilton's *The Scale of Perfection*, etc. Date: c. 1450–1468; R.M. Thomson, *A Descriptive Catalogue of the Medieval Manuscripts in Worcester Cathedral Library* (Cambridge: Brewer, 2001), pp. 114–16.

pp. 63, 120, 124, 129, 202

Worcester Cathedral Q. 84 **140** Part of Lectionary, NT, OT lections in LV

Thomson, *Medieval Manuscripts in Worcester Cathedral Library*, p. 178.

YORK

[York Minster XVI. D. 2		Sunday gospels in EV from *Glossed Gospels*]
York Minster XVI. N. 7	**141**	Lect. (second half of sanctoral only) in EV; NT, OT lections in LV. Ker, *MMBL*, IV.751–2.
p. 62 York Minster XVI. O. 1	**142**	Lectionary in LV, NT in LV

Date: s.xiv/xv; Ker, *MMBL*, IV.755.

PLACE UNKNOWN

170	Apocalypse (*olim* J. H. Todd, Trin. Coll. Dublin)
173	Gospels in LV (*olim* Lord Lindsay)
174	NT (*olim* H.O. Coxe, Canterbury)
180	Parts of NT (*olim* Marquess of Hastings)
181	NT (*olim* Mrs Bagot of Standestone)
192	Rom.6:13-Apoc. in LV (*olim* Bristol Baptist College Z. d. 37; Sotheby's 12.77). Date: s.xv med, Ker, *MMBL*, II.191.
216	NT (Sotheby's 16.10.45. lot 2035)
220	Epistles in LV (Maggs cat. 687, no. 166, 1930–1)
222	NT (Sotheby's, 6.50, lot 218)
223	Lectionary, Matt.–Hebrews 13 in LV

Date: c. 1400, Sotheby's catalogue, 3.12.51, lot 18.

230	Psalms in LV (?) (*olim* Wilbraham, Cheshire)

Total number of MSS **c. 253**

This total excludes manuscripts of the *Glossed Gospels*, transcripts, summaries, glossary and concordance, but includes fragments. It counts as one MS parts of MSS known to have belonged together, but counts as separate MSS portions of Bibles which probably belonged together.

General index

CAMBRIDGE STUDIES IN MEDIEVAL LITERATURE

1 Robin Kirkpatrick *Dante's Inferno: Difficulty and Dead Poetry*
2 Jeremy Tambling *Dante and Difference: Writing in the 'Commedia'*
3 Simon Gaunt *Troubadours and Irony*
4 Wendy Scase *'Piers Plowman' and the New Anticlericalism*
5 Joseph Duggan *The 'Cantar De Mio Cid': Poetic Creation in its Economic and Social Contexts*
6 Roderick Beaton *The Medieval Greek Romance*
7 Kathryn Kerby-Fulton *Reformist Apocalypticism and 'Piers Plowman'*
8 Alison Morgan *Dante & the Medieval Other World*
9 Eckehard Simon (ed.) *The Theatre of Medieval Europe: New Research in Early Drama*
10 Mary Carruthers *The Book of Memory: A Study of Memory in Medieval Culture*
11 Rita Copeland *Rhetoric, Hermeneutics and Translation in the Middle Ages: Academic Traditions and Vernacular Texts*
12 Donald Maddox *The Arthurian Romances of Chrétien de Troyes: Once and Future, Fictions*
13 Nicholas Watson *Richard Rolle and the Invention of Authority*
14 Steven F. Kruger *Dreaming in the Middle Ages*
15 Barbara Nolan *Chaucer and the Tradition of the 'Roman Antique'*
16 Sylvia Huot *The 'Romance of the Rose' and its Medieval Readers: Interpretations, Reception, Manuscript Transmission*
17 Carol M. Meale (ed.) *Women and Literature in Britain, 1150–1500*
18 Henry Ansgar Kelly *Ideas and Forms of Tragedy from Aristotle to the Middle Ages*
19 Martin Irvine *The Making of Textual Culture: Grammatica and Literary Theory, 350- 1100*
20 Larry Scanlon *Narrative, Authority and Power: The Medieval Exemplum and the Chaucerian Tradition*
21 Erik Kooper *Medieval Dutch Literature in its European Context*
22 Steven Botterill *Dante and the Mystical Tradition: Bernard of Clairvaux in the 'Commedia'*
23 Peter Biller and Anne Hudson (eds.) *Heresy and Literacy, 1000–1530*

24 Christopher Baswell *Virgil in Medieval England: Figuring the 'Aeneid' from the Twelfth Century to Chaucer*

25 James Simpson *Sciences and Self in Medieval Poetry: Alan of Lille's 'Anticlaudianus' and John Gower's 'Confessio Amantis'*

26 Joyce Coleman *Public Reading and the Reading Public in Late Medieval England and France*

27 Suzanne Reynolds *Medieval Reading: Grammar, Rhetoric and the Classical Text*

28 Charlotte Brewer *Editing 'Piers Plowman': The Evolution of the Text*

29 Walter Haug *Vernacular Literary Theory in the Middle Ages: The German Tradition in its European Context*

30 Sarah Spence *Texts and the Self in the Twelfth Century*

31 Edwin Craun *Lies, Slander and Obscenity in Medieval English Literature: Pastoral Rhetoric and the Deviant Speaker*

32 Patricia E. Grieve *'Floire and Blancheflor' and the European Romance*

33 Huw Pryce (ed.) *Literacy in Medieval Celtic Societies*

34 Mary Carruthers *The Craft of Thought: Meditation, Rhetoric, and the Making of Images, 400–1200*

35 Beate Schmolke-Hasselman *The Evolution of Arthurian Romance: The Verse Tradition from Chrétien to Froissart*

36 Siân Echard *Arthurian Narrative in the Latin Tradition*

37 Fiona Somerset *Clerical Discourse and Lay Audience in Late Medieval England*

38 Florence Percival *Chaucer's Legendary Good Women*

39 Christopher Cannon *The Making of Chaucer's English: A Study of Words*

40 Rosalind Brown-Grant *Christine de Pizan and the Moral Defence of Women: Reading Beyond Gender*

41 Richard Newhauser *The Early History of Greed: the Sin of Avarice in Early Medieval Thought and Literature*

42 Margaret Clunies Ross *Old Icelandic Literature and Society*

43 Donald Maddox *Fictions of Identity in Medieval France*

44 Rita Copeland *Pedagogy, Intellectuals, and Dissent in the Later Middle Ages: Lollardy and Ideas of Learning*

45 Kantik Ghosh *The Wycliffite Heresy: Authority and the Interpretation of Texts*

46 Mary C. Erler *Women, Reading, and Piety in Late Medieval England*

47 D. H. Green *The Beginnings of Medieval Romance: Fact and Fiction 1150–1220*
48 J. A. Burrow *Gestures and Looks in Medieval Narrative*
49 Ardis Butterfield *Poetry and Music in Medieval France: From Jean Renart to Guillaume de Machaut*
50 Emily Steiner *Documentary Culture and the Making of Medieval English Literature*
51 William E. Burgwinkle *Sodomy, Masculinity, and Law in Medieval Literature*
52 Nick Havely *Dante and the Franciscans: Poverty and the Papacy in the 'Commedia'*
53 Siegfried Wenzel *Latin Sermon Collections from Later Medieval England*
54 Ananya Jahanara Kabir and Deanne Williams (eds.) *Postcolonial Approaches to the European Middle Ages: Translating Cultures*
55 Mark Miller *Philosophical Chaucer: Love, Sex, and Agency in the 'Canterbury Tales'*
56 Simon Gilson *Dante and Renaissance Florence*
57 Ralph Hanna *London Literature, 1300–1380*
58 Maura Nolan *John Lydgate and the Making of Public Culture*
59 Nicolette Zeeman *Piers Plowman and the Medieval Discourse of Desire*
60 Anthony Bale *The Jew in the Medieval Book: English Antisemitisms 1300–1500*
61 Robert J. Meyer-Lee *Poets and Power from Chaucer to Wyatt*
62 Isabel Davis *Writing Masculinity in the Later Middle Ages*
63 John M. Fyler *Language and the Declining World in Chaucer, Dante and Jean de Meun*
64 Matthew Giancarlo *Parliament and Literature in Late Medieval England*
65 D. H. Green *Women Readers in the Middle Ages*
66 Mary Dove *The First English Bible: The Text and Context of the Wycliffite Versions*